Psychologic Cues
in Forecasting
Physical Illness

APPLETON PSYCHIATRY SERIES

EDITED BY

THOMAS F. DWYER, M.D.
FRED H. FRANKEL, M.D.
MICHAEL T. McGUIRE, M.D.

Department of Psychiatry
Harvard Medical School
Boston, Massachusetts

Psychologic Cues in Forecasting Physical Illness

SAMUEL SILVERMAN, M.D.

Assistant Clinical Professor of
Psychiatry, Faculty of Medicine,
Harvard University; Training
Analyst, Boston Psychoanalytic
Society and Institute, Inc.

APPLETON-CENTURY-CROFTS
Educational Division/MEREDITH CORPORATION
New York

Library of Congress Catalog Card Number: 77-110160

PRINTED IN THE UNITED STATES OF AMERICA
390-80980-2

Contents

Psychologic Cues
in Forecasting
Physical Illness

General Introduction

In recent years more and more clinical data have been replacing anecdotal observations about the relationship between psychologic stress and physical dysfunction in man. Insofar as they depart from a romantic or fanciful approach to the problem, these studies are useful. However, they often are subject to criticism because of retrospective bias, inadequate controls, and other questions of statistical validity. Frequently the involved psychiatric or psychologic data are also highly edited, condensed, or descriptive. When observations are more detailed and dynamically oriented, they usually have been taken from only one or a few interviews in each case, although the total number of cases may be relatively large. In those instances where the approach has been analytic and intensive, the raw data have not been included and the patients invariably have been ones in whom physical illness was already established before treatment started. Nevertheless, particularly as a result of such clinical research, the loss of a significant human relationship, overwhelming feelings of hopelessness-helplessness, and repressed hostility all have gained greater acceptance and credibility as psychologic factors important in triggering the onset of somatic disease and influencing its subsequent exacerbations and remissions. However, it is well known that people exposed to these emotional stresses may develop psychiatric rather than physical illness. Many others, following such exposure, have only minor, transient psychologic difficulties or do not become ill in any notable way. These exceptions have often been used to discredit the significance of emotional disturbance in the development of physical illness. While this is an extreme position, it touches on a fundamental problem. The complexities of health and disease in man cannot be adequately explained by any single system, organization, or function. This has led to an increased emphasis on the

1

multifactorial approach which includes internal physical processes such as heredity and genetic coding, social environment controlled by economic, cultural, and political influences, and physicochemical and biologic agents affecting the environment. While it is true that these data should be incorporated in a comprehensive overview of health, disease, and dis-ease, this does not invalidate the need for more detailed information about the essential role that psychologic factors play in the development of physical sickness. Hitherto, research into this particular relationship has come up with conclusions that are still simplistic and largely retrospective, limiting their usefulness, especially in the prediction and prevention of such disease.

This book presents a *prospective study in depth* of the psychologic processes *preceding* the occurrence of physical dysfunction in the individual analysis of eight patients, five men and three women, conducted by the author though not necessarily at the same time. Only subjects who had been in excellent health for at least a year prior to the beginning of treatment and for at least six months thereafter were chosen. It was considered desirable to begin the investigation at a point in the analysis, if possible, when (1) no somatic illness had as yet occurred; (2) certain psychologic manifestations such as instinctual drive dispositions, long- and short-term defense mechanisms, superego manifestations, and transference development had become clearly defined; and (3) changes directly attributable to the treatment itself were only in their early phases. The first part of the study, involving four patients, is concerned basically with the *search* for specific psychologic indicators which signal impending physical illness. This is carried out over a period of from six months to a year with reporting of raw data from consecutive analytic interviews, especially before the onset of somatic dysfunction. Summaries of interim periods provide continuity where space simply does not permit detailed accounts, and these in any event are not relevant. The second part of the study, also involving four patients, is concerned with testing and validating the predictive factors that have been worked out. Similar raw data are presented. Whenever physical illness occurred during the analysis of each of the eight patients, information about the diagnosis and treatment of the condition was obtained from the internist or other specialist consulted by the patient. In a number of instances, the patient's emotional responses during and after each episode of somatic illness were also studied. In addition, the case material permitted a survey of day-to-day stresses and the accompanying shifts in psychophysical equilibrium in each patient. This made it possible to throw more light on how these factors may signal development of transient physical symptoms and minor ills and discomforts which not only these patients but everyone experiences more or less. Finally, in a number of analytic hours, very detailed psychologic observations were available which could be used to study some aspects of the complex interface between the physical and the mental from this particular vantage point.

Each case is presented in three parts. First, there is a brief history including past physical illnesses, and a summary of the major psychologic configurations and trends noted in the consultation period before the detailed reporting of the analytic material begins. Then, the raw data of the patient's associations with relevant interlinking summaries are reproduced. A series of notes following each case presentation specifies the detailed meaning and significance attributed to these associations. Finally, a third section is devoted to comments on the general and specific relationships observed between psychologic factors and the development of physical dysfunction—its time of occurrence, site, and severity. Predictive psychologic variables are specified from the data of the first four cases and used in each of the last four cases to forecast somatic disorder.

The psychoanalytic interviews reported are in the patient's own words, except where summarized. Most analytic hours have had material deleted from them because it was not pertinent to or necessary for the particular points to be illustrated and, otherwise, because of space limitations. Representative interventions by the analyst appear in abbreviated form where relevant to an understanding of their influence on the analytic process and, in turn, on the psychophysical shifts; but no attempt has been made to fully illustrate or discuss the technique of treatment. Certain changes have been made in each case history, not interfering with the essential data, for the purpose of preserving confidentiality and the patient's anonymity.

Although the number of cases here is small compared with subject populations in other studies of a macroscopic nature, it is possible to derive significant conclusions from this clinical research because it is prospective, microscopic, extends over relatively long periods of time, and tests the results in other cases under generally similar conditions. In 1935 Lewin and, more recently, Chassan (1960) and Knapp (1962) pointed out that the intensive individual approach is an important, yet neglected one in formal clinical research. Frequent detailed observation in any given patient who is being studied over a considerable period of time can lead to a better understanding of the complicated psychologic processes which are involved, compared with an approach in which large numbers of subjects are used but in which only limited observations can be made.

In the last section of the book, helpful psychologic cues found in forecasting physical illness are considered in detail. It should be emphasized that they are not being presented as etiologic factors. In the discussion, it is suggested that these indicators, though discovered during psychoanalytic treatment, also can be elicited and meaningfully applied by the informed physician under other circumstances, e.g. during medical examination, survey, or research. These physiologic signals add a new dimension to the resources of medical science already being utilized in early detection of somatic disorder and prevention of serious or fatal sequelae. Greater awareness of their presence can lead to development of preventive psychologic measures which, when used in conjunction with those already known in the physical sphere, will make it possible to further reduce the incidence of somatic illness.

SEARCH FOR
PREDICTIVE CUES

E. F.

Rage in the Joints

INTRODUCTION

E. F. is a single, 31-year-old engineer. He entered analysis because of continuing difficulty in his relationships with women and concern about periodic preoccupation with homosexual fantasies.

He is the younger of two children. There is a married sister five years older who has one child; her husband is an important business executive. She has been in good health since her youth. The parents have been separated for ten years—their marriage having been an unhappy one almost from the beginning. Mother is described as an emotionally unstable person, who makes many demands of the patient and who is a hypochondriac in addition to having chronic, minor gynecologic problems. She has had low-grade osteoarthritis since the patient's childhood. Father, an architect, appears as a bright but withdrawn man; he has been so preoccupied with his work that he has had little time for the patient during his childhood. He suffered for years from kidney disease and then from a recurrent osteomyelitis of the left arm which finally healed after several surgical procedures.

E. F.'s emotional difficulties extend back many years. He has a severe character neurosis with obsessional features. Confusion over sexual identity has been a core problem. He has experienced frequent episodes of anxiety and depression. Successful in his work as an engineer, he has also had a lively interest in art, music, literature, and current affairs, so that his intellectual pursuits have been many and varied. A period of psychotherapy produced some symptomatic relief five years previously. Actually, the patient has not had any major physical sickness. He had the usual childhood illnesses without sequelae and at age five self-limited episode of joint pain, never definitely diagnosed.

In the first eight months of analysis, the patient's marked ambivalence toward women was prominent in his associations. There were expectations of being nurtured by them and also of conquering them sexually. Actual disappointments in woman were followed by vivid homosexual fantasies in which the patient's feminine identifications and his search for an omnipotent nurturing father appeared prominently. This was reflected in the transference. A strongly narcissistic trend, oral components, and projective tendencies were much in evidence. Self-pity and tearfulness without actual crying also could be noted on numerous occasions. Somatic manifestations, chiefly tachycardia and generalized malaise, though frequent and principally equivalents of anxiety, were transient during this phase of the analysis. Masturbation was intermittent, usually after unsatisfactory intercourse with his current girlfriend. Evidence of moderately severe ego-superego tensions was reflected in frequent references to guilt. However, apart from mild anxiety and depression, no intense feelings had occurred during this phase, and there was little affective expression of hostility. Despite severe internal conflict, the patient was able to pursue a number of his interests in art, literature, and music.

The patient was in the midst of another ambivalent stalemate about what to do with his current relationship to Laura, a girl he had been going with for two years, as detailed reporting of subsequent analytic hours begins.

CASE MATERIAL

6/2 *

1†   Plenty of anger. I'm bursting with it—just furious. I had a dream last night about shit and about being shit on. But it's too nice an afternoon to be talking about this. I'm tired and you're tired, so let's call it quits and go out and have a beer. If I can eat with you, I don't need to do any work here.

2   I called mother last night, as usual she complained, literally clutching at me, wanting me to give, give her all my time and attention. I got mad and told her she needs a man. That upset her, and she launched into a tirade which I didn't listen to. I said that I hoped she would have a nice week. Another tirade followed, which I treated with more avoidance. Then there was a third tirade with my again putting the receiver away from my ear. At the end I repeated my hope that she would have a nice week and said goodbye. Then I was in a fucking

*These numbers refer to the dates of the analytic hours.
†These numbers refer to marginal notes at the end of each case.

rage, but it soon petered out and I felt guilty. I probably provoked her. I originally tried to be kind but when she cast aspersions about how my desk at home used to look like a little girl's, I had to counterpunch with that remark about her needing a man. ["You felt attacked and then counterattacked."] When anyone criticizes me I fly into a rage which boils over into Laura, my body, you, everybody, and anything that gets in my way. I feel very sensitive since the time I lived with Laura in her apartment and was so dependent on her, a disgusting role. She herself is both dependent and demanding, and even though I'm living by myself now, I'm submitting to a lot of her crap when I see her. If only I could give Laura up and move on, but it's like giving up my mother. Right now I feel like leaving here.

You know, after my call to mother, I then wanted to call father for support 3 against that overpowering bitch of a mother—that lonely, old lady. Father wasn't in his apartment. I thought—he must be out with his girlfriend. That's what he did to me. He left me alone with this devouring thing of a mother, when I was a kid. I was just 17. I knew he wasn't coming back to her. I remember how she quizzed me then about where he was and if he wasn't coming back. To the latter all I could say was, "I guess not." I felt like a piece of shit and helpless as well [hands placed behind head]. I met the bastard and asked him if he was going to leave it to me to tell her he had left her for good. He said no, that he would take care of that. The fucker didn't. I can never forgive him for that. I feel like cracking their skulls together. They were separated for a while before I was born, and if things had remained that way, I wouldn't have been born.

What do I have now? Nothing but a half-respectable apartment. All my 4 friends are going away. Well, that's a gross exaggeration. I feel like smashing Jim [a colleague at work] on the head with a bat for leaving. He's got more on the ball. He's going out to Chicago to a bigger and better job, but I'm like the playboy of the Western world. I seem to be stuck in my work. I feel like a girl. I have the fantasy now of taking a knife with my two hands and plunging it into Laura's, into mother's chest, not her vagina. Now I'm back to feeling helpless, like a little girl. I hate that.

6/6

My back aches quite a bit. A couple of days ago I was out rowing with one 1 of my girlfriends. I did most of it but didn't have any immediate aftereffects until I noticed the aching last night. It seemed to interfere with my sleeping, and I felt tense anyway, so finally I masturbated and that gave me some feeling of relaxation. Then I was able to fall asleep. I don't seem to have the depression that usually comes on afterwards. When I was masturbating, I was thinking about a girl—Maude—I used to know before I met Laura. She was a nurse, big and blonde, several years older than me. Her body reminded me somehow of my mother's. Maude was quite an experienced girl sexually. She had had several abortions, so she knew what it was all about. In a mechanical way sex was most satisfactory with her. We both had mutual orgasm every time. She was the kind of person who did a lot of mothering too and that's something I just eat up. But when she began introducing me to her high society, blueblooded relatives, I felt so dreadfully inferior that I was in a panic all the time. I couldn't stand it, and I began to give her the business by telling her that I knew a cute French girl who was superior to her and whom I preferred. Maude couldn't take that very long, and one evening she slapped my face and the affair was over. She was a girl with whom I had felt like a man, at least for a while. Then she left me. It makes me think that a number of people, some of whom I knew quite well, are leaving the firm to go on to better jobs. I just feel rotten at such times. It brings up a lot of memories of the breakups I've had with girls. Now I'm thinking of leaving Laura, trying to do something about that relationship instead of just floating along.

6/7

1   I have a funny feeling in my body, but I don't feel sick. Last night I had a compulsion to get to know a girl who was a guest at Laura's. She's tall, slim, and good-looking, but she's not going to be around. Now that feeling is in my stomach; I'm aware of strange, wavelike sensations, but I don't mind. Curiously, at the same time I have a sense of well-being. I keep thinking of what it's like to be the kind of mother who tries to beat men into submission by a torrent of words. That's my mother. If you submit, you're unmanly. So then I get thoughts that I have to be tough with women like that, not only tough but kill them.

2   I had a dream that I was in a slum dwelling. The landlord was told to fix the walls—to hide the defects but not really repair them. The landlord seems cynical, a real bastard. I guess that's me. That's the way I've been trying to fix things up. On the other hand, maybe it's you who are doing a poor job.

3   I'm worried about people leaving me, about me leaving them. Dick [a colleague] told me yesterday that he had consulted you about his problems. That made me jealous, competitive, and I kept feeling that you must like him better. It's as if he were like a brother. He's a real person, and I'm a coward. My father is a coward, too, the son-of-a-bitch; we both are. That bitch mother of mine makes me feel completely helpless. The thing I'm not sure of is whether my problems with Laura are so great that I really can't handle them or whether I'm reacting neurotically to her. It's just hard for me to separate from Laura or from my mother and be on my own. Laura made dinner last night for five people, and there just wasn't enough food. That gets me mad—the stingy bitch. Guess I'm feeling hungry right now. My stomach feels empty, and I sure could eat.

4   I took a shower before coming here. I wanted to be clean and pure. Now I think I've exposed myself—my hungry, selfish ways—that I don't really want to go to work, but to bed, to sleep, and to be taken care of. Getting up early in the

morning makes me think of father—that was one of his ways. All he thought about was work. My thoughts go back to the fishing I did the other day. I remember once catching a great big fish, and everybody else, including my father, was so envious. I'd rather fish than play tennis with father. But what's the use? I feel that people lack respect for me as a person. For me, growing up meant being alone. Father gave me the dirty work of telling mother that he had left her. Liking Laura seems to me to be associated with pleasing father.

6/8

I don't feel like talking today. Am I angry at you? Yet, it's on my mind that there may be a cease-fire. I seem to want to talk about that. Maybe I want to bring good news. I feel that there's a cease-fire in effect here, a temporary relaxation. 1

I keep thinking that Laura doesn't take contraceptive pills and her diaphragm is a year old. She really should check it. I'll probably have to use condoms for a while. 2

Last night we had a party in honor of Dick's going away at a fancy restaurant and I got high. I said bad things. Dick has been my supervisor at work. I feel embarassed. I said to Dick that he didn't send out enough cards on Mother's Day—that he's got mothers everywhere. 3

I have a conference after the interview here. Tomorrow there's another dinner to which Laura and I are going. You know, I've had a toothache now for the past six days, a lower right wisdom tooth. The lower left one has been pulled. Anyway it hasn't bothered me much. Maybe that's why I haven't mentioned it before. 4

I talked with Dick yesterday and told him he had been the most important person in my life this past year. I shouldn't have hurt him last night. At one point, I started to cry in his presence. I feel like crying right now. I told him that even though it's been a struggle, my working with him has been the most joyous thing this year. I think his eyes were watering too. It all brings back memories of my closest friend in school. These relationships with other fellows make me think of my playing the role of little brother. Then I wonder if I have any homosexual tendencies. In school I felt all my friends were much brighter than I was. I don't like the idea of saying goodbye to Dick. I keep thinking of Dick as a brother of mine and that I like him better than my own sister. I talked with him about his coming here and my being in competition with him. When I was drunk, I told him of thinking that the three Scotches I drank were like three nipples. I was running my mouth off incessantly, and it made me look like an asshole. I have a vision of cutting off my own scrotum and holding it up. I feel like pulling my own tooth out myself, so it would stop hurting. 5

Now I'm back to thinking about father. I could never understand why father 6 never gave me anything but necessities. Now I think I'm trying to control what I'm saying. Actually I'm having associations about one of my friends. He's also being analyzed. He seems to be able to get right down to bedrock quickly and with plenty of feeling. I guess he's gone further than me. I feel uncertain about myself. Am trying to get you to see the witty, easygoing side, in addition to my sadistic side. But I better stop trying to suck you. Now dizziness and anxiety are sweeping over me. This backache is starting up also. It feels like a spasm and must be from the rowing I did the other day.

6/12

I feel speechless [pause].

1   Thursday night Laura and I went to a banquet, then to a friend's house, and then to bed at home. Did I say Thursday? I think it was Friday. She said no to my sexual advances. I became enraged and didn't want to be with her. So I went and slept on the living room couch. About 4 A.M. she woke me up. First, I said I wanted to be alone. Then I got excited and anxious. I went back to bed with her. My heart is pounding right now. We fell asleep without intercourse. On waking in the morning I had many homosexual thoughts. They bombard me now, especially those about screwing in the rear end. Laura was furious at me; she kept saying that we were supposed to live apart, why did I keep coming back? I became enraged myself and sarcastic and said, "Thanks for letting me know." She then said outright that she doesn't have any more sexual feeling for me and that we ought to live apart. I furiously told her that it wasn't a bad idea and felt that it was all over between us. We parted angrily, but I felt terribly lonely, and finally called Laura back and invited her to a party next Saturday night. I didn't get a definite answer, and I haven't seen her since or heard from her. My feeling is that it's all over.

2   There's confusion in my mind, a desire to start a relationship with another woman, and yet I'm afraid I won't succeed. Now I keep thinking of Laura. I have a fantasy that she's got a penis, that something's wrong with her genitals, that she has a big clitoris, and she's built almost like a slender boy.

[Pause.]

3   My thoughts go back to loneliness. The air conditioner here isn't doing a good job. It's very humid [actually not] and oppressive here—don't you feel it? Now I'm getting angry at you; you're not giving me any help with the Laura business. ["What isn't clear?"] I want to know what I feel about her. There seem to be no positive feelings yet there must be because we wouldn't have stayed together for two years. There must be positives. ["But there are also negatives, especially when you feel you're not being mothered enough."]

6/13

Feeling very anxious. I'm thinking of how I got aroused by some of the girls   1
at the conference this morning. I gave them the eye. Some good-lookers were
there, and it was hard to keep my mind on what was being presented. Haven't
had any real sexual activity for several weeks now [pause].

Now I'm feeling sad about Dick's leaving. He's probably the most important   2
person I've met in a long while. Maybe if I just let all my feelings really come
out, if I got angry at you, I'd feel better.

One of the things I do when I feel anxious is to get a haircut; it seems to   3
relieve my anxiety a bit. It used to be the opposite—I would have homosexual
fears in a barber shop, feeling helpless, at the barber's mercy; he could cut and
stab at will if he should suddenly lose control. I really can't comb my hair
[which is very thick and worn somewhat long] except for a week after a haircut.
I need to get a crewcut because if I'm neatly groomed, I feel more like a man.
[The patient has put the index finger of his right hand on his lips.] Right now
I'm concerned about what's life going to be like without leaning on Laura. Does
it mean I'll move back to the previous state of being a Don Juan? Getting
pleasure in any way I can. At times I need so much [pause].

Now look what I'm doing, running the hangnail on my finger on my top lip.   4
It's painful and pleasurable at the same time, like masturbation. Don't you hate
having patients who've been with previous therapists? Why should I think that
way? It occurs to me that I hate you for not giving me things on some level that
I want. You don't have a farm. You don't invite me to dinner. ["Like your
previous therapist."] Yes. Why do you charge me so much money [standard fee,
which the patient is realistically able to pay]? Your office is so far to get to [not
in fact]. Besides I'm just plain jealous of your success.

I'm beginning to feel hungry for food. I notice that I'm pinning my hands   5
down to prevent my fingers from getting to my lips and mouth. I think you'll
say, "Stop playing with your thing." I remember my father telling me, "Stop
playing with your dingus," but I was just scratching my crotch then [pause].

My thoughts are about cars. An uncle of mine had a 13-year-old car when I   6
was a kid, and my father didn't have a car at all. When he did get one, it was a
junky, smoky car, and I felt like passing out. When I was older, an adolescent,
I'd often be out very late Saturday night, till 3 A.M., and then lie around all
Sunday morning, and my father didn't like that at all. [Interpretations about
activity-passivity, masculinity-feminity, masturbatory practice and guilt, and
father transference are made.]

6/14

1   Thinking about Laura. What I'm doing now is trying not to break up with her. There's a girl I knew in Philadelphia who recently asked about me, and so I've been trying to find out what her address is and what she's doing. I feel tense in my stomach. That girl is the only one I ended with decently. I said to her if there's no sex, there would be no relationship. She told me she wasn't ready yet. I said, "No hard feelings but no sex, no relationship." Having said that now I don't feel so tense. That girl's name is Phoebe, and she never led me on sexually. Her attitude about cars was so different. Father used to say, "Don't lend your car to anyone." Phoebe just tossed the keys of her car to me and said, "Let's go." Now it makes me think all over how lacking as a man I am. A whole year has gone by and nothing has changed. I took Laura out to dinner last night even though we're now living apart. Then we went back to her place, listened to records. All the time I wondered what I was doing there. Finally, she went to visit a girlfriend, and I went back to my own apartment. Neither Laura nor I were really happy to see each other [pause].

2   When I'm not successful with girls, I get homosexual fantasies. Am I mad at you for not being a sexual partner of mine? Every corner I turn I see homosexuality—but I'm exaggerating, being histrionic. I remember as a child kissing father goodbye and other times asking to comb his hair, which he let me do. When I was 4 or 5, I used to clomp around in mother's shoes. I'm really embarrassed by these thoughts of what I did later when I was 10 or 12. I used to read about women with high-heeled spikes, boots, and whips. Then I would get my belt and see how tight I could make it around my waist, like the women in the book. I'd put a hole in the belt to mark the thinnest point. I'd do this in front of a mirror, without clothes and get an erection. Sometimes while I was naked I'd wrap a vacuum cleaner hose around me like a boa constrictor. I don't like to think of myself as not a man, and I keep trying to reassure myself that I am. The memories of what I did with the belt keep coming back. I think of a belt around my penis, cutting off its circulation. Now I think of putting the belt around your neck. I'm mad at you for being a passive, nongiving, meticulous spook.

6/16

1   This morning while shaving I had the fantasy that Phoebe had been a patient of yours when she had been in Boston some years ago, and that she didn't like you as much as her Philadelphia analyst. She said her doctor in Boston had not been very giving. Maybe you're the most non-giving analyst in Boston. I'm getting angry thinking about it. It makes me think of doctors I went to as a kid.

When I was five, I had joint pains and was taken to a doctor, an orthopedist, for this condition. He said nothing was wrong, but my mother wasn't satisfied, and she took me to another doctor who wanted to draw blood out of a vein in my arm, and I didn't want that, so I raised holy hell in that office, so much that my mother and a nurse had to hold me down. I still remember the gum rubber tubing that was held around my arm to make the vein stand up. I was so shaken up by that experience that I wouldn't let anyone draw blood from me for years afterward. That workup was negative too, but, oh, what a frightening experience! My tonsils must have been taken out when I was four. It was in a small, private hospital, and all I remember is that I hated being there.

Now I have a vivid fantasy of getting a wisdom tooth pulled and feeling 2 utterly weak and helpless. Now my joints seem to be hurting me a little. I remember when I had my tonsils out, my throat hurt badly, and I was given ice cream at home. I have another fantasy now of ice cream going down and feeling good. Like my father's ejaculate. Disgusting. I actually had a tooth pulled when I was much older, a sophomore in college. I went, again with mother, thinking it would be nothing, but it turned out to be something alright! The dentist had this most sexy nurse who kept rubbing up against me. Everybody around was so serious. They kept sucking blood out of my mouth. It seemed that the nurse's job was to hit the bone chisel with the hammer. The tooth was taken out in two pieces, the gum was sewed up, but I felt faint for a while afterward. Then I was sick three to four days because I got an infection there and I had to go back. It was a real mess. I had another tooth when I was eight or nine that was a real fang, an extra tooth in the middle of my palate. I remember liking it, rubbing my lower lip against it. Anyway the dentist chiseled, cut, slashed, but without hurting me, and got out the fang. I was glad it was gone. It had made me feel different from all the other kids. I had had this thing there in my mouth, and they didn't. That dentist's office was next to the camp office, the camp where I went as a kid. I used to sneak up to the camp office, overhearing what the counsellors were saying, spying on their meeting. The counsellors used to beat the kids. It's like when I'm waiting to come in for my hour. I tend to listen sometimes, trying to overhear what's going on in your office [pause].

As a kid I never felt I could make it in games like soccer. I had much less 3 breath than my friends, and I would get sick with pains in my chest. Also, I couldn't keep up with them in basketball. Yet I always excelled in crafts. I really wanted to do as well as the others in sports but didn't seem to have the stamina. I had a friend with asthma who had the same problem I had but was a better athlete. He had a mother who was crazy, drinking all the time, and the house always smelled of wine. By the time I was in high school, I felt stronger and became active in a lot of school affairs [pause].

Back to the present. There are two things on my mind. My friend Dick left 4 yesterday. That makes me feel very sad and lonely. I told him he was probably the most influential person in my life since adolescence, when John R was a counsellor of mine. John made me feel like a man. But I don't want to talk about this because of something else—the quandary I'm in with Laura. She went to Philadelphia for a few days and didn't say goodbye. You know, after I was so mad at you Wednesday and told you, much of the steam went out of me, and I wasn't so angry with Laura. Now I feel very lonely. When I called on Laura Wednesday, she was crying and crying over her problems with her father. I'm going to Philadelphia myself next weekend to show I don't have to put up with her. I don't feel so angry, but hurt that she left without saying goodbye. Should I remain loyal to Laura? I think I'll go to Philadelphia and test out my fantasies of being welcomed by Phoebe as the long-lost hero, conquering her, falling madly in love, having perfect sex, and living happily ever after [puts right hand in mouth]. Here I am again with my hand in my mouth. I just feel lonely and am trying to fill the void up desperately somehow.

6/19

1   I had some confusion about today's hour. The weekend was just dreadful. I couldn't reach Phoebe by phone. Bad luck. I had a feeling there was a plot against me; the situation made me mad, and there was nothing I could do about it. Meanwhile Laura came back and asked me if I knew a girl named Phoebe who's renting a country place with Jean who's Laura's best friend. It's uncanny how these two girls have a mutual friend. At first I felt like laughing, then was angry at fate.

2   Things are all mixed up. I screw up my schedule—a sign of irresponsibility. It makes me feel like a horse's ass. It reminds me of a fantasy I had while masturbating Friday evening—wanting to suck myself off rather than just masturbate.

3   Anyway, last night I went to bed with Laura for the first time in two weeks. I felt excited and anxious. I bought a prophylactic for contraception. We had intercourse, but she wasn't too excited, didn't have an orgasm, and kept complaining that it hurt. I then had a strong feeling that I should leave, otherwise, I'd feel depressed and drained the next day. Yet I was in no hurry to leave. I just wanted to lie in bed for a long time. When I finally got ready to leave, she started to cry. I asked why. She told me it was because I was leaving. When I reminded her of our agreement, she became very angry [pause].

4   Why did I get the hour mixed up today? Perhaps I was worried you wouldn't be here, and I had a great need for you to be here. There's been so much changing in the past week, I wanted the hour to hold on to. Tomorrow is Laura's birthday. I bought her a card on the way here. I still miss her and feel confused about Phoebe. Right now I feel anxious, but not depressed. There's a tightness in my stomach. The beers last night didn't loosen Laura up, but she's got a tiger in

her tank. Something in my balls tells me to call her up, but in my heart I'm undecided. My head says no. My heart feels sad [tears]. I'm thinking about Laura and the sadness of our predicament [more tears]. I think I love her, but yet we can't seem to make it. I want to be with her, yet when I am, I can't stand it [more tears]. ["Does it not seem likely that what you both need is an opportunity to reflect on and work out the meaning of the relationship?"] Yes, but it's difficult. I don't want to move. She keeps crying that I'm leaving.

6/20

I just had my teeth filled. My mouth is kind of numb. So, if I don't speak   1
well, you'll understand [pause]. Whatever's cooking smells fine [has become aware of faint odor of cooking which drifted into the room before the hour began]. Today, Laura's birthday doesn't make it easier. I want to go to Philadelphia this weekend. All my friends are leaving. Laura doesn't care to go to Philadelphia with me. If I go alone, would I dare have a date with Phoebe? It might get back to Laura who wouldn't understand why I did it, nor could she be expected to. She might fly into a cold rage, and then I would get angry at her. That would lead to a complete breakup because of a casual date that I've had. I don't feel ready to do that.

I've been very anxious today. There's a new chief engineer. I missed an   2
important meeting with him this morning because of my dental appointment. I feel guilty at running out on my responsibilities. Yet on the surface I don't show it. Others ask how I can come and go so casually. I never looked on that as much of an asset, because I know what's bubbling inside.

I continue to feel very tense. I want to understand more of this business with   3
the girls. I'd like to get Laura a present for her birthday and take her out to a concert. There's lots of guilt. That makes it harder for me to see if I really want to get her a present. I can't afford more than five dollars—that's baloney. My schedule makes it difficult to get to Laura's place until later in the evening [pause].

My dentist is the same one that Dick used. He's very nice. Most of the time   4
he talks with me about music. I don't know if he's a good dentist; he seems very casual about filling teeth. I think you're a better analyst than Dr. X who treated me before. But he was better at giving me certain things which I needed. I really like him. He was my friend, cared about me, was on my side. He helped me feel more like a man. Sometimes I think you can be tough—right now, for instance. Maybe my head has been clouded by the dentistry. Half of my face feels numb; there are the beginnings of a headache, and my eye hurts—all on the left side. I feel as if my head has been through the wringer. I can't decide about calling that girl in Philadelphia [pause].

Now I'm aware of an uneasy feeling. A stomach feeling, tightness and   5 crampiness. I'm very uncertain where I stand with Laura. I've been so furious with her. She's not sexually exciting or excited, but she's working on the problems that interfere. I guess I've had strong feelings she doesn't like me, and that's made me feel mightly low. It's all related to Laura's behavior. She gets excited, seems just about to have an orgasm, at which point I usually do, then she just doesn't and backs off. If I hold back, then intercourse gets stretched out, stays on a plateau, and then tapers off with neither of us coming. I still find her body exciting. But there are times when she completely turns me off. The last time we had intercourse she said it was hurting her, and I didn't know what to do. I said to myself, "You bitch, how typical! It's like throwing cold water on me. Why don't you drop dead?" ["Who's you?"] Before the question it was Laura, now it's you. You're supposed to do analyses and I want more. But in life there's a reasonable entitlement. I don't want to deny myself that right.

6/21

1   It's warm here today. Very good. I sense a contrast between the warmth of this heated room and the coldness of the analysis. I was late today [by eight minutes] maybe because I took what you said yesterday as meaning I was no good, a rejection. Last night Laura had her birthday. She's really got a nonsupportive family, but I was nice to her. Later we had sex. It worked out very well for a change. We went to my place. She at first wanted only to be held and gently caressed. She's very fearful of penetration. But after being held a while, she got very excited. She had an orgasm with me on the outside, using my penis to masturbate. Then she wanted me to come in, and I came afterward. Then we both went to sleep. After I left her I was still mad and yet also glad that I could act more freely. Last night I tried to make clear to Laura what I considered our arrangement to be. One reason we've stayed together so long has been my guilt. I had a fantasy last night that Laura wanted to rip my penis off, and I found that very exciting.

2   I had a dream of a person I haven't seen for at least eight months. He's a selfish binge alcoholic—a clinging, sucking guy, in some ways like me [loud stomach rumble of which the patient is unaware]. In the dream, he flies an old-fashioned airplane, but not well. It seems he's soon to be fired from whatever he's doing. I just now feel a tremendous, sharp, knife-like pain in my left hip. Ouch! I'll cross my legs; there, that's better. The pain is going away. In the rest of the dream, I'm driving a car with this fellow, and then another person appears—a pretty, seductive, 18-year-old girl. That's all there was to it. The girl is this fellow's daughter. She can never get angry with him, just laughs things off—a habit which I have too, from way back. I feel I'm off the subject—how I came to be angry in the first place. You can't win; I'm angry whatever you do—whether you're quiet and not giving, or talk and give what I think is not enough or right. [Transference interpretation: Analyst seen as frustrating parent.]

To be a patient in psychoanalysis is an admission I'm no good. I hate you for your silence, and I hate you for telling me things that make me feel I'm no good. If I were any good, I wouldn't have to come. [Clarification: Goal of work here is factual understanding, not moral and judgmental understanding.] Now I'm mad at you for criticizing me, even though reason tells me you're not criticizing. The last time I got angry at you I got an attack of arthritis. That's ridiculous. I never heard anything so ridiculous in my whole mind [laughing] —I mean, in my whole life. I was going to mouth the party line, but suddenly I think of mother calling me endearing names. Anyhow I was going to say that it's like mouthing the sayings of the little red book of Mao Tse Tung—only in this case it's the sayings of psychosomatic medicine. You've talked about anger, guilt, and suffering. I'm not wholly convinced, though there's lots of evidence to prove that's what's going on in me. I find myself not enjoying this session [pause]. 3

How did I ever get to feeling that I'm no good? I remember vomiting several times on the way to school when I was a kid. It seems I had to eat mashed bananas for a long time afterwards. What made me feel no good? I saw my parents fight when I was four years old. One fight I'll never forget—my father smashing my mother. Now I have an image of father sitting in his chair, not wanting anything to do with me. I often wondered if I was adopted. Why was I born? It was accidental. Father must have resented my presence. [Interpretation of transference implications.] 4

6/22

I'm late. I drove here with a splitting headache which began two hours ago. I stopped to get a hot dog. I had a choice. If I got here early, I could urinate. But then maybe if I got some food into myself, it would make the headache better. I could have been on time if I hadn't eaten. Things are winding up—there are terminations all over the place. I have no wife, no children, just a dingy hole of a place to live and an effeminate relationship with a girl who has many problems. It's easier to get angry than to feel loneliness and sadness. I can stand only two hours of it. I'm thinking now that there's a carton of potato salad in the car, and I'm wondering if it'll get spoiled. I have nothing for myself in terms of people. That's an exaggeration. I really don't believe that. Yet I ate dinner alone last night. I hate that: eating alone, walking alone, living alone. But you have to do it. So I resolved to live alone for a while—apart from Laura—and to experience loneliness to see if I could bear it. I told Laura last night that I wouldn't be around for dinner. There are some projects at work that are going well, and I mean to make a study of the meaningful things that are happening there. 1

Last night mother called. At this point I feel as if I want to leave this room. I have the fantasy of wanting to finish the hot dog. Now I feel like urinating. She called—so—now I feel dizzy—it was an anger-provoking call. I was so furious, I didn't know what to do. Her tone of voice, clawing at me: "So sad I'm not with 2 you. What did you do with the money I gave you?" I didn't get angry on the phone with her, but within I felt furious. To give a kid with a bellyache a sundae isn't doing him a favor. My rage was unbelievable; I felt like killing her. After my mother called, it became a matter of urgency for me to be with Laura, with somebody. So Laura and I went for a walk. I felt sad after I was mad. I'm already over 30, but I want to be treated like a prince, yet feel deprived of lots of things. Mother is trying to turn me into her dead, long-lost brother who, I think, committed suicide. I sound just like my mother, whining, "Woe is me." Fuck it, woe is not me. It was a nice walk I took. What's the big deal if Laura is frigid or not frigid? She's a nice girl, except when she's depressed. Every little fucking thing gets me so mad. I keep thinking of that hot dog sitting on the front seat of my car, getting cold; that gets me mad. You won't let me go out and get the hot dog and finish it now.

3   I'm feeling dizzy, headachy. I feel like I'm getting arthritis. For the first time in weeks a pall of depression is settling over me. Now I have the fantasy of chopping telephone wire with an axe. That phone conversation with mother. I can't leave her angrily without feeling guilty. Well, I'm not leaving her just yet. I can hear you asking—is it your mother or Laura you're talking about? I wish I knew what the fuck was coming off. My real problem is my uncertainty.

4   Now I'm aware my elbows hurt. I feel like screaming. I'm angry about that phone call, about the food that I can't have when I want it, angry because everybody's leaving. I can't stand the loneliness. I'm undecided about going out with the other girl in Philadelphia this weekend because I haven't finished this thing with Laura here. I'm damned if I go out and damned if I don't. I'm damned because I hate mother. I'm the son-of-a-bitch who hates his mother because she's a farthead [bangs couch]. I hate my whole fucking family, Laura, you, the universe. I hate because I have nothing. It's not so simple with mother. She gives and gives. I hate the giving. She gives more than I'm entitled to, of a certain variety. She doesn't give respect—but food, yes. She gives money till it makes me vomit, except I don't. I feel I've got her inside my fucking little joints. I feel like an infant for talking like this, but I feel it, I feel it! I should be cool, calm, and collected, but I'm in a fucking rage. Hell has no fury like a woman scorned. The woman is me who is scorned by mother. I was an unwanted child, probably accidentally born. Father was thinking of divorce, then I came along, and he couldn't get it till much later. He must hate me. Mother didn't really want me either, just wanted me to keep the marriage together.

6/26

1   Been thinking about when your vacation will occur. I thought I was falling apart last Friday, the day after our last interview. I got joint pains on Friday as plain as ever. I've been blaming you for them. I figured you should be able to

cure them and you haven't—so I've been mad at you. I remember getting up last Thursday morning depressed and developing a headache by the time I arrived for my hour. I had an uneasy feeling that the joint pains were coming on. Then I had the idea that if I got mad it would avert the joint pains, but though I got mad at mother, they came on anyway the next day.

I went to Philadelphia this past weekend. I was scheduled to say goodbye to Mike, a roommate from the university. I was also going to say goodbye to my sister who was going to Europe with her family for six weeks. When I did, I found myself growing mad at them. I just had a brief twinge of pain in my elbows and shoulders. Otherwise right now I feel O.K.   2

I called Phoebe in Philadelphia Friday, and she was happy to hear from me. I invited her to dinner Saturday evening, but she said she was going to be away in the country for the weekend. My father and I had a long talk on Sunday. We talked about Laura and where I stood with her. I was glad to do it. I told him there was a problem between us, that she was wrapped up in herself. My angry view of her called for distance. He concluded that things between Laura and me were all over, but I said that wasn't so. When I mentioned her frigidity, he suggested there was more to it than that and asked if she took pride in my work. I said, "Not much." I didn't get in touch with my mother. Since she doesn't talk to my father, sister, or friends, she wouldn't know I had been in town. I didn't want to insult her, just kill her. The reason I can't get involved with a girl for marriage is that in some ways it's equated with the murder of mother—not equated, but associated with it.   3

My joint pains went away after I saw my sister. I found myself very angry at seeing her on Saturday. I let fly at her for going off and leaving mother all to me. I'm so disgusted with both of them. By Sunday morning the pains had gone. This episode of arthritis was a short one: Thursday evening, Friday, and Saturday. It was very bad on the train going to Philadelphia, very painful. But it doesn't seem to be coming back. Maybe I have a mother in my joints. It sounds funny that that's what came to mind. These joint pains date back to longer than her joint pains, if what I had at age four or five was the same thing.   4

I felt that as long as I had the joint pains, I was an invalid and passive, and couldn't get the girl I wanted. I would have to choose a neurotic girl who would accept a guy with joint pains. I inquired how Mr. Z was; he's had very severe rheumatoid arthritis—a very great gentleman. Now at 45 he's in a wheelchair. Oh shit! There but for the grace of God, go I! These joint pains which I should learn to live with turn me into an emotional cripple. Going down on the train to Philadelphia I kept saying to myself, "Oh shit, here they come again." Yet here I am back without them. I thought maybe I did something to avert them, I don't know. [Pause. Right index finger in mouth.]   5

I notice my finger's in my mouth. I think of father's apartment and mine; mine's much nicer. It's not for me to have such an adult-like apartment. Maybe   6

I'm more identified with father than I like to think. I asked him what he was going to do about his situation—whether he's going to get married again, now that I've talked about myself. He hedged. I told him that I've heard that stalling before. If he wouldn't hedge, maybe I wouldn't hedge. I've got pains in my knees right now. If my father wants to marry the woman he's going around with now, then he and mother would have to get divorced, and that would leave mother and me alone. At this point I want to leave your office, but I won't. I suspect that I don't want to face my feelings around what I'm talking about. Maybe I want mother for myself alone. It's not nice to have your mother alone, if she's a sucking bitch. But father and sister ran out on me, left me handling her, holding the bag. That's why I'm so much in a rage at them. They left me with that bag. That pain in the knees is bothering me.

7   Now I have the fantasy of getting a hot pastrami sandwich before I return to work. I keep thinking I won't get a chance to eat tonight, but I don't work late tonight. Laura offered to help me move into my new apartment. I appreciated that. Now my right elbow hurts. Talking to one of my friends in Philly, he commented that it must have placed a large strain on Laura; not only did she have to be my girlfriend, but she had to replace all of my friends when I left that city. When I lived there I had lots of friends and didn't have to depend solely on Laura for emotional contacts. After leaving Philly, I was very lonely and expected her to fill the void, and she couldn't. She was away from her friends too, and so we did a job on each other. She turned me on last night—the bitch [laughter]. She looked so pretty. I suggested we spend the night at my place. She refused, and I felt myself getting mad. But I said, "Don't" to myself, "You know she's going through a difficult time herself. She can't replace all your departing friends this time again. You don't need sex as much as you think." So I kissed her goodnight and went to bed alone. Now I feel a bit like crying. I felt proud I could do what I did, as if I have some integrity. I have a suspicion if I can learn to face loneliness for a while, it'll be a great help. If Laura doesn't become less frigid, I will move on. She wanted to be held last night like a little baby. In a strange way I enjoy being a mother, and she enjoys the mothering.

8   That's so sick. I think I'm trying to avoid something—guilty feeling about not calling my mother when I was in Philadelphia. I had a conversation with myself: "Do you want to see her? No. Do it for her sake, just to say hello. I don't have the time nor do I want to see her." I guess I didn't want the pain that comes along with it. If I had called, she would have asked me to come up. I could have said that I just can't, don't have the time. If she knew I were there but didn't come, she'd flip her lid so it would be easier, actually less cruel not to call, thus not tantalize and not come [bitter laughter]. That's what Laura did to me last night.

6/27–7/2, Interim Summary

Strong wishes for treatment to be subsidized by the analyst appear in the patient's associations. He then remembers his father's severe kidney infection which occurred when the patient was seven years old and which was followed by disintegration of the marriage shortly afterwards. June 27 excerpt: "After father's return from the hospital and his recovery from illness, the family would never sit down together for meals. These memories make me feel empty and dizzy. I want to leave the office, not think about these things. The sun is in my eyes. [He stands up and partially closes drapes of adjacent window, then lies down again on couch.] I shouldn't have stood up. I feel dizzier than before. Besides I didn't do a good job. [He closes the drapes still more.] It's painful to remember those days. Father would come home depressed and tired, and would have to take his meals by himself. I remember eating with mother mostly, not much with sister around. She used to go off to her girlfriend's house. The times we were together were angry dinners where everyone got indigestion. Claws were dug in so deep that their extrication was even more painful. I'm angry at you again now—do you realize how much I work and still have a marginal existence? Anyway it's easier to talk about my current troubles that those horrible mealtimes years ago."

There is further rage at Laura whom he blames for not giving him enough and for not helping him, as he is in the process of moving from his old apartment to a better one. He verbalizes continued resentment at the analyst for not loaning him money and being supportive in other ways. These irrational accusations clash with his realistic appraisal of the analysis.

7/3

I was grateful that you changed the time. I had a sort of enjoyable weekend. You had damn well better have changed it, or I would have killed you. That's all talk, you know. It's stuffy in here. Can I open the window?   1

Saturday Laura went out of town to a wedding. I went on my first date with another girl for the first time in two and one-half years. I took out one of the secretaries, Fran. She had been going out with a guy who's leaving for the West Coast. I invited her out to dinner, but she had already eaten. So we went for drinks and spent a very nice evening talking. I guess I acted like a little kid. Didn't know whether to kiss her goodnight or not.   2

Friday night I had a dream in which you told me to stop going out with Laura. I was surprised that I dreamt it like that. It enabled me to be freer. But Sunday morning I felt a bit queasy. The night previously I had experienced   2 extreme excitement—sweaty hands and a persistent erection. I felt funny because I was staying in Laura's house in her absence; you see, my own bed in the new apartment hadn't been set up yet. I thought you wouldn't approve. I had the strange feeling of being a kept man. Yet I had made it clear to Laura that we had an understanding that we could go out with other people. Fran is aware of my setup. Still I feel guilty.

4   I haven't heard from mother in three weeks. Fran looks like my mother, but she's of a different religion. With Fran I feel a sense of release—as if I could be a man and have a family. But all is not perfect. Afterwards I had doubts; Fran seemed inappropriate for me intellectually—not bright enough. Now I feel excited in my genitals. When we walked out of the bar, we were both a little high. I offered my arm. She took it, and it was alive. I had almost forgotten that feeling—like electricity. I kissed her goodbye in a warm way but not so that we would have to follow this up. On Sunday I had fantasies all day about her. I remembered a bite mark on her arm—at least she's not been shy with somebody. That excited me, but give it time and it'll get me down. Fran told me I was well thought of at work. I've found it so hard to hear positive things from others. If you want to be superman, just being yourself is crummy. I feel like crying. It's possible to be loved for one's self. I don't read enough. I feel I have to be great—better than my father, better than Laura's father who also makes me feel less than nothing. Now I'm getting into the intellectual sphere. The heart of the matter is that I was very mad at Laura for going away this weekend. The loneliness became too much for me, and I saw somebody else.

7/5

1   I've been experiencing pain in my right side, front and back [right upper quadrant]. It's like a spasm. In the last two days I've had it twice. It's something I've had before. It's a dull, constant, dragging sensation, radiating into the groin, and there's slight nausea. It feels as if I'd been kicked in the groin. Strange, just as I said that it eased up.

Last night I masturbated. I started thinking of Fran, but my fantasies then went in a homosexual direction, and I thought of mutual masturbation with men, including my father and you. Had an unusual ejaculation; it went a mile, and I caught it in the neck. It made me feel dirty. I couldn't get to sleep until late. Then I dreamt and I woke up with the pain and lots of anxiety. It was the first night I had slept in my apartment. The dream: I got a call from my father and was very curt with him on the phone.

The pain just went away again for a few seconds. It must be a spasm.

2   Yesterday I felt quite miserable. It was a different kind of pain—the pain of being with Laura who returned terribly depressed. We went to the beach and I picked up her mood. I kept thinking I wish I were with Fran instead of her.

Then I was thinking of last week's hours. I didn't quite understand the look you gave me as I left. I took it to be a look of disgust. I was feeling unwanted and criticized for my inability to do good work here. I tried to understand my anger yesterday, but I would get lost in the pleasure of hatred. I thought of a movie about German troops who treated women sadistically. The fantasies included putting knives in vaginas and were accompanied by sexual excitement and anxiety. It seems to me that Laura is really doing analysis on herself, and I'm not able to. She can sustain a terribly deep depression, but I can't. I think—the hell with psychiatry. All I need is to find the right relationship, but then that's coupled with the fear that it's all a lot of baloney.

Yesterday I had a memory of punching mother when I was ten or eleven   3
years old, on the arm mostly, and she didn't do anything about it. I keep asking, what am I so angry at Laura for? And why at mother in those days? It seems like it was mostly temper tantrums, not getting something I wanted. I feel like crying all of a sudden [pause].

If I'm really going to analyze my relationships with girls, I'm afraid they'll   4
turn out to have been empty ones. Now I have the fantasy of a small ship in a stormy sea with ups and downs. I hate you for what's happening to me. I came for analysis, and now I'm full of hatred. Analysis means waiting, being unable to get married and have a family until I understand myself better. It could go on forever.

It's too late to get what I want. Again I have the memory of being in the   5
kitchen with mother and punching her—my wanting to go outside and her not letting me. Now I have the fantasy of putting my penis between her legs. Thinking back to mother makes me cry internally. I have memories of lying in bed with her and touching her. I remember her giving me an enema. She herself was always taking enemas. I remember when I was a student in Europe, I had dysentery and returned to the U. S. with some blood in my stools. I thought I had cancer at the time. I was run through all the x-rays and lab tests. That damn pain is still there in my right side. I remember enjoying giving enemas to myself when I was younger [pause].

Fran's build reminds me of mother's—having a little spare tire around the   6
middle. Mother used to walk around with hardly any clothes, and I wasn't supposed to look. Now I feel like crying. One of my friends tried to punch his mother, when we were kids, and she wouldn't have any part of it. My sister and I used to play games where I tried to hit her hand, but she was too quick for me, and I would hurt myself, my wrist, not her. ["You talk about inflicting or trying to inflict pain on others for not giving you all you want, and then you talk of experiencing bodily pain now—it is an expression of your guilt feelings."] [Pause.]

I feel I'm not able to work at my analysis. I'm too sick, too babyish. I'm not   7
willing to bear the pain. Maybe I'm a psychopath—you can't do analysis with a

psychopath. I'm just a shallow person, but Laura is not. She's really able to do something with her treatment. I'm asking for you to tell me that I'm not inferior to Laura and capable of continuing in analysis. Mistakes have been made about treatment. Perhaps I should have had more psychotherapy. Somehow the inscrutable women are right, and men don't stand a chance. This lady consultant that saw me before I came here wasn't sure I should undergo analysis.

7/6

1   It's going to be a crummy day for me and you. The schedule I have now is too hectic. Had no dreams last night. I'm unable to make a decision about going to Philadelphia and seeing Phoebe. That horn blowing outside makes me think I'm wanted out there and not in here.

2   I felt great pressure to have a date last night. I asked myself why I didn't call Fran to drop over for a cup of tea after work. My reply was that I shouldn't get involved with her unless I really meant it. I asked myself whether I couldn't bear a little loneliness. Well, I couldn't make up my mind. I just thought of Philadelphia and Phoebe, but I haven't got the money for the trip.

3   The pain went away when I got up this morning. Actually, no. It went away around one o'clock yesterday, though it was very sharp around noon when I had to attend a conference [several hours after yesterday's interview]. I'll bet it was from masturbating—that's a dirty business.

4   Instead of an idealized picture of Fran, I have one that's negative to neutral, limp to limpid. It's as though I'm afraid to ask her out again. I would like to take her out both days this weekend. But I feel guilty—as if I owe the weekends to Laura. I'm getting an erection as I say this. I'm not sure that I have any obligation to Laura. I've taken your remarks to mean that I don't have this obligation. Thinking of taking Fran out gets me sexually excited [part of right hand is put in mouth]. [Pause.] Hand's in mouth. Now I have a fantasy of sucking a penis—yours. For some reason Fran today looked like a mean, nagging bitch, just like mother. I can't stand such images of women. It occurs to me that father was warmer than mother. But that wasn't so when I was younger. It's true now. I'm worried whether I'll have time to get a sandwich on the way back.

5   I feel I've got to show consistency and loyalty to Laura—evidence that I'm not shallow, so I can't abandon her. It's like an obligation to myself: by being disloyal to her, I also am to myself. There seems to be a semi-agreement between us. She's so depressed though. Fran may not be as bright, but she's a lot healthier in her own way; she's enjoyable to be with. Only two people know how I felt when I had the joint pain, you and Dick. Fran thinks I'm healthy and robust. She's going out with some athlete as well as me. The feeling I have is wouldn't she be doing to me what I do to Laura? Here's this virile athlete, bright enough for her, and along comes this passive, mealy-mouthed, so-called intellectual, me. She'll leave me. The tables will be turned with the woman

having the penis. Still that sounds way out, I really don't know this girl; we've had only one short date. Maybe Fran will nurture me.

7/7 - 7/27, Interim Summary (Followed by summer interruption)

Negative transference is manifest around late payment of the fee—related to intense oral needs and their frustration; it is also manifested in coming late to the analytic hour. The relationship with Fran continues to develop with greater sexual contact but no intercourse, while the relationship with Laura deteriorates. The patient becomes concerned that homosexual feelings are being warded off by this changing relationship with girls. There are recollections of fishing with father and competition with him. In the analysis the patient now tries to give pleasing associations and formulations. He recalls an ideal father-figure in the person of one of his teachers who had been analyzed, a married man whose wife is also remembered in an idealized way. There has, however, been no contact with them for several years. The patient remembers the motherly aspects of his former therapist toward whom, however, there is strong ambivalence. Affect in the form of transient sadness is expressed in connection with a hostile, dependent relationship to father. There is another unsatisfactory date with Laura followed by fantasies of sucking on breasts which is sexually stimulating, but when this is associated with mother, it becomes revolting to him. The patient's tiredness, passivity, and tendency to almost fall asleep during an hour are linked with memories of father's falling asleep and concern that the analyst will. He reproaches himself for indecision, babyishness, and sucking-clawing tendencies alternating with hostility toward his bitch-mother, as he calls her. There are also references to the summer interruption and missing the analyst. Laura and Fran are compared, and the former is seen as intellectual and cold, the latter as not so bright but more giving. The patient verbalizes his repetitive concern about being left alone and not having his intense narcissistic needs fulfilled. This is followed by memories of mutually angry scenes with mother, her postmenopausal depression, and her inadequate treatment. He has recollections of high school and the need to excel in extracurricular activities, mostly seen as effeminate; yet he is obsessed with proving he wasn't and isn't a fairy. There are other recollections of summer vacations. He expresses concern and rage about regressing during this period, being left to the mercy of women [his mother and the girls].

9/6

[Preliminary discussion of schedule.]
[Blows nose.] I think I'm coming down with a cold. It's good to be back. In   1

the past week I've had masturbation fantasies which, though they were homosexual, didn't frighten me.

2   I've been acting out or playing around in the past five weeks or so. I've been going out with Fran. There's been lots of rubbing but no intercourse. Once I came in my pants—it was bloody. I guess I'd been rubbing too hard. I was frightened. It was ridiculous, like high school stuff. With your coming back, I haven't asked Fran out lately, and she's mad as hell at me. I've also started going out with another girl—Ruth, daughter of a famous industrialist. My previous therapist's middle name was Larry. I went from Larry to Laura, then to Fran. Now, in the past two weeks I've been seeing Ruth. If I can't have an important, great father, I at least will have his daughter. Just to make things more complicated I've also been seeing Laura again. When she came back from vacation, we had an elegant dinner and then went to bed. She wasn't frigid, but not exactly a flame. Before that we had been having a cold war. When I was with her I cried, said I wanted more from her, felt this need intensely, felt like a slave to it. But she really can't give what I crave. Now I feel like crying here. She too is the daughter of a famous man.

3   Last week for the first time in my life I felt able to handle my homosexual fantasies directly and effectively. I'm not as frightened of them as I thought I'd be. I have a notion that they're related to your coming back and to my sexual escapades with the woman I've been talking about. Having said this, I have the fear of being thrown out of analysis. It's as if I'm asking for reassurance that you won't do it.

4   Ruth has quite an interest in food. She put together an amazing picnic lunch. But I find myself sexually inhibited with her, as she is with me. I wonder if it has anything to do with her father. Am I somehow afraid of him?

5   I missed you, yet was relieved I didn't have to come in—saving all that time and money. Yet there were occasions this summer when loneliness was very difficult to deal with, especially when I got the flu-diarrhea thing and was alone and away from everyone for a week. Just this past Sunday mother called me because she had a letter from me and thought I sounded lonely in it.

9/7

1   I have a cold, a head cold with running nose, stuffy sinuses. It seems to have started yesterday. I've been taking a cold pill and feel a little out of it. [He is quite slowed up and there are frequent pauses.]

2   I felt depressed most of last month and still do. It's mostly about feeling my need for so much and the realization I can't get it. At times I've cried inwardly. During vacation I was propositioned by several lonely prostitutes, but I didn't get involved. No V.D. for me. Then I would have thoughts of being close to father, and they would turn into sexual fantasies of anal intercourse.

I feel like crying, remembering the times Fran has held my hand   **3**
sympathetically. It's hard to think now because I feel stuffed up, wrapped up in
my symptoms and my bodily misery. Other thoughts seem to have become
fleeting, scattered. I keep thinking you don't understand my feelings and needs.
[Begins to cry]. It generates a fury in me. I have you to take care of me and you
don't. [Transference aspects of child-parent relationship interpreted.] I don't
want words. I want love. I feel like crying again; but I won't. I'll show you I'm
tough and don't need to be taken care of like a baby.

9/8

How can you bear to listen to all this so early in the morning? I would find it   **1**
hard to do. I shifted my date with Ruth from Saturday night to tonight. Ruth
gave me the name of her cleaning woman. I haven't been able to get in touch
with her. The idea of having her in my apartment makes me anxious. Do I really
want her cleaning it? Evidence of any of my activities there, especially with
other girls, would get reported back to Ruth. It's like having your mother in the
apartment.

I've got three women: Laura, Fran, and now Ruth. I can't go out with three   **2**
women. Last night, when I was with Fran, I told her I can't go out with her on a
dating basis any more until I resolve things between Laura and myself. I got
frightened of Fran, I think. It has to do with a masturbation fantasy of mine
that she's going to suck me dry. I was also frightened by all the sexual rubbing
around that caused me to ejaculate blood. But I guess that's just due to some
local irritation. However, I was very worried for a while. She's not had
intercourse with anyone, but she's not a cold person. I've been seeing more of
her than anybody else in a long while. That sucking dry fantasy arouses me. But
then I also get scared that she's getting too involved with me.

I have difficulty in talking about Ruth here. I keep having the fantasy that   **3**
she's your daughter. One problem is that her father is a famous industrialist—a
big shot in the business world. I feel guilty that I keep wanting to make him my
father. I want to suck off the famous father. The daughter is a means to get to
the father. [Interpretation: To give—in role of parent—is to be sucked on; to
receive—in role of child—is to suck from; both roles appear in associations.] As I
think it over, Ruth represents the girl with the most supplies—the most to
offer—although she's got small breasts. But she offers food, and she offers
intellectual stuff.

Now I keep thinking of myself in the active and passive roles in penetrating   **4**
anal intercourse. I recall the time my mother tried to give me an enema. Fran
really gives me support, a kind of love. I feel sexually aroused talking about her,
but she's not pretty and she's overweight. Even as I feel excited, I'm afraid of
getting sucked dry and ending up with a bloody penis. Ruth is nice but doesn't

arouse me sexually the way Fran does. Still she has lots of other things going: there are many interests that we have in common and can talk about. We come from the same area. She both lets me lead and yet lets me know if she doesn't like some things. While I'm telling you all this, there are fantasies about her father, the famous, yet kooky industrialist, the great inventor, who's a little bit crazy. I felt guilty revealing this to you, as if I'm telling secrets Ruth has confided in me. I really feel guilty because I have this desire to suck off him. You see, Ruth is frigid.

9/11 - 9/24, Interim Summary

There is continued comparison of the girls and indecision about which one is most suitable for him. He considers how they may remind him of mother's good and bad qualities. Despite a negative reaction to Laura's passivity and coldness, he resumes sexual intercourse with her, using condoms with the fantasy that they prevent him from giving anything to her. Immediately afterwards he has a somatic reaction—a brief spasm of the anal sphincter, coupled with fantasies of anal intercourse in which he assumes the passive role in a disguised way. His marked concern about having a basic defect is manifested in many ways: being a poor analysand, doesn't dream, may require an interminable analysis, and in the end remain an "unmarried, homosexual, bachelor prick." There is resentment at not being given enough by everyone, including the analyst, followed by a strong need to shout and threaten or plead in order somehow to get attention. At times he resorts to masturbation with hostile and incestuous impulses toward mother figures as well as identification with them as screaming, demanding, and seductive. Anger is mixed with guilt following a phone call from mother who spoke of how much she is suffering and has suffered. Fran being away for two weeks reinforces his lonely feelings and turns him toward Ruth. Dreams reveal that a powerful motivation in coming to analysis is to be both fed and in the process to surreptitiously get a big penis which people will think he always had; they will not know he wants to use it destructively. Superego activity interferes with constructive and understanding use of analysis, decreases self-esteem, and increases feelings of isolation and loneliness.

9/25

1   It's stupid and ridiculous just talking. My life stinks. No amount of talk will do any good. Friday night I went out to dinner with an older woman who looks like my mother. Then to her apartment for a drink. It was screwy because there's nothing going on between us. Yet I get sexually aroused and anxious after a couple of drinks. I wanted to go home and be alone. I did and masturbated with different fantasies—in some I was in bed with this woman who

was sucking my penis and biting it. Also fantasies about another woman I know who wanted me very much and would do anything for me. I was tied in a chair and immobilized by her. She danced nude in front of me as I developed an erection, with her slapping it. In another scene she was beating me and also giving me enemas—which was very arousing and brought me to a climax as I thought of torture enemas with colon filled almost to bursting. Now I have associations of mother giving me enemas when I was six or seven, while I was lying on the floor. I'll kill any woman who gives a son of mine enemas. Now I feel like crying [pause]. Now I feel the beginning of a spasm near my anus. The muscles of my right buttock are twitching [pause].

That's stopped. Saturday night I was out with Ruth—very nice. Because it   2
was so late, I asked to stay over because I was afraid of being mugged on the way home. I had a dream of a lake. One side was shady, the other sunny. I was walking around with Ruth. I encountered mother about to go swimming in the murky water. Some associations occur to me in the middle here. A woman whom I know is smearing feces over me, and it's both exciting and degrading. I think of my previous therapist, that I identify with him in so many ways. Back to the dream: I refuse to go swimming with mother, duck the cold part, and go to the other side of the lake where it's warm, good, and there are lots of people around. Other associations occur to me: I'm thinking of the good and the bad mother. If Ruth and I got married that would be warm and gregarious. Now I feel like crying. Ruth and I went out for lunch yesterday, on a little picnic along the river, but it was cold. I guess Ruth is the good mother and Laura the bad one.

9/26

I have a toothache this morning. Last night I went to see Laura. I didn't   1
quite know why. I guess it was to say I wouldn't see her any more, but nothing was decided. When I got there, she was not her usual depressed self, but quite happy, while I wasn't. My toothache is bothering me. I hadn't eaten dinner. I had also told Ruth I would call her. I better go to the dentist right after here. Anyway, I went out for a sandwich last night, then came back to Laura's. We talked. I said I didn't see why this torture should be continued. There was so much resentment going back so far, even if I didn't feel that way to begin with—it developed later. Ever since two years ago there have been frequent battles between us with few lulls. I kept a diary of a trip we made together, and we fought all the time.

I had a dream about men getting killed. Didn't want to come here this   2
morning. I keep wondering whether I'll be able to work with my second therapist—you. The anger towards the first one interferes and makes work with you difficult. Maybe I'll need a third.

3   With Laura I felt passive and whiny as I was talking. She was making light of a lot of things. I wanted to hurt her badly, but all I said was it would be best to have a moratorium on dates. This was coupled with the feeling that I don't want that—I want to patch things up and get back to living with her. I couldn't completely remove myself. I also wanted time to clear myself with Ruth. But I didn't get to call her. I fell asleep, still dressed, about 2 A.M. Then I had several dreams. First, I dreamt of Mary whom I knew years ago. She was engaged but not married as she actually is. I felt very happy about her. I associate Mary and Laura. A breakup with Laura is a breakup with Mary, so I guess five years from now I'll be talking this way about Laura. Then in another dream, Mary is getting married but to someone other than her actual husband. I'm in the audience. Guess I wish it were me. I'm reminded of a letter from mother enclosing a birth announcement for a little boy born to my friend Mike in Philadelphia. That made me sad—he could and I couldn't.

4   I'm in a bind with Laura and Ruth. Ouch, my toothache! Fran is coming back from her vacation today, and I plan to pick her up at the airport. Cut the shit—I say to myself. Are you really interested in that girl? Not really. Why the fuck are you going to the airport? What do you want from her? Lots of love. The trouble with Laura started the first time I went to bed with her. Before that the relationship between us had been a light-hearted one. Afterwards, it was as if my penis were caught in her. Very painful to her and to me. She's demanding and spoiled. Not getting enough many years ago was a real loss, and I didn't work it out in my previous therapy. [Shows picture of himself at age ten with mother in a boat near a dock at a summer resort, and another picture of himself and father at the same place.] When I was going with Mary, I first developed spasm of the colon—a spastic colon, they called it. I remember being examined, a tube was inserted and air blown in; I felt my insides would burst. Mary wanted, insisted on our getting married. I was scared stiff, spastic. I do know this, that when I got rid of Mary, I got rid of my bowel trouble, and then got very anxious about the possibility of being homosexual. That's when I first went to see my previous therapist. I was able to find another girl who helped me get over the panic. She was a substitute for Mary.

9/28 - 10/8, Interim Summary

There is continued indecision about which girl to stay with, reflecting the intensity of Oedipal conflicts. Fear of getting involved with anyone is repetitive. Further references to guilt are brought up, especially in connection with intense hostility to mother, a major source of his severe superego formation: "If I don't please mother, I'm nothing, but there's no way to please her." Almost uncontrollable tearfulness follows a telephone conversation with his sister about getting together, with her absolute refusal to include their mother in the meeting and fury at him for suggesting it. Activation of negative transference is verbally and partially affectively expressed, because he feels he isn't being given enough. Self-devaluation continues. Intrusion of homosexual fantasies occurs along with the wish for greater closeness to father and father-figures. There is added guilt over this, and fear that nothing can help, including analysis. The patient reverts to masturbation with fantasies of being a girl, looking at himself, and feeling confused about what sex he is. There is ejaculation at the point of thinking himself a girl in whose rectum father has put his penis. He goes to Philadelphia to visit his relatives.

10/9

I got a cold which I picked up in Philadelphia. I feel like a child. It reminds **1** me of being sick when I was a kid. I could stay home and go to bed. Then nothing would be expected of me. I would try to forget about everything. Mother would take care of whatever I needed. She'd give me aspirin and cough syrup or help me feel comfortable. Right now I'd rather go to sleep than talk. The cold's bothering me too much.

Friday I visited my mother. Then that night I went to my sister's and saw **2** her. I slept over there. The cold then started the next morning with a fever, chills, and a big running nose. I left her house later in the day. I had no place to go, and I wanted to be alone. So I checked into a hotel, sick as a dog. I didn't know what was going to happen. I went to bed. Ruth had also come up to Philadelphia, and I had a date with her that night. After I had slept a couple of hours, the fever went down. I went to her place in a cab. We sat around for a while. Ruth was very considerate, and I began to feel good, in fact, better than now. So we went out to dinner. When we got back, we went to bed together in her place, but with the understanding that there'd be no intercourse. I didn't like it, but agreed. There we were, screwing around under the picture of her father. Through manipulation, I had an orgasm, but she didn't. I felt somewhat disappointed. Now I have a noise in my ears that's terribly annoying. I just want to go to bed and forget everything, but can't possibly do it. I can't admit I'm a patient.

She's a real fucking pain in the ass—my mother. To be bound so closely to **3** her and want so much to get away. I don't get a whole shit load of support from anyone else. I was with her and my sister's mother-in-law, two old ladies. I took them to church. In five minutes my mother was trying to get me to go from the side I picked to the side she wanted. I was furious, and told her to beat it, to get off my back. Then she kept dragging friends of hers over to meet me.

It's difficult to work with a stuffed nose. I just keep thinking of myself **4** today. That means I've grown up too attached to mother and not well related to other people, fearful and lonely. Mother is there at the expense of my peers. I have no friends but acquaintances [bitterly]. Do I feel to hell with the hour or not? I'll act up and blow my nose [he does]. Lying down this way is tough. Going to work will be tougher. I have this cold in my chest, besides my nose. But I'll get through somehow. I'm trying to paint a dismal picture, trying to impress you.

5   God punished me for going to Philadelphia when I had so much to do back here. Though I got angry with mother, I didn't feel any guilt over it. It's been a long time since I've had a cold like this. I remember having something like this when I was much younger, when father and sister went away on a pleasure trip. I was glad to see father back. It turned out to be chickenpox [pause].

6   Ruth treated me very nicely. I had fantasies of marrying her this weekend. I like her a lot. With Laura there's too much resentment. It's a relief not having spoken to her in a week. My right sinus was so painful, I couldn't sleep last night. Did I pick Ruth because she was frigid? How come I picked two girls in a row with charismatic fathers? My own family seems like nothing to me. I seek another family through these girls. I want not just a wife, but a father. I have a great longing to be taken care of, mothered, held. If it isn't an opulent father, it's a copulant cow.

10/10

1   I'm afraid to start. Guess I've been pretty angry and feeling hopeless. Angry at you for not saying anything yesterday. I keep feeling you don't like me—that's a projection. When you don't say anything, that gets me mad as hell. What the fuck is it all about? What I want is a treatment that supports; yet I really don't want just that. I want to find out more about myself [blows nose]. I feel better today than yesterday. I had an apple and spiced doughnut to eat. Apple mouth. Again I'm aware of your presence—would like to kill you. I'm not sure why. Jabbing at you with a right cross and a left hook [pause]. Feel like crying [nose sounds stuffed up, with heavy, loud breathing]. I want to kill you because I don't feel you care about me. But I realize how selfish I am. I keep asking myself: Isn't it enough to have your mother, and now your analyst, you narcissistic prick? Getting up this morning, I felt that what I wanted from Ruth is to borrow her father's prick, become the son-in-law of a famous industrialist. Is it worth paying the price to marry someone frigid? I want what I want so much. [Interpretation about intense orality which if ungratified provokes intense anger at the frustrating object; then the anger may be turned on himself for wanting so much.]

2   When I was younger, a lot was given to me of a certain variety—material things, food,—but not enough of another variety—a real interest in me. It's as if I grew up in an armed camp. That's what my home was like, with father and mother hating each other. I was treated as very special in some ways, but that

masks what's missing. Instead of a well-balanced meal, you get hot fudge sundaes. You feel something is missing, but it's hard to see it—all you see is hot fudge sundaes. There was, then and now, the feeling of not being backed up by the chief persons in my family and of being afraid I was going to be chopped up into little pieces.

Somehow for a while earlier today, even with my cold, I was effective, not thinking of other things that have anxiously preoccupied me.   **3**

When I was much younger, there was a period, for about a year, that I had terrible dreams—fear of dying. Sister was nice to me then. She would try to comfort me, saying it's something that happens to everybody. I felt more at ease, not so alone when she did that. I don't want to lose sister as a friend. But now sister's house itself is like an armed camp. Her husband is a furious man. He treats his kid as if she were the scum of the earth. I feel for that kid.   **4**

10/11

I come in here today feeling the patient before me is a better person on the couch than I am. I feel jealous. I want to control this hour, not go any place or do anything. When I talk about loving Ruth, it has to do with loving fathers. You know, it's characteristic of all relationships with women that I don't love any of them. No wonder I have such a hard time making up my mind about them. Now Fran is not frigid; she's very warm sexually, and I like that. But as a person Fran is not for me. Yet because she gives so much, I want her. What's the result? I feel guilty. She understands where I stand. When I turn to Ruth, I'm not at all clear. I feel like crying. I would really like to try and work at this.   **1**

Last night I was feeling sick again. Had fever. I kept thinking that I want someone to take care of me, to make me comfortable. It didn't make any difference whom I called. I had the thought of calling my mother and not screwing around with other people. But I didn't do that. I just wanted someone to come over and hold my hand. Then I wanted to talk to Ruth, but without letting her know how sick I was. So I called her, and we talked about other matters—talked shop. After quite a talk, my dinner was ready and I hung up. I realized I wanted more contact with her. But shitty and sick as I felt, I could still cook my own dinner, and take care of myself. Yet I continued to have the fantasy that I'll marry Ruth and depend on her for things to work out right.   **2**

It seems now as if I'm going around in circles. I keep thinking how you said a long time ago that my associations get stuck. But when I'm feeling so miserable, all I can think about is myself. I wonder whether I want to butter you up so you'll pay more attention to me or whether things are really improved. I keep thinking that to say something positive is to be insincere in a sense. Then I feel guilty, which makes me think I have to disavow the positive feeling. There must be a neurotic purpose in buttering you up and that is to cover up my anger.   **3**

4   Some queer thoughts are passing through my mind. Father's illness. I've been told people with kidney trouble may not have symptoms for years before. If Dad can't pee, Mommy can't pee, I can't pee. He had that trouble a long time ago, when I was a kid. Then there was that business with his arm—the bone infection that hung on for a long time no matter what they did for it.

10/12

[Comes late—25 minutes.]

1   Wasn't sure of whether there was an hour today or not. Yesterday I had some fever. I had some very necessary work to do at the office, but I was burning up with temperature and could hardly concentrate.

2   Last night I saw Fran. We just talked a little. I felt frustrated, restless all night. This morning I masturbated. Guess I didn't want to tell you and didn't want to come here. One fantasy was of having sexual intercourse with that older woman I took out some time ago. I treated her to a dinner unwillingly. She reminded me of my mother—a shrewish type. Why didn't I ask her to hop into bed with me that night? Anyway this morning I had the fantasy I did. That was followed by the desire to masturbate. Then I had wild thoughts of sex with you, being sucked by Ruth, finally intercourse with Fran.

3   Now I'm all the more aware of how physically sick I feel. I want Ruth to take care of me. Such passivity. I feel flaked out, tired, as if I'm getting over the flu. I don't want to go anywhere today, just stay put and have her take care of me.

4   There's a rising tide of anger in me again. Why am I so mad at you? I'm mad at your having an hour today so that I had to leave Ruth and that warm, cuddly feeling. I feel like crying. My passivity, my needs, my anger, my guilt are all so great.

10/16

[Four days since last interview]

1   I got my arthritis back today. Actually last night. It's most disconcerting. I just feel like crying.

2   I remember mother's sitting on my legs when, as a little boy, I had similar pain. I was taken to the doctor. Blood was drawn. It's been many months since I last had this pain. I had hoped it was gone. I'm very depressed by its return. It's like receiving a punch in the nose. I'm wondering how long and how bad it'll be this time. Trying to think—whom am I angry at? I'm furious at Ruth. Maybe I'm paranoid. Thursday night we got very close. We didn't go anywhere because I was still sick from the flu. After my interview here last Thursday, I returned to her. We both had such close, warm feelings and felt like crying. She wept hard.

Then later I had a feeling of well-being. I left her that night at 12 and had a good night's sleep. But on Friday I again felt crummy, though not as sick as earlier. We went out Friday night, had drinks at a cocktail lounge, but I felt uneasy, because I'd been there with Fran. Then we went back to her place. We started to make out, and she got sick and dizzy. So she took some medicine, felt better, and encouraged me to stay. We went to bed together. It started out O.K., with her masturbating me. It was exciting, but I didn't like it. I came. I started to masturbate her, and I didn't like that either. It went on and on. After 20 to 25 minutes she was getting aroused and finally had an orgasm. Then we went to sleep. In the morning I took a shower and went out to keep an appointment. But I noticed I felt depressed, sad, and angry.

While I was working Saturday I got the flu back, again with a running nose. I   3
went back to Ruth's on Sunday. We had a hard climb to the top of a small mountain. That's when my joints began to ache. Maybe it's got something to do with lower barometric pressure. Anyway I must have been absorbed with myself because, on returning home, Ruth said she was angry with me—that I was distant. I got mad as hell at the implication.

If the arthritis persists more than a week, I'll see someone here. I can stand   4
the worst flu, but this constant nagging pain is impossible. All I do is think of it, it seems. Every minute I associate to it. Nothing helps it. I feel: Aw, shit, it's better to be dead than a cripple in a chair. Last night I felt very close to Ruth who again treated me with loving tenderness and understanding. We sat down and talked about what had been going on. I seemed to feel better—but only for a while. This morning I woke very early with a feeling of doom.

10/17

I haven't paid your bill yet. I must be reluctant to pay you. I had to pay a   1
premium on very heavy disability insurance.

Last night I had a dream about Ruth—but can't remember it. I got a good night's sleep.

There must be something going on between you and me. I want to know   2
more about you, but don't want to find that you're weak like me. My joints still hurt. Yesterday I killed you off—in my thoughts—not once but twice. I feel sorry for myself when I have these joint pains. Helpless. But even if this develops into rheumatoid arthritis, it's not the end of the world. However, it will mean there's something wrong with me for the world to see. I'll be wearing the pink badge of weakness, associated with utter helplessness, clinging, and sucking. Have you read "A Mother's Kisses," about a mother who follows her son around everywhere? Ouch! That pain!

It's a constant, low-grade, dull ache in my wrists, elbows, shoulders, knees,   3
ankles, fingers, pip and dip joints. I have it when I move and when I rest. There

are also feelings of malaise and fatigue, worse in the morning than in the afternoon. The doses of painkillers I've taken so far haven't relieved the pain. It's associated with a desire to go to bed and sleep. If I'm sitting, I don't want to move. It hurts even if I don't move. There's a fast heartbeat with it. In the past it's usually lasted 2 to 3 weeks at a time. When I've taken my temperature, it's 99.2° or 99.4°. I get it mostly in the spring or fall. I'm scared. I've been thoroughly examined twice because of it, but nobody committed themselves to a definite diagnosis. I'm convinced it's early rheumatoid arthritis, even though the doctors hedged about it. There's a slow, gradual onset. What it does or can do to the rest of my life is horrendous to consider. Everything becomes a strain. I feel like crying again. I'm afraid to talk about it here. Not just you, but anybody wouldn't like me for it. To have this thing means to be alone. Who wants a cripple? Nothing helps. If I were married, it would be a good time to get away from the house. No one could stand it except maybe Laura. She was with me and at least tolerated it when I had it before. If Ruth knew about it, forget it. It's better to fight it than just to give in to it.

4   I feel sick, tired, lonely, whining, clinging, and my enormous inertia is right out in the open. A lot of hatred for you comes because I think you don't like me for it. A whining, clinging adult male is a disgusting sight. I'd rather be alone, than have anyone have to see that about myself. How I'd like to climb into bed with Fran, sucking away for a week. Anybody that doesn't provide that for me is seen as a cause of my trouble [pause].

5   ["How was it when you had the sickness in childhood?"] It wasn't really that I was neglected. When I got sick, I got lots of attention. I was sort of doted upon. Father came back with sister from a trip once when I had chickenpox. I used to be very anxious when I got sick, until the doctor came. I never went to school when I was sick. Mother would cook for me, shop for me, take care of me, and sit on my legs when they ached. You see, I had pains like this when I was four or five, and they went away. I hope that'll happen again.

6   When I had scarlet fever, I was three—a year that we moved from one part of Philadelphia to another. I remember lying in the back seat of a cab with my head in mother's lap, not knowing where I was going. We had a new apartment with new people around us. I remember Ricky; his brother got polio, couldn't move his legs. I liked to go to Ricky's house, liked his father, but his mother was a kind of a drag. Ricky had a train set and a chemistry set, and we played a lot together. I met him a couple of years ago after a long separation. Laura didn't like him, but he's my oldest friend in the world. I feel like crying, thinking about him.

7   When I had chickenpox, a big blister formed between my toes, and I scratched it a lot. [At this point, he starts scratching the right side of his nose without being aware of it.] Finally, it burst. I remember liking the sensation. Then a scab formed.

10/18

I forgot my tie today. I also forgot to give a message to one of my associates. **1**
I almost forgot to come here. Generally, I feel miserable, but my joints seem
better, though they still hurt.

Saw Fran yesterday. We did a lot of heavy petting with orgasm. I felt guilty **2**
afterwards. I went to see her because somehow I had the idea that she might
help my arthritis, if I could suck enough—and to hell with anything contrary. I
did a lot of sucking and had a lot of fantastic sucking fantasies. Your silence is
like a judgment—that it's no good, that I don't consider the other person, that
it's not fair to egg her on because she's a susceptible person. I really loved Mary
who mothered me, not Laura. Laura the brain—cold, frigid bitch.

Having these sophisticated conversations with Ruth is a bunch of garbage. **3**
There's not enough sucking there. I got so fucking angry at her last night for
being so full of shit. She doesn't enjoy sex, so why does she have to pretend?
Sick of playing games. Here, too. I should talk about my real fucking
associations, my hatred of Ruth—a girl who doesn't get alive. I'm sick of
pretending I'm somebody I'm not. I'm a demanding bastard, and Ruth is frigid.
Her father, no father in the world will make any difference. I'm a guy who wants
to suck hard and long and wants to screw with it. I feel like a prick, a class A
horse's ass. If there's no response from you, that's a fucking judgment. I'm
trying to get a response out of you, come hell or high water. ["Why?"] I keep
thinking of you as my fucking father in his fucking silent chair. [Nose sounds
very stuffy; eyes suffused.]

10/20

I still have the joint pains. I still feel crummy. It could be some form of **1**
rheumatoid arthritis. If it persists much longer, I'll go to the best expert on it in
the East.

I had a dream that I was walking down a suburban road, and went by a **2**
blond-headed guy in the grass who made a homosexual advance to me—he
slapped his thigh. I acted as if to say—not now. I lingered a while, but then
moved on. My associations go to my former therapist who's blond. I once had an
association which he interpreted as my wanting to wrestle with him, have bodily
contact.

Right before this dream, I had another: Mother was showing me off to a **3**
bunch of people and directing me. I grabbed and lifted her by the neck, then
threw her to the ground. She's also got blond hair. It reminds me of this
professor I had at college who's blond with red cheeks. I saw him once nervously
waiting for a cab outside one of the university buildings. He was pacing up and

down, and I thought he was going to have a heart attack. He was supposed to be above all that, a man in an important position; yet here he was looking nervous. You must be the professor. I guess I'm still mad at you, and I'm finding fault with you. I don't think you appreciate the real distress I'm having. Instead of recognizing my suffering, comforting me, making me feel good, you don't say anything, or else you make with the interpretations.

4   I had an auto accident Thursday night. Was acting like a fiend, like a complete and utter asshole. Anger covers a terrible feeling of desperation. I'm terrified of being helpless, a crotchety, old rheumatic at the age of thirty-one. The pain became worse yesterday. On the basis of what I used in previous episodes, I began to take two aspirins and half a Miltown every three or four hours. That tones the pain down somewhat; and I don't get so panicky. I keep medicating myself even though I know I should see an internist. But I'm afraid that this time he'll tell me I've got rheumatoid arthritis. Anyway, the accident: I was in the left lane, and a guy made a left turn from the right-hand lane. Creased fenders—not much. This pain interferes with my reflexes and with my thinking. I feel nutty each night. Things don't seem real in a sense. I'm like an automaton; I've got to talk to somebody, and I keep thinking that there's nobody I can really unload to. I'm driven to have hates when that's the last thing I want. Finally, last night I played cards with some of the fellows for a while and that helped me forget the pain a little. But when it was over and I came back to my room, it was like every one of my joints was screaming. Yet my knees and wrists didn't look particularly swollen. Again aspirin helped. I began feeling lonely for Laura. So much has transpired between the two of us. Tonight I have a date with Fran and don't want to go. Here it is again: All I want is to be loved and taken care of, and Laura has lived through the arthritis with me. Maybe she's the girl for me after all.

10/23

1   I still have the arthritis. I'm taking lots of aspirin. I'm giving it one more week. If it doesn't get better, I'll see someone. It's getting in the way of the analysis. It seems that's all I want to talk about.

2   This past weekend I tried to rest and Laura visited me. It was very pleasant. You see, she knows about the arthritis from before, and it's very comforting. I don't have to worry about a reaction from her on that score. Yet she's such a defensive girl. On Sunday she wanted to go climbing to the top of the Blue Hills when she knew I had these pains and needed to take it easy. It's sadistic on her part to push for it—she wasn't thinking of me. But later things relaxed, and I ordered some food sent up to the apartment. The more I think about Laura, the more I can't be sure whether she's truly feminine or not. She certainly looks womanly, and has a softness that's womanly. I can say that she's become much

more feminine in bed. She's not frigid the way she was before. She stayed over at my apartment, and we had sex in the morning. She doesn't like mouth things that Fran and Ruth and I like—you know, like French kissing and so on. She's more excited by below-the-waist touching. This last time we were together she had an orgasm before I even had a chance to get in. She's built different from Ruth and especially from Fran. She doesn't have a lot of flesh. It makes me feel tearful when I remember being with her this past weekend. I didn't feel lonely with her around [begins crying]. It's you that I'm angriest at. [Transference interpretation.] I know what you say sounds right, but it's very difficult to separate what's neurotic and what's reasonable.

10/24

My joints don't hurt but my ears are ringing. This morning I was sitting in   1
Howard Johnson's waiting endlessly for breakfast. I recall when I was eight years old, I was at a Howard Johnson's in Philadelphia with my sister, father, and mother. It was some kind of special occasion. Sister had graduated from something—music school, I guess. Everybody seemed unhappy about it. The dinner was at a Howard Johnson's instead of some elegant restaurant because they couldn't decide or agree on where to go. Howard Johnson's pleased me no end, but they didn't seem happy.

I know if I stopped taking aspirins, my joints would start to hurt. That's   2
been the pattern before. I hadn't been taking them regularly before Sunday. Since then, I've been taking two every four hours. It's helped, though I feel shaky and perspiring. It's comforting to know that there's something that can help relieve the pain. What do you think I've got? What am I asking you for—you don't know about arthritis? Do you think it's purely in the mind? ["A thorough evaluation by a specialist is in order as I've suggested before; then, depending on the findings, the condition can be considered more accurately in terms of what's causing it."] Well, I've had evaluations in the past and enough physical tests that are negative. But I suppose I would be wise to be checked over again [pause].

I'm thinking now about the fee. I have the fantasy—what if I could afford   3
double the present fee or more? Then I'd be paying the highest fee and be the most special patient. It's as if I would be putting a fast one over on everyone [pause].

I've read up on arthritis. One theory refers to muscle tension pulling on the   4
capsule of a joint. I went to an expert in the field before. He treated me with great consideration. But he couldn't be sure of the diagnosis. Knowing that it's rheumatoid arthritis seems to me to be better than uncertainty. I feel like crying. What if it turns out that I have it? I'd have to change my whole way of life, because I know that rheumatoid arthritis is an incurable, chronic disease. One of my associates has been complaining of pain in his joints, and I was naturally

interested. He described the same symptoms I have. What if I become a crock? Psychoanalysis is hell. I've not expected psychoanalysis to cure the pains, but I'll be mad and disappointed every time I get them. I feel bogged down. I'll have to wait till it's over. I know other people have said there are times when they can't associate, but they haven't been kicked out. I guess I'm asking for reassurance you won't kick me out while I'm in this difficult situation [pause].

5   That ugly secretary at the office is waiting for me to give her my notes on a project I've been working on. She gives me an uneasy feeling. She has a funny way of looking at me. I feel like relaxing and falling asleep on her chest. Sucking at her tits. Mothers everywhere. I want desperately for you to take care of me because I have no one else to do it. In the past I got over measles, mumps, pains in the legs, if someone took care of me. It was mother. I told you she sat on my legs. She and father would give me alcohol rubs, and she fed me aspirin. This expert who saw me looked like a fellow I knew who eventually died of cancer of the testicles. I guess I don't trust him. I want to hear something definite about this condition.

10/25

1   I got the name of a good arthritis doctor and will arrange to see him. I have the thought that it won't make any difference, but at least there'll be someone I can turn to. A relative of mine, an uncle, died some days ago, but the family didn't reach me in time for me to be able to attend the funeral yesterday out of town. I feel dizzy now. I spoke to my father last night about my aches and pains. Mother doesn't know yet. He asked me, "Are you sure it isn't psychosomatic?" He said it in a tone of voice as if he didn't want to hear that I'm not perfect. Yet he talks about his diabetes or his urine tests. You're on his side. You're both bastards [pause]. Tell me that you're alive [he suddenly turns around and looks]. I had the fantasy that you died suddenly, quickly, and quietly—of a heart attack, like my uncle. I feel like crying. He was a nice man and though dominated by his wife, had an inner strength. Quietly and despite ridicule, he made good. He was a kind man, and I'm going to miss him.

2   Now I'm aware of my elbows and wrists hurting. I'm scared. I feel anxious in the stomach. I finally told Ruth on the phone last night about my joint pain. I also wrote to my sister about it. This was before she phoned me about my uncle's death [pause].

3   I'm afraid of homosexual feelings. I'm afraid you're going to hurt me. I have a fantasy of your whipping me as I lie on the couch. I'd better be careful of what I say. You don't like my demands. I have to hold in a murderous rage [pause].

4   I remember father telling me once that his mother had an acute form of arthritis. My own mother complains of arthritis, but in her case it's been diagnosed as osteoarthritis. I wonder if I'm like a woman in this respect. I have

read that people with repressed rage have arthritis; so if I can unrepress my rage, the arthritis will go away. Yesterday I almost keeled over, talking to some people. I felt dizzy from too much aspirin. When I stop the aspirin, the pain is back. I'm going to let a doctor manage my medicine. Will see him this afternoon. I'm having a hard time accepting the symptoms. I want someone to make them go away with a kiss. Enough love and they'll go away.

10/26

I saw an excellent specialist yesterday afternoon. I'm very satisfied with him. He told me that the history I give is typical for rheumatoid arthritis, but that he could never make the diagnosis on history alone without swelling, tenderness, or pain. He would not say that I had it. However, he couldn't tell what the future would bring. Since it has gone on and off without blossoming into a hot joint, the chances were better than 50:50 that it would not. He talked about such things as a three-year prodrome and poor correlation with severity of eventual possible rheumatoid arthritis, for example, just one hot joint for six weeks and none thereafter. He indicated that it's just as likely that I would have a couple more years of this, and it would fade out. He told me he's seen other people with this condition. He didn't ask for lab tests because he knew what they would show. The rheumatoid factor was negative last time, and it would be unchanged now. One other possibility he mentioned was that joint reaction is one way I might respond to a viral infection. He officially put me on aspirin, 3 tablets four times a day. Since I get bothered by aspirin, I'll start with 2 tablets and gradually increase to 3 tablets. One test I did get was an E.S.R., whatever that is [erythrocyte sedimentation rate]. That doctor is on my side. He doesn't look at me as if I were a kook, like you do. That's my thought. Still I'm not sure. Just as I'm not sure at times about your being alive or dead. Yet I'm glad that you forced me to be an adult, though I don't like it. In my bones [!] that's the only thing that's going to make any difference. **1**

I sent my uncle a telegram—no, he's dead. I sent it to his wife. One of the engineers at work attempted suicide and had to be hospitalized. I seem to have some things in common with him, though we were only casual acquaintances. He slept in a bedroom with his mother, he told me, and also had had treatment before coming to work here. I feel dizzy. He's married, but he's been surrounded by all kinds of trouble. He's had a bad back, developed some kind of pulmonary trouble, and his father's had two strokes [stomach rumbling loudly]. I sound hungry. When am I going to get some food in? I need to take some aspirins—my joints are hurting again. **2**

I think back to the difference between myself and other kids. They had happy fathers who got things for them. My parents slept together in the same bedroom until I was 15 or 16 years old, but they were always quarreling. This **3** fellow's mother and wife did anything and everything for him.

4   This Saturday I'm going with Ruth to a meeting. I'm uneasy you might be there. If you're there, I can say hello to you as a social equal, get close to you. You'll see me and Ruth and approve our marriage, and we'll live happily ever after, though she's not sexy. I guess I want you to see me and Ruth, then you'll let me know how it looks. I could also see what your wife looks like. I would find out what you look like outside the office. Now I have a fantasy of lying naked on the couch with you. Are you sure that you can take this? I'm avoiding—am I sure *I* can take it? That could be a masturbation fantasy. I never masturbated till I was a sophomore in college—age 18, late.

10/30

1   [Late] Car broke down. Everything's breaking down like me. It needs to be overhauled. I'd better not wait too long with it either. In one sense I want to deny there's anything wrong, and in another sense, I have a need to be unnecessarily uncomfortable.

2   I think of how my joints hurt me in between aspirins. They really zonk me then. Twelve aspirins a day really get me dizzy. I keep thinking I might fall over. I'm going to try to do with less medicine.

3   Saturday night I had a dream in which you told me not to come, if I keep up this farting around. When I told father about my joint pains, his advice was to go to the "baths" where his mother had got relief. He just doesn't like to hear about defects, about sickness. Now I again think of the dream in which you tell me not to come. [Transference interpretation.]

4   I didn't see you at the meeting on Saturday. I guess you weren't there because the subject was chiefly biophysics and your major field of interest is psychoanalysis. So I keep thinking you're not around, keep getting rid of you, thinking you're dead. Saturday night, after the meeting, Ruth and I had a nice dinner and then went over to my place. I'd been having sexual thoughts about her since Friday, wanting her to stimulate me, to pull on my penis. Which girl would I really choose? That's become a major question. If only I could make the right decision and live happily ever after. As I think about these girls, especially Fran, I get a double feeling, one like crying, the other like sexual excitement. But having sex relations means getting hooked. I've got bad impressions of what happened to my parents and their marriage.

10/31

1   I've been thinking about the fee again. I must have some self-destructive thoughts about it. I've had the fantasy of a $100 an hour fee. It seems I have to hurt myself to get special protection. That old business about the doctor who

charges a high fee is the better doctor keeps bugging me. Maybe I could get away with more if I paid a higher fee. It seems as if I'm trying to convince you to charge a lower fee, so I could buy a new car and get out of debt sooner. I'm worried about the arthritis—it's making me stingy. When I have it, I'm not too generous, with time, money, or effort. I'm doubly unsure of what the future will bring, and I have to hoard my resources.

My feet started to hurt yesterday. That really got me worried—that I may not be able to walk, that's the dread fear. With my knees involved, I could still walk, but it's down to my toes now. It's a new pain, sharp, with tenderness and it's getting worse. It's relieved pretty much by Bufferin after each meal, but the effect wears off about 10 A.M., 4 P.M., and 11 P.M. Then it really hurts. **2**

I'm thinking about very little these days, except arthritis. I still do my job, even though minimally these days. I rest as much as I can and spend a good deal of time at home. I get some paper work done there. I don't want to be at their mercy. ["Whose?"] My parents. I feel like crying. I can't stand the thought of being at their mercy, being a cripple who is dependent on them. I'm on the edge of a real feeling of grief, a mixed feeling. I'm trying to concentrate on something else in order to stay away from it. I'm looking at the ceiling hard, but it's no use. My wrists are aching, as well as my elbows and shoulders. What did I do to deserve it? I was struggling to make a go of things, when this fucking pain came along. It's punishment, I tell you, for all the rotten, greedy, angry things I ever thought and did. **3**

Now I think back to mother—that white-haired bitch—trying to remember what it was like when I was seven, eight, or nine. What was it like, day to day? Did I have any friends? I remember in the fourth grade I was a very special pupil—bright, cooperative, obedient. I was the teacher's pet. I felt very attached to her even after I left her class. I have a deep longing for those good old days. I felt important, capable, very good in conduct, though I couldn't play punch ball. Those were the better days, with no responsibility and lots of praise. School was something I always liked to go to. In the ninth grade I also had a wonderful teacher who invited us to her house once, and served a special luncheon. If I had had a mother like her, things would have been a lot different for me. Now I notice that I'm chewing my cheek. I do that when I'm tense. It goes back, way back to age three, and I still do it. [Interpretation: Longing for an ideal mother and ideal conditions. There is a familiar sequence: Uncertainty, impending loss of Laura, no adequate substitute, upsurge of longing for the past, accompanied by a sense of frustration and fury, with a tendency for the hostility to be submerged.] I feel if I could jump just once and release this pent-up fury, maybe I'd not ache so much. **4**

I just see arthritis as a stroke of bad luck. It doesn't let me discharge my aggression through other means. I'm just repeating words. The connections are present in my associations, as you said. But what it means to me, how I use it, is **5** another thing. For a year we've talked about pent-up rage. I don't yet feel it most of the time, though occasionally I do. It must come out disguised, somehow in the form of guilt. I don't know what to do about it. Mostly it isn't experienced directly as yet. It's like chasing a wispy object. What am I supposed to do with it? I want action right away. So I'm back to feeling frustrated and I say—angry.

6 Each of my joints feels as if there's a little man in it, sticking me with a sword. They're all shrieking with pain. Now again I feel like I'm going to bust out crying. It's as if an anger is drilling in me. The pain is like pain when a dentist drills without novocaine. In each joint. Thoughts come rapidly now: I feel as if I'm in the process of losing all my teeth. What does that mean? Loss of my looks—is that self-love? I recall an old dream in which two front teeth fell out. I'm afraid I'll become a helpless woman, unable to screw, to initiate anything—relegated to a wheelchair, like Lionel Barrymore, the great actor, which is how I feel [said with histrionic flair]. Damned if I'll cry in front of you or anybody else. You'll make some annoying interpretation about it. I can't afford to feel sorry for myself [Cries].

11/1

1 I had a dream last night and remember quite a lot of detail. I didn't start today with the subject of my arthritis, because I think it's going away. After I left here yesterday, it got worse than it had ever in my life. It was so bad that I stopped the aspirins. I thought there was no use continuing them, if they didn't help. Then a most extraordinary thing happened: By nine that evening I felt much better. I began to wonder if taking aspirin could make the pain worse. After the pain had pretty much subsided for a while, I cautiously resumed taking the aspirins but the pain didn't get worse again.

2 Well, here is the dream: I wrote it down on this card—it's a dentist's card for a prophylaxis. The dream was about war. I was on the front lines. A funny bombardment was going on. Howitzers were shooting shells straight up in the air. There was a forest in front, and the enemy were in the bushes. That's it. In the last battle dream I had no weapons, so the howitzer is an improvement. Last night before going to bed I saw a taped TV show on war.

3 Today I feel light-hearted. The arthritis isn't troublesome. I feel I'm getting back to myself. What you said yesterday made a real impression on me—my wanting to go back to a time when things seemed so much better for me. My favorite chum was in the same class where I had that wonderful teacher. Now I feel like crying for the good old days.

4 I wanted to write the dream down. I felt it was important. The forest reminds me of the house where I lived as a youngster, near a thickly-wooded park. Oh! I forgot the most important thing. Last night I masturbated in a most

unusual way. I did it in the bathroom, with a light on over the sink. While I was sitting on the toilet seat I had a compulsion to masturbate in the old way. I overcame my reluctance by telling myself that I felt so alone and lonely that I couldn't care less. I had finished my TV dinner, took my aspirins, and listened to a recording of La Traviata. I kept thinking of my first love, Mary, and also about the girls I have now. I wondered if Mary was divorced. I was obsessed with the idea of looking for a perfect mother. I sat around this way for a long time, and finally cleaned up my room. Then I went into the bathroom and masturbated over the sink [pause]. I don't like to talk about it. Masturbating over the sink enables me to see something come out. There's a part of me that I can see coming out. Wouldn't you call that real self-love? When I was a sophomore in college and a counsellor at summer camp, I remember once sneaking off with the desire to masturbate. Last night I remembered that incident and the fear I had of being discovered. In my home in Philadelphia, I used to masturbate over the sink and in front of a mirror. There was a line of fire, which, if it was extended through the wall of the bathroom, would land right on my father's bed. Shooting semen. A wall between us. There was an aggressive, killing component to it. I'm again reminded of shells being lobbed. I first thought that it was mother I was shelling, killing.

[The patient continued to take aspirin for a few more days, then stopped. The joint pain subsided completely.]

11/2 - 1/15 Interim Summary

Increased work demands and further difficulties with his girlfriends again activate the patient's dependent, passive-feminine tendencies. There is little overt affect where much anger would be expected. Marked intellectualization and increased use of projection can be noted in the defensive constellation. The analyst continues to be seen as a judge, an external representation of the patient's superego.

Sexual release is attempted through masturbation, accompanied by fantasies of making girls pregnant, alternating with fellatio fantasies. Both oral and phallic aspects of aggression can be noted in these. Angry demands with little affect are verbalized more frequently in the transference. These are in contrast to references to the previous therapist's supportive but also infantilizing attitudes.

A week or so before the detailed reporting begins again, the patient became sexually more intimate with his latest girlfriend, Fran, with much mutual sucking and kissing but no intercourse. Concomitantly increased guilt began to be indirectly expressed, linked with a forbidding mother image. A few days later the patient did a great deal of skiing. Following this a mild cough, more a throat tickle, began to bother the patient.

1/16

1   [Coughing.] I've got a cold. I was mad as hell on the job yesterday after I left here, mainly because of the stupidity of some of the people that work for me. They screwed up some important blueprints and when their mistakes were pointed out to them, instead of correcting them, they botched things up even worse. Just stupidity and carelessness.

2   I want to ask you if you ever had a heart attack. I'm worried. I compare you with this other doctor who's had two. It must be hard as hell to be in analysis with a guy who's had two. I keep having these fears that you would die and go away before giving me anything.

3   This morning my car made funny noises. I blew out the heat riser on the car's carburetor. As the car warms up, a temperature sensing device which comes off the manifold closes a valve down and adjusts the mixture coming into the engine so it doesn't race when it gets hot. It's like a thermostat for the gas mixture. When the heat riser blows out, it sounds like a hot rod. So now there's something wrong with my car too.

4   I had a brief dream about one of my earliest friends, Rik. I was at a party with him. That's all I remember. There was something in the dream about music [coughs]. Rik had a brother, Harry, who was fond of Zenith TV sets. Fran has one. I was always at Rik's house watching his Zenith TV. Rik and I would watch TV for hours sitting or lying on the rug together. Harry had polio from the waist down. He'd ride me like a horse. It was lots of fun—sometimes I would get a hard on and have to hide it. Now Rik's a chemist—rents a house with another scientist. He's quiet, got lots of problems. His father was a very nice guy, an activist, while Rik turned out to be shy. I felt he was lucky to have a father like that. You keep pointing out to me about my wanting so much, without my showing anger if I don't get it. I guess it's related to the heart attack talk—you might die—and also the possibility of your just going away and leaving me.

5   My own father was very sick when I was seven years old. I understand he had a serious bone ailment in his left arm and that was before they had the newer wonder drugs. What I remember is being in that waiting room downstairs from the ward where he was. When father came home from the hospital he had a beard. I wanted him to cut it off. He didn't look like the father who had gone into the hospital. When he got home, he didn't seem to care about us kids. He never liked my sleeping late on Sunday which I still do—in fact, did it yesterday. He was up early, playing tennis. Sometimes he would take a lesson and I would watch. You know, I was embarrassed for him, he was so bad [much coughing; sits up briefly]. I have the fantasy that I'm contaminating the office with germs and that you want to leave. I want you to leave because I don't want you to get the virus. At work everybody's got real bad flu. This notion of hurting you,

killing you off, must be because you don't give me the magic answer about what I should do, especially about girls. Father never taught me a fucking thing about them, how to handle them, what they're all about. In his relationship with my mother, he showed me how to be ground down under by a woman and then crawl out of it by having his son, me, do the dirty work of telling her he was through. ["You've had a longstanding disappointment about not getting the right answers and guidance from your father, and this affects your relationships with all men and specifically your relationship with me."]

I recall father's starting to take me to a football game once and then   6
stopping and turning back before we ever got there. He brought me a rocking horse when I was just a tot, and I kept it until I was 14, even though it was long since broken. I couldn't give it up. It's sad. I used to get some things, but not others—the important ones. I remember father's telling me how selfish I was, and my reaction of rage, my thinking: Fuck you. But he couldn't solve his own problems about women. I wonder how much I'm like him.

1/18

There's a new thing wrong with my car. I told you about the heat riser not   1
working. Well, it had to be fixed and it cost me $30.

I feel like I'm getting arthritis again. Just the beginnings. It seemed to   2
coincide with the weather starting to get warmer. This morning I felt I was going to have a temper tantrum at the world. Here I want to rip the place apart, but then I feel like crying. Maybe it would relieve the ache in my joints if I smashed things, which indeed it wouldn't. I'm angry at you for not fixing them. What kind of a doctor are you anyway? One of my colleagues at work got caught in traffic and he was all upset about being late. I could sympathize with him because I had my own feeling of rage, right inside, wanting to destroy. It wells up in me. I can't remember what happened the last time I was here. Now I can. I didn't tell you of a basic reaction I had yesterday. I felt you were telling me that I shouldn't go out with girls until I understood my relationships with men better. At least that's what I think you said. I imagined that you said I shouldn't go out with Ruth. Well, fuck you. After I left, I continued to be mad at you because of what I thought you were saying, ordering me around.

I remember when I was at college that my father insisted on my joining the   3
ROTC. What splitting headaches I had every Friday when I had to go to the parade grounds! I hated the drilling, the regimentation, the military atmosphere, and most of all, father's ordering me—in effect, to participate. At that time I had developed trouble urinating in public toilets and was concerned about how I would manage that if I had to go into military service. You see, I used to sit down when I urinated—just like a woman. I finally got out of ROTC training and also changed my career plans so that I would not have to take up father's

profession. I did well in my new career after my fucking father told me I couldn't. I feel enraged at you now for not treating me like a good doctor should. [Pounds couch.] I also feel like crying. First there's anger, then guilt.

1/22

[20 minutes late.]

1   My car was blocked in the parking lot, and I got a late start. Then I ran into traffic difficulties. Actually I should have left work earlier.

2   My ears are ringing. I'm back on aspirin. The fucking arthritis came back on Friday [1/19—no scheduled analytic hour]. I'm pissed off at you for its coming back. That's not fair; it's not really your fault. Friday night I had a disturbing dream: In the beginning I was in bed with Fran. Then it shifted and I was in bed with Max, a childhood friend of mine. We were having homosexual relations. Actually it was sex from behind. I was rubbing my penis between his legs, but it wasn't anal intercourse. It ended as a wet dream. It was the first homosexual wet dream I ever had. Well, I didn't hold that back from you.

It seems as if my joints are relaxing now, except that they're not really in normal shape.

3   There was a visitor at our office today. His name was Selwin. I was impressed by his knowledge and experience. I wondered if he knew Mr. Selwin, my physics teacher in high school, whom I liked. I asked him. He said it was probably a second cousin. My feeling was that he's very bright, not dogmatic or judgmental. Last week I thought you were not judgmental and my attitude then shifted. For a while last week I didn't seem to need so much from you. I was coming here for analysis rather than gratification of my needs. Then on Friday my joints started to hurt, and Oh shit! That homosexual dream—it wasn't Friday night. It was Thursday night I had that dream.

4   If only I didn't feel you should cure my arthritis and take care of me ["Is that a way to get me to take care of you?"] I don't think it is [silence]. Those remarks bother me, get me furious. ["Why?"] If it is my need and really subconscious, I don't know about it. It's your tone of voice. You're telling—not asking—me. On a previous occasion I saw my arthritis as being related to a change in the weather. When it started getting warm, I first got the symptoms. I wonder if the pain comes first because I want to be taken care of or does it make me want to be taken care of? I've read stuff about it. What do they call it—Oh, yes, psychosomatic medicine. Don't you subscribe to Alexander and Dunbar, all that shit? Actually when I feel this way, my need to be taken care of is greatly increased. You know, this is a painful illness. It seems to have no end point and makes me afraid I'll want to be taken care of for years and years, forever. Fran is the motherly type of girl, so I keep thinking she can take care of me if I get arthritis. I can't keep my hands off her. Sunday night after the movie I wanted

to have sexual intercourse badly. Maybe it was to counter Thursday's dream of homosexuality which has been bothering me ever since. I was very aggressive in bed with her. I took the initiative. I gave her a lot of affection, though we didn't have sexual intercourse. She made dinner for me Saturday night. Sunday, when I woke up in my apartment, I was hurting quite a bit. Fran's car was on the blink. I tried to get it fixed, but couldn't. Then I went up to her apartment for a while, but couldn't stay long.

Now I feel like crying and at the same time have a little feeling of excitement   5
in my penis. I called up Laura Thursday night before the dream. I hadn't seen her in quite a while and thought it would make her feel good. It was a mistake. I got into an obsessive rage talking with her. Shit! "I don't want to get into it," I said to her. After she started in on me, whining about herself, I said to myself that nothing has changed. Finally, I told her to skip it. "If you want contact," I said to her, "let's get together and play some music or have some other fun." I was quite enraged at her, though it ended fairly well.

I remember that I also called Ruth Thursday night and also that before   6
seeing Laura, I had spoken with my mother. Last of all, I got in touch with Fran. All the women—contacted the same night. I was feeling lonely, needy, and wasn't getting enough satisfaction from anything or anyone. That's the mood I've been in for a while.

1/23

I need to change the hour tomorrow. I have a must conference at the office which will make it impossible for me to keep the regular time.

I left something relating to Thursday out of what I was talking about   1
yesterday. It's somehow connected with that dream I had because that evening before I went to sleep I had thoughts of trying to outdo father and my favorite cousin. I wanted to make a bigger mark on the world than they have.

Yesterday I had the feeling we might have a fight. I thought you were trying   2
to provoke an argument and figured on how I was going to retaliate today. I thought at one point that I'd say nothing for the whole hour in the spirit of fuck you. I also thought of not coming, but that's the chicken way. The other person has no control over the situation, since you're not there. I keep thinking—what was he [analyst] all hot and bothered about yesterday? He was jumping down my throat for saying things I wasn't saying.

I can't dismiss my feelings about arthritis. You can call it the need to be   3
taken care of. Call it a rage in the joints. I've read some books on this subject. I think I told you that. I find myself arguing with you as though you were Flanders Dunbar. After reading her exaggerated claims, I thought analysis would prevent my incipient arthritis from becoming a chronic disease. ["You say all this quite calmly."] I know I feel angry, but it doesn't come out.

4   Anger came out once *really*. Then the arthritis did go away. When I finally exploded, it got better. Now I try to produce explosions, but they have the quality of an artifact. They don't have the same quality as the other one did. I feel like crying. Why should I cry when I'm angry? Can't get angry at one's father. I, at least, never could [hands behind head, yawning]. No place to let it out. I hate his fucking guts and don't know what to do with it. I don't hate my mother as much. She's sick and not as malicious. A sick, old lady with an immense appetite; still she has some warmth. It's different with him. I've been longing for a human being for a father for many years. One of my uncles told me I don't understand father, that he's got a good heart, so then I felt terrible. Yet this generous guy, so-called, wouldn't pay for any treatment for me when I really needed it years ago. I've been so angry at him on the phone that I've wanted to rip it out. My whole body shook. I couldn't look him in the eye on his last visit. I wanted to smash him around the room, I was so angry. ["Why?"] Because he's not what a father should be. For leaving me when I needed him most, for being like putty with that woman, my mother. He's never remarried, but he's been going out with another woman for years, just piddling his way into the grave. I had the feeling I had to produce honors in school for him to tolerate me. I remember once on orientation day at college he made a fool of me in front of my friends. I vowed to pay him in spades. When I was 10 or 12, when mother was seducing me and he could have been around and prevented it, he defaulted; he left. I used to scream at night that I wanted my daddy. I remember once when I was around 10 years old, I got dreadfully afraid of dying after hearing a program about brain tumors on the radio. I couldn't sleep, was crying, felt nauseated. My sister came into the room and said, "Who do you think you are? Everyone dies." Remembering this makes me sad. But I can't forget the hurts I've had in my life. ["The desire to get revenge is often with you."] Almost everything I do is motivated by that, including coming here. Just think, father's supposedly perfect son, with honors, has to see a psychiatrist. Well, that makes him suffer a bit. A lot of my revenge is conscious and deliberately executed. ["A lot is not so obvious."] Maybe. I know it's so strong I can't bear to look at him or speak to him. I try to control myself. About once a year it breaks forth and clears the air a bit.

5   He refused me a loan for the analysis outright, saying I shouldn't have to go through it. I said, "Fuck you." It's the lowest, dirtiest, most cutting thing he's ever done. That's what I told him on the phone when I was shaking so. [right hand under head]. But I can't get it out of my system. Telling him off doesn't do it. I even told him he wanted to keep me sick and childish. Now I have a fantasy of stringing him up by the feet to a tree and hitting his head with a baseball bat [rapid breathing]. I guess a lot of that rubs off onto you. On the outside I don't show it, and I'm a very well-liked person. ["Inside you're consumed by hate."]

1/24

Five minutes late. 1

I allowed myself plenty of time to come here. But a series of things 2
interfered. I got jammed into a parking space. Rage. My elbow hurt so much, I
could hardly turn the wheel. I took a short cut and got caught behind a garbage
truck. Then I was held up by school traffic. I managed to make every red light.
Rage, rage. I keep blaming others, accusing the world and you of being against
me. You're a hard-hearted s.o.b. You can't cure my arthritis. You can't get me
here in time. You don't help me rise in my work. You don't help me find a wife,
or how to be a man. Let's analyze while my life goes wasting away. It's a fucking
mess.

Yet last night I got a lot of work done, for the first time in a long while. I 3
also got a phone call from my father. It was like all the other calls. I had nothing
to say to him and avoided charged issues. He doesn't see anyone but his
girlfriend, and there's nothing to talk about. Right now I sound like my god
damn mother.

I'm in a special rage about not having intercourse with Fran, even though 4
she's not got all the qualities I look for in a girl. I'm also sore about the $45 bill I
got for having to fix my car.

I'm really so fucking tired of being pissed off. You haven't said anything 5
and, I keep wondering whether you are asleep—not wanting to hear this shit I'm
putting out. I don't like to hear other people's anger. I want a nice big breast so I
can go to sleep next to it, sucking contentedly away. ["And have all your wishes
fulfilled without any effort on your part."] I'm in a rage at everyone who wants
to take anything from me.

I'm exaggerating for a studio audience—for you—to get attention and 6
sympathy. I'm so fucking mad. There's no point to it. I feel as if I've been in a
crazy rage.

I want so much, and I get nothing. Yet what have I been doing here but
trying to cut myself down before you? In self-defense I must say I never missed
a day's work because of the arthritis.

1/25

I give up. I can't help it. I get angry all the time; there's no end to it. I'm 1
especially angry at you—and for illogical reasons. I'm much angrier than I sound.
I took pleasure in dumping all the snow on that front mat.

A dream I had last night comes back to me. I was skiing. One of my 2
associates at work was along. I had some kind of drawings of faces or metal

masks. I asked what he thought of them. He said they represented the work of a crazy person.

When I awoke from that dream, I felt sick—felt that I'm sicker than I had thought. My associate had given a lecture about a business trip he had made to Africa and had thrown in some of his interesting experiences in the areas away from the cities with some of the tribes. What can I talk about that's anywhere near as interesting?

3   I drove Fran to pick up her car. We stopped for a bite to eat. I got very angry at not being able to find a parking space on our return. I tried hard to get into one space that really was too small. People were watching, and Fran was getting annoyed at my childishness. I'm also mad as hell at her for not letting me get into her without any effort—the rage is at not having sexual intercourse.

4   Another dream: I was visiting an old girlfriend at her home. She was there with her baby and her parents. They seemed to watching a TV program which wasn't very good. This girlfriend looked old, too mixed up with her father and mother. That's all I remember of the dream. I was telling Fran how angry I've been, also mentioning the pattern of going out with daughters of famous fathers. I don't know Fran's father and wouldn't want to meet him in a long while. We got to talking about love, and I told her I wasn't sure about whether I loved her for who she is or for other reasons.

5   Now I feel like crying. Guilt, that's what does it. Guilt over my rages. Guilt over going out with girls whose fathers are famous. I'm afraid I'll be cut down for having such ideas. Maybe you'll do it because I'm challenging the big shots. It occurs to me that I keep having such thoughts both ways, cutting others down and being cut down by others. There's something almost enjoyable in such thoughts. As if I enjoy the idea of pain, pain itself. I have no pain now, but there is a sensation of the room turning. It's probably from the aspirin. The aspirin seems to be controlling the pain quite well.

6   There's something else. It's most important. Last night when we were at the restaurant, I had to go to the bathroom. Well, it's a public toilet with stalls. I couldn't urinate until a Puerto Rican and some others had left. The original problem for which I first went to a psychiatrist was that I couldn't urinate in public toilets. That hasn't changed. It makes me feel so sad. I keep thinking—I got the idea somewhere and fixed it in my mind—it means I'm homosexual. I'm not really homosexual, yet I can't shake the idea. It becomes the main thing on my mind, and all my sadness centers around it. After I was finally able to urinate, I had to go back to our table in the restaurant and pretend I'm a man. I don't know what causes me to be so inhibited in the toilet. I kept wondering while I was there whether I was better or not. I opened up my fly but thought: Don't start while the Puerto Rican is drying his hands; wait until he leaves. One part of the trouble seems to be making a noise—the noise of urinating. Sitting down and doing it, there's less of a problem. I remember trying to listen to

mother and sister urinate. They often flushed the toilet while doing it so the sound would be drowned out. I'm just afraid that my female interests will be found out.

1/29, Summary

Ten minutes late. Considerable reference to anxiety, but little affect exhibited. Need for reassurance about manliness and about being loved—especially in transference context. Many dreams with heterosexual content. No mention of somatic complaints. Ambivalence about Fran continues.

1/30, Summary

Much concern about being an adequate husband-father, resentful of the competitive, sucking kids. Wish for a dominant mother figure to be his wife, in charge of him and of home. Continued fear of impotence and projective reference to Fran's frigidity. No somatic complaints.

1/31, Summary

Five minutes late. Differences between Fran and himself detailed and compared with differences between his own father and mother. The intellectual inferiority of women is defensively emphasized. Concern about being obligated to marry Fran because of premarital sexual relations. Accompanying fantasy: penis getting hooked in the vagina.

2/1, Summary

Ten minutes late. Angry thoughts, without affect, that he will not be given an extra ten minutes. Rationalization: He gives [money] but doesn't get [cure]. Whining, complaining, feeling guilty. Fran serious about going on the pill, prior to regular sexual relationships. He may have to commit himself as far as marriage is concerned. Complaining of pain in right testicle for first time, though it started two days ago. It comes and goes, accompanied by dragging sensation in scrotum. Fantasies of biting on nipples and being punished. No mention of joint symptoms.

2/5

Thursday night I masturbated with fantasies of Fran and my mother pulling my penis, then sucking on me, and giving me enemas. It's the first time I've directly felt excitement thinking of mother and the sexual activities I mentioned. It crept on me, like the homosexuality, by surprise. The enema part was the most exciting, reminding me of time she gave me an enema while I was fighting her and writhing on the floor.

2   Friday night I went out with Fran. We were both tired. We had an after-dinner drink at a local bar. She and I talked about sex, and she wants to see a gynecologist first before we go to bed again. I had been taking a lot of aspirins and that together with the drinks knocked me out. I went to sleep on her couch. She told me I kept talking in my sleep, saying, "More, more juice." She slept in her bedroom.

3   I had troublesome dreams. In one dream there's a scene with my mother where I feel intense rage at her for suffocating me, and I stamp my heel near her head as she lies on the floor. She tries to attack me with a butcher knife, and I subdue her. Now that all the rage is out, I can love her. In another dream there's an iron superstructure with scaffolding going up very high. I climb it with a woman—maybe mother or Fran—and then we start swinging. I have to hold on for dear life, feeling that this is it, that I'm going to die. Finally, I manage to get back and climb down. The dreams make me think of my relationship with Fran. It seems to me that stomping on mother's head is a cover for wanting to stomp on Fran's head. We had a pillow fight Saturday. I criticized the dress she wore Friday night. She wondered if I felt entitled to go to bed with her whenever I want. We were banging away at each other.

4   Mother telephoned that night that she doesn't feel well, is constipated, and will take an enema. Important news! What a nerve! There was no sex with Fran on Saturday night either. I get a suffocating feeling from mother that I don't do enough. It's as if I'm destined to bear all the hostility she had toward others. In turn my anger is directed toward Fran. I manage to find fault with her for one reason or another, especially when she withholds anything from me. ["Need to be mothered and given to."]

2/6

1   Should I pay you today or tomorrow? I have money, but it's not yet in the bank. If I wrote a check today and didn't deposit the covering money today, you might cash the check and it would bounce. Actually it wouldn't, since my checks are insured up to $1,000. I'm worried about money, even though I really have enough. I'd better not deplete it too much or I'll get into trouble. I need a good reserve.

2   When I left here yesterday I was mad once again because, despite my hearing what you said, I felt you were telling me I was going out with the wrong girl. ["You put your own interpretation on my remarks. What I was talking about referred to your continuing strong need to be mothered."] That's what I'm

really troubled about as far as Fran is concerned. I've got awfully strong babyish needs that I expect her to satisfy.

I keep thinking I'm being hounded here, treated like a kid. ["As if I were   3
your parent."] It's as if I hear an incantation to action. Why don't I quit analysis? It's hopeless. I keep on feeling hounded. That's a tricky maneuver because it's meant to elicit sympathy and attention without which I feel I can't live.

I seem to still get very strong visceral feelings about the matter of my   4
relationship with girls. It's as if my body is reacting negatively to this problem with Fran. Actually, I should need less mothering, whoever the girl is. I should choose a girl on the basis of other qualities. It's a struggle to decide whether it should be a child-parent or an adult-adult relationship. On the other hand, I think of the mutual respect we seem to have for each other. Then I have negative thoughts about her—that she's a big baby herself and wants to suck even more than I.

The arthritis has gone away. It left this past weekend. It had been under   5
control. Now I can go skiing with Fran again.

2/7, Summary

Angry (no affect) at having his infantile oral needs pointed out. Despondent over how immature his relationships are. Fran is going away for five days, evoking his anger and a threat to act out while she's away. He keeps referring to his leaving the analysis again. A pending loss of an ambivalently reacted to object activates the defense of acting out, possibly in the transference.

2/8, Excerpt

I've got to get some things straight. Am I being judged or treated here? You said that it's not nice for me to be a mother's boy. You called me an adult baby. I don't believe it's safe to talk up. I don't believe I can say anything here without retaliation [projections]. Somehow I came away from here with the belief that you were saying Fran is no good for me. Well, part of me, the reasonable side, knows that none of this is really so—that what I'm attributing to you and accusing you of is a distortion. That part hears you correctly and agrees with you. I won't be ready for marriage for a long time, not until my neurosis really changes. Yet my relationship with Fran isn't just a sham, a desire to suck from a breast. There's a give-and-take, an openness between us that's different from relationships I've had with any other woman. I miss her being away, even though it's for only a short time. [The burst of negative transference and use of projection to defend against activated oral needs are modified by some degree of insight.]

2/12

1   [Four day interval.]

I'm back on aspirins. I've been having general malaise, tiredness, dizziness, some swollen glands, a lot of depression, rage, discouragement, and fear. [Said blandly with hands in pockets and legs crossed.] It's a long time that I've been having this trouble. I keep thinking of it as hopeless. With the aspirins I drink so much milk and eat so much that I'm getting fat. Everything seems hopeless—my family, my relationships with girls, the analysis—everything. My work is discouraging. I keep hoping you'll make it less hopeless for me, and I get mad when you don't. I have this great yearning to have someone make the pain go away. It recurred late Thursday after a short period of improvement, and it's been much worse and different. Previously my joints were painful, but not my whole being. Now I've got the old pain back, the one that's much deeper, together with the swollen glands. My life seems destined to be full of pain.

2   Sunday night Fran came back, and I saw her. She's back and I still have the pain. I was very happy to see her and I told her that. I couldn't keep my hands off her, and we wound up in bed. It felt good. Her body was warm and soothing. She was mad afterwards, because I had some gratification and she didn't. She said she felt like a prostitute, hopping in and out of bed. That upset me. I thanked her sarcastically for doing me a favor.

3   My sister and I had a long talk when I went to Philadelphia. She had been able to get a consultation for her daughter, my niece. It seems as though my niece has a compulsion to see my mother. It's as if she was afraid the old lady would die if she didn't see her every day. It's as if she has to go through this ritual. My niece expressed rage which I think is similar to mine. I've been thinking about my mother a lot. The things she used to do which would enrage me. My niece said, "Grandma isn't nice to the family." She's only 14 years old, but she senses that I have the same problem as she does—that I can't break away from mother, much as I'd want to. I feel just as mad about my mother as my sister does, but she expresses it and I don't, and I guess I must pay a price. Anyhow I have trouble trusting people—not only women, but men too.

2/13

1   I feel afraid of you. You're angry at me for those two black spots on the rug, mud I must have tracked in. You must be thinking—what's he doing here; he screws up the rugs. I'm very careful to wipe my feet ever since you told me that I dirtied the rug [projection]. It's not really true; you didn't say that. I'm annoyed that I'm sick with this fucking disease. Three weeks of it, and it's getting worse. Aspirins don't do much. I'm taking a lot of aspirins and still feel

sick. I'm not thinking straight. I want to go to bed for a day and be taken care of, but I can't seem to get away from my work. I think marriage would be dangerous because I'd tend to get into the position of complaining and whining, and I'd be turned into a dependent child by my wife with my help. I would never marry, feeling this way. As you see I have a great yearning to be taken care of, but at the same time I'm terrified of it. Given the nature of this thing, cropping up periodically when things seem to be going well, I shouldn't impose it on anybody. When it gets this bad, it's hard for me to do anything. I feel so sick, really sick. It's like having an inflamed tooth in each major joint—elbow, knees, hips—together with this awful malaise as if I had some kind of infection.

I'm afraid to discuss this illness with Fran. It's the one thing that would drive   2
her away. It could be something serious, or it could be nothing. It could go on for the rest of my life. I've been wondering why I went to Philadelphia when I wasn't feeling well. Of course, I'd already made plans, and I didn't want to get held up by this arthritis business again. I've had it so many times my attitude is—so long as I can be up and around—it won't get better if I take to bed and don't go. So I went. I would love to take the day off and go to sleep, but from past experience I know I'll feel just as bad tomorrow, so what's the point?

2/14

Are we ten minutes late? I guess I've gone and confused it with another time.   1
You must be annoyed at my suspiciousness. That statement in itself is more evidence of suspiciousness.

I want to talk about Fran. My mother called last night, and she was   2
hysterical. She was saying bad things about my sister. They had had an argument during which my sister lost her temper. Last night I felt rage at my mother, my sister, and my father. It's as if I have to sweep up after these people. If I didn't do it, if I weren't at all accessible, my mother'd kill herself. Fran was in my apartment and overheard part of it. Am I involved with my family because I want to be in it—partly—or because I have to be in it? Of all the people in the family around mother, I'm the only one on talking terms with her. Fran and I were discussing sexual intercourse, and she told me how mad she was Sunday at not having any satisfaction. I told her how resentful I was about her remark in which she felt as if she were a prostitute. She's still terrified to go to a gynecologist. When she talks with her own mother about sex, her old, rigid position about intercourse gets reinforced. So she's in a lot of conflict about this. When she gets so rigid, it pisses me off and I won't buy it. So I told her off. I walked away not sure whether I was mad at mother or at her. I think it's good that the feeling came out, but why at this time? Fran was shocked, but not too shocked. She asked if I didn't believe in a God, and I told her I was agnostic. She's mad because she's not getting gratification. I know I want to be with her

all the time—it's a frightening feeling. It might mean my mind would shrivel up, and I'd become an intellectual nothing. But she turns me on sexually [Pause].

3   ["Your physical condition hasn't been mentioned today."] Perhaps I don't feel quite as sick as yesterday. Maybe I'm a little better, though I still have some discomfort. I slept a little more yesterday. It's like your saying: "See, a little of the real feeling comes out in life and not so much goes into the joints." Well, I won't admit it. I know, I know, you didn't really say it. I'll try to keep an open mind. But I get enraged when I hear all this talk and people going out on a limb about mind over matter.

2/15 - 2/26, (Summary)

Ambivalent rumination about his relationship with Fran continues. Guilt about hostile and sexual impulses toward her increases and is reinforced by recollections about forbidden sexual activities during childhood. A call from father evokes fresh rage and anxiety. More associations about distrusting women come up. The neurosis frequently interferes with realistic perception at this time. There is a transference dream of an Hitlerian analyst who is becoming more benevolent. The patient starts smoking a pipe again.

2/27

1   The pain was being controlled by 12 aspirin until this weekend—Saturday, when I cut it down to 8. Saturday night I got emotionally upset, and Sunday I felt as if I hadn't slept at all though I got 8 hours sleep. Sunday morning my joints again became tender to touch. I discussed my illness with Fran [tears]. I feel so bad about it. Last night it was O.K. for a while, then it started coming back. Now I'm back to 3 aspirin four times a day and a couple extra, so it adds up to 14. No matter who I go out with, I feel it's a glaring defect to be crippled with arthritis. To be alive is to be in great pain, to be unable to walk, to have a short temper. I expect the worst consequences. A teacher of mine who developed arthritis and got progressively worse, no matter what medicine he took, with all the complications, finally had to resort to a wheelchair and then had to give that up. He became bedridden.

2   I want to start a new life, and I feel like a piece of shit. I told Fran I felt terribly embarrassed and no good. She said, "Whenever we get closer, you tell me you're no good." I'm beginning to think that she looks like the healthy one. I can't ski with her because of these damn joints, so we went to a movie instead. The afternoon was nice but I felt inadequate. Fran showed me her album of pictures with many happy-looking ones of herself. I don't know much about such happiness. I don't feel I could or should have a girl like that if I'm a cripple. I see myself as infecting her. The happy pictures would turn to sad ones. When

I'm like this, the only safe way is to be alone. There's a dramatic quality, but also a truth to it. I don't think you understand how awful I feel and I have to impress you. The real feeling you don't understand is the desperation I feel with the pain. Supposing the symptoms hit me really hard and I couldn't work; that's what I'm afraid of. When I was 8 or 10, I was terrified of dying, so terrified that I couldn't sleep at night. My sister kept telling me I wasn't alone, that the family was around, but I couldn't be convinced [tearful, crying]. It's the fear that I would be alone, that no one could stand being with me, like mother who's alone; nobody can stand being with her. She's got some kind of arthritis herself: I believe it's called osteoarthritis. ["The great fear of your life is that you will become helpless and will be abandoned, so you are forced to look constantly for reassurance, proofs, or guarantees that this will not happen to you. Even a slight change in tone of voice is enough to make you think that you'll be deserted."]

Yet I have a conviction that if Fran and I got married, she wouldn't leave   3 me. Have you ever read the *Beast in the Jungle*? This guy has a relationship with a woman but never marries her because a beast awaits him in the jungle— something dreadful. At age 60 she dies without consummation of the marriage. Then he realizes what the beast in the jungle is—that this woman dies and he didn't do anything while she was alive and now he has nothing, nothing at all. I feel identified with that story.

When I was in the sixth grade, I wanted father to live forever, mother to live   4 forever, and for us to have a million dollars. I remember my teacher noticed how preoccupied I was and asked me if anything was wrong at home. I couldn't tell her how bad things were there. Then my penmanship got very bad, and that was a way to get her mad and distracted, by slanting the letters wrong.

2/28

Went to a belated bachelor party last night. John, for whom it was given, is   1 already married. The rest of us were single men, and there was one secretary from the office. Afterwards I had a strong desire to see Fran, but I didn't, though I strongly missed her. At the party I felt awfully uneasy, as though I were a little kid without his mother. That's silly, isn't it? After all I'm a grown man and yet I feel that way. My friend John, at whose apartment it was, lives in a rough neighborhood. He has two doors with four locks and a crossbar. Maybe that made me uneasy too—that somebody was after me. When I telephoned Fran later in the evening, she didn't recognize my voice at first. I was hurt by that, and now as I tell you about it, I feel like crying. Yet at the party I was attracted to Anna, the secretary, but she wasn't playing around. Actually she's a very tight, constrained sort of person. I have a fantasy now that Fran is like a big baby. Is sex with any woman a way of fending off homosexual fantasies? I've had such fantasies toward some of the men there—mostly about engaging in mutual masturbation. If they only knew what thoughts I had about them.

2   At the party I was much better than I usually am. I was quiet, but when I had something to say, I did and I meant it. I felt sorry for Anna. I go for her physical charms. I guess I also hated her for her smartness and her upper-class manners, even though I really don't know Anna and have never been close to her.

3   Believe it or not, the arthritis this morning was much worse when I got up. I couldn't make a fist. Last night I didn't take any aspirins. Well, I didn't get away with it. This morning while eating breakfast I took three aspirins and by the time I got here, I was better—not worse than usual. If it would be like this, it wouldn't be too bad. I'm not really fine, but I'd settle for the way it is now. I feel you don't understand, and I want to get into a fight with you.

"You make up excuses," was something my mother would shout at me for not visiting her. I feel like crying, screaming, running out on you, just as I used to do with her.

4   I still have a desire to hurt Fran. This was brought out in part by a phone call last night. I guess it was because she was teasing me, playing with me. That's it. She plays little girl games with me. Yet Fran has some awareness of her emotional problems. I guess I had a lot of rage at stopping when I was three-quarters of the way in when we had sexual intercourse. But what do I do with all that rage [tearful]? I guess I haven't been doing anything with it, but I think that it has something to do with the arthritis. I don't go kill anyone. Yet I would like to take Fran by the shoulders and shake her and say, "Do you know what you're doing to me with that hysterical three-quarters of the way in?" If I hurt her and leave her, I'll wind up being lonely. Yet I'm in a rage at her for fooling around with me. But there must be a lot of unwarranted suspiciousness on my part, because she wouldn't have refused complete relations if I had insisted.

2/29

1   I felt so sick that I finally called my internist for an appointment tomorrow. I almost didn't go to work today. I felt awful, just like a person with a temperature of 103°, only I didn't have any fever at all when I checked it with a thermometer. Yesterday I had a headache and a lot of malaise. I was taking so much aspirin I thought maybe it was from the aspirin, so I decided to stop them and see my doctor. I have a wisdom tooth that I've been told is impacted. It's the right lower side, and it's very painful. It's been bothering me for about 10 days but I haven't mentioned it, I guess. I hesitate to get my wisdom tooth pulled, because I had a very bad infection once on the left side.

2   I couldn't work this morning, couldn't concentrate on what was being said to me. Gradually as the day wears on, I feel somewhat better. I got up feeling worse than before, though I slept through the night. I had trouble concentrating

on talking even to Fran for an hour last night. Maybe the aspirin was making me sick. I had some ringing in my ears before I went to bed. I discussed with Fran how much commitment it would be if she and I had sexual intercourse. She said it would be a 60 percent commitment. She said that a girl should have intercourse with only one person in her life, and she would want to marry the man she had sex relations with. She said it would be harder to break up if we had intercourse. I have fantasies of starting all over again with someone new. I need a vacation. I want to go where it's warm, lie in the sun, and go fishing. Yesterday I was going to ask you if I was crazy; when the physical side gets worse, I get to thinking my emotional troubles are too much.

3/4

[Four-day interval.]

I'm hesitant to talk about what happened since Thursday. I'm ashamed and 1 embarrassed. After I left here the last time I had a sudden desire to see Laura, the girl I used to go with before I met Fran. I talked myself into thinking it was because I wanted to understand the differences between them. Laura is such a bright girl compared to Fran and so highly educated. Coupled with this was rage at Fran and myself for not completing the act of intercourse when we had a chance.

When I saw Laura last night she almost immediately said to me, "Let's go to 2 bed." I almost flipped. That was a remarkable show of spontaneity for her. First, however, I took her for a ride in my car. I got some prophylactics. Then we went to bed. She was so horny and wanted to be on top. It's still hard for her to have an orgasm. She seemed like a man with her body, going after me as if she had a penis. Then she wanted to suck off me. She was so tense, and there was a driving quality to her actions as if she had to come, no matter what. I don't like the smell of Laura's genitals compared with Fran's. I don't like to rub her with my hand either. Afterwards I fell asleep and had a frightening dream of a woman coming at me with a spoon as though it were a sword. It reminds me of a time when I was a kid, maybe five or six years old; my mother was coming at me with a spoon, insisting that I have some more to eat, and it seems to me I had a fantasy of her ramming the spoon and all down my throat. Laura is a sucking kind of girl, sucking dry. Fran wants to feed me till I choke. I don't think Fran has a penis, but I certainly have that idea about Laura. Still, it felt good in a way to be back, and I enjoyed talking with her. We recalled some happy times together [tears].

My wisdom tooth is still bothering me a lot, and I'll have to squeeze an 3 appointment in with the dentist and have it taken care of. However, since last Friday [the day after the last hour] I've been feeling much better. [No mention is made of his visit to the internist that day.]

3/5

1   [Five minutes late.]
It takes quiet diligence to be an analyst, I guess. I envy you for that. I'm much longer on sheer flamboyance. My father is a diligent worker, a good technician, but less personable than his boss. I wanted to get my father's love by being what he was—an architect—but I could never get interested in that stuff. It seems to me that I keep wanting to be what these older men have achieved.

2   My tooth still hurts. I saw the oral surgeon yesterday, and he burnished the molar hitting on the half-erupted tooth below. There's still a swelling there. I'm late today because I put my car through a wash before getting here. I remember mother taking me home in a taxi from the dentist, about 15 years ago. I was so dependent on her. I had an impacted molar extracted, and I was weak and dizzy from shock. I was aroused by the dentist's technician who seemed to be rubbing all over me, but she had to hit the chisel with the hammer. I dread teeth extraction—that's why I delayed doing anything about this one. Then, after the tooth was out I had a big infection there. I have some kind of idea about the tooth that's bothering me now: If I have it removed, the arthritis will go away. Fran said she would take care of me, if I needed it, after the operation. I just keep having fear of a terrible outcome if the tooth is extracted, even if it were done by the best oral surgeon [pause].

3   My thoughts are turning to the time I first came to have sexual intercourse. I had been very much afraid of it. When I was in college, one of my friends who was a medical student, insisted that I watch an autopsy. I really didn't want to but he finally had his way and I went. It was done on an old lady who had died of cancer. When they opened her abdomen, it was the worst smell I had ever experienced in my life, worse than the worst shit smell or outhouse smell. I got so sick, I had to leave. I felt like throwing up and just made it to a toilet. I was terribly upset afterwards. What had I seen there? A smelly old body in the end. I could die too. That became a persistent thought. I'm mortal. I wondered what I was waiting for. I'll screw everybody. I was confronted by mortality, that everyone dies, but maybe I would die early. I remember the fellow who was doing the autopsy—what do you call him—the pathologist, asking if the old lady was a virgin. She was a mess, an old nurse. I went from that autopsy room, shocked, with a determination to have sex, come what may.

4   I was going out with one girl, but we were just playing around, getting nowhere. In back of my mind was another girl, Wendy, who I knew went down. I was aware that she liked me. I thought I could make her. I was 21 and hadn't had sexual intercourse. I went out on a number of dates with Wendy and then seduced her in my college dormitory room. I borrowed a radio because I thought that quiet music would make a nice background. I remember when I went to the

drugstore to buy prophylactics, the clerk seemed to leer at me in a knowing way, and I was terribly anxious. I arranged the bed and the light in just the right position. We had some cognac and then I said to myself, "This is it!" By golly, that's what happened. She was a lot more experienced than I and really great in bed. I came very quickly that first time, but then later less quickly. She was a good dancer, somewhat ugly but not unbearably so. Once she had the crabs. Underneath it all I thought she was a slut. We were together for two years, and then she got married. I always feel like crying when I talk about a girl I've lost. If I commit myself to Fran, then Laura will hate me, and my mother will hate me. I can't bear it, if she doesn't love me.

3/6

1　　The matter of homosexuality has been on my mind since yesterday. But it's easier to fight about your bill than to talk about that. I haven't paid you yet, but you sent me two bills this month, and I thought you were mad at me. [Explanation of double billing error.] It seems to me that the thoughts I had about being in bed with Laura, her acting as if she had a penis and her seeming to be like a man, were all of a homosexual nature. I've made up my own private theory about this. As I tried to act the man with Fran and our sexual life approached a culmination point, I guess I got panicky. So I ran to have relations with a girl who has a penis. You see, in my thinking Fran doesn't have one. But in reality neither does Laura.

2　　I had a dream about Mike—a sweet, soft guy—who's married to a girl with the largest penis I've ever seen, figuratively speaking. She's a business executive and likes to cut up people, goes horseback riding, gets dozens of traffic tickets, and is really tough sounding. In the dream Mike and I arrive in Paris. I suggest we stay in a special hotel, and I tell the concierge that I stayed there some years ago. There's talk that Mike and I are two homosexuals looking for a place to shack up. I say, "No, two single rooms, please!" I get one for $2 and go to it, and it's a pretty good deal. That's the dream. I've been thinking about what to do about my vacation time and where to go, which I haven't decided yet.

3　　I keep thinking, wishfully maybe, that women feed you and take care of you when you're sick. At such times my feelings about mother are not all negative.

4　　I have no arthritis today. I'm cured—after that homosexual encounter with Laura—to be exact. That was Thursday night. On Friday I saw the doctor. He said it wasn't the aspirin, but that I had a virus on top of my joint pains and that I could continue with the aspirins. But, since I felt better on Friday, I wasn't going to start up with the aspirins again, and I haven't taken them since. Actually during last Thursday I started feeling better and better, and then went out to Laura's that night. By Friday I was much better. Yet I still have a worry about becoming a cripple. Essentially Fran is a woman while Laura to me is like a man. Fran doesn't like—what do you call it—fellatio. Well, Laura did a lot of kissing and sucking of my penis, and I wasn't asking for it. Then she kept wanting me to rub her clitoris with my hand until she had orgasm without my actually being inside. If I should try intercourse, she wants to be on top. I keep thinking now that I'm giving in to my own fantasies about having homosexual experiences with you through this kind of disguised sex with Laura and then going to see my internist the next day. When I was in bed with Laura and after the sexual activity, I asked her if she had a lot of dolls when she was a little girl. She said she had only one doll which wet its pants when it got a bottle. I kept thinking of her as unfeminine, like a man trying to emulate his famous father. My father isn't famous. When I think of it, most of the girls I've had a relationship with have had important fathers.

3/7

1   I'm a little better in the teeth, but worse in the joints. That pain recurred right after the last hour. It just makes me feel I'm destined to lead a life of loneliness and suffering. I should tell you that I felt awful sick when I left yesterday after making references to homosexuality. In fact, I feel awful now, just like crying. Last night I got a letter from one of my friends inviting me to his wedding and that's when I really got depressed. I can't face it. If he gets married why can't I? I thought him to be sick and depressed. But I'm the last of all my friends who isn't married. I feel I'm the worst, the craziest, terribly in pain, each day a struggle. I keep thinking of a nonexistent penis. I'm capable of no love for anybody.

2   Last night I hated Fran with a passion. I was sitting in a reclining chair and a spring broke on it. The previous night she had been jumping up and down in it and broke it. I was very mad at her and wanted to kill her. She isn't so heavy now; she weighs 110 pounds, down from 124. She's quite an eater. The broken chair—well, I tried to fix it seven different times and felt frustrated each time, and wound up wanting to rip the chair!

I can't stand hating so much. My chair that Fran jumped on and broke is like me, full of arthritis and homosexual feelings. It's as if she did it to me.

3   Tonight I play poker with some of the fellows from the office. Though I'm busy and feel sick, I don't want to turn them down. I guess I'd like to do my work while Fran is holding my hand. This homosexual business has troubled me before, but in a vague way. There's concealed interest in my male friends. Then there's this not seeming to want to settle for a woman and get married. I talk angry, but I feel shitty, worthless, incompetent, crazy, helpless, and hopeless. That's when I hate everybody, men and woman. In yesterday's hour those hidden homosexual fantasies came out. You've been intimating at my being mad at you. Well, I've been mad at you for not helping me deal with those feelings. It all came out that way—queer.

3/11, Excerpt

You know, I did something I'm not supposed to. I got hold of a book just   1
published, and it's on rheumatoid arthritis. Well, I just had to read it, even
though I didn't understand most of the technical stuff. There's a type which
starts off with 3 to 4 years of symptoms of discomfort and joint pains for
periods of 1 to 2 months with free intervals for longer. It seems that 50 percent
of patients have this form first. It also seems that almost nobody has the disease
during the summer, and the most common time when it kicks up is during March
and October. I've had dizziness and this discomfort on and off for quite some
time now. Realistically, from that book, it looks as if I have an excellent chance
of being hospitalized some day. I don't think you understand how it feels, how
this expectation can permeate my whole outlook.

3/12 - 5/14, Interim Summary

Concern about forming new relationships with women is again rising:
Discovery of his defects—neurosis and arthritis—will lead to their rejecting him.
Castration fear with oral overtures—wisdom tooth pain—reappears in the
transference. Continued anxiety and hostility are linked with a general slowing
up. Regressive wishes to be taken care of by a loving father are reactivated.
Arthritis symptoms continue to be absent. Masturbation fantasies focus on oral
and anal practices with resultant guilt. The patient tries going out with a sexually
attractive, bright, new girl, but she is quite immature, and he feels dissatisfied.
Still he is concerned about his manliness when with her. This concern is followed
by a feeling of despair and a drift into homosexual fantasies. A date with an old
flame, with both inhibited, turns out to be a sad experience. There is a brief
return of mild, joint pains which continue as he visits relatives out of town and is
aware of, but doesn't feel anger toward them. These symptoms subside as he
returns to Boston. A persistent question troubles him: Can he be a man if he has
arthritis? He takes a week's vacation. On return he feels better. Finally sexual
relations with Fran are complete, but ambivalence toward her persists. He visits
with her parents. He sees his own father as an arch-villain responsible for
dumping the patient's mother onto the patient's lap.

5/15

[Late five minutes].   1
I got up this morning with a headache. It began last night when I attended a   2
meeting on violence in the streets. The headache rapidly became very severe.
They were talking about riots and killing. A lady lawyer began haranguing the

audience, and she was followed by a Negro actor. I had the impression that there were sharp differences of opinion and that feelings were running high. I myself really got pissed off. Now, suddenly, I feel like crying. I got a traffic ticket for parking in a crosswalk, while going up to Fran's to get her for the meeting. That's what started it off—rage at the cop who gave me the ticket. I blamed it on Fran: You bitch, if you don't come downstairs in time I'll get a ticket. But it really wasn't her fault. Yet all evening I kept having bad thoughts about her, the stupid bitch. She kept asking me what it was all about; she had trouble in following the speakers. I raged inside: You ignorant country girl, what do know about this. Where she comes from, there is no race problem. She also asked me about what certain words meant that she should have known. Yet, when I wanted to leave the meeting, she wanted to stay. I finally insisted, because of a splitting headache. Then we slept together without intercourse. Meanwhile, some of my friends are trying to fix me up with new girls which leads to a conflict too.

3   Today my joints hurt. Whenever I get one of these headaches, I think I'll get my arthritis back. It's as if there's something eating away at my joints. I wonder if it's part of the headache. When the headache goes away, the joint pains seem to go away.

4   I was so mad at the cop for giving me a ticket. In fact, I saw him writing it. When I discussed it with him, the cop said he had already started it and couldn't stop it. I was pissed off. That was my neighborhood, but all of these outsiders that come to watch sports activities are parked illegally and don't get parking tickets. I sympathize with the Negroes who say: Kill the cops. Yet the cop wasn't that tough, and he had already started writing the ticket. I told Fran about the ticket, attacking it instead of her. Then I got mad at her for defending the cop when she said, "Well, you parked in the crosswalk, you're not special." So I said to her, "You bitch," with a smile. But she was right and the cop was right: I'm not special. The idea that I'm somehow mysteriously above the law is not realistic. Yet I got into a fury about that.

5   There's a realistic problem, an intellectual gap, between me and mother, just as between mother and father. I think that if my mother were smarter, more resourceful, less dependent, then she and father would have made it together, somehow. She just didn't make any attempt. She never completed high school. I can't get away from that feeling that Fran isn't smart. Yet I keep thinking she's intuitively brilliant. I have mixed feelings now. I feel like crying and I'm getting excited in the genitals about the thought that she wants to get married and I want to marry her. She's talking about not being able to continue this way much longer, insisting that we make plans or stop seeing each other. I think of stringing her along. Yet the thought of actually marrying her excites me. However, when I get to feel as I did last night and this morning, I start wondering. What if we got married and I started hating her on a regular basis as I

did last night? Father got married in his balls because my mother was attractive. But there were no common interests and the marriage fell apart leaving the children all fucked up. I'm so hateful. When I experience this white-hot hatred, I don't feel like marrying anyone. All I can think of is that I've been frustrated and not getting what I think is due me.

5/16

I've got the bloody arthritis now. The headache went away, but I was left 1 with arthritis. Am I to consider that my life will be that of a person with this disease or a variant of it, or nothing? If I have to figure every four months that I'll be sick for a month, I have to plan my life differently. When I feel sick, I don't react normally, though most people may not notice it. If I really have arthritis, I should give up a lot of things and change my way of life. But, if I don't have it, I would like to be much more active [rumbling stomach]. That noise is the bottle of Coke I had before coming here. But there's a much more important question: If I have the disease, should I get married and have children? A good person would never marry a guy with this disease, wouldn't want the shit that comes with it. When I have the sickness, all my desire to be mothered becomes overwhelming. Yet neither mothering or nonmothering is acceptable, and I have a strong need to be alone [more stomach rumbling]. Everything becomes an effort and aspirins don't help that much. How strange! When I don't have the pain, I don't take it into account. Out of my body, out of my mind. Maybe I'm working too hard. I keep getting these repeated knockdowns. Fran doesn't want to be a controlling, dominating woman. She really has taken my interests into account. Yet she doesn't live up to my goal in intellectual, social, and sophisticated terms.

5/20

I have had a further return of the arthritis symptoms over the weekend. I can 1 hardly listen to what the people at the office are saying. I start thinking of my pain and then can't think of much else. I have that feverish feeling which lasts anywhere from a week to a month, with ups and downs. At times it seems I'm running a high temperature, but when I go and actually take it, it's either normal or 99.4° or 99.6°. But every joint aches, though I can move them. Then I load up with aspirins, but it makes me dizzy so I can't concentrate, and then I have trouble with my memory and will power. I'm mad at one of the executives at the office for not showing up for a conference with me after I had prepared a report he requested, though I felt so sick. When I contemplate years of this torture and suffering as lying ahead, it's extremely disturbing. I have no deformity yet. But if this is the beginning, how will it be when it gets really bad?

Maybe it's something worse than arthritis; what, I don't know. I've been wondering whether I should move to Arizona or some hot climate, though I don't like the South. The specialist I consulted about this told me to take three aspirins every four hours when these symptoms start up, but I hesitate because the effect of the aspirins on my work is like the illness itself pretty much. The symptoms are worse on arising, but better by afternoon, and aspirin in that dosage has a doping effect on me.

2   Contemplating marriage with me having this condition is very difficult. If it didn't threaten me with the eventual helplessness of a baby, it wouldn't be so bad. It's worsened by Fran's babying tendencies, which, however, she can turn off. Also, if it got bad, she could get a divorce and marry someone else. She's a girl who comes from a happy background, but I've grown up with unhappiness; it's part of my life. But she really doesn't know about unhappiness. It's hard to forget moroseness this morning when I'm not feeling well. I can't rid myself of the idea of having pain all my life, which is a real possibility, because it seems to me medicine can't cure my condition with what's known now. Here I am, though, hanging on to a magical belief that analysis can cure arthritis, that if I ever analyzed out what was going on, it would go away, that you have the answers.

3   I've got a lot of pain, and I'm being hit by forces I have no control over. It started at the meeting when I got a splitting headache. That had something to do with my rage because of the traffic ticket. I'm saying this to please you, but what I'm really saying to myself is that I've got this mysterious disease whose cause is unknown and whose cure is unknown. I've had it a number of times and it keeps coming back. I'm so mad about its recurrence. Feel like Job. Self-pity. Lots of self-pity. It's happening at a time now when I'm considering marriage and separation from mother. If I could only reconcile Fran's not being intellectual enough with my love for her. I'm in conflict about it. Now I'm getting tearful. I don't think you understand. I believe Fran and I could work together. I really like her. But I'm afraid you don't think it's really love, that you're saying: How can he love her—she's below his intellectual and social standards; it's his self-love over and over again, he doesn't want to give up his mother. ["Those are your own thoughts."]

5/22

1   I'm still feeling sick. Last night Fran called me; said an old friend of hers was coming to town with her husband, would I like to go out for a drink with them. I said yes, but felt no. I got a headache and was very tired. I didn't too much like the people. That was the worst part of it. They've been married a year. They fight about the wife's manner of speaking—she has a bad accent. He, on the other hand, doesn't pick up after himself. So they fight about these things. He also doesn't like his wife's habit of talking with her hands.

Afterwards I took Fran to her apartment, and I was dead beat. I wanted so   2
much to rest. My head was splitting, and I ached all over. I lay down on the
couch, and she lay down next to me. I had no energy at all, but she wanted to
make out. I got mad, mad as could be and said I have to go. But she wanted
more kisses and embraces. I protested because I could barely keep my eyes open.
In the process of leaving I said something about not wanting to go out because I
had been sick and depressed, and besides, I didn't like her friends even though
they were really nice to me. I was getting madder and madder at Fran's wanting
more from me because I had nothing to give. Actually I wanted more and more
from her because of my sickness.

When I feel as I do, everything looks shitty, no good, grim. I had fantasies   3
last night of getting rid of Fran. I keep thinking of her as either too giving or too
demanding.

But I'm mad at you, mad at psychoanalysis. It's been a long time in   4
treatment and I'm still sick. I don't see any hope. Really, what can I expect of
analysis as far as this pain is concerned? I have two sets of expectations: That
it'll do nothing or that it'll do everything. I'm saying it over and over again—it's
not good enough for me. I want you to be an authority. I know about your
interest in psychosomatic medicine. Wish my friends hadn't told me about it.
Then I wouldn't have to worry so much about whether or not you have the final
answers. I read somewhere about a patient who had arthritis; the psychological
meanings of his symptoms were discussed. It seems that there is a desire to sleep,
and the hands being bent into a special position indicates such a desire. That's a
lot of garbage. I think it's the need to get away from pain that causes the desire
for sleep and for the hands to be held in such a bent position. I was really
annoyed by the article.

You have no idea how angry I am at this. ["I couldn't tell that you're that   5
angry."] [Bland actually.] Well, how can I tell you how angry I am? I'll get
kicked out [laughing] as being too self-preoccupied and untreatable. My anger
does come out, but not here; I'm afraid. ["Why are you afraid of me?"] Well,
I'm afraid you'll kick me out. I have such a hostile attitude that you'll say to me,
"If you feel that way, get out and don't waste my time and yours." I keep
thinking it won't work and a lot of it is garbage. I think I can be on this couch
till Kingdom Come, and it won't affect the arthritis, just my adjustment to it,
maybe. The only honest people in psychiatry are those that treat people with
drugs. They say: That's all we know about, and they don't mess around. I have
an acquaintance who's a psychiatrist. I think he's a sham. He has trouble
organizing his thoughts, often says things I question, but he plays a good game
of tennis.

Now that meeting has come into my mind again. I'm so fucking tired of   6
hearing all this shit about racial strife! You'd think that some people created the
fucking world the way they parade their sense of entitlement. I can understand
my sense of entitlement but not theirs. When I spoke up at that meeting, that's
when I got the headache and these pains started.

7   I'm angry at Fran. Last night I was with her, the stupid cow, deluding myself I'm in love. We just want to feed each other—there's nothing else in common. What am I wasting my time for, sitting around, deluding myself with shitty rationalizations?

Since I'm pouring out my anger, I might as well throw some at my friend Dick who's been away and came into town briefly. He was supposed to stay over at my house, and at the last minute he reneged after all my efforts.

5/23

1   Last night I told Fran what I told you and more. When I have this pain, I can't give anything. I just want. Perhaps the best solution is not to get married. Look at Dr. A, famous analyst! He would have been luckier if he had never gotten married, what with all the tragedy in his family. I think that sometimes loneliness is better than closeness, if in closeness nothing is given or one's own woes are inflicted on others. I asked Fran if she wants to marry someone who could be a cripple in fifteen years and told her how mad I am at normal people. I added that I hated orthodoxy of all religions when I'm in this mood. I think it's so much hocus-pocus, and she might as well know how I feel, since she's a religious person. I'm sick of talking to my colleagues at work when I feel like this, yet I don't want to be hateful. I kept up this angry barrage for an hour with Fran to the point where she started to cry. For a while I didn't feel sympathy, just cold, thinking it would be better to break up because there was no future. I told her I felt like Job in the beginning—railing against the Lord. I told her I believed in *nothing* when I feel like this. Anyone who'd like a person who's this way has got to be crazy. This pain is driving me crazy. I get so fucking mad. I might have driven Fran away last night. When the pain is great, all I care about is myself, my joints, and the hurting. Everything else can take a back seat to that. I kept telling myself to shut up, but I didn't. I just kept on going.

2   Everything is enveloped in hatred, even my good friend, Dick. At the last minute he tells me he won't be staying over, after our plans had been made long in advance. I felt so damn mad. He and I got into a couple of arguments that Thursday night. I can't concentrate well. I'm mad that nothing can be done. I feel like hitting a punching bag. You can write, I can't. You can organize, concentrate, and I can't. You're smart and I'm stupid. I feel like crying [pause]. It doesn't hurt so much today, and I think you're trying to gloat because I got angry and that led to some relief.

5/27

1   Driving here today I felt very dizzy, especially going through tunnels and on curves. I almost had to pull over to the side. I slowed down and began to feel

better. I finally stopped at the bank to cash a check and the dizziness went away. Maybe it's from the aspirin I've been taking. Two before bed. two at 2 A.M., two at 10 A.M., and two at noon.

I'm concerned that you don't understand my pain. I feel far away from **2** marriage. Who can marry me? What do I have to offer anyone? I'm not very aggressive or manly. I can satisfy Fran in bed, but not as often as she wants. I want to leave her before she rejects me because of my arthritis. Why am I so sure she'd marry me, anyway? Would I marry her if she had the illness. I don't think I would. I'd run out. Saturday night Fran and I had sexual intercourse, very enjoyable. But the next day she said something disturbing. She wanted to know if I were making love to her or to you. I had mentioned being married to the analysis. Actually it's because my life is so much in turmoil that I think about the analysis so much.

5/28

I still have the arthritis. It isn't better or worse, but it doesn't get in the way **1** and I'm not so depressed.

I had a long dream: It was in the apartment of an old college roommate. I **2** was living there with Fran but wasn't married. She was out that morning. A very thin, small girl was there and I was getting sexually excited. She had on panties and a bra. I went in back of her, put my penis between her legs, and embraced her. My thought was I would not have sexual intercourse with this girl. Her body shape was like that of my sister. We go into bed and make out. Then to a sink where Fran has been washing out my socks and underwear. I let the water out of the sink; something gets caught in the drain, a comb. I toss the socks out of the sink. I hurry. Fran is due back at 10. I tell the girl: Let's go to your place. I leave. Then I'm awakened by a phone call.

Associations: It's as if I was no longer interested in Fran. She had become like mother, taking care of me. I was out for more excitement. I thought she's too fat, weighs about 118 pounds, heavy around the waist. The other girl is very slim and in a sense more sexy. I had a feeling toward Fran like I used to have to my previous girlfriends. The apartment in the dream reminds me of a seduction I engineered there. The girl was looking out of the window. I approached her from behind, put my arms around her, and we finally got to bed. I was so frightened of success I was almost impotent. I was also frightened then that someone would come in. But it turned out O.K.

I'm still in a rage at you for not curing my arthritis. I had fantasies last night **3** about seeing some out-of-town specialists who'll diagnose it as something else, curable with some specific medicine, and I'll live happily ever after. But I have a good internist in Boston. Why do I have to see these great names?

My turning on Fran is related to my lousy physical condition. I seem to want **4** to run out on her. She's been eating a lot more than usual. I'll bet she's getting ready to say we're not compatible, which is really what I'm getting ready to say. I question my motives in seeking out any woman. The only person who could stand me this way is mother. She wants to come to Boston this weekend. I don't want to see her. She can't keep her hands off me, makes me feel like a little boy. She talks about her own poor physical condition, her wrinkled skin. I feel threatened by the memories of lying down in bed beside her when I was a kid. There is the sadness of her telling me her skin is wrinkled. This is in contrast to my rage at her for her threats of suicide and her lack of reasonableness. She will not listen to anything but her own needs. I'm also afraid of her meeting with Fran. God knows what will come of that. You know, silly as it may sound, I'm still afraid that she'll kill me if she doesn't get what she wants. Then I'll get it in the neck. She never really wanted me to begin with. If I hadn't come along, maybe she could have fixed things up with father. I want her, and I don't want her. That's my dilemma. She's my insurance policy against disaster—against complete helplessness—because she'd take care of me if I got sick. She'd provide a place where I'm safe. I long for that haven. You know, when I was sick as a child she waited on me hand and foot. ["Your extremities are involved physically now. The symptoms you have are linked to the wish to be taken care of hand and foot, a reproduction of the childhood days when mother provided such care. It's as if in this way a reunion with mother will be possible. Yet, while that's longed for, it's also dreaded—this remainder of your extreme dependency."]

5   I had this attention whenever I was sick as a child, with measles, mumps, scarlet fever, and joint pains. When I had the joint pains then, mother would sit on my legs and warm them with her body heat. Father would rub them with alcohol, I got this care from both of them, but mostly mother, when I was four or five. I remember once—I must have been seven—her holding me while a doctor drew blood, or tried to, from my arm. I fought so hard they couldn't get blood. I fought tooth and nail. Mostly, though, I remember the pleasures of being sick. These pains I had as a child were never diagnosed either. It was mostly in my feet then, my calves. It wasn't limited to the joints, more in the muscles. Pressure from weight and aspirins made it feel better. I often asked mother to sit on my legs and she would. Both father and mother would give me alcohol rubs. It felt good. My sister didn't like my getting that attention at all. Now I want that mothering stuff from Fran something awful and though she gives me a lot, it isn't enough. I don't want to be helpless, and yet there's a strong need to be that way.

5/29

1   I've been sick since last night with a splitting headache and feverish feeling, but no fever. I got up feeling much worse than now. I started crying a little over

what's happening to me. I want to be taken care of. But it seems to be becoming a reality that every three months I'll be sick for a month or more. That means every year for four months I'll be sick, feel like hell, have to go on aspirins, feel dizzy, and not be able to enjoy anything. I can't stand the limitations it imposes. The aspirin doesn't help this feeling of malaise, though it seems to reduce the pain. The way I feel now is the way my friends tell me they felt with mononucleosis. I remember how many times I was checked for such symptoms, and nobody knew what I had. I think I've got some glands in my neck now. I always get them when I feel this way. It must be a virus. One doctor thought my joint pain was due to muscle spasm and prescribed what he called a muscle relaxant which I took faithfully without any effect except sleepiness. All blood tests have been called normal. Actually last year when I had the joint pains they were worse. Then, finally, this specialist examined me very carefully and said he couldn't call it rheumatoid arthritis, though the story sounds that way. Now here I am, scared stiff. But look at Biggs, the organist, and surgeons that operate despite their arthritis. But others, like Barrymore and Bobby Jones, sit in their wheelchairs.

What am I going to do about marriage? If Fran were around this morning, I'd   2
be more babyish. This way, in her absence, I had to get up, get going. So there's nobody to complain to and no occasion to hate myself for it.

Exercise helps my general mood. I don't feel so helpless or hopeless, and I'm   3
not as depressed. It gets rid of some of the stiffness. If I can play tennis, all is not lost.

I had a dream: I was in an office building looking for father. I look in a room   4
and there are toys there. Father is on the sixth floor. I get off on the fifth floor, wanting to buy a tennis racquet.

Associations: there's a cut-rate tennis equipment store near father's office. Recently I got another racquet from a friend and am doing very well with it. Father buys things cut-rate, but doesn't always get a good deal. Since I've gotten a new racquet my game is much better. When my father went into the hospital five years ago for his kidneys, I remember driving him there. I don't think I've told you about that. He looked awful, as if he were going to die. I had the fantasy he had transferred funds from his account to my account, as if he were preparing to die [tears, sobbing]. I didn't want him to die [tears]. He loved me [sobbing]. But I treated him like a shit bag. I hate him so much for buying used tennis racquets, for having no force or style, for being so distant with me. when he left the house, I had no man to model myself after, just my sticky mother ["You've been looking for a strong, nurturing father for many years, trying to establish a hoped-for ideal relationship."] [Violent sobbing.] I hate him for leaving me with her. ["For another woman."] [Violent sobbing.] ["This emotional reaction is a small indication of what a sense of loss you've experienced over the years."] I used to cry out at night when I was younger that I wanted my daddy, and my mother would use that to beat him with for leaving, so finally I had to give up crying [violent sobbing]. What a change there was in him when he was sick with that urinary trouble! He came out of the hospital looking so debilitated. I hadn't seen him in six weeks. They thought he was going to die [violent sobbing].

6/3

1   After I left here the last hour, I felt pretty bad for a while. Then I suddenly decided to play some tennis. As I waited at the tennis courts with a friend for my turn, the bad feelings gradually dissipated. The feeling of sickness and joint pains diminished as well as the sad feelings. And they have been considerably better since then, though I'm afraid to say it. Instead, I've felt lots of anxiety coming here. I've had thoughts of wanting to kill. I've been with Fran, and I've had fantasies of putting her in a meat slicer and slicing her, piece by piece, one piece at a time. I'm beset with fantasies of what I'm doing with this stupid girl, wanting to get rid of her. She really isn't stupid. Feeling as I did toward my father means that I've been acting something out, as you call it, with Fran. My going out with her is an expression of animosity toward him. She's not the ultra-bright girl that I want and that he wants. I'll show him, the bastard, and not go out with any highly educated girls, although some I've known have seemed to me to be nongiving and cold. I think you're mad at me for all this. As if you were implying that you've had enough of my fuzzy thinking. Now I'm thinking of the revolutionary movements that are in the news. I'm an old conservative. Analysis is a thing of the past. We're entering the age of entitlement instead of enlightenment. There'll be a revolution after which there'll be no analysis.

2   I've invited father for a weekend of tennis and he'll meet Fran then. I wonder what that will be like. He'll say she's stupid, too fat, and not good enough for me. I haven't invited mother to come up because I can't handle her right now.

3   I'm not as sexually aroused as I used to be by Fran. She now needs support herself. I keep having more and more fantasies of going back to the other girls I used to know.

4   I'm getting a headache. I wish I could cry. I think I feel the emotion, but it's inside. If only I could cry like I did the last time, because it's still there. After that crying, I felt more relaxed, though sad, than I have all year. I felt bad because I couldn't sustain the sadness, but I've been feeling blue periodically. A headache's coming on. There've been a few times when I've felt like crying again. I keep thinking of having had some good things and then having lost them. I'm beginning to appreciate how powerful a force a loss can be. But right now the feeling has gone underground. Instead I'm preoccupied more with furnishing my new office.

Meanwhile I keep having thoughts of hurting Fran by going back to my old girlfriends who can talk with me on the same level. I feel I'm talking down to Fran but I don't believe that it's realistic to think she's stupid. Maybe it's really mother I feel so concerned about; she's not bright but knows how to maneuver and manipulate. It did father no good. Am I following in his footsteps? I can't sustain the feelings of sadness that pop through to the surface from time to time. I feel the sadness now again. I think the real sadness is not in relation to father as much as it is to mother. It seems that all the feeling I can drum up now is hatred. I hate her so much I can't see the loss, although it peeps at me. You're not doing enough for me, says mother, see how I suffer. Yet how can you feel sad, really sad, for someone like that?

* * * * * *

The joint symptoms subsided completely after a few more days, but returned again though only briefly and in shadowy form twice more during the remainder of the analysis.

MARGINAL NOTES

6/2

1. Melodramatic references to hostility, but little feeling expressed. Masochistic dream. Oral transference wishes.
2. Mother's oral sadism coped with initially by avoidance, but rage and guilt manifestations break through in verbal form. Frustration of own dependency needs evokes impulses to leave the rejecting women; transference aspects.
3. Turning to father who is still unavailable, having deserted him and mother for another woman. Affect discharge continues to be only partial.
4. Losses. Shifts from passivity to reactive sadism back to girlish helplessness.

6/6

1. Somatic dysfunction preceded by unusual muscular exertion. Subsequent restlessness and masturbation with thinly disguised incestuous fantasies. Recollections of former girlfriend: Shifts from manly to inferiority feelings with reactive hostility resulting in breakup of the relationship. Current losses. Attempts to overcome passivity.

6/7

1. Bodily sensations, probably erotic. Fantasies of oral-sadistic mother, activating defense of being a killer-type man.
2. Dream: Self-devaluation masking transference hostility.

3. Separation anxiety. Sibling rivalry. Helpless males, depriving mother-figures. Hunger pain percepts.

4. Fear of exposure, regressive wishes. Defensive recollections about manly skills insufficient to compensate for inferiority, feeling of being deserted by father.

6/8

1. Transference aspects of war and cease-fire.

2. Concern about impregnating Laura.

3. Envy of sibling surrogate's oral oversupply, followed by defensive devaluation of him.

4. First reference to somatic symptom, though present several days.

5. Guilt, retraction of hostility, expression of positive feeling toward sibling figures. Concern over homosexual aspects. Oral imagery and activity. Self-devaluation. Self-castration fantasies linked with tooth extraction.

6. Father's withholding. Transference envy about what another sibling figure is getting. Concern about his own orality. Somatic manifestations as expression of anxiety.

6/12

1. Rage and anxiety about repulsed heterosexual advances, now reactivated. Regression to homosexual fantasies with anal elements. Rejection. Ambivalence.

2. Anatomic references to Laura's masculinity.

3. Hostile transference, feelings of deprivation. Sensory percepts. Ambivalence interpreted.

6/13

1. Anxiety in affective form activated by recollection of voyeurism. Heterosexual frustration.

2. Being left by older sibling figure—partial affect discharge only.

3. Haircut now symbolizes manliness, relieves anxiety; formerly activated castration and homosexual fears. Motor response outside patient's awareness. References to dependency or overcompensatory heterosexuality.

4. Belated awareness of finger activity linked with masturbatory equivalent. Transference: jealous, competitive, and frustrated hostile dependent attitudes.

5. Awareness of hunger percepts and immobilization of hands. Transference: expectation of punishment for sexual play.

6. Negative recollections of father. Interpretations.

6/14

1. References to ambivalent relationship with Laura and with old girlfriend. Interoceptive percepts. Father's symbolic warning about phallus.

2. Heterosexual frustration and inadequacy activate homosexual fantasies. Recollections of feminine identification: secret acting out and looking at self in that role with intense sexual excitement. Castration anxiety. Defensively hostile transference.

6/16

1. Hostile transference related to oral frustrations. Linked with early fear of and disappointment in doctors. Specific anxiety about venipuncture symbolizing sexual attack. Tonsillectomy also linked with negative recollections.

2. Symbolic castration anxiety. First awareness of pain percepts. Further references to oropharynx and teeth extraction with sexualized associations, both homosexual, heterosexual, and masturbatory, linked with symbolic castration. Recollections of voyeuristic activities at camp, with current transference implications.

3. Competitive difficulties in sports, compensatory success in crafts and extracurricular activities.

4. Losses, with partial affect discharge. Compensatory fantasies of substitute women, self as hero, linked with activation of infantile oral motor activity.

6/19

1. Frustrations, hostility, paranoid reaction, confusion.
2. Self-accusation. Narcissistic masturbatory fantasies.
3. Sexual intercourse disappointing; continuing ambivalence.
4. Transference confusion. Further reference to ambivalence. Affect discharge—tearfulness. Intervention. Acting out conflicts about mother with Laura.

6/20

1. Direct reference to teeth. Sensory and olfactory percepts. Continuing ambivalence.

2. Verbalization of anxiety and guilt in relation to a new father figure.

3. More guilt and ambivalence.

4. Comparison of father-figures. Intellectualization. Somatic manifestations of transference.

5. Somatic shift, interoceptive percepts. More ambivalence. Feelings of being rejected, low self-esteem. Sexual frustration, anger. Hostile transference.

6/21

1. Temperature percepts. Hostile transference expressed ideationally and behaviorally. Manipulated sexual activity. Continuing ambivalence. Guilt. Masochistic sexual fantasy.

2. Dream about narcissistic orally demanding ineffectual person—identified with self. First somatic manifestation, not in patient's awareness. Second brief somatic manifestation: pain percepts. Another identification: the girl who cannot be angry. Again hostile transference. Interpretation.

3. Further transference hostility. Further interpretation. Link between anger and arthritis indicated.

4. Low self-esteem. Recollections of childhood vomiting linked with family quarrels, violence, feelings of being unwanted. Transference implications interpreted.

6/22

1. Resistance. Somatic manifestation. Rationalization. Continuing sense of loss, frustrated oral needs, hostility, testing loneliness and seeking compensations.
2. Reference to mother activates oral needs, somatic equivalents of anxiety, hostility, guilt and need for reassurance. Narcissism. Identification with passive-aggressive mother. Further verbalization of anger, without affect discharge. Transference implications.
3. Further somatic manifestations with first cognitive reference in current associations to arthritis. Verbalization of depression, sadistic impulses, ambivalence, guilt, insecurity.
4. First awareness of actual pain in elbow joints, linked with deprivation, verbalized hostility and continuing indecision. Pseudoaffective discharge of universal hostility related to intense narcissistic needs. Mother represented as an introjected object. More references to being unwanted.

6/26

1. Anticipating summer interruption. Severe joint pains have become established. Projection in transference. Recollection of psychophysical prodromata. Verbalization of anger insufficient to prevent somatic dysfunction.
2. Hostility to sibling linked with awareness of pain percepts.
3. Frustration. Turning to father. Avoidance of mother. Intellectualization about transfer of intense hostility from mother to women in general.
4. Relief of pain following angry abreaction. Probable somatic identification with mother.
5. Secondary reaction to joint pains, seeing self as potential cripple, forever dependent on neurotic women. Further somatic identification. Motor activity— an oral indicator.
6. Identification with father's evasiveness and hedging about remarriage. Recurrent awareness of joint pain. Oedipal fantasies with hostility toward mother, father, and sister.
7. Oral needs. Seeking impossible narcissistic gratifications from Laura— seen as a replacement for loss of other objects. Reversal of roles of mother and child.
8. Guilt about mother linked intellectually with pain. Partial affect discharge.

6/27 - 7/2 Summarized in text with dynamic formulations.

7/3

1. Hostile transference without affect.
2. New girl—Fran—substitute object.
3. Transference dream shifting responsibility for his actions. Reference to sexual excitement and guilt.
4. Partial identification of new girl with mother. Ambivalence. Self-doubts and self-pity. Competition with fathers. Intellectualization. Hostility at being left and need for substitute (mother).

7/5

1. Somatic manifestations following masturbation with homosexual fantasies; transference implications. Immediate guilt. Subsequent dream of hostility to father recalled. Sudden subsidence of pain.
2. Ideational and affective precursors of pain. Transference: being rejected and criticized as inadequate analysand. Sadistic sexual fantasies toward women. Comparisons with Laura unfavorable to self. More hostility with transference implications.
3. Recollections, prior to somatic dysfunction, of physical violence toward mother because of frustrated oral needs, now followed by guilt and surge of affect.
4. Transference fears and hostility.
5. Further recollections of mutual hostility in early relationships with mother. Current and past erotic fantasies about her. Anal practices of the past linked with memories of gastrointestinal illness, examinations, fears of dying, and current physical symptoms.
6. Further identification of new girl with mother. More recollections of childhood violence. Interpretation.
7. Inadequacies as an analysand compared with Laura. Superiority of women. Self-devaluation.

7/6

1. Reference to transference difficulties.
2. Indecisiveness.
3. Subsidence of pain which is directly linked with masturbation and guilt.
4. Ambivalence, guilt, sexual excitation. Motor activity associated with oral sexual fantasies. Repulsive mother-images. More positive father image currently.
5. Superego elements. Comparison of women friends. Self-devaluation. Passivity in relation to phallic women. Hope of getting oral supplies.

7/7 - 7/26 Summarized in text with dynamic formulations.

9/6

1. Somatic dysfunctions associated with homosexual masturbation fantasies.
2. Traumatic sexual activity. Seeking new narcissistic gratification through the daughter of a powerful father. Partial affect discharge.
3. Reassuring self. Intellectualization.
4. New girl's oral interests. Mutual sexual inhibition. Paternal threat.
5. Ambivalent transference responses. Recollective links between loneliness, depression, and physical symptoms.

9/7

1. Somatic manifestation. Retarded state probably related to both drug ingestion and depression.

2. Frustrated narcissistic needs. Avoidance of loose women (mother), turning to homosexual fantasies (father).

3. Preoccupation with body. Affect breakthrough linked to frustration and hostility in the transference, self-pity, secondary gain. Attempts to deny infantile needs.

9/8

1. Fear of being exposed by mother-figure.

2. Uncertainty about relationship with women. Castration anxiety with oral sadistic overtones.

3. Continued search for omnipotent nurturing father via fantasies of feminine identification. Dual roles of feeding parent and sucking child interpreted.

4. Anal fantasies linked with mother. Fran: supportive, sexually exciting, and associated with castration anxiety. Ruth: frigid, intellectually stimulating, with a famous father seen as an omnipotent source of supplies. No further mention of the upper respiratory infection (which has largely subsided).

9/11 - 9/24 Summarized in text with accompanying dynamic formulation.

9/25

1. Resistance. Date with mother figure activates anxiety and sexual excitement, followed by masturbation with passive, masochistic, oral, and anal sadistic fantasies. Linked with recollections about mother's anal practices. Incipient affect, transient perineal and gluteal muscle spasms.

2. Dream reflects the good mother image: warm, nurturing—and the bad mother image: devaluating and sexually seductive.

9/26

1. Somatic manifestation linked with visit to Laura with whom an ambivalent relationship continues.

2. Transference doubts, continuing search for a rescuing father.

3. More ambivalence about women. Envy of potent, virile men.

4. Heightened pain perception. Conflicted relationship with Laura. Childhood deprivation. Links between anxiety about marriage and development of spastic colon. Elimination of this stress accompanied by subsidence of physical symptoms and onset of homosexual panic, in turn relieved by substitute girlfriend.

9/28 - 10/8 Summarized in text with dynamic formulation.

10/9

1. Another upper respiratory illness linked with memories of childhood colds, being cared for by mother, and freedom from responsibilities.

2. Onset of illness follows stressful visit to mother and sister, with temporary remission linked to partial gratification of activated oral needs.

Tinnitus a somatic expression of not wanting to hear himself, related to transference stress.

3. Dependency on and rebelliousness against mother expressed in anal terms.

4. Increased narcissism, regression, secondary gain.

5. Superego elements. Past illness linked with separation from father.

6. Continued search for nurturing father through relationship with Ruth.

10/10

1. Partial awareness of anger, its meaning, and defense against it (projection). Frustration and hostility in the transference. Cognitive anticipation of crying followed by nasal congestion: affect discharge blocked. Self-accusations. Interpretation.

2. Overgratification mixed with deprivation. Appropriate metaphor stressing orality.

3. Temporary denial of stress.

4. Recollection of night terrors and sister's protectiveness. Identification with niece mistreated by father.

10/11

1. Transference: sibling rivalry, omnipotent wishes. Again, search for nurturing father through the daughter, complicating the relationship with women. Guilt. Self-pity.

2. Return of physical symptoms previous night with further intensification of oral needs. Frustration. Attempts at self-satisfaction. Ruth a possible source of oral gratification.

3. Narcissistic preoccupation. Difficulty in expressing positive transference feelings.

4. Fantasies of somatic identification.

10/12

1. Resistance. Previous day's interfering physical symptoms.

2. Incestuous, perverse masturbation fantasies.

3. Regressive intensification of infantile needs with current somatic malaise.

4. Rising transference hostility and guilt verbally expressed but with affect discharge blocked.

10/16

1. Return of joint pains. Self-pity.

2. Sexualized recollection of similar joint symptoms during childhood. Pain compared with physical attack. Attempts at understanding—intellectualization. Temporary improvement in current physical state associated intellectually with partial gratification of infantile needs and absolution of guilt. Relapse associated similarly with sexual activity and Ruth's own physical illness. Mutual masturbation followed by hostility and guilt.

3. Return of physical malaise on weekend. Unusual physical exertion followed by onset of joint pains, self-preoccupation evoking mutual hostility.

4. Total absorption with joint symptoms, expectation of the worst consequences. Temporary remission associated with mothering.

10/17

1. Resistance.

2. Hostile transference. Persistence of physical symptoms. Self-pity. Secondary gain. Fantasies of extreme passive dependency in an indissoluble bond with mother. Intense pain percepts.

3. Obsessional reporting of clinical details. Expectations of the worst outcome. Further self-pity. Reinforced expectations of rejection.

4. Self-devaluation. More transference hostility. Wish to hide. Fantasies of prolonged oral gratification. Projection.

5. Childhood illness: marked anxiety; secondary gain, especially from mother.

6. Another childhood illness linked with closeness to mother, recollections of motor paralysis of chum's sibling.

7. Regressive motor pattern activated, with displacement and possible sexual element.

10/18

1. Transference resistance.

2. Acting out fantasies that intense oral activity would help alleviate physical symptoms. Guilt. Expectation of transference condemnation. Hostility toward masculine women.

3. Insufficient mothering, too much intellectualization evokes hostility. Self-accusations and devaluation. Silence equated with condemnation: transference. Partial affect discharge.

10/20

1. Continuing physical symptoms.

2. Homosexual dream.

3. Hostile dream involving phallic mother with transference implications.

4. Acting out of hostility at prospect of invalidism. Self-medication. Brief depersonalization episodes. Transient compensatory masculine social contacts. Loneliness. Personification of joints. Continued ambivalence about current relationships with women.

10/23

1. Weekend interruption. Resistance: continuing preoccupation with bodily symptoms, but delaying medical consultation.

2. Still doubtful about Laura's femininity and motherly concern for him,

thought she temporarily mitigated his loneliness. Reiteration of hostile transference with affect discharge. Interpretation.

10/24

1. Waiting for oral supplies, actually and symbolically. Recollection of unpleasant eating experiences with family.
2. Medication, an actual and symbolic comfort. Speculation about emotional factors. Need for physical checkup emphasized.
3. Fantasy of buying special treatment privileges.
4. Clinical details. Self-pity. Expectation of the worst. Transference: disappointed expectations (of infantile wishes and needs); need for reassurance.
5. Need for constant mothering, especially during physical illness. Recollection of parental care. Distrust of doctors linked with castration anxiety.

10/25

1. Ambivalence about medical consultation, search for paternal figure. Reference to loss of favorite uncle, followed almost immediately by vertigo. Hostility toward father for lack of support, linked with transference associations, followed by motor activity—looking, verbalization of death fantasies, identification of analyst with dead relative. Verbal reference to affect.
2. Shifting attention to physical symptoms, associated with anxiety. Disclosure of illness.
3. Concerned about homosexual, oral, hostile fantasies: expectation of punishment.
4. Hereditary aspects of arthritis: in women relatives; somatic identification. Intellectualization.

10/26

1. Positive reaction to internist. Clinical details. Awareness of tendencies to project, ambivalence in transference.
2. Verbalized identification with a sick colleague, followed by multiple somatic manifestations of anxiety and need for reassurance.
3. Contrasting childhoods.
4. Transference: search for guidance and approval, comparisons, erotic fantasies, further awareness of tendency to project.

10/30

1. Four-day interruption. Continued anxiety about physical breakdown involves car, seen as extension of self. Denial and need to suffer.
2. Aspirin side reaction during increase in anxiety.
3. Transference dream of rejection. Paternal (superego) admonitions and insufficient support.
4. Further transference associations: hostility. Continued ambivalence about choosing a wife is related to parents' unhappy marriage.

10/31

1. Transference: common theme in conflicting thoughts about fee: how to get the most narcissistic gratification.
2. Fear of the worst somatic consequences.
3. Preoccupation with physical illness. Forced activity to defend against intense passive needs. Self-pity. Sharp affect discharge seems imminent. Attempts at distraction. Punitive superego aspects of pain.
4. Further distraction: forced reminiscences of happy childhood experiences with loving, idealized mother figure. Infantile motor activity. Interpretation. Awareness of accumulated hostility.
5. Mixed intellectualization and growing awareness of links between rage, guilt, and joint symptoms.
6. Personification of body parts and symptoms. Sexualization of (oral) pain. Intellectualization: castration anxiety and narcissistic needs. Expectation of the worst. Then denial of need for sympathy. Affect breakthrough.

11/1

1. Intensification, then dramatic reversal of symptoms—a delayed response to massive affect discharge.
2. Dream of sexual symbols.
3. Lifting of depressive feelings. Greater awareness of regressive longing for an idealized childhood.
4. Dream linked with repetition of childhood masturbatory practice, intensely narcissistic and voyeuristic, with sadistic overtones directed toward the parents. This regressive act preceded by marked loneliness and preoccupation with search for ideal mother.

11/2-1/15 Summarized in text with dynamic formulations.

1/16

1. Upper respiratory infection linked with hostility.
2. Thinly disguised negative transference; without affect; related to frustrated oral wishes.
3. Identification of car with self.
4. Recollections of eroticized relationships with boyhood chums and envy of their having the good father; transference implications.
5. Somatic identification with sick father and other related recollections of father's appearance, prohibitions, inadequacies, especially in relation to women; further transference aspects and guilt. Interpretation.
6. More positive memories of father, but hostility predominates. Identification.

1/18

1. Further reference to defects.
2. Premonitory associations about joint pains linked with verbalized transference hostility and guilt, but affect discharge less than what may occur at times outside the analysis.
3. Headache associated with father's commands. Further link with inhibition of urination and feminine identification. Adolescent defiance of father. Further transference implications, some dramatized affect discharge.

1/22

1. Resistance and rationalization.
2. Tinnitus related to medication for recurrence of joint pains. Confessional about shift from heterosexual to homosexual dream activity followed by some remission of physical symptoms.
3. Temporary positive transference shift.
4. Secondary gain interpretation evokes hostility and projection. Primary and secondary psychologic aspects of pain. Hopeful expectation of maternal care. Heterosexual activity: an unsatisfactory attempt to neutralize upsurge of homosexual libido.
5. Self-pity linked with perception of sexual excitement. Narcissistic rage.
6. Reaching out for maternal care.

1/23

1. Competitive aspects of previous dream.
2. Projective and hostile transference elements.
3. Intellectualization. Frustration of expectations and resultant hostility without affect. Interpretation.
4. Angry memories about father. Increasing affect discharge. Interpretation.
5. More hostility toward nongiving father. Need to control feelings. Interpretation.

1/24

1. Resistance.
2. External events reinforce hostility which is linked with exacerbation of physical symptoms. Projective mechanisms activated. Transference implications.
3. Mechanism of avoidance. Identification with mother.
4. Sexual frustration.
5. More hostile transference. Orality and narcissism interpreted.
6. "Affect displays" exaggerated to gain attention and sympathy.

1/25

1. More transference hostility verbalized and acted out.

2. Dream of being defective, especially in comparison with colleagues at work.

3. Infantile temper tantrums.

4. Another dream linked with the search for omnipotent nurturing father through alliance with his daughter.

5. Pain a symbol of punishment and in the service of superego function. Vertigo—a somatic anxiety manifestation.

6. Inhibition of urination related to homosexual impulses and castration anxiety. Reference to auditory percepts linked with inhibition and recollections of curiosity about feminine toilet functions.

1/29 - 2/4 Summarized in text with dynamic formulations.

2/5

1. Passive masturbation fantasies: phallic, oral, and anal; incestuous implications. Recollections of anal-sadistic experiences.

2. Continued sexual frustration.

3. Dreams suggest sadomasochistic conflicts with mother being reenacted with Fran.

4. "S-mothering" and withholding evokes hostility which is displaced onto Fran also. Interpretation.

2/6

1. Transference resistance.

2. Projection. Interpretation. Infantile expectations.

3. Further transference associations, principally for attention-gaining effect.

4. Bodily reactions linked to conflict over relationship with women.

5. First mention of joint symptoms in about ten days. They are in remission.

2/7 - 2/8 Summarized in text with dynamic formulations.

2/12

1. Return of somatic and psychologic symptoms verbalized without affect. Increased oral intake linked with heightened pessimism, especially because of recurrence of joint pain.

2. Fran's return insufficient substitute gratification.

3. Unable to vent angry feelings, but otherwise identified with niece in relating to mother.

2/13

1. Transference manifestations: fear of retaliation for hostility; projective tendencies, quickly modified. Regressive wishes—a secondary reaction to persisting physical dysfunction. Oral aspects.

2. Anxiety about secondary gain fantasies. Activity as an attempted defense against intensified passivity.

2/14

1. More projective tendencies in the transference.
2. More verbalized hostility at family, particularly mother, concerning his assuming responsibilities when his needs for mothering are so great. Displacement of hostility onto Fran with mutual recrimination.
3. Confrontation reveals somatic improvement, grudgingly admitted because of transference distortion.

2/15 - 2/26 Summarized in text with dynamic formulations.

2/27

1. Return of joint symptoms. Confession. Partial affect discharge linked with secondary concern about progressive individualism.
2. Low self-esteem, marked self-accusation, partly in the service of eliciting sympathy, expectation of the worst: helplessness and abandonment. Recollection of childhood tears. Affect discharge. Identifications with mother, including somatic. Interpretation.
3. Wish for mothering linked with passivity. Narcissistic need blocks marriage.
4. Childhood fantasies of ideal family as a defense against full impact of bitter parental discord. Hostility toward inquisitive teacher; transference implications.

2/28

1. Concern about inferiority. Fears of being attacked. Identity anxiety. Self-pity. Devaluation of women. Questioning of heterosexuality as a defense against homosexual wishes.
2. Presentation of a confident front. Ambivalence.
3. Preoccupation with physical symptoms and medication. Provocative transference associations linked with mother.
4. Hostility to Fran linked with sexual frustration. Partial affect discharge. Intellectualization about connection between rage and joint symptoms. Consequences of unleashed hostility. Greater awareness of his projective tendencies.

2/29

1. Worsening symptoms force medical consultation. Rationalization about toothache actually a defense against castration anxiety.
2. More preoccupation with symptoms and medication. Continued sexual frustration linked with fantasies of a new relationship. Wishes for nurture and a passive existence. Concern about mental state.

3/4

1. Four-day interruption includes weekend. Impulsivity despite rationalizations.
2. Fulfillment of sexual fantasies. Laura's masculinity. Unpleasant olfactory percept recollection associated with her genitalia. Subsequent anxiety dream linked with childhood recollection of being attacked by a phallic mother. Contrasting oral fantasies. Self-pity.
3. Shift in somatic symptoms. Medical consultation unmentioned.

3/5

1. Resistance. Transference envy. Histrionic tendencies. Competitiveness.
2. Persisting toothache linked with recollection of adolescent dependency on mother, sexual excitement, physical shock with complicating infection, and castration anxiety. Expectation of the worst unmitigated by magical wishes.
3. Anticipatory anxiety—first sexual intercourse. Recollections of olfactory percepts linked with nausea, anal associations, the imminence of death, and urge for sexual gratification.
4. Further memories of first seduction and sexual intercourse with *ejaculatio praecox*. Later devaluation of love-object.

3/6

1. Upsurge of homosexual fantasies. Transference distortion of realistic billing error. Clarification. Intellectualization about turning to phallic woman because of lack of self-confidence with a feminine woman.
2. Dream of homosexuality and its denial. Associated references to phallic woman.
3. Wish for nurturing mother during physical illness.
4. Improvement in joint symptoms, though fear of invalidism lingers. Further contrast of feminine and phallic women. Relationship with latter seen as disguised homosexual transference. Again reference to finding omnipotent father through daughter.

3/7

1. Shifting somatic sites. Recurrence of joint pain linked with upsurge of homosexual ideation. Concern about not being married associated with depression and self-devaluation, melodramatically expressed.
2. Upsurge of hostility to Fran related to her activity and orality seen as destructive to him and extensions of himself.
3. Further concern about homosexual fantasies. Self-devaluation. Transference hostility.

3/11 Excerpt.

1. Curiosity, intellectualization referable to physical symptoms. Expectation of disaster, long-standing, now expressed in terms of chronic illness.

3/12 - 5/14 Summarized in text with dynamic formulations.

5/15

1. Resistance.
2. Somatic symptom linked with references to violence, law and order, and specific rage at an authority figure for punitive action. Projection tempered but not eliminated by rational ego. Devaluation of Fran marked in ambivalence toward her.
3. Return of joint pain signalled by tension headache. Oral reference.
4. More rage because of narcissistic hurt.
5. Devaluation of mother's and Fran's intellect; identification with father. Masochistic reaction and sexual excitement at prospect of marriage. Recollection of parents' incompatibility, own narcissistic needs interfere with his getting married.

5/16

1. Recurrence of severe joint pain. Again expectation of the worst. Auditory percept, interoceptive stimulus. Fears of hereditary transmission. Fears of rejection. Increased regressive needs. Ambivalence about Fran.

5/20

1. Four-day interruption, as in other instances, activates symptoms. Preoccupation with bodily sensations and effect of medication. Intense secondary anxiety about uncertain diagnoses, sequelae, and possible invalidism.
2. Concern about marriage under regressive conditions, complicated by Fran's infantilizing ways. Discouraging, depressive thoughts—also secondary to illness. Belittling the possibility of analytic help—devaluating father interference.
3. Intellectualized insight in the service of ingratiation. Masochistic references. More ambivalence about Fran. References to narcissism and dependence on mother projected onto analyst.

5/22

1. Reinforcement of pessimism about marriage, a rationalization against fears of unmanliness.
2. Intensified hostility, partly secondary to illness, partly primary-frustration of longstanding dependency needs, reinforced by demands on him.
3. More depressive thoughts, ambivalence.
4. Upsurge of transference hostility verbalized. Intellectualization.
5. Unmistakable hostile ideational content, but bland affect due to fear of rejection. More verbalized devaluation of psychiatry and psychiatrists.
6. Projection of own sense of narcissistic entitlement onto others. Exhibitionism linked with headache.
7. More devaluation of self and others.

5/23

1. Needs—limitless; ability to give—nil during illness. Rationalizations about avoiding marriage and disastrous consequences. Impact of anger on Fran disregarded at first because of narcissism, greatly intensified by physical illness.

2. Narcissistic hurt further intensified by recollection of friend's behavior. Anger is linked with guilt and approaches point of affect discharge. Projective tendencies in the transference.

5/27

1. Somatic manifestation of transference anxiety.

2. Self-devaluation. Leaving first—a defense against being rejected. Heterosexual success insufficiently reassuring. Reference to homosexual transference. homosexual transference.

5/28

1. Temporary stabilization in somatic dysfunction.

2. Dream equating Fran with mother: providing for dependency needs but sexually unattractive. Sexual interest in other girls complicated by anxiety over potency. Fear of being caught by mother (or substitute) in sexual activity with sister (or surrogate). Anal elements.

3. Defensive hostile transference: devaluation of analyst's potency. Reassuring fantasies are questioned.

4. Ambivalence about all women, originating with mother. Need to avoid her seductiveness, complaints, and hostility mixed with need for nurture from her, his insurance policy against utter loneliness—all evoking guilt and infantile fears. Interpretation.

5. Further specific recollection of childhood illnesses linked with anxiety, sexual and secondary gain elements. Current physical illness accentuates already existing dependency and narcissism which in turn are defended against by still insufficiently effective avoidance and denial.

5/29

1. Physical relapse. Self-pity. Concern about imposed passivity continuing indefinitely. Recapitulation of diagnostic possibilities and treatments. Appropriate description of the reinforcing somatic effect of secondary anxiety.

2. Absence of nurturing object mobilizes him from dependency which otherwise might be enhanced.

3. Forced activity a defense against passivity.

4. Dream of father with sexualized elements, longed-for closeness to him, fear of losing him, and memories of rejection evoke dramatic discharge of affect. Interpretations. The liquefaction (crying-affect discharge) of physical symptoms is likely.

6/3

1. This four-day interruption is one of physical and psychologic improvement. Anxiety replaces physical symptoms and depression. It is related to hostility and sadistic fantasies involving, alternately, mother (and surrogate) and father in the oedipal situation. Fear of retaliation and rebelliousness in the transference.

2. Planned reunion with father linked with memories of their once closeness together.

3. Diminishing sexual interest in Fran, maternal figure.

4. Somatic symptom linked with underlying guilt and depressive feelings. Wished for abreaction. Affect discharge more likely though. Greater awareness of effects of loss. Continued, though modified, blocking of affect.

5. Ambivalence about Fran linked with mother. Cyclic partial discharge and blocking of affect. Shift from depression to hostility to guilt.

COMMENT

This patient has not had any major physical illness. However, at age five he experienced a self-limited episode of joint pain never definitely diagnosed and without sequelae. Several similar somatic responses have followed exposure to unusual stress in later years, but the patient has also had frequent episodes of anxiety which at times have been quite severe.

During the early months of analysis, the patient was in good physical health, except for transient somatic manifestations, principally tachycardia and generalized malaise, representing anxiety equivalents.

On 6/8 the patient makes his first reference to toothache, a somatic symptom that already has been present for several days but apparently blocked off from associative recall during the analytic hours. Actually an upsurge in oral needs can be noted in the patient's material, beginning a week before. On 6/2 and 6/7 there are references to his mother's oral sadism, his identification with this aspect of her emotional makeup and his frustrated dependency accompanied by hostility all guilt. All these are expressed largely in ideational form with partial affect discharge and transient somatic manifestations due to stomach dysfunction. Evidently the continued high level of largely oral tensions is being insufficiently relieved because an additional outlet becomes necessary. This is in the form of further somatic involvement and the principle site is, appropriately, the teeth. The possibility of extraction is linked with castration anxiety, a response evoked by visits to the dentist in the past, and another indication of the patient's intense concern with his body integrity.

Shifts between different outlets for discharge of tension are clearly evident on 6/12. Ideational references to being rejected sexually by a woman several nights before are followed by somatic equivalents (cardiovascular) of anxiety. These, in turn, precede the sudden emergence of forbidden homosexual fantasies in which anal elements are prominent. Later in the interview sensory percepts, probably respiratory—related to oppressiveness, are linked with previously expressed ideas of deprivation and loneliness. A sensory percept, as in this instance, can enter consciousness as an expression of a repressed transference response. It usually reinforces what has already been or is being verbalized or affectively expressed about the transference without the patient's being aware of the connection. Such sensory manifestations of transference are generally overlooked.

As the patient's relationship with Laura worsens, his homosexual impulses increase, and he is flooded with fantasies of feminine identification. On 6/16 recollections of his first episode of joint pains are brought up and linked with intense castration anxiety while being examined and treated by doctors and dentists. These associations are followed by awareness of "shadowy" joint pains. This sequence of manifestations may be due to dysfunction already begun in the joints but of such minimal degree that clearcut symptoms have not yet developed and broken into awareness. In the same hour there are references to losses, and partial affect discharge (sadness). The next few days are filled with frustrations, rising potential for hostility, and feelings of confusion. The patient attempts unsuccessfully to escape from his tensions by narcissistic, masturbatory fantasies and sexual intercourse with Laura. His disappointment in her is becoming intense, and there is another partial affect discharge (sadness). On 6/20 the patient reports that he has just had fillings put into several of his teeth, something he has postponed doing for a long time, largely because of the associated castration anxiety evoked each time he has planned to visit the dentist. The numbness, eye pain and headache that he now describes as sequelae of the dental work are most likely conversion symptoms associated with repressed homosexual fantasies.

By 6/21 the patient's activated feelings of being deprived and deserted have extended deeply into the transference with hostility reaching a high level, but unexpressed directly. The psychophysical equilibrium has shown increased instability during the past week as external stresses mount and internal conflicts intensify. A critical shift seems to be impending as partial affect discharge, sexual acting out and fantasy formation, intellectualization, and projective tendencies are insufficient to relieve the accumulating psychologic tensions. Physical symptoms have been on the increase, and in this hour (6/12) two more somatic manifestations appear, following a dream about a narcissistic, orally demanding, and ineffectual person—identified as the patient. The first is gastrointestinal, but the patient is unaware of the loud stomach rumbling. The second is a sudden, severe left hip pain of which he is acutely aware. Though the patient then links anger at the analyst with arthritis, he is forced to deny vigorously any meaningful association. Low self-esteem and recollections of family violence follow. Although a number of transference interpretations have been made, their modifying influence on the impending psychophysical shift remains to be seen. On 6/22 the patient reports further massive preoccupation with loneliness and deprivation, especially after an anger-provoking call from mother the previous evening. He mentions depressive thoughts and sadistic impulses. Then the patient becomes aware of pain in his elbow joints which continues despite verbalized hostility. In retrospect there has indeed been a critical shift in psychophysical equilibrium in the direction of activated and continued physical dysfunction. Could the site have been predicted? On 6/16 traumatic emotional experiences in childhood involving venipuncture, being forcibly held, and examination for joint pain are recalled. They are associated with memories of tonsillectomy and then tooth extraction. In the latter instance, the upper extremities are referred to indirectly and linked with a sexual theme. Recollections again dealing indirectly with the use of the extremities, particularly the upper ones in sports and handicraft, continue. On 6/21 there are further recollections involving the upper extremities—father's striking mother. The prominence of these references about a particular part of the body could, retrospectively, be an indication of the site of impending physical dysfunction.

The joint pains persist for the next few days and then remit following an outburst of anger at his sister. However, the notion that the venting or abreactive discharge of anger will bring essential modification of its internal source is incorrectly simplistic. In the inverview of 6/26, there are indications that the joint pains have not completely subsided and that the somatic dysfunction is continuing though at a "subclinical level." A somatic identification with mother who herself has had joint symptoms for years appears in the patient's associations. There is also a secondary reaction to his illness in which he sees himself as a potential cripple, forever dependent on neurotic women.

In the next week the patient recalls his father's severe kidney infection when the patient was seven years old. It marked a turning point in his life; his parents became more and more distant from each other, and finally the father left the home for good. The patient's current rage at Laura continues unabated, and again he looks for a rescuing male figure.

On 7/5 the patient reports right upper quadrant pain. At first there seems to be no antecedent material that can be related to it specifically. However, further associations indicate that it began after an uneasy sleep which followed masturbation. This sexual activity had been accompanied by intense homosexual fantasies about father-figures, including the analyst, and subsequently by a strong sense of guilt. The description of the pain is suggestive of irregularly intermittent spasm and relaxation of the right ureter, possibly ascending colon. The previous afternoon, while with Laura, the patient experienced pain in ideational and affective form evoked by the "painful relationship" with her.

Later he had specific, sadistic fantasies involving women in general and his mother in particular. There were also memories of actual physical violence toward her. When relating these, the patient experiences a surge of affect and becomes tearful. The memories include getting enemas—highly sexualized—from mother as well as giving them to himself. He also recalls gastrointestinal illness and bowel and anal examinations, accompanied by fears of dying. The right upper quadrant site may also have some relationship to the act of masturbation itself how it is done, i.e., the particular postular fix or position (but this material is not available). Another possibility to consider about the right side is that symbolically it refers to manliness; the patient's doubts about the masculine adequacy have been currently reinforced. The pain subsides altogether the next day, though it has begun to diminish during the hour of 7/5. At that time his confession and the noncritical atmosphere in which he has made it apparently provides sufficient neutralization of his guilt feelings which have been linked with the somatic dysfunction previously.

During the summer interruption the patient's relationships with two new girls, Fran and Ruth, continue to develop, while that with Laura deteriorates. He experiences a low-grade depression and unsuccessfully tries to ward it off by fantasies, at times sexualized, of being rescued by an omnipotent father-figure. On the day he resumes analysis (9/6) he notes the beginning of an upper respiratory infection, is preoccupied with his bodily symptoms, and is quite tearful. There is a mixture of ideational, affective, and somatic components. Orality is prominent in his associations. After a few days the cold subsides without sequelae. For the next few weeks there is continued indecision about which girl is most suitable for him and a nagging preoccupation with the idea of being basically defective. Narcissistic needs remain strong. At times the patient resorts to masturbation with fantasies about mother-figures in which there are incestuous, hostile, and identification elements. Continued superego-ego tensions interfere with constructive and understanding use of the analysis and increase feelings of isolation and loneliness.

On 9/25 the patient reports that, following a date with an older woman clearly representing a mother figure, he feels both sexually aroused and anxious. He then resorts to a familiar, regressive sexual activity, masturbation, which is then accompanied by a rich variety of fantasies, sadomasochistic in nature involving mother-figures. There follows an upsurge of recollections about mother's insistence on giving him enemas. At this point in the analytic hour, the patient is aware of an imminent affect discharge (tearfulness) which is rapidly followed by perineal and genital muscle spasms. One wonders if both these responses were present originally during the late Oedipal period when the patient was being given enemas by his mother. They occur right after such recollections which seem to act as triggering stimuli, and they represent a "somatic remembrance of things past." On 9/26 toothache is a troublesome symptom. It follows a disagreeable visit with Laura the preceding night. It is also linked with transference disappointment in the search for a rescuing father. As the patient continues to associate about his painful relationships with girls, there is a concomitant increase in somatic pain—the toothache hurts much more. An earlier experience with a girl was highly stressful, and there were somatic consequences in the form of spastic colon. When he got rid of the girl, he got rid of the physical symptoms, but they were replaced by homosexual fantasies with accompanying anxiety which in turn were relieved when he developed a new relationship with another girl. The sequence here is psychologic conflict→somatic expression → elimination of stressful object → subsidence of physical dysfunction → appearance of another psychologic conflict and its subsidence → formation of temporarily adequate substitute object relationship. The dysfunction of the colon is related to ambivalence toward the loved object: wanting to keep the girl for himself, a narcissistic retention, and need to control; this is in conflict with the wish to get rid of, eliminate the (fecalized) object. This alternation is reflected in shifting spasm and explosive expulsion.

In the next few weeks indecision about girls continues. Hostility towards mother again increases with accompanying guilt. Frustration of oral, narcissistic wishes in the transference evokes verbal and partial affective expression. More guilt develops over homosexual fantasies and masturbation. A trip to visit relatives is highly stressful. He returns with another upper respiratory infection (10/9). For a week prior to its onset, dependency needs and homosexual fantasies had both been strongly activated, with reflections in the transference responses. The visit to his mother and sister represent elements of further loss, frustration, sibling rivalry, and hostility. This stress is the psychologic trigger in the development of the physical illness. Other outlets—ideational, affective, and behavioral—had proven insufficient.

Tinnitus, a primary physical symptom during the interview of 10/9, is well-known as a side reaction of high aspirin dosage. Any drug, apart from the varying efficacy of its specific effect from person to person, may produce a variety of side effects. The kind and location of side reactions have been thought in the past to be due essentially to physicochemical factors, hypersensitivity or allergic responsiveness, overall physical state, etc. Generally, the individual's psychologic state at the time the drug is being taken has been considered as not pertinent or significant. In my opinion, it cannot be disregarded as a factor influencing both efficacy and side-reactions of a given drug. At the beginning of the hour (on 10/9) the patient directly states his strong need to avoid his troublesome thoughts. This actually has been a chronic and often unspoken attitude, being expressed in the past in a variety of ways such as blocking, focusing on trivia, denying of problems, etc. Later in the hour tinnitus begins, and the patient finds it difficult to hear himself. This suggests the possibility that a psychologic factor (stress and its avoidance) is sufficiently facilitative so that a sensitive vestibular response evoked by aspirin in this patient then becomes reinforced enough to produce symptoms.

In the same hour the cold assumes a punitive significance. In addition, its symptoms are drawn into the service of secondary gain.

On 10/10 the cognitive anticipation of crying is followed not by tears but by nasal congestion. An affect discharge has been blocked, but concomitantly somatic dysfunction and symptoms have increased. On 10/11 there is an increase in physical malaise linked with an intensification of oral needs and their frustration. The patient attempts self-gratification through masturbation with perverse (oral) fantasies but ends up feeling more guilty—an invariable sequel. He comes very late to the analytic hour (10/12) and indicates, in this way and verbally, his rising hostility. On 10/16 the patient reports with much self-pity the return of joint symptoms the preceding night. It should be noted that there has been a four-day lapse since the last interview. Such interruptions favor a buildup of stress centered around frustration of oral needs, separation anxiety, and activated hostility and guilt, often reflected in transference shifts. The retrospective recollection of the childhood episode of joint symptoms contains sexualized elements. Currently, his acting out sexually with Ruth—seen as a mothering figure only in part and more basically as a means of getting to the powerful nurturing father (through passive-feminine identifications)—imitates and precedes the above-mentioned recollections. The current episode of joint dysfunction actually begins after unusual musculoskeletal activity involved in mountain climbing. This ordinarily would produce only some muscle and tendon stretching or minor strain and normal fatigue. However, the musculoskeletal system is a target organ; it has been linked with psychologic conflict and tension in the past. Currently the unusual physical exertion reinforces its potential as a site for possible organ system dysfunction. The psychologic disturbances may also influence "host resistance" in an unfavorable direction. The combination of all these factors in turn may favor the development of the palindromic state noted in this patient. It should be noted, however, that muscular effort may also represent, again symbolically, a means for adequately relieving psychologic tensions, especially those due to pent-up aggression (though not at this time in this patient).

Hostile transference is closely linked with persistence of the physical symptoms. Secondary gain becomes an especially prominent element in the patient's reaction to his physical illness (10/17). In the next hour there is increased expression of hostility both verbally and affectively. The patient's reluctance to seek medical consultation continues; he is deterred by his very strong expectations of having his worst fears confirmed. He has been medicating himself with aspirin which has helped in the past.

On 10/25 the patient reports being notified of a favorite uncle's death. There is no immediate emotional response; instead he experiences sudden vertigo—a somatic equivalent, probably of anxiety. The reaction that follows suggests this anxiety is related to the activation of transference hostility in the form of death wishes. These are expressed during the hour in part by motor activity—turning around to see if the analyst is alive, and in part verbalized. An intensification of joint symptoms can then be noted. This may be a somatic expression of superego-ego tensions and have a symbolic, punitive meaning. In this interview hereditary factors are brought up by the patient. Paternal grandmother and mother each have had some form of arthritis. Both genetic coding and psychologic processes of somatic identification should be considered as possible factors involved in determination of the target organ site.

The patient reveals (10/26) that he has finally had a consultation with a medical specialist to whom he has a positive reaction. He is advised that a diagnosis of rheumatoid arthritis can not be absolutely made at this time, though the history he gave was typical. The clinical findings and laboratory tests do not yield any confirmatory evidence. A 50-50 prognosis for the future is given; the consultation will either subside in a few years or flare into unmistakable rheumatoid arthritis.

On 10/30 a marked shift in psychophysical equilibrium occurs again. This time under the favoring influence of interpretations, it is in the direction of a considerable affect discharge and a greater cognitive awareness of the repressed conflicts. The next day a dramatic worsening and then subsidence of the physical symptoms are reported. The patient is more aware of his regressive longing for an idealized childhood and reality-imposed frustration of this wish. At the same time there is a lifting of the depressive mood. The patient continues on aspirin for several more days and then stops taking the medication. By then the joint symptoms have completely subsided.

In subsequent weeks, increased work demands and further difficulties with his girlfriends appear again as stresses. Marked intellectualization and increased use of projective tendencies can be noted in the patient's defensive constellation. Affect is once more largely blocked off. The analyst continues to be seen often as a judge, an external representation of the patient's superego. Sexual release is attempted largely through masturbation accompanied by fantasies in which both oral and phallic aspects of aggression can be noted. Demands for nurture are verbalized more frequently in the transference and are contrasted with references to the previous therapist's supportive, but also infantilizing, attitudes.

On 1/16 the patient reports still another respiratory infection. The preceding week has been characterized by further stress at work; more is expected of him. His dependency needs increase, are reflected in the transference, and encounter frustration; as a result, a considerable degree of potential hostility and guilt is mobilized. The patient attempts some sexual activity to escape from his troublesome thoughts and feelings. Masturbation and increased sexual intimacy with Fran, the new girl, through mutual sucking—oral contact—are unsatisfactory. All coping mechanisms mobilized seem insufficient to contain the additional stresses. Meanwhile superego-ego tensions have perceptibly increased. A shift in psychophysical equilibrium again is in the offing, and the patient becomes ill with a cold. In this hour there is further indication that transference frustration and hostility are still increasing. There is also considerable preoccupation with father's past illnesses. Multiple aspects of identification with this parent appear in the associations: somatic (bone dysfunction), attitudinal, and behavioral with marked, negative features. Also to be noted is the reference to unusual muscular exertion which occurred several days previously. On 1/18 there is continued reference to defects and premonitory associations about joint symptoms. This takes place amidst histrionic but partial affect discharges.

The joint pains return the day after the last analytic interview and persist. The prior references to the musculoskeletal system, thus, seem to have been cues that if further physical dysfunction occurs, it will be in that system.

The night before the symptoms recur, the patient has frustrating, verbally angry encounters with Laura, Ruth, and his mother—all of whom he has hoped would be the nurturing parental figure he has sought for so long. These stressful exchanges act as a cumulative, triggering factor which shift the psychophysical equilibrium still further in a somatic direction. In all likelihood the onset of the physical symptoms also increases his needs to be nurtured. In addition, a sexual element is involved. On 1/22 the patient reports that he has had a dream preceding the return of his somatic difficulties. It began as heterosexual but then changed to homosexual. Again this portrays his need for a close relationship in which he turns from women to men, but is disappointed by both, as he had been by his mother and father. The presence of such sexual elements in fantasies, dreams, and behavior, apart from their more specific significance, suggests a less intense aggressiveness and, in turn, a less serious impact on physical functioning if adequate discharge of psychologic tensions is not otherwise possible.

As the somatic dysfunction becomes established, a large secondary gain aspect again appears, predictable on the basis of the patient's narcissism and already frequently manifested self-pity. It also represents a means of maintaining the symbiotic tie between himself and his mother or mother-substitutes.

The patient calls his physical dysfunction both "arthritis" and "a rage in the joints." He recalls anger *really* coming out once, exploding, and then the physical symptoms improving. This sequence of events is a simplistic and overly generalized explanation. Also, forcing outbursts of affect in therapy is unproductive of lasting results and may even contribute to undesirable complications, e.g., in the transference. In any event, emotional abreactions have limited usefulness in or out of treatment. Awareness and understanding of the repressed origins and significance of hostility are necessary for effectively discharging their noxious tensions and, thereby, shunting them away from organs and organ systems where they cause dysfunction. Another factor in lessening the impact of hostility may be the actual decrease of external stress, through chance, manipulation, inherent limitations, or other reasons. Such an occurrence would tend to deactivate the individual's internal conflicts and any resultant aggressiveness. On 1/24, while there is evidence that the patient has had an emotional discharge of rage, he also is consciously exaggerating his outbursts of affect to get attention and sympathy. Thus, a secondary gain factor interferes with the sufficiency of emotional discharge through nonsomatic channels.

As before, the joint symptoms continue to serve as a symbol of punishment (1/25).

In the next few weeks the physical manifestations gradually fade out in the associations as the stresses to which the patient has been exposed also diminish, and there is some further affect discharge and continuation of work on his emotional conflicts.

On 2/7 he reacts to his girl Fran going away for five days with verbal expressions of anger and threats of acting out in the transference: he will leave the analysis. There are associated, strong, projective tendencies, mobilized to defend against his activated oral needs. The burst of negative transference and use of projection are modified by some degree of insight.

After a four-day interval, the patient reports (2/12) the return of somatic and psychologic symptoms, but without affect. Amongst the physical manifestations is joint pain which flared up after the last analytic interview (2/8). The patient had experienced only a short period of freedom from this recurrent symptom. However, it does not intensify and shows evidence of remitting again. The following association of the patient's is most pertinent: "A little of my real feeling comes out in life and not so much goes into the joints." In the following month there is intermittent improvement and relapse in the physical dysfunction, as the blocking of ideational, affective, and behavioral outlets of psychologic tension varies. A basic, persisting, infantile need continues to be the search for a nurturing parent, shifting from mother to father and back again, and subject to repeated disappointment and complicated by sexualized elements which have become associated with it. Again the physical dysfunction subsides as stresses abate and the patient remains essentially free of somatic manifestations for the next few months.

On 5/15 the patient reports a sharp upsurge of hostility which precedes the latest exacerbation of joint symptoms. The hostility is felt, but its unconscious significance is not yet sufficiently understood nor worked through by the patient. An argument with a policeman about a minor parking violation was neurotically distorted into a critical, traumatic experience with a parental authority who was punishing the patient for a major misdeed which others were committing and getting away with without being caught or punished. The patient reacted with severe narcissistic hurt to this incident against the background of listening to a discussion in a public forum on law and order in which mitigating factors were introduced to explain away the lawlessness of others. But there have been other stresses also. The patient faces a decision about whether to get married or not. This activates memories of his parents' incompatibility and marital breakup and the expectation of the same fate for himself. Meanwhile, his superego-ego tensions have again built up over homosexual fantasies activated in flight from fears of heterosexual inadequacy. Additionally, guilt over oral needs is present. Projective defenses against internalization of rages are insufficient.

On 5/16 the patient reports that he has the "bloody arthritis" again. But he also has relatively more awareness and insight into the conflicts causing his psychologic tensions than he had during previous episodes. There has been a gradual shift over the months of reported analysis in which the energies of the repressed have been diminished and the defensive ego energies have gradually become less necessary and modified into less pathologic forms. Also, as previously, the libidinal drives are strong enough and so disposed through the mediation of the ego, that they exert a mitigating influence on the impact of pent-up aggression. This episode of physical dysfunction and manifestations is shorter and less severe than the previous ones. On 5/29 reporting a dream about his father, which expressed a longed-for closeness to him, the fear of losing him, and memories of past rejections by him, evokes a dramatic and extensive discharge of affect. The occasion is used for further interpretations of the patient's sensitivity to loss. The liquefaction of his joint symptoms (crying) is under way. After a few days they subside.

G. H.

A Spinster's Private Dilemma

INTRODUCTION

G. H. is a single, 34-year-old junior executive. She entered analysis because of a persistent inability to develop a satisfactory relationship with a man.

She is the older of two children. There is a married sister, three years younger, with one child. This sibling had had intermittent episodes of physical illness diagnosed as regional ileitis. The patient's parents have had a troubled married life but have remained together. Mother has hearing problems and father has had a chronic duodenal ulcer. He is a successful stockbroker, and the family has always been in comfortable financial circumstances.

G. H. was a very bright, intellectually precocious, musically gifted child. As she grew up, her talents were continually highlighted and put on exhibition, particularly by her father whose favorite she tried very hard to be, thereby overshadowing her sister who was only an average student. Both parents encouraged the importance of a career for her and did not seem to emphasize marriage and raising a family as they did for the younger sister.

Physical illness had occurred during the patient's late adolescence in the form of an anemia of undetermined etiology, requiring at one time hospitalization and transfusions for several weeks. A careful check on blood levels has been kept since then; although the hemoglobin level had dipped several grams below normal at times, the patient has not subsequently been incapacitated because of this, nor has her internist prescribed any medication. However, in her early twenties, shortly after an unsuccessful love affair, the patient rapidly developed the symptoms and signs of an acute duodenal ulcer which was confirmed by x-ray. The condition responded to a conservative medical regime of antispasmodics, antacids, and tranquilizers. The ulcer healed, and there has been no recurrence, although the patient from time to time has been troubled with mild to moderate stomach symptoms, particularly epigastric distress.

The preliminary clinical impression was that of a moderately severe character neurosis with mixed obsessional and hysterical traits. In the first six months of analysis, the patient presented an overly polite attitude, was excessively thankful, and was seemingly compliant with the fundamental rule. It soon became clear, however, that these were massive reaction formations concealing intense hostility, toward both men and women authority figures. There was marked penis envy as well as envy of other women's feminine accomplishments and conquests. A deep, passive dependency was defended against, though thinly, by a drive to achieve success, especially in competition with a largely male group of junior executives in her company. The patient was extremely well read in psychology, having majored in that subject in college and also used intellectualization as a major defense. Her hypersensitivity was marked, and she was easily hurt, tears coming quickly on those occasions. Ambivalence was moderate in degree and reflected in the developing transference neurosis. Superego-ego tensions were severe. Although there had been several affairs with men in the past, these had not been sexually satisfying. Masturbation was a primary sexual outlet. Considerable guilt was associated with masturbatory practices which, in the early phases of the analysis, were referred to only briefly and reluctantly.

As the detailed reporting of analytic hours begins, the patient is faced with an ever-increasing psychologic crisis: the return of a man-friend whom she looks on as a kind of "last hope" marriage prospect. The summer interruption of the analysis is only some six weeks or so away.

CASE MATERIAL

6/2

1, 2   It's so beautiful out. Funny, my stomach's churning and twisting. I read a magazine article that was so moving, such an honest outpouring of feelings that I had tears in my eyes when I finished it. I thought it was a lovely piece of writing. It conveyed a sense of tragedy, loss, and sadness, but the spirit of spring was coming through it all. On the way here it felt as if I was starting on a long journey, and I wanted to drive forever.

I remember a fragment of a dream. Judy, my colleague at work, was in it, wearing a jeweled pin—in the form of a sword. Yesterday I actually saw her wearing a lovely jade pendant. I'll inherit some precious jade when mother dies. It doesn't seem possible my thoughts go back to this, mother's death.

3   I read an article in one of the yellow journals on "How to Make him Marry you." I also bought the *Atlantic*. I have to show I don't read just junk. Lately I've been eating wholesome food and less candy so I can look healthier. That article in the paper says that in order to make a man propose marriage, you must create the fantasy that life with you is more appealing than without you. Well, I

want to look my best. I'm disappointed that I've had only a card so far from Brad.

I started off full of energy last night—did a lot of errands but after supper felt 4 drained. Evelyn dropped in, and I didn't do another thing that evening. Just played cards. Yesterday was the first day of my period. When I get to feeling so limp, I get worried about my blood count and being unable to keep up with Brad, just like the little girl unable to keep up with her daddy. I see to much of my father in all men. Feeling tired scares me, although I don't now consciously feel I'm going to die. I never consciously thought of death even when I had my anemia. I would block it out, although it was a realistic threat. Fantasy number 6,003: I imagine being married to Brad, having little children, taking care of the house, cooking good meals, being lively, but then because of anemia and tiredness can't keep up with it and he gets fed up with me. My sister Dottie's tiredness—she still takes a nap every day. She and her husband, Dan, are always wrangling about that.

I've just read an article which is an up-to-date guide to contraception. 5 Obviously I'm still conflicted about sex, about Brad's making a sexual move toward me. I should have gotten contraceptive advice by now. It would be dumb if I got involved sexually without doing that first. It'll be just my luck to have the timing off when I see him, and then I'll be fertile Myrtle. I'm tempted to buy this contraceptive foam. It's like taking an umbrella so you're damn sure it's not going to rain. Yet he's hardly even touched me. I could manage it. It's crazy not to take some precautionary measures. Yet I'm not sure I can avoid getting into trouble sexually. If Brad knew I was conflicted, he wouldn't force it.

["Conflicted?"] Jeepers [pause]. Wish I knew what that meant at the 6 moment. Fearing and yet wishing the same thing. I'm really scared of being the victim of a sex onslaught by a man. Yet I've set it up that way in the past. It's a dreadful way to think about sex. Makes me feel very angry at men. They're lechers, want only physical release, just using me. Yet I have a sense of suppressing my own desires. I get into a situation where I get sort of melty—almost as if I can't say no. I also feel like arousing and controlling the 7 man. Too much of me doesn't find sex pleasurable. I keep wondering whether I've actually reached a climax. I know I pretended with the last man I was serious about [several years ago]. ["How do you mean?"] I voluntarily tensed my vaginal muscles. Partly I put on a dramatic act. Partly I felt physically stirred by him, but to what point I'm not sure. I felt him inside me, and it was exciting, but not the point of orgasm. The pleasure was mostly in feeling the penis inside me, feeling full. As if I had this part of myself back again, and that's all that 8 mattered. I probably permitted past encounters only because I wanted restoration of that part, the missing part. The person didn't matter [tears].

I seem to have a split. The tender feelings are really paramount. I'm scared 9 that if I give way to the sexual feelings, the tender feelings will disappear. The tender feelings are associated with mother; the sexual feelings belong to father. I keep thinking that if I indulge in sexual feelings for father, I will lose tender feelings for him. Mother used to say our prayers with us. She would sing a hymn on leaving us. Dottie and I shared a room until I was 12. I thought mother had the most beautiful voice in the world. She doesn't, but I felt bathed in tenderness at such times.

6/6

1   I had some things happen Friday that made me feel guilty. Some work didn't go right, and I felt it was my fault though I had spent a lot of time and effort on it. I was mad at the people who were involved; they didn't act right and didn't bother to get in touch with me. One person in particular made me feel guilty because of her attitude [coughs]. She was pulling rank on me, pointing out deficiencies in the report I had written, though I was simply including other people's comments and observations. I filled up with tears. If I had only been more aggressive. I just couldn't stand this lady's controlled, patronizing manner.

2   The thought of it all gives me an uneasy feeling in general. Now I feel something in the pit of my stomach. My stomach's really bothering me; it's twisting and turning. I'm thinking of what happened the day before—on Thursday. That interview I had with Debbie. I've had pains on and off since then in my stomach. I've been chewing Gelusil, taking Belladonna, and when I'm awakened at night with that tight stomach feeling, I take milk. It was like a starter button when I had this emotional interview with Debbie—the girl who's in training to be an assistant junior executive and whose work I supervise. I felt guilty when she told me she went home every day crying, she was in such turmoil. Husband trouble was getting her down. I didn't realize she was so upset. I feel as if I had failed her because I wasn't aware of her emotional state. I've not been as available to her as I should have been. But, after all, it wasn't my role to be a doctor to her. She has problems with her marriage, and she's not been married very long. It seems that for some time now she's been experiencing severe anxiety and nobody was helping her. I knew in a vague way that she was having troubles, but I felt that we should focus on her work and not discuss her personal problems. Last Thursday she told me she'll have to give up her work [pause].

3   ["Is there anything else on your mind?"] Well, there's all this business about Brad. That's funny. Tina, who's going to a job in England soon, cooked dinner for me the other night and mentioned Brad's coming back from South America where he's been on a business assignment. When I heard about that, my stomach did a flip-flop. It was a sensation quite different from the ulcery feeling. It was wave-like and didn't have the unpleasantness of pain. Brad is a person I've thought of seriously as a husband.

I finally got a haircut Saturday. That's one positive thing, although I don't like it as much as the haircuts I've gotten from my regular hair stylist.

6/7

I can't come in at a different hour [in response to previous discussion about   **1** possible change in hour]. Maybe somebody needs my hour, or else you'll be out late and not want to get up so early to see me. An acquaintance of mine, Jim, switched analysts in midstream a year ago. He had been considering whether to take a Boston or Cambridge job. When we spoke recently, he inferred that he knew I was coming to see you. I mentioned seeing your wife at a concert recently and added that she was beautifully dressed on my fees. I advised Jim to be nice to his analyst, and he would get more from him. He told me of an analyst who married one of his patients. I said he shouldn't have mentioned that—it clutches me. He insisted it was different for women: just as they don't get over their attachment to father, they don't get over their attachment to the analyst. Do I feel attached to you? I do and I don't. Let's say that I finally get through the analysis. Would I be able to come back to you if I were in trouble? Yes, I suppose if it were for a sensible reason. There are moments when I feel so supported and grateful to you. At other times I feel so damn critical of you, without rational basis. Occasionally you look or sound sort of apprehensive, for example, when talking about time. I feel then as though you're warding something off—as if you're scared of me. More likely I'm scared of you.

I heard a story about a married couple who had a fight about buying a new   **2** car. The wife thought her husband was being taken in by the salesman and opposed it. He blew up at her and made her feel like a doormat. The son joined his father in ganging up on her. It's so obvious she feels inadequate as a woman. If it weren't for her sick daughter, she'd pack up and leave. Here I am still struggling, in treatment, trying to say what I think without being concerned about the consequences. That woman is an unattractive person, and she must feel so inadequate and defensive. She must have quite a wall around her feelings. Here I am talking of her as I do of myself. She—that woman—is fighting against her anger [pause].

I think of my ulcer. Generally I feel pretty good. But the ulcer, or at least   **3** my stomach, hurts at times. I see it being like an expression of feelings. Is it worse to have pain in the belly, or to have the pain in my mind, in the form of feelings? Why should I be having pain? It occurs to me that Brad's coming home. But why pain then? That business with Debbie really turned it on. That emotional session with her. She was mothering *me* after a while. My mother—I mean Debbie—actually was doing it. I couldn't bear it [tears]. Was it that I was going to lose her? After all, I was her supervisor and I feel guilty about not giving more to her and also about having her actually console me. It's as if when people are kind and good to me, I feel I don't deserve it. I have a knife-like pain now in my stomach.

4   Am I angry at my mother? All the little things she used to do for me, adjusting my clothes, my hair—and I'd get furious. This damn stomach pain. It's the guilt feeling that gives me the pain. The attention and kindness these various people give me makes it worse. Debbie was trying to tell me that I wasn't meeting her needs from the beginning, and I feel responsible. My feelings toward men also are wrapped in guilt, guilt over sexual impulses and wanting to hurt them. I believe my mother felt guilty about not feeding me properly as an infant. I never asked for a damned thing for myself as I grew up. At times I notice I raise my hand up and back. It's reaching out toward you. It's aggressive, but also reaching for help. As if reaching for help is an aggressive demand. I did cry to be fed as a baby, I'm told. I've always liked to be indoors. It's comforting—back to the womb.

5   I talked to Jane last night; her baby is going to be a few weeks late. She asked if I wanted to meet Brad at the airport by myself. If she hasn't delivered by then, she offered to go and take care of the car. I'm scared to meet Brad alone. He might look around and ask where Jane and Fred were. What do I want? I want time with him by myself if that would make him happy [pause, touches epigastric area]. ["Are you still having pain?"] It's still there—not so bad. When you mention it, I'm more aware of it. But now it feels more like too much acid, and not like ulcer pain.

6/8 - 7/5, Summary

There is gradual lessening of stomach symptoms but continued preoccupation with Brad's arrival. Brad is seen as her baby—a defense against feeling a baby herself. Acting as the adult at this time is felt as a strain and associated with stomach symptoms. There is nagging doubt about whether she is grown-up or not. There is also identification with an adolescent girl who has sexual problems and is caught up in a mother-daughter conflict in which symbiotic ties and attempts to establish her own identity clash. One friend has a positive Pap smear indicating that a hysterectomy might have to be done, and this news activates great tension in the patient who relates it to consequences of masturbation. Another friend is about to deliver, and the patient is urged by this woman to have dinner with her husband. Patient does, but then feels involved and guilty. She found it both exciting and inappropriate, a reenactment of the Oedipal situation. There follow recollections of how she, the first-born, reacted with great jealousy (and narcissistic hurt) when at age four she was displaced in mother's affections by the birth of a sibling. Patient then realizes belatedly that she and her married friends were involved in a mutual acting out episode. The thrilling part of it is ascribed to the identification with the woman having the baby and also to being the one who took a husband away from his wife. Anxiety dreams immediately precede Brad's arrival. The patient is not prepared emotionally for sexual relations. The night before his coming, she experiences severe epigastric pain which wakes her several times. There is an associated concern about losing him, or if she gets him, that she will lose mother. Anger is associated with not being able to have her cake and eat it too.

Brad's return—after a year in South America—evokes an intensely ambivalent reaction in her. He is not as demonstrative as she has hoped. She has expected instant magic and is greatly disappointed at his general coolness, frequent silence, and sexual disinterest. After a few days things warm up a bit. By the time he leaves to return to his home in New York, a somewhat easier relationship between them has been reestablished, but there is still no real closeness.

A mild depressive response and concurrent somatic manifestations of stomach dysfunction follow in the wake of Brad's departure, but the patient has a better understanding of her neurotic expectations and of Brad's neurotic behavior. She plans to talk things out with him at the next opportunity. She rereads some books on sex. There is rumination over Brad's having feminine traits. Word comes from her sister about a threatened miscarriage which activates old guilt over sibling rivalry. Her mother calls and insists that if she doesn't step in and somehow help the patient, she will never "land Brad." But the patient finds herself able to handle mother's domineering ways better than on prior occasions. There are regressive fantasies of being cuddled and protected by father. Depressive rumination continues with return of intermittent stomach pain for a few days.

Brad calls to say he's located himself in New York, his hometown. There is still much hostility between them. Her relationships with men continue to be difficult, those with girls more comfortable and supportive. Men appear as competitors, adversaries. She is concerned about what people expect of her and what she puts out, feeling guilty and inadequate. There are recollections about "going to potty" as a child, sitting there for a long time, and stubbornly holding the bowel movement in until a red ring showed on her bottom, thereby making her mother feel bad: a stubborn defiance of mother's domineering ways during the toilet-training period.

Interpretations focus on the patient's tendency to intellectualize—a defense against being flooded by the intense emotions which the relationship with Brad evokes. She fears the possibility of losing him, of being rejected by him, and then being alone and abandoned.

Sex and food are symbolically interrelated and seen as filling one orifice or another, filling a space within her which seems continually to be empty.

7/6

The weatherman said it would be sunny today, but it doesn't look it. 1
George, this friend whom I've seen occasionally, called last night and invited me to go on a trip out West. That gave me a boost and helped make me feel less depressed and less tired. I felt I was wanted by someone.

2   I can hear my stomach gurgling now. It's maddening to think how strained things have been between Brad and me. I really understand what you've said about my clutching at him as if he were the last man. I must feel terribly desperate to think he's offering me anything tangible in terms of marriage [tears]. Just thinking of it makes me cry. It is so different with George, who does things that seem as if he wants to take care of me. It's the caring for me, looking out for me—that's what I really love. When we went shopping, he carried the box of groceries and vegetables for me. Brad never did that. Then there's the cuddly part. George is very affectionate. That's mothering me too.

3   Yet the whole sex question scares me and puts me off. I'm bothered by rape fantasies. I remember when my car got smashed up. I talked of my car being violated, as if it were part of myself. This forcible seizure business is like caveman stuff. It both scares and attracts me. I remember this other fellow, Johnny, who was so sexually exciting, and I had lots of fantasies about him. The same double pull—attracted and scared at the same time. I never could relate to him as a person. I had the fantasy that he would grab me in a corridor, hold me tight in his arms, fix his smoldering eyes on me, and kiss me passionately. Why, even if he had just asked me for a date, I would have run. I don't think he had the faintest interest in me actually. Violent men, big men, fascinate me. It makes me think of father, my seeing him in the nude so often, with such big private parts.

4   The whole sex question is confused in my thinking. The way I've behaved with George is that it's all right as long as I'm the one that controls it. As long as I felt he wouldn't push me too far for sexual intimacy, I wanted him. What am I going to do if I go on this trip out West with him next month?

5   At times I feel a real sexual longing physically. What I could really kill my father for is that there was so much overstimulation in my house when I was growing up. That stimulation led to real fear. My father to this day will walk around without clothes upstairs in the family house. Now I stay out of his way. But what's a little kid of six supposed to do? I was fascinated—the size, the shape, the difference—I'm sure I was just flooded with feelings then. Millions of times I was in the bathtub and father would go to the john and I would watch avidly. Wouldn't you suppose a grown man would have the sense not to expose a child to all this? I feel flushed all over now, warm, and perspiring. The way I poured through books as a youngster looking for pictures of naked male statues. What did I want as a kid? Maybe to feel that sense of excitement and stimulation. I got so preoccupied with the idea of male genitalia. For years it was on my mind.

7/7

1   [Late ten minutes.]
I hate to get moving in the morning. That's been the case since I was a

youngster. Mother used to get after me for this, and the more she did, the more I'd stall. Maybe I'll get over being late. I need to be more aware of this childish tendency. It's such a sly way of being hostile.

Brad hasn't called me yet this week though he promised. But I'm not   2
desolate over it. My reaction seems to be: isn't that typical of him? My second thought is: he's depressed. I hate this distance business, our being separated. I like people who are warm, giving, and relate to you. Brad's real close friends—if he has any—are married couples. With George, real communication and rapport are possible. Brad seems to relate to people through his professional identity, not personally. His birthday is very soon. I thought of getting him a slide sorter; that's a neutral thing. But why should I send him one? Is it to pressure a relationship that's crumbling? Hell—who wants this? I wonder if I've changed that much. I really got along with him before he went to South America. But on his return he wasn't strikingly different. All of a sudden I take a look, and I don't want the relationship. What did I think was so marvelous to begin with? He liked me—that was flattering. But how much? And look at the crap you put up with. If it weren't for our mutual friends, the relationship wouldn't have gotten off the ground. He wouldn't have taken the initiative on his own. He's passivity personified. I think of how I am scared of aggressive men. My relationship with Brad is like a seething, bubbling cauldron of angry feelings. I don't get that feeling about George. Brad and I seemed alike. Have I changed so much?

I listen to myself dissecting my problems intellectually, and I say, "Quit it"   3
[tears]. I must—it isn't just the passage of time—I must be different to have reacted to Brad this past weekend by not just tears, but by getting mad at him because of his awful behavior. Maybe what I'm saying isn't important. I guess I need to switch gears. I need to please. The hardest thing for me to say yesterday was that I felt like killing my father.

About 18 years ago I was on a boat with Phyllis Martin and her husband. My   4
mother was along. The Martins had two sons. The one my age was on the fringe of social acceptance, kind of like I was. We were in swimming and he tried to duck me. I got panicked at first, then very competitive, and ducked him. Afterwards I felt awful about it.

I've always had this very strong competitive need to win out. ["And here too by trying to analyze and formulate everything that you say before I do."] [Tears.] Now I feel like you're scolding me. ["Clarification and interpretation are for the sake of better understanding, not criticism."] I know, I've got to stop this sensitivity, but I still don't see how. I keep feeling at such times as though you're pulling the rug out from under me.

7/11

I've just been to see Dr. M., my internist. I had an appointment with him today which somehow I didn't mention previously here.

1   Brad called yesterday. He sounded better. We talked for almost an hour. It was a friendly talk. He was more with it. He's so damned undecided; he never does anything—at least as far as I'm concerned. He still wants to arrange a vacation next month, but he talks about what we might do in such a vague way. I have to be direct with him. I told him we needed time together to sort things out. I also told him there were weekends and we didn't have to force everything into a short time while we were on vacation together. If he really cared about me—why didn't he ask me down to New York or come down here, since our last meeting together? When I got off of the phone—and I also feel it returning right now—I started to feel ulcery. It's tantalizing; the whole situation is like a carrot on a string. It was a nice conversation, but nothing deeper in terms of a relationship.

2   Dr. M. asked about my love life. I told him there was no active one now. I wondered if he was being tactful, when he said he'd be available for gynecologic advice. He told me he'd been trying to get me happily married for the past eight years. I replied that I'd been working on it. I still have fantasies about Dr. M. But I was disconcerted that he wanted to see me as early as October again. My hemoglobin, he told me, was 9.9 g and the hematocrit was 29. I said to him, "Let me call you in September to arrange it, when I have my schedule straight." Really, what I was doing was temporizing, to put the appointment off. Perhaps I don't want to hear allusions to my love life, or maybe it's my positive attachment to him. [Reference is made to the patient's intellectualizing and analytic guessing.] I know that's true, but it's hard for me to take it [tears]. I know I do this, and I'm upset about it, yet when you point it out, I feel attacked. It's my sensitivity. I feel so criticized. It's really like being chipped away at. I want to explain what I'm thinking, and every time I open my mouth you do this to me. ["Every time?"] That's an exaggeration, of course. I try so hard to please you. That's so you won't accuse me of being hostile. I guess it's one thing if I say it, and it's another if you do. It makes me so mad to hear it from you. I just want to shut up and say nothing to you. Now I feel I'm getting mad. Another part of me is sitting there, saying—that's an improvement—but it's the same damn thing, intellectualizing. Can't do anything right.

3   There is a problem I'm reluctant to tell you, but I will, nevertheless. I feel as though you'll slap me in the face with this stuff. Well, I know that isn't so. I got an invitation in the mail to a party being given by the Social Club—it's a beach party—a week from Friday. The admission is three dollars per person, and you bring a bathing suit and your food. If I wanted to expand, to create social contacts, that's where the eligible, attractive guys can be found. I've talked about it for years. I ought to do it, but I can't get started. I don't know if it's acceptable to go without a date. I could ask Sheila who's a member, but I haven't been able to locate her. I guess the issue is that I want to do it, but I'm scared to. I probably won't take action about that party, but for the first time

I'm thinking it would be to my advantage to join that club. It takes such courage to apply. Then when you start in explaining my problems to me I feel so vulnerable. ["It is an asset to be bright, but a disadvantage when it is used defensively."]

I don't parade my intelligence in front of George. That's not the level at which we relate. I'm also afraid of being competitive and aggressive with him; I don't think he's as smart as I am. Yet with Brad it's different; we get caught in a cross-intellectualizing. The fear of how men will react to me gets stirred up when I think of joining that club. It's the way each sex looks over possible new members of the other sex. Men will see me as C.F., the class freak. 4

7/12

Monday night I ran into a friend who used to work with me. She remarked that she met somebody who knew you and recommended you highly. I like to have outside confirmation that you're good. Here I go analyzing. I like to hear it about myself—that I'm good [pause]. 1

I'm feeling ulcery now. I must still be mad at you. It's not actual ulcer pain, but on the way here I started getting vague heartburn. I really was upset yesterday. During the hour and afterwards. Somehow I begrudge admitting that I'm getting help here [pause]. I still tend to see it as criticism. 2

I went down to the political headquarters of one of the mayoralty candidates to check signatures and addresses. It's not just political but also social. The other candidate is so awful that there is no choice. I found an attractive group of men and women at the headquarters. I got teamed up with a married man, big, husky; he didn't seem to be too smart, but turned out to be pretty nice after all. I thought I made a favorable impression and that made me feel good. It's a boost to my ego to work out well with a man. Unfortunately, most of the men there were married. There were a few single fellows, and I felt comfortable with them too. I didn't feel like the class freak. 3

Honestly, I get upset when I think how scared I am of men in general, even with the inoffensive, meek ones. No wonder I latch on to the most passive sorts. Otherwise I fear I'm going to be laughed at and rejected. 4

7/18

Last night was quite a business. I was going to try out for the amateur symphony orchestra, and the audition took place last night. I became nervous and scared about it in advance. Then at the audition, while filling out the application, I got very nervous. I listened to the girl ahead of me. She was of soloist quality, and my heart sank. The more I heard her, the more nervous I got until I was shaking. Then when I started to play, I was so frightened that my 1 hands shook. It was really upsetting, even though the audition committee was so nice. As I'm telling you this now, I can feel my insides churning. I felt insecure except for the sightreading which I did O.K. I told them I wished I wasn't so nervous. I left there at 7:30, wanting to escape from it all and go sailing on the river. By the time I was ready I had doubts if there'd be any boats going out, so I went to my other musical group. I feel so superior in this group and so secure. If it isn't one extreme, it's another. Maybe the symphony orchestra is way out of my class. It's the way I feel about men.

2   I wanted to talk about joining the Social Club to one of my friends who's a member. I got tearful and thinking how scared I'd been at the auditions and how gentle those guys were. I thought it meant they considered me so fragile that I had to be let down easily. Why is it that other girls new in the musical group are able to attract the attention of the stand-offish men and walk away with them? That never happens to me. On the way back home I stopped to buy a couple of paperbacks to bolster myself. I bought a potboiler whose heroine has a first name similar to mine. The other one was by Robert Murphy: *Diplomat Among Warriors.*

3   I woke at 5 A.M. this morning. The audition was on my mind. I read for a while, then fell back asleep and overslept. I had the most unbelievable dream. I dreamt that I was having intercourse with Carl, this old, old love of mine. All of a sudden he stopped. I looked to the left, and there up on a platform or hanging from a lamppost was a girl who had set herself on fire. I watched horrified. There was something inflammable around her neck. She had lit this, starting a ring of fire around her neck, spreading to her waist, and flashing back and forth. This girl was alive and had done this to herself. I thought desperately, "What should we do?" While we were there, her head caught on fire. It seemed like some political happening. Then I heard a whimpering voice. The sound was like that of the girl who was raped by the bandits in the movie *Virgin Spring*: "Why would this girl do such a thing to herself, this poor girl whose father wouldn't protect her?" It was at this point that I awoke.

I thought, that girl was me. What a dreadful association: engaged in sexual activity and seeing that girl doing such a horrible thing to herself, not expressing pain or trying to save herself—a real nightmare. The flames seemed to explode, to get out of control. The whimpering voice reminds me of my awful fear at the audition, my anxiety at not knowing what to say to men at social gatherings. I think I'm sticking my neck out for a rebuff each time I try to start a relationship with a man. I'm scared of rejection. I'm terrified of being destructively damaged. So I've got to withdraw, to hole up with a book. When I get some support and reassurance, I can venture forth again. ["What occurs to you about the fire?"] It was self-immolation. It's like sexual feelings I get scared of—hot, fiery feelings. I want tenderness, support, caring. Can't put sex and that together. ["Need to hurt yourself may be involved."] I didn't think of that. The girl is me. I need to punish myself, thinking I am a bad little girl sexually and a failure in my musical ambition.

7/20

I'm mad. I put too much bleach in the water to wash my blouse. It's   1 carelessness. I'm ruining stuff left and right. I feel like Lady Macbeth, washing her hands. I feel I'm bad. Why else would I pour buckets of bleach in? My self-image is that of a hunk of feces. I'm systematically ruining things I want to wear when I'm with Brad—with anyone. After his call inviting me to New York, my stomach was upset. I wondered if my ulcer were coming back. It's a real threat to go down to New York. It has to be from the way I'm reacting. Wanting to whitewash my clothes myself, and I wind up ruining them, even though I want to look well. Those Lady Macbeth lines are running through my mind [loud, persisting stomach gurgles]. Oh, listen to my stomach. I get mad at that part of myself that acts so dumb. [Silence.] I'm worrying a lot about dirtiness   2 and cleanliness [again loud, persisting stomach gurgles]. My stomach's talking too. I guess sex is the dirty theme. I remember telltale spots on the sheets of my bed. Probably a nocturnal emission by George when he stayed over. Spots on my nightgown after masturbation, when my period was not quite over. I have a fantasy of my insides as a yawning cavern, bloody and messy.

Now I'm thinking of your vacation schedule. I wonder what will happen in   3 my gut this summer. Last year Brad went away, and my sister got sick. Now I recall as a little girl sticking my finger in an electric socket and getting a shock, when father and mother went away on vacation.

I remember as a youngster making drawings of an imaginary family, with the   4 father urinating and defecating, the kids doing the same. Actually, when I was a youngster, my father would come into the bathroom so many times when I was there. I would often be taking a bath, and he would come in to urinate. He walked around exposed many times. As a youngster I thought of the penis just as an organ of elimination, and I believed that during sexual intercourse the man would urinate into the woman's body. I started with sex being associated with food, and now my thoughts are centered around sex being dirty.

Marge and Dave are going to get married, they're so happy. When will that   5 happen to me? I was a blah girl fifteen years ago and today. Now I feel ulcery again. My stomach's churning. What's bothering me? [Pause]. I just remembered: today is father's birthday. I haven't sent him a gift or even a card. I must be mad at him for not paying attention to me recently.

7/21

I saw a nun with a lovely face today. It sticks in my mind. I'm really scared   1 of men—powerful, aggressive men who can hurt you. Get thee to a nunnery, girl.

I can see myself running for mother instead of father in crises, when the chips are really down.

2   I was so mad at Brad last night. He said he'd call me and didn't. I was supposed to tell him when I was arriving. So I called him. "Oh," he said lightly, "I knew it would be you; I've been discussing great psychologic truths with a couple of friends." As if that was more important than calling me. I told him when I would be arriving in New York. He puts himself almost in a worse position than me. When he's so passive, he makes me act aggressive. At least since I called, he'll know when to pick me up. Otherwise, I might be stuck at LaGuardia. Not calling was his fault. He sets it up. Then he says: you make me feel guilty. I'm good at that. My mother was a past master, that is, mistress, at being the martyr, and her behavior made me feel I was responsible for the way she felt so many times. I get much too wrought up about it. Brad gets scared, then hostile to women, and I toward men. We're using each other to work out problems about the opposite sex. If we were both healthier, we'd move on to more worthwhile things. I keep recalling how mother used to set me on the potty, and I would sit there for hours doing nothing. When I got up, I'd have a red welt on my bottom. When she saw that she'd feel sorry for me. Then I'd pop it in my pants.

3   At least I slept well last night, though for some time now my sleep has been disturbed. Jane called. I told her I was going to New York. That relationship is really shifting, not only because of my awareness of the neurotic elements in it, but Jane is absorbed with her baby. There'll be a gradual loosening of the bond between us, though we'll still be friends.

4   My mother also called. It was father's birthday. She wanted to know if I was coming down. Father was unable to come to the phone because he was at a meeting. Mother's hard of hearing, and she talks practically nonstop on the phone. I guess I'm really in a lousy mood. I'm bothered by Brad's not calling—really mad. It reminds me of hanging breathlessly on. Now I feel short of breath, pressure on my chest. I remember an earlier boyfriend of mine pulling away. One weekend he didn't call, and I just about went out of my mind. I keep hoping that Brad will take over the initiative and show a spontaneous interest in me. I expect more from George than I'm willing to give him. With Brad I extend myself just to get a pat on the head. What a difference in my reactions. But even anger is better than not being recognized at all. Chasing after Brad is like chasing after father. This myth of being father's favorite. I achieved that at such cost. It involved subordinating myself to please him. That word *please* hits me right in the face [tears]. He had a tremendous interest in light opera which I would play over and over for him at the piano. If I hadn't played it, he wouldn't have jumped to come over and be close to me. I remember when I made Phi Beta Kappa, I raced to the phone to tell father. I think I really got conditioned to behave in certain ways with men. You've got to knock yourself out to please them, and then you'll get a puppy dog pat on the head. It means such

subordinating of one's self. Yet cuddling with father was not only my need but partly his wish too.

7/25

When I saw Brad this weekend he had a cold. I don't know if I caught it. We 1 finally had intercourse. I practically didn't feel a thing. I can't dismiss lightly what's going on between Brad and myself. I don't know if I really love him. How much are we drawn to each other for sick reasons? Being almost without feeling during intercourse bothered me. There are so many ways in which he reminds me of my father. Yet, in spite of all the troublesome things, we had a good time. On Friday night he showed he really liked me. I was so surprised when he asked me into his bed. Then we began to be physically close. I've made an appointment with a gynecologist, something I've been thinking about for years.

At the party for Brad, I met one of our mutual friends who told me that I'd 2 changed. He also asked why Brad and I don't get married. I blushed and passed it off lightly. Brad and I got to bed very late that night, but he didn't want sex though I did. I was surprised in view of the past night when he had initiated it. All he said though was that he was confused. I didn't sleep well that night, and today I feel as if it's caught up with me—this feeling of fatigue.

I had a call from my sister who's two months pregnant and taking shots to 3 keep from spotting and maybe miscarrying. I can remember all the trouble I got myself into when she was pregnant four years ago. I got so anxious about myself then. I had been having intercourse with this former boyfriend, and though he was very careful, I was scared that I was pregnant. At one point I was so upset that I tried to abort myself with a skewer. That was a self-destructive thing, and it turned out I wasn't even pregnant.

I don't know if all this depresses me or what. I feel cruddy. Before I came 4 here, one of the lady doctors at the company saw me. She's sharp. She asked me if I was pregnant. I thought: Jesus Christ! But Brad wore a condom. I don't want to risk becoming pregnant. Anyway she struck the fear of God into me. I remember being embarrassed to see Brad walk around without a stitch on. I've set him up for this fatherly business. He may have his troubles, but I do, too. I really couldn't look at him, I, who have been so curious about male genitals. I 5 just thought this is our last meeting before summer vacation, and I won't be coming here after my appointment next week with the gynecologist. Dammit, I wish you wouldn't be gone, with all this pregnancy and sex and Brad business on my mind. I'm concerned about getting into sexual trouble, getting pregnant. My sister is pregnant.

I couldn't sleep well last night—was as high as a kite. Kept thinking of how 6 I'm scared to admit my interest in sex. Sometime in the middle of the night my throat began to feel sore. I used to have sore throats a lot when I was younger. I'm reminded of little children being scared of eating, who keep saying,

"Mommie has a baby in her tummy; did it get there from something Mommie ate?" I finally got out of bed and took some orange juice to relieve my throat. It did just that, though you'd think it wouldn't. Orange marmalade has been a favorite of mine for years. I used to eat sandwiches made of it every day for a long time. Now I'm feeling hungry [stomach rumbling]. I would like something to eat.

7/26 - 9/6, Summer Interruption

9/7 - 10/19, Interim Summary

The ambivalent relationship with Brad continues. The patient is on "the pill." Stomach symptoms have been less troublesome. Her relationship with men continues to be influenced by infantile fixations. Strong voyeuristic tendencies are becoming activated in the transference, especially with reference to many details about the analyst's office. There is continued expectation of the worst happening at work, socially, and in the treatment. Brief episodes of tearfulness occur both in and out of the analytic hours. There is a persisting fantasy that mother needs her to keep father happy. Sexual matters were never discussed by mother. The patient is more aware of resenting the position and privileges of men and of using her brains and intellect to compete with them. She has a vivid dream about a cotton-mouth moccasin snake with a white belly and white mouth behind a bathroom door and the wish that someone would come with a forked stick, catch the snake, and chop its head off. Associations to this dream contain references to the many times when she was in the bathtub as a child, and as father walked into the bathroom to urinate, her eyes would be fixed on his penis. Father often wore moccasins with white tennis socks. There are also links with intense voyeuristic, oral-incorporative, and castrating wishes centered around a huge phallus. She compares herself with the analyst, feeling bigger, superior, and able to control him. These fantasies compensate for opposite attitudes in the transference. The sensory and sensual memories of father keep recurring—his tallness, the size of his genitalia, the veins on his hands, his big shoes, and vivid imagery [visual and auditory] of his urinating. At the same time there is also increasing transference anxiety about sexual attack and a need to deny the analyst's presence.

Men are visualized as either giants with great destructive power or as cut down to size and controllable, dominated by her. There are narcissistic fantasies of using Tampax to masturbate with. In a dream she is being given ornate jewelry—symbolic of male genitalia. She continues to be unable to experience orgasm with Brad—almost anesthetic. This activates concern about defect and the need to compensate by brilliant analytic interpretations. There is envy of a friend who is so feminine and so sharp at the same time, seen as a marvelous example of combining job and family successfully. The patient begins to feel keenly the need to shift from her masculine, phallic strivings, but is fearful of great passivity, dependency, and masochism which might then come to the fore. The latter seems very close to the surface. Following a weekend of physical malaise and slight fever, the patient develops a cold with postnasal drip and cough, taking antihistamines, cough syrup, and many cough drops. She is involved in a minor accident, hitting a boy on a bike with her car, resulting in slight injury to his hand. She had been feeling angry about and preoccupied with an incident at work prior to the accident. The cold causes her to blow her nose frequently, checking the Kleenex to see what she's produced. She notes being preoccupied with every body orifice. She keeps reminding herself of the need to interpose her mind-intellect between feelings, being afraid otherwise she'll be at the mercy of primitive impulses.

10/20

Watched a show on TV. It had a lot of violence in it—one of those private-eye things. That night I had two dreams.

The first dream was in a department store. There was a big display of flowered briefcases. I kept pouring through them and trying to decide. I kept looking for a blue one because Brad likes that color. Then I saw an olive-colored one, which I prefer, but couldn't finally decide.

The second dream was about a little kid needing a change of diapers. I was going somewhere with somebody, but I had to take this little one home for a change of diapers and avoid a mess along the way.

I remember once, when I was in my teens and hospitalized for anemia, that I suddenly fainted while walking in the corridor and defecated while I was out. Gee! It looks like that little kid in the dream was me—all that anal stuff. Pardon me for interpreting. Yet part of me recognizes that these dreams and thoughts come from inside and are not just intellectual exercises. Now I think of mother's hands doing things to me, cleaning me up, straightening my clothes. It's like being a lifeless puppet manipulated by her. I feel very uncomfortable and angry at her to this day. You know, reading about bowel movements and a child's reactions to them makes me very uncomfortable. I can't let you do the interpreting because I feel the same way about it as I do about my mother. If I start letting you think about these things for me, it's as if you're taking over control of my thoughts. I get really mad if you make interpretations for me, whereas if you'd only wait, I'd get there myself. That's like my reaction to mother—her saying I should do something, just before I'm about to do it. That evokes intense anger. I can't let you do this work for me because then I'll feel it's not my own. Accepting help means losing my identity. I can't let you say anything to me, otherwise I'd feel diminished. I've dragged my heels so, when mother has wanted me to do something because it meant I was failing to assist myself as a person. With all this, there's another part of me that understands that you only point things out—you don't say I'm supposed to or not. You don't threaten my autonomy really. Here I am using up all the time talking about this.

2   When I think of the dreams again, the first thing that comes to my mind is the kitchen in my childhood home. I remember a real sensual pleasure in kneading dough in the kitchen, the sensation of sinking my fingers into that soft, yielding stuff. But mother wouldn't let me do that. As far as the briefcase is concerned, the one I have now is pretty worn out. That's why I'm thinking I'll get a new one. I want to be different in many ways so Brad will be attracted to me sexually. I keep wondering if my body really excites him.

10/24

This matter of what's done for me and to me has to be separated out. Now I'm thinking of some books hostile to psychiatry that a friend of mine told me about.

1   I went shopping yesterday and bought a feminine bag to substitute for the mannish briefcase I've been carrying around. I looked over quite a few before I made my selection. I've had the other one for so long; it's worn out, but I couldn't give it up till now. There are other changes that I'll have to make, especially in the way I look.

2   [Shuts window.] I feel a cold draft on me. Reminds me of being out in the cold. As a little kid I never liked to play outside, especially in the cold. Like the wish to crawl back inside my mother. Feels cold here. ["Is it possible that you feel exposed, unprotected here in the analysis?"] I'm afraid of something coming up on me from behind—well, there you are. These thoughts keep running through my mind: being born, being wet, feeling a draft, feeling cold, a shock. I had a fantasy as a child of witches or cannibals dancing around a pot, and then they would come for me as I was cowering behind a bush. I also had fears of someone coming up behind me. I feel that now, too, when I'm outside and it's cold. Once when I was younger, a man with an erection stood behind me, but I was unaware of what it was all about then. I keep thinking of sexual assault. A male dog will climb on a female dog from behind. Skiing has helped me. I can now stand being outdoors. It's a protection, having the slope of a mountain behind me. Climbing is more threatening. There's danger of falling back. I can remember the fear of falling out of the back of a rumble seat.

3   On my right hand, inside the little finger, there's a little mole—an identifying mark which is practically gone now. When I was ten or eleven, I had warts on my right thumb and index finger; they finally went away. I didn't like them. I associated them with something unclean. That reminds me of the bad acne I had. I used to think it was an outward manifestation of dirty sexual thoughts and masturbation.

10/25

I started out here tense, with symptoms in my stomach that made me think   1
of the ulcer. There's a big conference at work about personnel practices. It's all a
niggling debate over pay, especially for part-time employees. As I lie here, I feel
a slight draft [closes window]. They told me at work that I had been out the
day after a holiday three times in the past year. That got me very upset. I felt I
was being accused of cadging on time. I got very tense and knotted up in my
stomach until I thought the whole thing through. I spend so much overtime
without pay at work, and then I bring stuff home to do. I don't feel so tense
now. When I talked to Brad I felt he wasn't interested enough in me. Dammit!   2
I'm getting upset all over again as I talk about it [teary]. I felt attacked at work,
but it was really grossly out of proportion to what really happened. On top of
that I felt that Brad wasn't so affectionate with me as I would have wanted. Do I
want blood? Yes, I do. Here I've been talking so long about this crummy
self-image I have, and it still gets me, though there are times when I think I've
gotten some distance from it.

Now I feel a vaginal itch. I seem to have some sort of infection there. I've   3
had it since yesterday. I have an appointment to see my internist in a couple of
weeks. This itch started suddenly. I have the fantasy it's because I masturbated
and had germs on my finger. When I had an affair years ago, I developed a
whitish discharge. At that time, on one occasion, I was looking up the word
"leukorrhea" in a medical book when a fellow came up behind me and surprised
me so that I slammed the book shut. This fellow said teasingly, "Aha! I caught
you in the act!" I felt terribly guilty then, and I guess now. It's guilt. What a
pain in the neck—in the ass—it is to be intellectual! I feel it's getting in the way.

I was talking with a girl who has an ulcer, had to have almost all her stomach   4
out because of a perforation. There was no pain; she just fainted and was rushed
to the hospital. She had a terrible experience there. She was so sick and out of
it: being able to hear the doctors say she might not live, yet being too weak to
protest. She described the surgery as if it were like an assault, without any
preparation. A battle-axe nurse told her to shut up when she cried, and she was
put in a room with an eighty-year-old lady dying of cancer. Her own family
couldn't tolerate the situation, but all they could say was, "Don't worry, dear."
The doctor sat down to talk with her after she was out of the woods and said
with tears in his eyes, "We thought we were going to lose you." There was a time   5
when I almost died from measles. I remember father was separated from the
family then, and I was delirious, out of it. Mother went through hell. Now I
remember another time—father was in the hospital. Children were not allowed in
there, but I thought it was because I was bad. I was very young then, maybe five
or six years old. Mother was pregnant then. ["What brings such thoughts about
serious illness, possible death, hospitals, to mind?"]

I've drifted away from this vaginal discharge. I keep having all sorts of   6 anxious thoughts about it. Maybe it's a sign of something very serious. Maybe I won't be able to get pregnant. Maybe masturbation brought it all on. I can't seem to get rid of the idea that I'm bad, that I've done bad things and have to pay for it.

10/27

1   The couch feels warm. The night before last I had a dream. It was a most conflicted, sexy dream. In it some friends, just married, have moved into a new apartment. The woman has dining room furniture I would not have chosen. Her husband said he didn't like it either. Then there is an abrupt change. I'm alone with him. He was scornful of my knowing what to do and how to behave sexually. I fondled the end of his penis, and he disdainfully said that I should move my hand down toward the shaft of the penis. I did and saw it become huge. I got scared. I've been so mixed up about what I would tell Brad about my sexual reactions. I felt in the dream that I had to go along with the man's condescending attitude. At the same time I had a strong sense of guilt. I thought that I would have to give Brad up.

2   Last night I woke up because of ulcery pain. Right now, telling you this, I feel as sharp a pain as I have felt for months. All I can think about is that pain, right in the pit of my stomach, as if I'd been stabbed. Now I'm thinking of this married couple that I visited Wednesday night. Lucy was indisposed, so Hal, her husband, invited me to go to the Symphony with him; he had two tickets and Lucy couldn't go. It reminded me of going out with my other friend's husband while she was in labor. Last night at the concert I felt more comfortable about it. I used Brad as a kind of protection. I couldn't see the ticket go to waste. I wanted to hear the concert. If I had said no, somebody else would have had the chance. But once I accepted the ticket, all the other stuff about the implications of what I had done flooded me. I was going out with another woman's husband. Hal should have sold the two tickets and stayed home with his wife. Would I have been so quick to say yes if he had offered me the two tickets? I'm not so sure. How I pay—I pay through the nose for this stuff when I get to feeling this pull toward married men. In the dream, the dark-haired man reminded me of the fellow I once had an affair with. My father has dark hair. In the dream I see myself as a worthless, stupid girl, forfeiting my relationship with Brad. I did enjoy the concert, but it's not worth the way it makes me feel. At the time it's actually happening, I don't see the implications. Wednesday night I felt lonesome, rebuffed, and I used Lucy and Hal to be with somebody. Right now, thank God, the pain is subsiding but I feel depressed.

10/30

I had a lovely weekend. I told Brad I loved him. We were in bed, and it's so   1
easy to say these things in bed. He told me how happy he was to see me. The
more I see him, the more comfortable and happy I am.

I must have some kind of mild gyn. infection. Even before I went to New   2
York, I looked these infections up in my medical encyclopedia. I kept seeing
myself as bad and dirty, and wondered if I would transmit it. I wondered if it
was a monilial infection. One of the symptoms listed was painful intercourse. It
did sting some when Brad and I had sexual relations. The book said it's apt to
happen if the acid-alkali balance is upset. It was just after my period. I'll call my
gynecologist this week. I feel terribly embarrassed and overinvest this kind of
thing the way I felt about my skin when I was younger and had acne. I think of
myself as a bad girl, and I don't want anyone to see that. With my first
boyfriend I really did feel like a bad person, having an affair with him. But that
word doesn't fit what's between Brad and me.

When I tend to shy away from men and keep moving toward girlfriends, the   3
whole idea of homosexuality creeps into my mind. It's as if I could get terribly
hurt by men or else they just wouldn't like me. Then I think of how relatively
safe it would be with other women.

I'm not used to sleeping with somebody else. Brad's bed is too short. He's   4
getting too chubby around the middle. His lying in bed beside me reminds me of
father because Brad is built like father. How many times father exposed himself
to me! It's so confusing. I really don't want a father in Brad, but in some ways I
do want this. I get scared of losing him. Who's the one I'm really scared of
losing? Is it Brad or is it father?

When I spoke with mother and told her that I had visited with Brad, she said   5
to me, "You're leading a dangerous life." She probably meant sex with Brad.
But I don't feel that way with him. It's homey, comfortable, and that's not
really dangerous. If my mother ever found out about my sex life! My stomach
does a flip-flop at the thought. Yet I feel I could work it out with her. I wish I
could really talk with her about my relationship with Brad. There's something
missing between mother and me which I wish could be restored.

10/31 - 11/7, Interim Summary

A gynecologic appointment is postponed because of pressure of work that
couldn't wait. She blames mother for not teaching her responsibility, not
allowing her to help at home, and yet constantly complaining. There is

continued concern over vaginal discharge, but fear of what the doctor will tell her has influenced her to delay seeing him. She has troublesome thoughts of herself as a nonentity. Masturbation reinforces feelings of guilt and hypersensitivity.

The patient is finally seen by her gynecologist about ten days after the vaginal symptoms began. A diagnosis of trichomonas vaginalis is made. There is continuing guilt about masturbation. It is still difficult for her to talk about it except in a general, cursory way. She is concerned about what will be done with this "information." As a child she had a fantasy of snakes coming out of the toilet into her anus, but she has consciously suppressed this in the analysis until now. Several years ago she was masturbating compulsively, using Tampax as an artificial penis. She had also used other substitutes, but had been unable to talk about it before. This was a way of retreating from involvement with men. The frequency of masturbation has been reduced now. She notes that her revelation sounds as if she were reporting in to a probation officer—the analyst [seen as external superego].

11/8

1   I walked by you with my head hung low, after telling you yesterday the one thing I had held back as a secret—how I masturbated. I was more scared to reveal that single conscious bit of information than anything else I can think of so far in the analysis. I certainly felt guilty as hell about it. It was a great relief not to have you react one way or another about it. But I still can't look at you straight. I've just noticed a funny eye tic. I connect it with having seen recently a woman whom I took to be your wife. The tic just started up in my left eye. Now I feel irritated, as though I want to hit out. Yesterday I had the thought—get out before you're thrown out. It's dark now when I come here, and the lights are on inside of the houses, when I look at them from the outside.

2   You didn't react to the stuff I unloaded yesterday [loud stomach gurgles]. Listen to my stomach! I thought you'd be angry, sick, and disgusted, and throw me out. My stomach is gurgling nonstop. It was so reassuring to me that you didn't react yesterday. I remember how my parents were upset and angry with me when they discovered that I didn't deliver a letter from the teacher about me to them. My stomach is gurgling on and on. I used to imagine your face as being so stern. Father came across as stern and hostile to friends that sister and I brought home. I had to keep explaining that he really isn't; he just acts that way.

3   I keep thinking about marrying Brad. Do I move to New York and switch analysts? Or do I stay here? I feel tension and my ulcer has been kicking up. The whole idea of leaving the analysis scares me. Today and last night I've been feeling jumpy. Just this moment I had a pain that was incredibly sharp and vivid. I had been thinking that the ulcery symptoms were related to work pressure. I

haven't had any when I'm with Brad. But when I talk about marrying him, going to New York, and leaving the analysis, the pain is as sharp as if a little gremlin nicked my stomach lining with a sharp knife just to remind me he was still there. The idea of marriage occurs more often than I mention it here, but when I say I'd go to New York, I get that sharp twinge. It's a strange thought, that there's someone inside me, in my stomach, ready to hurt me, if I should consider leaving here.

11/9-11/26, Interim Summary

She has had another visit with Brad, but is disappointed at his reluctance to be physically close, and reacts with aggressive and castrating remarks about him. She is using douches for the vaginal discharge. She continues to feel greatly relieved at having disclosed her masturbation secrets. She is becoming more aware of her tendency to deny the presence of the analyst. Another episode of masturbation occurs during which she seemed detached from what she was doing. The next day an upper respiratory infection develops. She received a list of Datamate names and some calls but is not eager to respond. There are memories of fights with her sibling, not tolerated by the parents—with mother frequently developing a sick headache whenever there was a family altercation. The patient emphasizes how difficult it is for her to part with anything she produces: hawks phlegm and swallows it with great ease; used to bite out nails, chew, and then swallow them; also picked nose and ears; couldn't let any secretions go. Several calls from Datamate seem to be from passive, unintelligent men and evoke a strong reaction in her of wanting to devaluate them. She is more aware of the tendency to overreact to hostility by the need to please everybody. Finally, she went out with one of the men who turned out to be a bore. A scheduled physical examination by her internist was seemingly negative.

11/27

My watch has been broken a long time, and I brought it to the store to be fixed today. It'll be two weeks before I get it back. Yesterday I did quite a lot. I regulate my life so much by the clock that I was surprised to find I did more and got more out of the day yesterday, when it broke. 1

It's funny—more pain. I've been having trouble with hemorrhoids this weekend. I didn't mention it to my internist whom I saw recently because I wasn't bothered then. I'll call him today to ask about the blood tests he took and then tell him about the hemorrhoids. It was frightening to wipe myself and see blood. In all my life I haven't had any bowel trouble like this. My ulcer isn't bothering me, and it seems as if my physical symptoms are shifting. I'll also have to call my gynecologist; I don't think I'm rid of that trichomonas. But my 2 tummy feels fine. I wish I didn't get physical symptoms so easily. The hemorrhoids began hurting more after I had a large bowel movement.

3   I had dinner with Jane and her husband Saturday night. I seemed to enjoy myself, but didn't feel so involved with them as I have in the past. I then had a dream about him and Kathy, the receptionist in my office. He got her into some kind of trouble, not pregnancy, in the dream. I wondered how she knew him. Maybe I had introduced them, then I realized that they had met independently. Kathy's mother is dead. Kathy lives in a big house with her father, seems well adjusted, and always nicely cheerful. I talked with Jane during the course of the week, and that's when she asked me over for dinner Saturday night. I felt funny because that's a traditional date night. My impression of her husband has changed. He was far more interested in the football game than he was in Jane's or my conversation. He always gives me a kiss and all this physical baloney. Last year I enjoyed it, but this year I look on it askance when it's coupled with nothing except a damn football game. Brad, though he's less demonstrative, is much more interested in me.

4   After dinner, Jane put out the lights except for three candles and put on Mozart's Requiem. Her husband fell asleep. When he woke, he announced that Jane would stop taking the pill next month. She was annoyed. I don't blame her; that's too private. I had the fantasy—suppose I stopped taking the pill and can't get pregnant right away. As I listened to the music, it made me unhappily nostalgic. It brought back the time when I was painfully uncomfortable with myself—such barren years. I want so much to get married to Brad. My cousin's pregnant. My sister's pregnant. I remember a fragment of a dream I had over the weekend in which I wanted to be pregnant. I seem obsessed with the idea.

5   I'm not feeling much as I talk about this. The words are just coming out. I'm aware of the pain from the hemorrhoids [pause]. I keep feeling conflicted about marriage and the analysis. If Brad wants to marry me soon, before the analysis is over, what would I do? Actually Brad wants me to finish analysis first. He's giving a party in a couple of weeks, so I'll be going down to New York then. Jane and her husband are also invited, but I'm not happy about that [coughs]. I feel blocked. Now I'm getting hoarse. That's aggravating, coming on like this [takes a cough drop]. When I talked with my family on the phone last night, I mentioned that I would be taking a trip with Brad in the near future. My father immediately asked where I was going to stay. I said, "In a lodge." I wouldn't tell them about the rented cottage. My father came out flatly and said, "You're going to stay with Brad." I said, "Don't be ridiculous." I just didn't feel like talking to them any more. Here I am with my parents kidding me. I've taken pains over the years to create the impression of a nun in a convent. If my mother ever knew about my first affair she'd have been desolated.

6   All the time I was growing up, mother was deaf, wearing cumbersome hearing aids, wearing clothes designed to cover the equipment. These aids are so much less obtrusive these days. You never knew what mother was going to hear

and what she wasn't. You had to be careful about what you said. When I listened to that Mozart Requiem it took me back to a time that was unhappy. I was so disturbed when I was a student at college though it was so sheltered there. But I wasn't really happy or well adjusted. I had such sick friends, and yet those were the kind of people I could relate to.

11/28

I have some very nice things to mention [closes window]. I called my   1
internist. He said my blood is the best it's ever been. He told me that the hematocrit is 35 and the hemoglobin is 12.1, for the first time at those levels in over 10 years. So exciting! If I feel sluggish or tired, I can't blame it on a low blood count now.

Brad called last night. I was so happy to hear from him. He and I were eating   3
avocados as we talked. I really do miss him. I spoke to my internist about the stupid hemorrhoids. Like describing my personality. He asked if they were painful and told me if they continue to bother me to get a surgeon to take a look. I told him that my ulcer was less troublesome and that I was hopeful that my hemorrhoids will give way. You know, the first time I had an indication of rectal bleeding was the time Brad visited my family with me after we'd been on a short trip. I was under tremendous tension then, got terribly tight, constipated. I wondered what they'd think of him; fortunately, though Brad and father had a few heated discussions about politics, things turned out better than I expected. I think my physical condition has changed. I don't feel the need to worry so much about my stomach. Even when I run out of milk. I don't know if my stomach is better or if I feel better in general. Anyway, I'm taking too many pills: Contac, Vitamin C, birth control pills, and Flagyl for the trichomonas. All these physical complaints get me so concerned at times. I feel now as though I'm just talking—about nothing that matters.

Oh! I had a dream about Joe. He's a fellow I used to know. In it a girl from   3
my high school class, Sandra, came up to join us. She had an engagement ring on, and I realized they were engaged [gesticulating right hand]. Sandra was redheaded with a round face. Makes me think of Brad [right hand on stomach, left hand by side]. I spoke to him about his fat face—maybe he's sensitive about it. He has a stubby nose. I have such a horsey face and long nose [right hand touches nose]. I look like father. Brad and I both are built on a large scale. When I think of raising a family with him, I wonder which features our children would inherit. I wouldn't want a child of mine to feel as unattractive as I did. Yet I remember that a homely girl in my class was very popular and married early and well. So I can't use that excuse of being unattractive.

It bothers me that I'm not working hard here. I'm not connecting [waves   4
arms around]. I'm lying here, not putting this disconnected stuff together, maybe leaving it to you. If you ask me if I'd said anything significant in the past

week, I couldn't think of it. There are loose ends to be tied up. It's sort of like not wearing my watch. I'm so used to these intellectual connections and putting intellectual packages together.

5   It's as if the world around me had no gravity. Here I am closed up in a tight, earthbound brick wall. If I broke down the walls, all kinds of terrible things would come rushing on me. I feel if I knocked down those walls, I'd float suspended in air. One wall I have to break down is the wall between you and me. I remember that redheaded girl that used to come before me. She'd leave the office and say goodbye in a soft voice, though she was hard-looking. I used to think—what's going on in there? Yesterday it occurred to me that you said goodbye to me in a soft tone. You're really nice, you've really helped me. I didn't think of the situation here in a personal way before. Now I see this place as more homelike. I must have been jealous of that other patient. ["Who has red hair like the girl in the dream."] That's right! Like a family situation: she's your favorite and I'm the outsider. It's funny. Now I have this strange sensation of floating, almost as if I were about to go off to sleep.

11/29

1   Yesterday started off without anxiety, but then I got a couple more calls from this Datamate thing. One of the fellows sounded very nice. He asked me for dinner Friday night and I agreed, but I feel tense about it.

2   [Closes window.] My hands are cold. I don't know whether I like the couch prewarmed or not. I don't like to share it.

3   To go or not to go. This is one situation which I can't figure out. The guy said he's forty and divorced and in personnel work. He sounds sophisticated. He's a stranger here—I feel sorry for him. He's from California. If it weren't for Brad, I wouldn't have this doubt. I get restless wishing he were around, but he's not around. Here I am with fantasies of marrying Brad, then catch myself in a position where I've agreed to go out with someone else [right hand gesticulating]. I'm all mixed up. Maybe I want the feeling that men like me [pause].

4   Maybe my hemoglobin of 12.1 might be in response to the pill—the steroids in it which, I understand, are supposed to be good for building up the blood. My bone marrow has been described as depressed. I know I've been feeling depressed on and off. If I get pregnant, will my blood drop? My internist doesn't know I'm taking the pill. I really don't know what will happen between Brad and me. Maybe you don't think it's such a terrible thing to go out with this other guy [both hands on stomach]. Things are O.K. one day, and then there's a crisis the next. Why the hell do I think going out with this guy is improper? [Gesticulates with right hand.] If he tries to kiss me, I'll freeze.

5   Ever since this afternoon, I've had vague stomach discomfort, right after I finished talking with an angry, depressed lady colleague at work who's being divorced. I remember mother's feeling sick if there was anger around her. I feel

anxious now. Here I am going off to do bad things with men. I must have been, still am, scared to death of mother's getting angry; it happened so rarely. I recall it when she told me about father's pursuing another woman [gesticulating right hand]. It's still hard to believe. I feel as though I've got to burp and can't. Thinking how people or kids want to get rid of something. It's an awful feeling. A burp brings real relief. I used to throw up with my period and also get bad cramps. After throwing up I'd feel better. Now I'm feeling mildly nauseated in here. I can't remember having this before. I think one Thanksgiving at my aunt's, where there was a lot of excitement, I threw up the whole dinner. The idea of my father pursuing another woman is unacceptable [rubs eyes, then leaves left hand on forehead]. I feel so damned uncomfortable inside—so nauseous, not ulcery. Introduce me to a man and I get sick. My mind's wandering. All I can think of is this nausea. I've got to pull my mind together intellectually. What's scaring me? [Men scare you and also make you angry.] They really do, beginning with father. Mother's scared of men. Brad turns out not to be so scary, but I'm afraid he's going to yell at me. I remember father's angry look. It makes me take my breath in.

12/1

I had an unbelievable dream the night before. I just thought of what I have   1
to wear for dinner. A real creep called last night. I told him I was busy and he got the clue. Anyway, in the dream, will you believe I was lying on a couch listening to a psychiatric lecture, not from you behind there? Instead there was a guy beside me on the left. It reminds me that when I sleep with Brad, he sleeps on the right. I turn around and talk to the guy beside me. Suddenly he rolls on top of me. The message was: let's go to bed, and I went along, feeling I couldn't say no, though I was scared. I followed him into a house where there were children around, though asleep. We went into an L-shaped room; at one end there was a little bed with a little girl. Around the corner was a double bed. I said that we'd wake the girl, but he said we wouldn't. He started to play with my nipples, using his teeth. Then he moved downward and started kissing my belly and then buried his face in my genitalia. The next thing, I thought, would be intercourse, with his penis inside me. I then woke up sexually aroused and scared. As I lay there awake, I thought of the little girl and how much I could have heard from my parents' room when I was a little girl. The dream room resembles my room; in it was a high bed—and I once had one [gesticulating as she describes location of her bed in relation to her parents' room].

I had another dream the same night about a brooding castle in which there   2
was a mysterious lord of the manor and a little governessy type, taking care of his children and both secretly admiring each other. The flavor of the dream was dark brown, and that characterizes father to a T. I get an ulcery feeling every time I think about my date: he has a stepchild in college. That takes me aback.

He's in his early forties—parental age. I'm in my mid-thirties, though I don't look it. I think I look like a young kid [left hand over mouth]. This mixup in generations gets me anxious and my stomach anxious [hands flat on stomach]. I suddenly think of all the stuff I have to do at work [rolls up sweater sleeves]. Now I'm in the past. There we are, sitting at the dinner table. Mother, the square, would ask father to make us behave. He really joked about it with us. We had an allegiance with him against mother.

3   In that first dream, the little girl would wake up frightened hearing the sexual stuff. I was both people in the dream—the little girl and the grownup girl. A frightening and exciting scene. You say how I'm scared of men. I know I am. Why do I get into such ghastly situations with them? [Partly to disprove you're scared; partly to ward off anticipated rejection.] I have to work so hard at feeling comfortable with men [tears; wipes eyes with lipsticky Kleenex in left hand]. I'm in conflict. I was scared when I was with the guy who took me to the movies last week. I'm worried about trying to disprove I'm scared when I'm with Brad [continues to wipe each eye separately]. Yet I don't think it's that way, because he's so passive. I don't know what it is I want, though I want it so badly. I'd better face it: I'm scared going out with this guy, previously married, over forty, with a college-age stepchild; he could possibly mean business.

4   I was listening to this doctor last night on TV, a real parental figure, talking about LSD with those college kids. What a rapport he had with them. My relationship with my colleagues and superiors is changing for the better. I talk up at meetings and take notes. I feel I understand what they're all talking about. I have to tell some of my assistants that they don't dress properly for the work situation. Dresses are too short, hair is flowing, lipstick is too pale. I feel very uncomfortable about this generation bit: they're very young, trying to emancipate themselves. ["Now you see yourself in another role—that of the forbidding, restricting parent."] All this is making me so sad: that I'm the parent instead of the child [wiping tears with right hand]. I don't want to stop being a child. I don't want to give that up. When I think of myself as still being a child, I can somehow think of avoiding responsibilities and danger. Being a parent means losing the child role. Growing up seems to mean losing, instead of gaining. Opening the window of my bedroom is going out into the vast, swirly emptiness of the outside world [loud stomach gurgling]. It makes me want to retreat. My stomach is grumbling, it sounds so empty. I remember as a child being afraid of the cars outside driving right into the bedroom window and killing me. There's something comforting about Brad's apartment. The walls keep him from going away [rests left hand on office wall]. I don't like it when I'm cold. There are times when I'm scared of being outdoors. I have to screw up my courage to get outside. Then, too, I'll lose contact with people if there aren't walls to hold them.

12/4 - 12/17, Interim Summary

Dates evoke no spark. Memories from the past: at age five, room and bed downstairs were backed up to wall of parents' bedroom; when new baby was born, patient was moved upstairs and remembers being in bed that whole summer with "bronchitis." She recalls that illness was her way of handling the loss of her room, her place in the family, and the presence of an intruder, the new baby, by whom she felt shoved out of her mother's affections.

Another episode of masturbation occurs during insomnia caused by anxious rumination about going to Brad's party. There is concern about further sexual relations with Brad and need for distance. The identification between Brad and her father is still too close. A fantasy develops that the penis has a separate identity with a destructive potential when it is put inside the woman—linked with recollection of father's huge penis and wondering how mother could accomodate all that bulk without some gross physiologic disruption. Another fantasy: poison from penis spreads through a man, changing him from a Dr. Jekyll to a Mr. Hyde, to be coped with by castration to preserve the nice man.

The patient leaves for New York and Brad, not sure her vaginal infection has been cleared up and feeling quite ambivalent about the relationship. She is also concerned about persistent trouble with hemorrhoids, some bleeding, and is reminded of her first menstrual flow about which mother told father in her embarrassed presence. Visit with Brad is somewhat better than usual; she is just beginning to feel a sexual sensation, though unable to have an orgasm as yet. On her return she continues to be concerned about itching genitals, visits gynecologist again, and is told that the infection has cleared up. This is specifically reported: "Felt itchy genitals." Went to see the doctor again today. He told me that there's nothing there. But it's itchy and twitchy. I thought there was still a whitish discharge, but the doctor said no. I guess I had talked myself into thinking I still had an infection. When I had intercourse with Brad, I couldn't be sure about it; I thought it stung a little but I couldn't be sure. The doctor rhapsodically described the beautiful, gorgeous state of my vagina. I thought to myself: turn it off! He said he had never seen a more perfect, healthy vagina. All I replied was thank you. I told him I would tell my analyst about this. He said, 'Then I don't have to counsel you.' He's homespun. He held my coat for me as I got ready to leave. But even as he was telling me I was O.K., I still itched. I thought that's different from having an ulcer which is something that's really there. In this situation I can't be sure that something is actually wrong there every time I have a twinge. . . . As a child I was greatly preoccupied with genitalia, with excretions, and I was very secretive and fascinated and guilty. Parents ran around without clothes. Father still does. I talk about this and Oh! do I itch. Recently father walked stark naked from the bathroom to his bedroom after taking a shower, just as I stepped out of my room. Maybe in my thirties I'll be able to handle it better than at thirteen, when I was startled and staggered by the size of father's genitalia. I can see mother being hysterical. It's like a blind spot in my home. People went around naked, but you weren't supposed to see. I still react that way, wanting to look and feeling I shouldn't."

12/18

[Late five minutes.]

1   I guess I overslept this morning. But I had such a disturbing dream. I dreamt I was in bed. This girl came into the room to interview me for a magazine, but I didn't want to be interviewed. She followed me around and when I couldn't shake her, I started hitting and scratching her. I got panicked. My father was sitting at a desk in a house in our hometown near the railroad station. The room was dark. He was answering the telephone—like I do at work. I asked him to help me. He said I shouldn't pay any attention to the girl, and she would go away. He told her to get out, so she disappeared but then came back. I crouched down behind a screen. It was narrow and I was scared I'd be discovered. She found me again. I wanted to sleep and she wouldn't let me. I was furious and pummelled her. I went to call the police and then woke up.

2   It sounds strange, homosexual. I resented mother doing things for me, fixing my collar, my clothes in general—when I wanted to do it myself. Once a roommate of mine, lushly built, was standing in my room with another girl, giggling while I was in bed reading. She had a devilish glint in her eyes, suddenly ran and jumped on me in bed. I had a furious reaction, gave her a big kick, and pushed her off. Same feeling as in the dream. It was a homosexual threat. When my sister was developing as an adolescent, she would come into my room in nothing but underpants and say she was in a bus, then stand there and jiggle. I would get upset and close my eyes, but she would persist. It was a combination of fascination and revulsion.

3   I had another Datamate date Saturday night. A bizarre experience. The guy was bright, in research at Harvard. He had a beard and wore a beret. He looked odd. We took public transportation, since he didn't have a car. He talked in a finicky, desiccated manner, enunciating too clearly and precisely. He emphasized details in such a way as to shut off communication and rambled on about himself almost nonstop all evening. His nice qualities tended to be hidden by this behavior. He was criticizing doctors in general. He liked only those who explained things carefully. While I was with him, he took three different kinds of pills. He had a cold. A lot about that fellow reminded me of myself in the old days. [Scratches back]. I have an itch there. This fellow was different from the others. He was more prone to touch me, put his hand on my arm, the small of my back to shepherd me through doors and through traffic. It was distasteful and reminds me of the dream. It has a sexual connotation. I respond more

favorably to the dates who wouldn't touch me with a ten-foot pole. I reacted violently to this other fellow's touching me. In fact, I shuddered violently at his touch.

Had a ball at the office party on Friday. Lots of fun talking with the fellows. There was one immature fellow who did some half-hearted propositioning. I cut him down verbally and then felt guilty [loud stomach gurgle]. This guy was so immature that I wasn't scared of him.

I was still so worried about that trichomonas infection that I went looking for a textbook on psychosomatic illness [!]. I found one by Dunbar for general practitioners and looked at the chapter on genitourinary disease. There was a paragraph on trichomonas, and it said that 80 percent of women who have this are diagnosed frigid. I reacted violently to that. I went back to my office and didn't have another itch the rest of the day. But it's very hard for me to feel any sensation during intercourse. When I masturbate, I find it easy to note to what I'm responding, and I feel more sensation through the clitoris. I'm very embarrassed to admit such sexual feelings.

12/19

I feel as though I'm coming down with something: achey, feverish, headachey and stuffed nose. I always wish that it's something going on emotionally. I had a very frustrating evening last night. Things were broken that had to be repaired, and I had a lot of errands to do. I finally came home after fruitlessly looking for a ski rack and a sweater stitcher. As soon as I came in, the phone rang and it was Brad. That pleased me and for a while I felt happy. Then, watching a TV documentary about a far-off land, I got a feeling of alienation one must experience in a foreign place. Everything was so different. Then I got to bed and had a nightmare.

In this dream I was setting up housekeeping in a two-room alcove apartment given to me by my landlady. It was open to the rest of the house and crammed with old furniture. The only thing in it was the sink. I remember rearranging the furniture. Then I brought father to look at it. When we got there, it was changed around again and lots of things had been taken away. I realized the bed—a great big canopied, Victorian one—had gone, and now there was a single bed, too short for me. Next to that was a double bed. I realized mother had switched this on me. The white kitchen sink was gone, replaced by a rose-colored bathroom sink. I was furious at mother. We screamed and fought with each other. Mother then rushed out, and I started to cry bitterly. Outside was a beach, and mother was lying on it. I went and lay beside her with outstretched hands. We told each other we didn't want to fight.

That dream just reminds me of how conflicted I've been about separating from my folks. It's as if I'm trying to rearrange my life, and there's still interference from them. That homosexual dream the night before—I wonder if it's connected with this reconciliation with mother. I've never been physically comfortable with her. I remember years ago it was on a beach where mother told me how upset she was about the other woman whom father was interested in. Father doesn't like the beach, neither does Brad. But I love it. Listen to my stomach gurgle, yet I'm not really hungry. I think of myself as having been the pawn between father and mother. Why did mother and I get into such a horrible fight? She had taken my life and tried to switch it around and make it indistinguishable from her life, trying to pull me back into a childish, dependent position. That sink—I'm reminded I have to douche tonight. I've been mildly itchy. I've sat on the bathtub douching, and it's as if I'm fusing my bathtub and that sink. Getting rid of the sink is like interrupting my independent life and being pulled back into the family nest. Just this minute I got an awful itch. Now I think of my feet getting cut off to fit the short bed. I think of that awful play, *The Devils*, with bloody torture and bloody feet. Things being cut off. Am I feminine or masculine? Now I'm back to thinking of that conflict between my desire to arrange things myself and fury at interference from mother, but then again there's that yearning for closeness with her. ["Any reference to the analytic situation?"] Hadn't thought of that.

12/20

1   I slept well and long, had dreams, but can't remember them. As I was leaving here yesterday and thought of your reference to my being very angry at you, I just remembered—I'll be missing the Friday before New Year's. If you can think of skipping an hour such as Christmas and New Year, I can tell you about missing one, too, but I had delayed doing it until now.

2   I was wondering as I was leaving yesterday whether I'm sick with a cold because I'm upset about being angry with my mother. Maybe I was coming down with something because of the troubles that were expressed in the dream. Last night I slept ten hours. I felt better today, but was woozy last night though I managed to do things about the apartment. After thinking out that conflict between mother and myself, and the anger that I felt, I immediately began to feel better. Mother used to say, "When you kids fight, you make me sick." As if anger is a quantity of some sort of substance—a noxious vapor. It reminds me of the fairy tale of the bad sister who spat out bad words, vipers, and frogs, and the good sister who spewed forth pearls. It's as if anger is a noxious gas, felling my mother. I think of flatulence and farting. If you have to fart, it's a relief when you do.

3   Now I hear my watch and the clock ticking [pause]. Now I'm blocking [pause].

4   I'm annoyed about Christmas in a way. I'm going home, but will be there only a short time, and then will visit with my sister [pause]. I have a tendency

to immerse myself in the other person's interests and neglect my own. I'm mad at myself for having put a blouse whose color ran with my nylons and then having to waste time getting the color out.

Reference to Christmas and church matters reminds me that you're Jewish. There are old remnants of snobbery cropping up. I feel I've got to put you in your place, cut you down to size all the time. Yet I feel so helped by you. So it's unrealistic to be angry. It's like you were my mother. I get this contemptuous feeling more about mother than father. I must have been in cahoots with father to derogate mother. Mother—ech—she's so emotional. I tolerate her with amused contempt. Yet this is what I'm afraid other people think of me. To take things from my mother means totally subjugating myself to her.

I feel far away today, talking in clouds of cotton wool. I'm giving out with a lot of words which don't mean very much. My friend, Lucy, asked me for dinner tonight. She was mad at her sister whom she asked for the use of a car, and her sister wouldn't lend it to her. Lucy sticks her neck out. She makes me feel she's panicky and manipulative, and I get ticked off at her right away.

12/22

I overslept this morning, but didn't panic. I just skipped breakfast. I feel depressed because I woke with a backache after having a depressing dream. Brad called Wednesday asking about whether I could go to Europe with him next spring. He suggested another couple might join us. Once again other people are mixing in and that irritates me. I'll be seeing Brad next weekend and talk it over with him. I think it would be better if just the two of us went.

I had a dream this morning. It must be in relation to Christmas and going home. It concerned my landlady and her daughter encroaching on my privacy. I felt helpless and depressed. They were saying that I've got to take garbage down every day. I hate to do it anyway. They said, "It stinks and you've got to get it out every day." I suggested that a garbage can be left near the back door, or else build a dolly on wheels. The apartment looked kind of empty. Then the landlady's daughter pointed out that I had left a light on in the hall and that I couldn't do it—so that was another mistake. I then went to their bathroom and had a bowel movement, feeling very guilty. I remember having a vivid impression of having a bowel movement in bed and half-awake reaching under to see if it was really there. I recall the time I was hospitalized with severe anemia, when I fainted and was incontinent. The dream seemed to be a continuation of the one I had about mother, but the quality was so different? [How do you mean?] I was so depressed, defeated, burdened with everybody imposing these rules. Mother used to tell us what to do. If anybody got angry at her, she would complain of sickness. I grew up feeling I couldn't express anger. Those two dreams are like the sequence of what happened! Mother tells me what to do; I get furious. Then the next thing she talks of is her distress, so what do you do—you feel guilty. There was one ray of hope in that dream: suggesting that the garbage can be kept in a more reasonable place. It's a pain to take the garbage can out. I have a pain in the back now, lifting all that garbage. What a cruddy job! Mothers give such chores to boys more often than to girls.

3   I remember as a kid when I left a light burning, my grandmother got after me for that. She was a good woman but a martinet who was very strict about wasting electricity. Mother would refer to our untidiness as children two weeks after she had been picking books up and putting our clothes away. She wanted us to be tidy without disciplining us. She vowed she wouldn't treat her kids the way she was treated, so she bent over backwards too far to avoid expressing her anger. [Can it be that you yourself in effect are bending over backwards to avoid expressing your hostility?] I'm so afraid I'll injure people—you know that dream where I was fighting with mother and found her lying on a beach, crying. I had to say I didn't mean it, although I did mean it.

4   Another part of this morning's dream involved going to the john in someone else's toilet. Thumbing my nose. Smelling up the house. That order to take the garbage out every day because I was smelling the house up too much. That makes half-assed sense to me [!]. As if, when I get confronted, I had to tell the dream backwards [!]. Having a bowel movement in their bathroom is an aggressive act so I had to disguise it.

5   I used to act in many ways to upset mother, and when she got upset it would be as if it were a personal attack on her. On the other hand, I would carry dirty dishes to the kitchen to please her and avoid her having a headache, rather than it being something that one does anyway. Mother never asked me to help her cook and that's one thing I really love to do, but had to learn it on my own.

12/27

1   I'm glad to be here this afternoon. I got so ticked off at the secretary of our department; she's a wordy old girl. But I'm beginning to assert myself. Not only that, but I'm trying to understand why I'm angry when I'm aware of feeling that way.

2   One of the things my mother said over the weekend made my hair stand on end. Mother told my niece, Helen, "Carry your coat yourself; your poor mother [that's my sister] is so tired carrying that new baby." I could see little Helen tense up. That was the wrong thing to say. I can hear my mother, when she was pregnant with my sister, saying to me, "Mommy is tired carrying the baby, so work harder and help out."

3   When I got home last night, I again noticed those damn hemorrhoids. They hadn't bothered me for a while, but now they're painful and bleeding again. I never filled my internist's prescription. I guess it's because it's a symptom that

depends on how I feel, and it should go away. I was so mad at that secretary at the office; I could have swatted her. She gave me unasked-for advice. I couldn't get a straight answer out of her without a thousand words of explanation. I feel as though she's a bottleneck who garbles things and is a bad channel of communication. But why do I get so worked up over this? I also felt frustrated about another matter at work. I was upset with myself getting so tensed up again. I was trying to reach a key executive at work and felt stymied. That's what I felt about father when I visited my folks and he had to have his way. He frustrated me unnecessarily when I wanted to stay with some friends a while longer, insisting we get to my sister's early. She was expecting us late. I feel like crying now. I have a lump in my throat, and it's painful to talk. I feel so frustrated that I want to kick, scream, and throw a tantrum like a two-year-old. What I want doesn't seem to matter, even now, unless it fits in with what my parents want.

When I was at my sister's, little Helen was terribly overexcited. Her father,   4
my brother-in-law, was tickling her when she was obviously already excited by its being Christmas and by all the guests. She started to hit him and he angrily said, "Don't raise your hands to me." He was joined in this by my sister.

[At this point the patient, who had herself been obviously tense and had   5
been speaking in a high-strung voice, suddenly calmed down.] I remember snuggling up to my father. Suddenly I feel as if all my anger has been drained off. I want to have control over my feelings [loud stomach gurgling]. Oh! Shut up, stomach! Crying is a release, sidetracking my angry feelings. I just started to think of sex with Brad—losing control in bed. How come when I get so furious and frustrated, I want to cry? It's like being reduced to being a baby.

I left my knitting, my camera, mother's goodies, all at my sister's . . .   6
thinking of four whole days with Brad . . . .

It's literally painful for me to say I get mad at my father—I get the lump in   7
the throat feeling. Father's order had to be obeyed, but it was a whim. It came down to whether he did what his daughter wanted or what he wanted. He didn't weigh the merits of the choices. He was tickled, however, that he got his own way. He was the boss—take it or leave it.

12/28 - 1/15, Interim Summary

She continues to be strongly ambivalent about Brad, wanting to gain his approval in a masculine direction as with father, yet also wanting to be cared for by him. There is concern about mutual sexual difficulties and particularly about latent masculine tendencies in herself. A depressive mood persists for several days, reinforced by the news of father's pulmonary difficulties. There is rumination about her tendency to be passive with men who are forceful and her need to defend herself against this by adopting an active role also. The more marriage seems likely, even in fantasy, the more anxious she gets. There is more rumination about being able to keep up with Brad, with father, and considerable stomach reactivity.

1/16

1   [Late five minutes.]

2   I've been driving aggressively, very angry at slow traffic and poky drivers. As I come to grips with problems about Brad, I swing from one extreme to another. For instance, tonight I'm looking forward to a Datamate date. I ought to be more involved with Brad, but distance interferes. Love needs to be nourished. I'd like him to woo me for a change. I've sent him three things in the mail. I guess it's true that I'm walking on eggs as far as he's concerned. It's more complicated than just a fear of being rejected myself. It refers to a fear of my being too aggressive and forcing him into passivity. I'm nervous about being together with him on a long trip. I guess that's another reason my feelings take a negative swing. I'm either ready for marriage, or I don't want to see him again. I sound as if I'm giving you a lecture on my own psychodynamics. I act as if I'm a living doormat [loud stomach rumbling]. Now even as I say it, my angry feelings are receding. I yelled at someone in my office today. This guy is an aggressive bastard who took my dictaphone without asking permission. Yet he was friendly to me later in the day.

It's a new experience for me to get mad. It's an exercise of power. I seem to be lining up on the side of the females versus the males. What would Brad do if I raised some questions about our relationship? I see him as either collapsing or saying we're not suited.

3   I had a dream last night about two children or dolls. The children were like rag dolls, live dolls. I wasn't sure if they were mine. One was smaller than the other, and its head kept drooping. It seemed as if I was taking them to the doctor. That was all there was to the dream. I've thought that if I touched an infant so that its fragile balance was disturbed, then its head would flop. Why were there two children? My sister's baby is due any minute, any day, though it may slide into February. One of my cousins is going to the obstetrician, might be pregnant, is what mother told me. Mother shouldn't have told me, she knows I'd be jealous; she's such a blabbermouth [loud stomach rumbling]. I'm the same way about my relationship with Brad. I have reasonable doubts about it,

4   but Brad and I will try to settle them between us. I'd like my mother to feel that the possibility of marriage is not for her special gratification [crying].

MARGINAL NOTES

6/2

1,2. Loss and restitution. Transference implications.

3. Shifting oral gratifications compensate for inferiority feelings. Anxiety about attracting men.

4. Activated concern about bodily integrity. Denial of death fears. Masochistic fantasy.

5. Fear of pregnancy, of dangers associated with femininity.

6. Hostility to men seen as selfish, exploiting, and sadistic; concurrent wish for power over men.

7. Frigidity and pseudo-orgasm.

8. Intellectualization.

9. Identity split and Oedipal conflict.

6/6

1. Self-devaluation and hypersensitivity to external criticism.

2. Interoceptive percepts: related to intermittent stomach dysfunction activated by stress interview; self-accustaion of not being a good mother.

3. Another kind of interoceptive percept, probably a conversion phenomenon, in the same body area.

6/7

1. Transference reaction: hostile, erotic, dependent elements. Defense mechanisms of denial and projection.

2. Identification with victimized woman and attempts to cope with hostility toward men.

3. Stomach dysfunction, linked with loss, hostility, guilt, and reversal of mother-child role in stress interview previously referred to.

4. Intellectualization: guilt related to aggressive and sexual impulses linked with interoceptive pain percepts, hunger, and motor activity.

5. Anticipatory stress anxiety linked with continuing interoceptive percepts.

6/8 - 7/5 Summarized in text with dynamic formulations.

7/6

1. Reassurance.

2. Interoceptive-auditory percepts linked with hostility at anticipated rejection instead of with hoped for nurture.

3. Masochistic sexual fantasies associated with intense voyeuristic stimulation in childhood.

4. Control a defense against fear of being overwhelmed.

5. Voyeuristic recollections activate vasomotor response, a somatic expression of mixed anxiety and sexual excitement.

7/7

1. Resistance: tardiness a repetition of defiance toward mother.
2. Intellectualization, devaluation.
3. Notes defensiveness; self-pity; reaction formation against hostility.
4. Adolescent competitiveness with boys.
5. Interpretation of transference competitiveness evokes hypersensitivity, tears.

7/11

1. Focus on Brad's problems and ambivalence; hostility ideationally but not affectively expressed; interoceptive percepts.
2. Intellectualization about father-figure. Interpretation followed by hypersensitive reaction. Reaction formation against hostility.
3. Fear of exposure of defects.
4. Anxiety over intellectual competition with men.

7/12

1. Ingratiation. Need for approval.
2. Interoceptive percepts linked with hostile transference.
3. Reassurance.
4. Inferiority feelings.

7/18

1. Marked stage fright. Vivid recollections linked with interoceptive percepts.
2. Increased feelings of feminine inadequacy, need for self-nurture.
3. Intensely masochistic associations linked with fear of loss of control, irrevocable rejection, further activating feelings of depletion and need for nurture.

7/20

1. Hostility; only partial affective discharge. Stress linked with stomach dysfunction, interoceptive-auditory percepts.
2. Sexual secretions, masturbation associated with anal elements.
3. Transference; separation stress and verbalized concern about effect on body connected with recollections of physical shock.
4. Voyeuristic recollections; excretory, anal aspects of male sexuality.
5. Interoceptive percepts linked with anniversary reaction, frustrated oral needs and hostility.

7/21

1. Fear of sadistic men.
2. Continued hostility: partial affective and partial behavioral discharge. Being the martyr and feeling guilty. Recollection of rebelliousness during toilet-training.
3. Detachment from an object relationship.
4. More hostility now linked to dyspnea. Need to ingratiate self with men, especially father.

7/25

1. Exposure to viral agent. Frigidity, linked with unresolved Oedipal remainders.
2. Sexual frustration, activated tension, and somatic reaction.
3. Identification with pregnant sister; self-destructive behavior.
4. Fear of pregnancy and its detection by mother-figure. Inhibition of voyeurism.
5. Transference: hostility at being left with activated dependency needs.
6. Anxiety: partial affective discharge and partial somatic discharge linked with infantile sexual concepts of oral impregnation. Interoceptive-auditory percepts.

7/26 - 9/6 Summer interruption.

9/7 - 10/19 Summarized in text with dynamic formulations.

10/20

1. Anal themes including loss of sphincter control, linked with hospitalization. Dependence on, domination by mother and reactive rebelliousness reflected in transference. Defenses against dependency: exaggerated independence and passive resistance. Attempts at rational understanding.
2. Screen memory of masturbation forbidden by mother. Concern about defective genitalia symbolized in briefcase associations.

10/24

1. Dream of 10/20 acted on.
2. Transference: feeling exposed and out in the cold, interpreted. Childhood fears: projection of own oral sadism; anal attack; intercourse *a tergo*; other symbolic anal libidinal references, both protective and dangerous.
3. References to stigmata associated with forbidden sexual activity.

10/25

1. Interoceptive percepts linked with anticipatory stress and persisting hostility activated by unjust accusations.

2. Hypersensitivity. Low self-esteem.

3. New physical symptom intellectually related to forbidden sexual activity and linked with guilt.

4. Somatic identification, but involving gastrointestinal tract, linked with masochistic fantasies of abandonment and death.

5. Recollections of serious illness, linked with separations from father.

6. Anxious rumination over physical symptom linked with consequences of masturbation.

10/27

1. An incestuous dream with masochistic elements, associated with guilt.

2. Sudden interoceptive pain percept related to being attacked. Subsidence of somatic reaction followed by affective response. Both linked with incestuous-like acting out the previous evening, defended against by rationalization, but insufficiently.

10/30

1. Reassurance.

2. Attempts at self-diagnosis, self-accusation, and devaluation; similar reaction to skin eruption; fear of exposure, partial affective discharge.

3. Activated heterosexual anxiety may lead to homosexual fantasies.

4. Incestuous associations.

5. Warning and possible discovery by mother activate Oedipal anxiety and guilt expressed in somatic equivalents.

10/31 - 11/7 Summarized in text with dynamic formulations.

11/8

1. Transference: continuing affect buildup and need for avoidance of looking despite partial relief after confessional. Additional discharge pathway activated: a somatic one.

2. Recollection of parental anger and expectation of rejection by analyst after confessional, linked with a second somatic discharge pathway; interoceptive-auditory percepts.

3. Associations involving stresses of possible marriage and transference loss linked with stomach symptoms and almost immediately followed by intense interoceptive pain percepts. Introjection and symptom personification with libidinal, symbolic elements.

11/9 - 11/26 Summarized in text with dynamic formulations.

11/27

1. Defective watch—extension of self—finally repaired.

2. First reference to painful hemorrhoids. Shifting site of organ dysfunction as somatic pathway of discharge.

3. Dream suggestive of incest but the incestuous figure appears to be increasingly detached and disinterested in women.

4. Fear of sterility.

5. Absence of affect. Pain percepts. Ambivalence. Reluctance to talk expressed somatically through laryngeal dysfunction.

6. Recollections of mother's physical defect; anxiety about her reactions. Recollections of tensions at college.

11/28

1. Reassurance about bodily integrity.

2. Onset of rectal symptoms linked with stress. Shifting site of physical dysfunction. Oral elements. Denial.

3. Comparison of her masculine appearance with Brad's feminine one, and anxiety about the effect on their children through inheritance.

4. Resistance: defense of intellectualization.

5. Claustrophobic defense against fearful consequences, linked with possible shift in resistance and emergence of erotic transference in an Oedipal setting. Proprioceptive, equilibratory percepts.

11/29

1. Anticipatory anxiety.

2. Temperature percepts: transference implications.

3. Conflict between guilt and need for reassurance.

4. Intellectualization.

5. Stomach symptoms activated by stress. Dual identification with angry mother and guilty daughter linked with father's infidelity—another Oedipal situation. Awareness of somatic response, followed by idea of what the response symbolizes. Recollection of association between vomiting and dysmenorrhea. Sudden onset of physical symptom linked with father's (men's) infidelity and anger as well as her own hostility.

12/1

1. Highly erotic dream with oral foreplay and transference implications, and linked with primal scene associations.

2. Second dream incestuous with anal implications. Associated with somatic reaction and anticipatory anxiety about date with father-figure. Further associations with childhood recollections of eating, misbehavior, and alliance with father against mother.

3. Fear of men, especially father-figures; counterphobic defense, ingratiation (interpreted). Self-pity.

4. Reversal of roles from child to parent. Longing for perpetual childhood and freedom from responsibility. Fear of growing up—seen as loss. Accompanying somatic reaction with interoceptive-auditory percepts. Need for protective environment.

12/4 - 12/17 Summarized in text with dynamic formulations.

12/18

1. Homosexual dream. Transference implications of asking for help with such deviant tendencies.
2. Recollection of mother's domineering ways and experiences which had homosexual overtones, while growing up. Accompanying excitation and guilt.
3. Devaluation of new male acquaintance who has a cold. Simultaneous identification with many of his aggressive, intellectualizing, pill-taking, and possibly somatic traits. Sensory perceptions and motor responses followed by reference to anxiety about sexualized contact.
4. Castrating tendencies, guilt, and somatic reaction.
5. Continued curiosity and concern about vaginal infection and frigidity during intercourse. Masturbatory gratification, guilt.

12/19

1. Physical prodromata, probably of an upper respiratory infection preceded by an evening of minor stresses.
2. Dream of fighting with, separation from mother, and yearning for, dependency on her.
3. Conflict between dependent needs and independent strivings. Dependency linked with erotic attachment to mother. Interoceptive-auditory percepts. Oedipal and pre-Oedipal aspects of relationship with mother. Independence linked with sexual freedom and possible consequences (somatic). Awareness of physical symptoms: vaginal itch, followed by castration fantasies and question of sexual identity. Further reference to dependence-independence conflict, with possible transference implications.

12/20

1. Retaliation for missing analytic hours on holidays.
2. Partial insight about relationship between guilt over hostility toward mother and development of respiratory infection. Mother's inability to tolerate anger. Hostility linked with oral and anal elements.
3. Auditory percepts. Blocking.
4. Tendency to identify with others. Hostility turned inward.
5. Ambivalent transference attitudes, linked with greater devaluation of mother than father.
6. Concern about intellectualizing. Ambivalence toward a woman friend.

12/22

1. Persistent physical symptom following dream. Hostile and depressive elements.
2. Dream concerns relationship with mother, her dominating ways, her refuge in illness when she evoked anger, leading to guilt and the construction of defenses against affective discharge of hostility in the patient. The infantile roots appear to be in the patient's toilet-training experiences. Backache is linked with having to do boy's work.

3. Further associations of domination by grandmother emphasizing no waste and mother emphasizing tidiness. The difference between the two was mother's bending over backward to avoid affective expression of anger. Patient's identification. Direct connection between backache and repressed hostility, interpreted. Fear of hurting people by expressing anger.

4. Anal-olfactory-sadistic elements.

5. Recollection of ambivalent behavior toward mother.

12/27

1. More expression and awareness of anger.

2. Mother's admonitions and guilt-producing remarks to grandchild reminiscent of patient's own early reactions when a sibling was expected.

3. Recurrence of anal somatic dysfunction, linked with hostility at a garrulous, domineering, ineffective mother-surrogate and further hostility at father's frustrating, narcissistic behavior. Interoceptive percepts. Impulse to duplicate infantile temper tantrum.

4. Identification with niece's erotic and hostile reactions.

5. Partial affective discharge shifts to partial somatic discharge. Interoceptive-auditory percepts. Fear of loss of control. Crying a means of discharging rage.

6. Losses, anticipation of more pleasant experiences.

7. Idea of hostility at father accompanied by interoceptive percepts probably due to oesophageal spasm. Father's egotism and narcissism evoke hostility.

12/28 - 1/15 Summarized in text with dynamic formulations.

1/16

1. Resistance.

2. Marked ambivalence. Fears of rejection alternate with fear of aggressiveness. References to passivity, masochism. Intellectualization. Shifting affective and somatic expression of anger. Recollection of earlier outspoken anger (without consequences)—a new experience; but concerned about Brad's reaction to her new confidence in expressing herself.

3. Dream about pregnancy, concern about being a mother. Jealousy of pregnant sister and cousin. Hostility toward mother followed by somatic dysfunction. Feeling pressured about marriage by parents and resenting their narcissistic interest.

4. As hostile affect recedes, stomach dysfunction increases, then as it diminishes, tearfulness sets in.

COMMENT

This patient has had two major episodes of physical illness: anemia of undetermined origin (late adolescence) and acute duodenal ulcer (early twenties), from both of which she recovered. However, minor dysfunction involving one or the other of these previously affected organ systems and an accentuation of psychologic manifestations have recurred as a mixed response to stress. It has been possible to follow and report on these and other shifts in the patient's psychophysical equilibrium in a large number of consecutive analytic hours.

During the first six months of analysis, the patient exhibited a massive reaction formation of politeness and compliance concealing intense hostility. There was also marked penis envy as well as jealousy of other women's femininity. A deep, passive dependency was defended against by a competitive drive to outdo the men in her firm. The patient's hypersensitivity was marked. Masturbation was practiced intermittently as a primary sexual outlet but was only briefly and reluctantly mentioned and was accompanied by considerable guilt. Physical symptoms, mostly epigastric distress and heartburn, were frequently associated with minor increases in tension. As the detailed reporting begins on 6/2, the patient is awaiting the return of a man-friend (Brad), seen as a "last hope" marriage prospect. The summer interruption of the analysis is about six weeks away.

In the first reported interview (6/2) interoceptive percepts linked to the gastrointestinal tract appear. They are associated with references to sadness. Also verbalized is a frequently activated concern about bodily integrity. In this hour, as in many others, an easy tearfulness is evident. It is usually an indication of hypersensitivity to criticism or expected criticism rather than an expression of true sadness. On 6/6 the patient reports two kinds of interoceptive percepts, again referable to the gastrointestinal system. The first is a twisting, turning kind of pain, called familiarly "my ulcery pain," frequently experienced and linked with loss, frustration, separation, and hostility. The second is wavelike, not painful, more an erotic-like sensation, less frequently experienced and representing a somatic equivalent of anxiety associated with repressed sexual tensions. The ulcery pain is again evident on 6/7.

In the next month there is but little decrease in the frequency of gastrointestinal symptoms. However, preoccupation with Brad's return continues. The patient is concerned about her immature tendencies, her masturbation, and her acting out in an Oedipal situation with the husband of a pregnant friend who is about to deliver. Anxiety dreams and epigastric distress immediately precede Brad's visit. After his arrival and departure, the patient experiences an intensely ambivalent reaction to him which diminishes only very slowly. There is mild depression accompanied by continuation of stomach dysfunction. However, she appears to have gained some insight into her own neurotic expectations and Brad's neurotic behavior. Meanwhile more stresses accumulate. Her sister may have a miscarriage. Her mother attempts to interfere in her relationship with Brad. There are intermittent episodes of depressive rumination and stomach pain as she and Brad continue to have difficulties adjusting to each other. Relationships with men are heavily laced with competitive elements. Recollections of resistance to toilet training appear. Interpretations are focused on the need to intellectualize, a defense against feeling the intensity of her emotions. Sex and food appear interrelated, filling what seems like a bottomless void of emotional needs.

On 7/6 masochistic sexual fantasies begin to break into awareness. They are associated with intense, voyeuristic experiences in childhood. These recollections activate a vasomotor response, a somatic expression of mixed anxiety equivalents and sexual excitement. In the next hour (7/7) there is a reaction to the highly charged material of the day before: the patient's defenses are very much in evidence, particularly intellectualization and reaction formation. Hostility toward Brad is manifest in the focus on his emotional difficulties and ambivalence, but there is little affect expressed. There is further development of the patient's competitive, aggressive relations with men in general. On 7/11 interoceptive percepts referable to the stomach are linked with hostile transference and guilt ideationally expressed. On 7/18 the patient reports intense stage fright while auditioning for a place in a local amateur symphony orchestra and reexperiences the marked physical manifestations of the previous evening. The incident leaves her shaken and she is increasingly preoccupied with thoughts of being inadequate and of being unwanted, activating her dependency needs. Anticipation of visiting Brad appears as another stress (7/19). Telephone conversation with him is followed by a surge of hostility expressed in an acute need to defecate. On 7/20 further stresses can be noted. One is referable to the belated recall of the anniversary of father's birthday, and a rush to send him a fitting token in time. Another and continuing stress is the upcoming summer interruption, linked with concern about being able to carry on without the direct help of the analysis. The activated oral needs now cannot be dealt with sufficiently by the usual psychologic defenses and have to find expression intermittently through conditioned somatic outlets.

The patient's hostility is on the increase and on 7/21 becomes mixed with anxiety, but the combined affects are expressed largely through a new somatic equivalent—dyspnea. This respiratory response is probably the result of shifting autonomic nervous system activity. On 7/25 the patient reports the stressful meeting with Brad who has a cold. She is frigid during sexual intercourse with him. Later, much concerned about becoming pregnant, she develops a sore throat. This is a conversion symptom, linked with activated infantile sexual concepts of oral impregnation which appear in disguised ideational form. It is another instance of the somatic breakthrough of an emotional conflict.

During these past seven weeks of analysis, there have been no major shifts in psychophysical equilibrium; however, minor shifts have occurred frequently, though all have been of short duration. The manifestations have been mixed, both psychologic and physical. The latter have represented brief, minimal dysfunction of various organ systems: gastrointestinal, cardiovascular, and respiratory. However, the principal target organ has been the stomach, already the focus of major but circumscribed dysfunction many years ago. Autonomic nervous system activity has appeared to be frequently involved, particularly when sexual tensions were mobilized. Somatic expressions of oral frustration linked with hostility have been reflected largely in stomach hyperperistalsis and hyperacidity. No discrete physical illness has been noted during this period of almost two months.

The ambivalent relationship with Brad continues through the summer and into the fall. The patient goes on "the pill." Her stomach symptoms gradually become less troublesome. However, as the detailed reporting of the analysis is resumed, she has growing expectations of the worst happening at work, socially, and in the treatment. This anxiety is related to an upsurge in infantile sexual conflicts. Many recollections of intense voyeuristic experiences appear linked with oral-incorporative and castrating fantasies centered around father's penis. Defensive comparisons of herself with men involve the need to control all situations involving them. Frigidity in sexual intercourse continues. Although there is a growing desire to be more womanly. she is fearful of the great passivity, dependency, and masochism which might then come to the fore. She next experiences an episode of minor somatic dysfunction: a weekend of physical malaise and slight fever is followed by an upper respiratory infection with persistent postnasal drip and cough. Again her activated oral needs are being expressed in somatic form. The patient takes a number of different cold remedies, sucks constantly on cough drops, and babies herself.

On 10/20 the patient has dreams which reflect her conflict about sexual identity, specifically referable to defective genitalia, and there are also anal themes which concern loss of sphincter control and resultant messiness. In this hour there can be noted a screen memory of masturbation forbidden by mother. Subsequently the patient buys a "feminine" briefcase, replacing the worn-out, "mannish" one she has been using. Again the feeling of being exposed and out in the cold is expressed in the transference. More anal themes appear: childhood fears of sexual attack are recalled as well as other libidinal associations. There is a rising tide of references to stigmata associated with forbidden sexual activity.

In the next hour (10/25) the patient reports a new physical symptom— vaginal pruritis [due to a condition later diagnosed as trichomonas vaginalis]. She has been aware of the itchiness since the previous day. The dream of 10/20 and the content of the hour on 10/24 are indicators of the site and the nature of the symptom before its actual appearance in the patient's awareness. These indicators appear against a background of increasing negative transference, insufficiency of the psychologic defensive alignment to contain the upsurge of repressed infantile sexual fantasies and activities, and an increasing sense of guilt.

On 10/27 there is a striking example of rapidly shifting representations of guilt. First, the patient is suddenly aware of an acute physical symptom—

epigastric pain. As it subsides, it is replaced by a partial discharge of affect. In turn, this is linked with recollections [ideational representations] of an incestuous-like episode several nights previously, which was the stimulus for a more specifically delineated expression of her sexual wishes in a subsequent dream.

During the next week the patient postpones an appointment for gynecologic examination. She is concerned over the continued vaginal discharge, but at the same time the fear of what the doctor will tell her has influenced her to delay seeing him. Persistent sexual pressures lead to attempted relief through masturbation which only reinforces her hypersensitivity and guilt. Finally, ten days after the condition is first noted, the patient is examined and the diagnosis of trichomonas vaginalis is made. In a subsequent hour there is a long-delayed confession about masturbation with an artifical phallus.

On 11/8 there is a vivid example of the behavioral and verbal expression of an idea—I must not look at the analyst or his wife—being followed by a somatic representation of the idea. This occurs against the background of the crucial confessions in the previous hour. Retrospectively, the discharge of guilt feeling then has been insufficient. Somatically, the organ of sight is involved and the eye tic is a transient conversion symptom. The eye has been a target organ from early childhood; it has been linked with frequent traumatic sexual experiences (voyeurism) and forbidden, infantile, libidinal impulses. In this same analytic hour, as more recollections of parental hostility with accompanying transference implications appear in the associations, still another but familiar somatic outlet is activated: stomach dysfunction reinforced by references to leaving the analysis. Then a secondary response to pain in the form of an unusual ideational representation follows. It is an infantile fantasy of being stuck with a knife wielded by a gremlin inside the stomach. This is a cognitive expression of the paternal introject highly personified and libidinized.

In the next few weeks the patient emphasizes her need to control and her difficulty letting go anything that is part of her. She is now more aware of the reaction formation of ingratiation and its use to ward off hostile responses. On 11/27 the first reference to painful hemorrhoids appears. There has been a shift from reference to activated dependency needs, although these are still present, to the theme of controlling and being dominated. Her parents, Brad, and the analyst are involved. It should be noted that the recent confessional about masturbation with an artificial phallus has been linked with anal elements. Concern about pregnancy is also associated with infantile, cloacal fantasies. Vaginal and anal orifices are now both involved in physical dysfunction. Trichomonas vaginalis appears as a consequence of dirty masturbation. Painful hemorrhoids are linked with the intensifying need to control and hold in, with hidden, sadistic implications. The punitive significance of the symptoms are clearly indicated. The first brief episode of bleeding hemorrhoids actually occurred during the summer interruption and was triggered by marked stress that the patient experienced when Brad first met her parents. At that time she was intensely concerned about whether they would approve of her choice of a man. Her tension then had become extreme and manifested itself in a general tightening of musculature, anal spasm, and an increasing and obdurate constipation which she had not subsequently mentioned until very recently.

In the interview of 11/27, there is a reference to another organ system—the respiratory—which is still malfunctioning as a consequence of a recent viral infection. The symptoms of coughing and increased hoarseness appear as additional, somatic outlets for escalating tensions specifically linked with the theme of not wanting to talk.

On 11/28 there is a clear example of the idea of a sensation—floating—followed by awareness of the sensation itself. The background is the emergence of erotic, Oedipal transference elements. Associations referring to claustrophobia first appear. They are followed by proprioceptive percepts which are a rather specific somatic expression of the erotic transference and the anxiety associated with it. Temperature percepts appear in a subsequent hour (11/29) as a somatic expression of the transference state. They are brief and, if not specifically looked for, could easily be missed. In the past, emphasis on the ideational, affective, and behavioral expressions of transference has tended to overshadow the physical indicators of this process. Deutsch (1962) has noted that the transference relationship influences the activation and appearance of perceptual complexes representing the emotionally significant object during therapy. This is based on the assumption that object relationships "originated from sensory perceptions of one's own body." According to this concept "any emotional relationship can be retraced to an abstract sensory awareness, of a certain quality and with a threshold depending on biologic and unconscious and preconscious factors." In the same analytic hour another physical symptom—nausea—represents a specific bodily expression of wanting to get rid of an undesirable object or relationship. Here the somatic response precedes the idea.

On 12/1 there can be noted an interesting variation of what constitutes a loss. There are many representations of loss—direct, indirect, and symbolic—often overlooked. In this instance there are associations which refer to the giving up of the child's role for that of the adult. It involves the loss of freedom from cares and responsibilities, the loss of childish, narcissistic gratifications. The activated idea of such loss is accompanied by evidence of somatic dysfunction in the stomach, a principal target organ, which responds sensitively to frustration of dependency needs and concomitant hostility. Such physical responses are often mixed in with psychologic manifestations, when the psychologic systems are insufficient to cope with the prevailing stress.

In the next few weeks the patient goes out on several dates with different men, but these are unenjoyable and stressful. There are many recollections from the past about her reactions to the birth of her sister, when she was five years old. She was ill with a respiratory disorder called bronchitis and remembers being in bed for many weeks. It was a response to the loss of her status in the family constellation as the only child, her being replaced in mother's affections by the new baby, and having to give up the room that had been hers till then. The patient also continues to be troubled by her relationship with Brad, especially the sexual aspects, with vaginal symptoms still present though the infection has cleared up. On 12/18, while associating about a date with a new man who has a cold, and in whom she finds much to devaluate as well as to identify with, the patient suddenly experiences intense sensory perceptions of itchiness localized to the back. There is a quick motor response in the form of violent scratching. In this instance, sensory perception and motor response occur first and then are followed by further associations about a specific, actual, unpleasant experience with her date involving the site of the somatic response. She remembers that when he put his arm on the small of her back to help her through doors, traffic, etc., she felt very anxious at the physical contact with its sexual implications of being taken advantage of and hurt. A further somatic sequel to this date is reported in the next hour (12/19). The patient notes the prodromata of what turns out to be another upper respiratory infection. The preceding night the patient has had a dream about intense conflict with her mother. There were elements of fighting with and separation from her as well as a yearning for and dependency on her. The concern about losing mother has been intensifying in the past several weeks and, as noted above, has been associated in the past with upper respiratory illness of long duration. The dream is a signal of an impending somatic reaction involving the same organ system.

On 12/22 there is another instance of a dream in which an impending somatic dysfunction is signaled. This dream basically concerns the patient's relationship especially identification with her mother. The associations deal with mother's dominating ways and her refuge in physical complaints when she evoked the patient's anger. These past experiences led to considerable guilt formation in the patient and the construction of defenses against affect discharge, especially anger. The conflict with mother seems to have been especially activated during the patient's toilet training experiences. Still further associations deal with other aspects of the theme of domination: grandmother's emphasis on frugality and mother's emphasis on tidiness. The difference between these two important figures is recalled as mother's bending over backwards to avoid affect expression of anger. The patient's current somatic complaint is backache. There is a direct connection between motion of the back and avoidance of hostility by the patient. Actually, the patient's own life style has been characterized by her inability to openly express anger and be aware of its deeper implications.

C. D.

Frustration from Bottom to Top

INTRODUCTION

C. D., a 29-year-old department store manager, entered analysis because of persistent feelings of inferiority, concern about being criticized and rejected by others, and difficulties in achieving sexual satisfaction with his wife. He had married several years before, and as yet there were no children.

His mother is described as a hard-driving, domineering woman, "wearing the pants" in the family and ambitious for her children to succeed in life. She had one major illness, from which she almost died, when the patient was seven. Father is a passive man, participating little in family affairs but a good provider, who had several bouts of pneumonia and subsequently underwent urologic surgery during the patient's adolescence. Both parents are now in fairly good health. There is a brother, six years younger, who is in graduate school, struggling scholastically, emotionally unstable, and who has been in psychiatric treatment for the past year.

Initial clinical evaluation indicated a moderately severe character neurosis in which there were both obsessional and mildly depressive tendencies together with prominent sadomasochistic and passive-feminine attitudes. There had been no previous episodes of psychologic decompensation and no previous psychotherapy. Physical history revealed constipation in early childhood, a T & A at four years of age, frequent colds later on, and an accidental brain concussion during adolescence. The patient has been myopic and worn glasses since childhood. He has always felt physically awkward and inferior to his peers and elders.

During the first eight months of analysis, the patient's central concern was about his masculinity, involving constant comparison and hostile competition with other men, and this was reflected with growing intensity in the transference. Accompanying this was fear of retaliatory criticism, physical attack (castration in fantasy), and rejection. Body areas and various activities and behavior of the patient were markedly sexualized. There were intermittent confessions of masturbatory activity during which, in childhood, he would use his mother's underwear and currently his wife's. Fantasies of assuming the feminine role and being passive began to appear more frequently as alternatives to thoughts of himself as the most aggressive and powerful of men. Headaches appeared as a somatic manifestation of castration anxiety after the patient had been involved in sexual activity such as masturbation, *soixante-neuf* (oral-genital contact), or intercourse with his wife assuming the top position. He had two brief upper respiratory illnesses following sharp transference reactions to anticipated criticism and rejection, concomitant with activated oral needs. At these times cognitive and affective discharge pathways were partially blocked and insufficient. Though there were a few explosive quarrels with his wife, hostile or anxious affect was expressed minimally in the analytic hour. The patient defended himself against such affective experience by humorous, flip attitudes and remarks—the "light touch." There was also a channel of emotional discharge available through teasing behavior, evident both in the analysis and elsewhere. Projection and intellectualization appeared intermittently as defenses. While ego-superego tensions were evident, these were in the moderate range of severity.

Anality overshadowed oral manifestations. On a number of occasions the patient referred to a parasitic anal infestation that he had had from the age of 10 to 13 years and to his mother's giving him presumably palliative and curative enemas for months during that interval of time. He picked his nose frequently in the analytic hours, equating this in his associations with the cleansing of his anus. He made frequent references to his entry into the analyst's office as one where the doctor brought up the rear on the way to the guillotine; at other times the fantasy was of authority (the analyst) breathing down the victim's (patient's) neck. There was frequent silent and noisy expulsion of flatus by the patient. Also noted were numerous descriptions of himself as an asshole, the analysis as a lot of crap, masturbation as an effective cathartic against constipation, being scared shitless, buggering and being buggered, etc.

Toward the end of the first eight months of analysis with the vacation interruption approaching, the patient's dependency became more marked. There were wordy unemotional accusations about not getting enough from the analyst. As yet, the patient had insufficient understanding of the deepening negative side of the transference. He was accompanied by the references to his failure as a man, more fantasies of himself in the feminine role, and continued curiosity about how a woman is fulfilled sexually and through pregnancy.

On the patient's return from four weeks of vacation interruption, deprivation appeared as a prominent theme. He also thought persistently that he would be more acceptable if he were a sissy (feminine). Then for two weeks, despite interpretive interventions by the analyst, the patient's associations became more and more scattered and descriptive. This defensive blocking represented an attempt to wall off intensifying sexual and hostile impulses and wishes. References were made by the patient to fears of being flooded and overwhelmed by his feelings. He was trying to avoid not only feelings but thoughts. He came late several times. He was informed his blocking was related to a variety of causes: fear of ridicule and criticism, fear of being too weak and defective to be able to make any effort, and an expectation that the work would be done for him. His reaction was to feel criticized. There was again an increase in sexual curiosity which he was able to reveal: how to get a penis inside him through an opening in his body; how to find out what it is to be a woman. At this point the more detailed account of the ensuing hours is presented largely *verbatim* as related by the patient, except where otherwise noted.

CASE MATERIAL

9/4

I'm not getting anywhere, and I want to blame analysis and you. Maybe it's   1
the weather. Ha! Ha! I just feel frustrated, here and on the outside. How does one get enough? You tell me. There I go, kidding and teasing, but I'm really bothered.

I had a dream last night. It seems as if I was in the house of one of the big   2
executives, in a bedroom. I was going to take a shower. I had a pink organdy towel and was afraid of what others would think of that. Then I saw an elevator shaft with cables and machinery, but no car. I became afraid that if I climbed up, I might fall and get hurt.

The dream makes me think of whether I'm a good boy or a bad boy, whether I'm producing enough or not. That's in relation to my boss—the one in the dream—and also in relation to you. I guess I value his and your opinion of me. I want to be like a son. In the dream I'm afraid that I'll be caught masquerading as a son—that I'll be found to be actually a woman underneath. The towel in the dream reminds me of the one I used in sexual relations with my wife, Ginny, last night. We practiced *soixante-neuf*. My nose was near her   3
bottom, seeing it and smelling it. She blew me and I licked her clitoris. I felt anxious while we were doing it. Then I took a shower, after which I had the urge to move my bowels and found I was constipated. It was as if I had to rid myself of something, and it was hard to do it. I finally managed to have a bowel movement but really had to strain.

The elevator shaft with no elevator in it. Like a woman's anatomy between   4
her legs. Looking in there, up there, and being terribly afraid of getting hurt there. Wondering if there really isn't an organ in that passageway, hidden away.

All these sexual thoughts make me feel guilty. I need someone to understand, to lighten the guilt. Well, it's only a dream. My uncle—he was a good man, good to his children. He had understanding. He treated me well when I was a kid, just as if I were his very own. Will you be considerate, not judge me?

That business of getting hurt reminds me of cuts and bruises I and my brother used to get as kids. Whenever I hear of blood or some injury associated with bleeding, I have a funny sensation in my anus—like a pinching or squeezing effect, which I can feel right now. [Acting out voyeuristic fantasies, identification with the woman, accompanied by much castration anxiety and guilt, concern over the consequences, especially involving the paternal transference.]

9/8

1   After I left the hour on Friday, I felt somewhat less anxious and guilty, but continued to feel under par. My abdomen seemed full. I was having an urge to move my bowels, an urge that came and went. When I actually went to the toilet, my constipation made me strain at stool. I thought that masturbating might relieve the tension and so I did. It wasn't much help. I kept on having to strain the next couple of days. Yesterday I felt something sticking out of my anus—funny sensation, though painful. I called my internist and told him about my condition. He referred me to a specialist and I went to see this surgeon, thinking I had a bad hemorrhoid. Well, he examined me, used instruments to look up there. I was scared as hell when he stuck a tube up my ass, and I thought I was going to pass out at any point. The whole business left me as weak as a kitten and shaky to boot. Finally, he said I had a polyp. Day after tomorrow I have to go to the hospital and have a barium enema—something I never had before. More stuff stuck up my ass. Here I've been having all kinds of fantasies about a penis up in the rear, and now this crappy business has to happen. Then in two weeks the doctor plans to do a biopsy and to use a cautery to remove the polyp. I don't like the idea of going into the hospital one bit.

2   These procedures make me think of being buggered. How does a penis feel up the rectum? Well, I'm going to have a chance to find out in a way I don't like. It serves me right for thinking and wanting unnatural sex. Since I had that consultation, I've been plagued by the gloomiest kind of thoughts: thoughts of cancer, of dying; that the condition in my rectum is not minor as the surgeon says, but that it's something fatal; and these ideas keep repeating themselves over and over. My mind's full of them. I also had a dream about going into a hospital through an arcade which looks like the hotel near where I lived when I was a youngster. It was a rundown place, like a flophouse with a bunch of near-derelicts living in it. Every once in a while they'd bring one of them out, dying or maybe dead. ["You expect the worst about your physical condition just as you expect the worst in so many other things you do or are involved in."]

9/9

Waiting to have that x-ray is murder. I keep thinking they're going to find a   1
cancer there. There's cancer in my family background. One of my aunts died
when I was a kid, and they said she had cancer of the stomach. How shriveled up
she became and yellow—something out of this world. What if I've got something
like that. Just suffering ahead, no hope. I get caught up in this morbid thinking,   2
and I can't tell anyone about it except you. I guess I'm going to pay for my sins
now. I had a nightmare last night. All I remember about it is that I was being   3
taken to a hospital where I was listed as an accident casualty. I was screaming in
my sleep until Ginny woke me up. That horrible dream reminded me of the time
I was in that automobile accident—when I was 18 and had just been driving a car
a short time. I snuck out and took the family car to a party which broke up late.
When I started driving home, there was an ice storm, and I couldn't handle the
car on those slippery roads. I wound up against a telephone pole with my head
on the windshield—skidded. I was knocked out and woke up in the hospital.
What a scene my mother made! Crying as if I were going any minute. That
scared me more than anything. But I only had to stay in the hospital a couple of
days; a concussion they called it.

I try to get away from all these unpleasant thoughts. One way is to get lost   4
in sexual thoughts. But then I'm in another kind of trouble. I keep having
fantasies of a penis being stuck into my rectum. Different men are doing it, and I
can't seem to figure out who they are. Here I am picking away at my nose. I've
been doing that a lot in the last few days and my nose is really irritated
[blocked].

The x-rays are tomorrow, and I keep thinking that I'm just doing the wrong   5
things to steady myself for what will happen then.

9/10

Well, I had that barium enema and thank heavens it was negative. It's quite a   1
pleasant, I mean unpleasant sensation. A technician gave it to me and made me
hold it in while the x-rays were being taken until I thought I would burst. Wow!
I wouldn't want that again in a hurry. I had to go to the toilet a number of times
to get rid of the stuff though not all of it came out. Whitish stuff—probably the
barium.

Last night I had two dreams—short ones. In the first I turned a knob and
some musical instruments unfolded. When I turned it in the opposite direction,
they came together again. In the second, a colleague of mine is talking to me in a
chastizing way; the scene is in an office at the place we work.

I keep thinking of the enemas I got from mother when I was very little. That   2
was something she was a great believer in. On one occasion, after I had already

started school, I developed a bad itch around my anus and for quite a while nobody knew what was causing it, even the doctor. It was my mother who finally discovered that I had pinworms which were causing all the trouble. She could diagnose conditions that a doctor couldn't. She was a terribly frustrated person. I guess she wanted to be famous, maybe in medicine or business. Well, she herself couldn't make it so she had big ambitions for me. I've had big ambitions myself. I keep wanting to take $25 and parlay it into $100,000. And once again I'm reminded of that little thing in my rectum—that polyp. Before I was twelve, I used to have a big fear of getting a heart attack. This came on after I had witnessed a neighbor having a terrible argument with his wife and shortly afterwards dropping dead of a heart attack. His wife went around with a beat-up look on her face for an awfully long time.

Those musical instruments in the dream; I used to try playing the saxophone when I was younger, but really didn't like it. Mother insisted on my practicing so much every day, and I'd pretend I was playing scales, but I was just making noises. I used to pass the time by thinking about sex and rubbing my penis between my legs. Finally my mother, after many months of trying to get me interested in the instrument and scolding me if I dodged practicing it, gave up on me. Will you give up on me? All these damn physical complications interrupting my work and the analysis.

9/11, Summary

Many pauses, afraid to talk, might be blackmailed. He has said too much. When he wants the analyst to talk, the analyst is silent. When he wants the analyst to be silent, the analyst talks critically.

9/14, Summary

Feeling sad, bleary-eyed. His best friend has left for a long trip. Is angry because he feels the analysis is rapidly nearing an end and the analyst points out his deficiencies coolly, without getting involved in an argument. Intercourse with wife: she is on top. Fantasies of a penis in his anus. Other fantasies of a twig in wife's vagina. Development of stomach pains and nausea. Several slips of the tongue in which he refers to himself in the feminine role.

9/15, Summary

After the hour yesterday he continues to feel nauseated, but eats dinner. He then feels very nauseated, sticks a finger in his throat, gagging and forcing himself to vomit. Continues to have abdominal pain, passing much flatus. Now feels quite detached. Preoccupied with thoughts about what women are like, whether they can be trusted. Blames one of them for the loss of a gold metal fountain pen he had received as a prize. Concerned about phallic woman; identification with them.

9/16 and 9/17, Summary

Marked tendency to block off feelings—in this instance, hostile ones—by laughing them off, making light of them, denying they have any significance. Detachment and avoidance of feelings altogether are other manifestations of these defenses.

9/18, Summary

Conflict between active and passive tendencies. More sexual fantasies breaking through about female genitalia, especially oral contact with them. Resultant: nausea. Recollections of rummaging through mother's personal belongings when he was a child. Recurrent, persistent fantasies of oral-genital contact. Fear of losing control over his impulses.

9/21, Excerpt

I've been tense, angry over the weekend. And I think of my brother's visit. 1 He's so damn inconsiderate and demanding. All his fancy talk. Who does he think he is—so superior in his attitude it makes me puke. He has the nerve to ask in that condescending way of his how my analysis is going. I just couldn't talk about it. ["That's the way it is here, too. You can't talk about your anger, particularly at the analysis and at me."] Maybe not. It's the fear of being told to get out. Same way at work. Get furious at my boss, and often, too. But I've got to clam up or I'll get bounced. He gives me a royal pain in the ass. ["You haven't 2 talked about your physical condition for a long time."] I just didn't want to think about it. Tomorrow's the day I go in to have that thing snipped out. The prospect gives me the creeps. I realize the whole thing won't amount to much but that's a real sensitive spot [wry laughter].

9/22, Excerpt

Well, it's over with. The doctor said there was no postoperative care, but he 1 advised me to have regular checkups, just in case of a recurrence. Right now I feel awful tired. I guess I want to be babied. That was a terribly uncomfortable state I was in. I kept having this horrible fear of being hurt during the procedure. It started from the moment I woke up. I kept anticipating what was going to happen and what they were going to find. I don't like hospitals and the atmosphere there. The operating room seemed so cold and threatening. The faces all so solemn. No one to turn to. At the mercy of the surgeon. Anyway the

2   whole thing didn't take very long. I was so concerned about what I had there, thinking of cancer and all, that I hardly paid any attention to the actual physical
3   sensations I experienced while the doctor was working on me. His looking right up there and putting instruments in there keep making me think of some crazy sexual act.

4   While waiting to come in I strained to hear what was going on in your office. Was the patient there—that pretty girl—being sexually used by you for perverse purposes? I guess it's that damn operation that makes me think such things. Maybe I want to take her place.

5   There are some big interviews coming up with the top executives in my firm about my promotion. I'm just worried that they might see my faults and be unbending in their judgment of me.

9/24 - 10/4, Interim Summary

The patient's postoperative course is without complications. His preoccupation with physical symptoms rapidly subsides. However, the postponement of a conference with top executives about his promotion leads again to angry frustration and disappointment accompanied by activation of dependency needs: he wants to be fed a cure. Concern about manliness and virility also increases. Persisting passive-feminine fantasies are weakly defended against by transient heterosexual impulses. Unusual behavior occurs: the patient takes medication prescribed for his wife's premenstrual tension. Regressive fantasies appear in which he sees himself as close to authoritative, powerful women who will supply him with what he needs through their big breasts. Growing anxiety leads to blocking and superficial rambling in several successive hours. There is, however, indication that hostility is being expressed toward his wife at home. The patient's understanding of the shifts that are taking place is still insufficient and cannot be used more effectively by him at this time because the negative transference continues to deepen.

10/5

1   I've been increasingly grouchy and irritable for the past week. Ginny and I seem to be fighting more. We've been accusing each other of thinking of infidelity. So there's been no intercourse and that leads to masturbating. it makes me feel immature, but I don't stop. I have fantasies of being like a woman, having breasts, wearing a brassiere and panties that belong to Ginny, or I recall the times I used to actually put mother's underclothes on when I was a
2   youngster. I guess I was pretty messed up in my teens, had bad headaches, especially in front—maybe sinus trouble—and in back. I remember cleaning my
3   vag—I mean my navel. There are other fantasies that plague me now that have to do with getting pregnant, especially when I'm constipated and feel bloated.

Ginny and I have been talking about having a baby. Who lays and who gets laid? If Ginny has a baby, will it be a Mongolian idiot? I remember when I was a youngster there was a kid in the neighborhood who was a Mongolian idiot. My mother would tell me to be nice to him, but I hated to be near him. Fortunately, his family moved away after they'd been living near us only a short time. I guess I'm concerned about defects. 4

[Scratches nose.] This nosepicking is a troublesome thing. I've been doing that ever since I can remember. Bad habit. I have an itchy nose. When I was a kid I had an itchy ass, due to pinworms. I've told you about that. I'd get frequent enemas. I would scratch down there, twist my ass, and wonder what people would think, seeing me do that. I became quite sensitive about what they'd see [right foot dangling over couch]. Talking this way I feel exposed here and want to leave, to run off, yet I can't. I'm afraid terrible things will happen to Ginny, that she'll be injured in the head, break her neck, something fatal. 5

6

10/6

I'm still wondering about what sensations Ginny has, especially in intercourse. We finally got together sexually last night, tried *soixante-neuf*. I had strong, sadistic impulses, wanting to ram my penis down her throat—down your throat too. Also fantasies of coming over Ginny's face. 1

[Nosepicking.] I guess you're critical of my nosepicking. It seems to me that I begin to do it the moment I park my car to come into your office. Maybe it's defiance, maybe it's devaluation. 2

I had a dream last night in which I was looking at myself and didn't seem like myself. I didn't have a receding jaw but the square jaw of an athletic young man and a powerful neck and shoulders. That's the way I used to think of myself when I was trying out for sports in school, but I never made any teams and didn't become an athlete. Now I've set my sights on intellectual achievement. I'm jealous of you with your Harvard background. I'm jealous of Ginny. She's fulfilling her role much more effectively than I am. She's a good housekeeper, will be a good mother, mostly cheerful, with generally sound judgment, in my opinion. 3

I want to keep my eyes closed so I don't have a chance to see you. Maybe I can shut out or shut off thoughts of being hurt by you. When I was in the fifth grade I gashed my thigh running into a sharp edge. Someone was chasing me—an older boy, a bully. It was a horrible mess, painful as could be, with blood all over my leg. I had to be taken to the hospital for some stitches. 4

5

Ginny seems so superior to me, and I wonder if she's the brains of the outfit. I remember how smart mother was. She read so much. Father was a plodding businessman who managed to make a living, but he was no match for mother. She could even diagnose illnesses in our family that baffled the doctors. I've wondered at times that maybe man is the inferior of the two sexes. 6

10/9

1   Today I've got a bad stiff neck. It came on suddenly. My neck is so painful on the right that I have to keep it turned to the left which gives me a little but not enough relief. Any movement hurts like the devil.

2   In the last couple of days my mind's been foggy. I haven't been thinking too clearly. I've kept busy with odd jobs at home, and I've been watching TV quite a

3   bit—escapist stuff. I feel stuck, don't know what to do. I'm really looking for help. I keep having the fantasy that you're stepping out of the picture and deserting me, that the women patients are getting knocked up here, but I'm getting nothing.

4   This pain came on yesterday morning after I woke up. The night before I was terribly restless, wanted sex, but Ginny was cold. We wound up by my masturbating her and then myself. I had to do all the work and it was quite an effort, especially since I craned my head to look at her genitals when she came. During the night I had several dreams, one was a wet one, but I don't remember what it was about. In another one I seemed to be on the roof of a building with suitcases piled high against it. I was afraid to move lest they go tumbling down.

5   I cancelled my appointments at work today. This morning I had another attack of severe pain; this time in the right side of my back, just below the ribs. I took five double scotches to deaden the pain. It was as if something were sitting there, maybe a stone. I kept thinking of father's trouble with his prostate. He had a hell of a time. I remember waiting to see him at the hospital. I noticed his chart was lying around and that was when I read something that wasn't meant for my eyes. It was about his habit of masturbating. I connected that up with his physical troubles. It makes me sweat to think that something like that might happen to me—all those surgical procedures down there. It gives me the creeps. If it's a stone, how will they get it out? The pain is so great, it seems to me to be worse than a woman would experience in labor.

6   Funny, I keep thinking how I like to tease people; you, right now. I feel like taking a cigarette, putting it in my mouth, and then I won't have to or be able to talk. Let's see you analyze that. To provoke—that's what I want to do.

10/14

1   [Is wearing a big plaster-of-paris collar around neck.] I had to cancel several appointments here because, as I phoned you, I had to go into the hospital. I spent four days and nights there. I was afraid of having a wet dream because the nurses might discover the evidence. Actually I dreamt that I was with Ginny and had a hard erection, but couldn't satisfy her. Then she left me for her father who was waiting outside the house. In another part I seemed to be in a second-floor apartment with the door open. I snuck over to the door with a short, stubby key

which had almost no stem and locked it. It was as if Ginny were coming toward the door with a guy she had picked up. I then tiptoed over to the front of the apartment, to a room with three people in it, and I wondered if they had broken through the door. I'm still plagued by thoughts that other guys are better than I am and will get the women.

I'm thinking of my room at the hospital. It was new and in a new wing. It   2
reminded me of a room in a hotel in Nashville where I spent a weekend with one of my former girlfriends. It also reminded me of a room in her house where we did a lot of necking. This girl and I talked about the possibility of pregnancy and how some of her friends had had to have abortions because they were careless. But we never got to the point of full sexual relations.

I keep wondering whether I went to the hospital so that I wouldn't face the   3
prospect of having intercourse with Ginny—or to get away from the analysis, from here. Actually there was a sound reason for me to be in the hospital: my   4
neck hurt so badly. The doctor called my condition a severe case of torticollis and said I needed traction. As you can see, I ended up with this collar around my neck. The pain in my back let up, and they told me there was nothing wrong with my kidneys. There'll be a hospital bill and that'll make it necessary to   5
postpone paying my landlord. A few nights ago I dreamt that I was living in a first-floor apartment with Ginny and our folks. The landlord came in enraged, demanding his rent, and I did something to him because he left in tears, and I had won my point. In fact, he is a bastard. He doesn't fix the tile in my bathroom, so I retaliate by not paying him. Maybe it's like the situation here. Maybe it was you in the dream. As if you were demanding your fee and I was giving you a cock-and-bull story about not being able to pay you.

The weird thought now occurs to me that maybe my penis would invaginate   6
in some peculiar way, and I would become like a woman sexually.

I've also had thoughts of how it would be nice to be a baby in your arms, rubbing my face against yours, being held and cuddled.

I think I've been furious at you, blaming my condition, this stiff neck, on   7
you. I then have the fantasy that you're a quack and maybe you've been suspended from practice.

I plan to go to New Haven to visit with my folks this weekend and I'll have   8
to wear this Goddamn collar. When they applied the traction, I felt my head was coming off, but I wouldn't let them know. At the hospital I tried to be as unobtrusive as possible. I didn't want them to think I was an aggressive, arrogant guy.

10/15

I find myself reluctant once again to express my feelings. I seem to be   1
concealing anger because you're going to be away for a couple of days. I'm pissed off with the analysis. It's interfering with my home life. Ginny wistfully

asks me if I would leave the analysis. I came home last night, grouchy. Later we had sexual intercourse, but it wasn't enjoyable. Ginny was very upset. I was needling and teasing her.

2   [Attention is called to his blandness, to the absence of feelings. "Who is angry?"] I am. Fuck the analysis, and fuck you with it! Just criticism. Poor Ginny, she's in the midst of the turmoil. Shit! Shit! Shit! I feel like breaking windows, throwing the furniture out, and you after it. All day I've felt pent up. Though calm outwardly, I was seething inwardly. I really felt like coming in and ripping you apart. I'm considering dropping the analysis. Right now I feel like killing you, damn it. Ginny says she has no sex life now, whereas the first years of our marriage we were happy together. It's this—the analysis; it's responsible. This is the troublemaker. We're going to New Haven for fun but we're not going to have any pleasure. It seems as if Ginny is telling me to choose—between her and you. I know I've tended to be cold toward her, but I've been so preoccupied with this damn shit. How do I get rid of you? You're becoming thoroughly obnoxious in my life. Ginny made some comment last night about my being too damn passive, but look at you—you sit there like an immobile turd. I'm just mad, just damn angry [unmistakably now]. I feel so tense. The only thing that can relieve it is to choke you—choke the guts out of you.

     I don't like being angry. I don't like being angry as I am now. I feel enraged. You encourage me to be in this turmoil situation. More concretely—go fuck yourself! This pain in my neck—you're actually the pain in my neck. The pain came on the morning after I couldn't have harmonious sexual intercourse with Ginny. You just sit back there and don't help. You're the goddamn pain in my neck, my ass, more concretely in my neck. I feel like ripping you limb from limb. You're worse than my mother. She at least could respond, but you just sit there in your slow, retarded, feeble-minded way. Dr. A, my friend's analyst, he's a real analyst, a real guy, nothing like you. I've never felt so enraged as I do against you now. I feel so helpless with the situation at home, and you do nothing. You're not the cream in my coffee, you're the pain in my ass, in my neck. Here I am, wearing a collar—it's a sort of atonement for coming and seeing you. God punished me for being in analysis by my having a wry neck, like an albatross. I picture you about to be hanged and tripped by me from the scaffold. I feel like taking the collar off my neck and sticking you with it, wringing your neck and strangling you. Tripping you into a vat of picric acid and seeing you disappear. God will right the wrong he's done to me in having you. There's no love, no nothing from you. I have no inhibition about this anger, but feel like wringing your neck, breaking it off, killing you, and washing my hands in your blood.

3   This rage reminds me how I once had such rages when I was a kid, how I'd terrify my younger brother and my mother. Then she'd tell my father and he'd threaten to break my neck if I did it again. One day my uncle gave me a terrific whack, no words, and that finished my rages.

["You've mentioned a number of times how you thought your brother was the favorite, got everything while you got nothing; also that the older men would always be superior. Don't you feel the same way here?"] I do. I want you to get rid of this neurosis, to make me a man. I've been so irritated at the situation at home. Ginny and I aren't getting along, especially in sex. Last night she was on top and I came just as she was getting warmed up. My penis dwindled down to nothing. Ginny accused me of being passive, and I wanted to shut her up. We quarreled. She stuck a finger in her throat to vomit and to get my sympathy. She said that I should do her one favor and quit the analysis. I said I can't. Later she said she was kidding. When we tried sex again and I got on top of her, then she called me a rapist. I can't win either way. 4

5

6

10/16

[Still wearing the collar.]

It's a horrible sight—this collar around my neck. It makes me look like a horrible, helpless creature. I feel trapped here with my neck and head in a sling, so I came here a bit late today. I'm stuck, feel sorry for myself and like crying. I'm going to New Haven tomorrow, and I know I won't enjoy it. When I got home last night I told Ginny what happened here and that I've never been so enraged at anyone. I also have some understanding what the rage is about. Anyway my neck is better. I can get along without the collar for an hour at a time now. Then my head and neck feel heavy and dragging, and I have to put the thing on. After I left here last night I took it off because my neck felt so much better, and I had the thought I wouldn't have to put it on again. After a while my neck felt heavy, and I put the collar back on. Today it isn't localized to the side. I've become ashamed of this goddamn thing. I'm ashamed of finding myself in this goddamn spot. Unfortunately, I've become a center of attention because of this. 1 2 3 4

I've just had a fantasy that you want to blow me, and if you come near me, I'll knock your goddamn head off. One of my bosses tells me I've loosened up. Maybe that job promotion will be given to me soon. Does that mean I don't need any more treatment? Yet, as far as analysis is concerned, I have a peculiar attachment to you or for you, despite all this uproar. I would like to extricate myself from my troubles, but it's discouraging. Dr. V said I should wear the collar and apply heat to my neck over the weekend. He thought I couldn't support my head without a crutch. I feel helpless and at your mercy. I want to kill you—not once but several times. ["Have you had such feelings toward others?"] Maybe towards my mother—but it's hazy. I remember being terribly mad at my father and wishing he were dead. Afterwards he got sick and almost died. That was a long time ago. For many years now I don't remember being too angry at anybody for any long interval. I'd get occasional short angry spells at my mother, my brother, and recently at my wife. 5

6

7   This collar makes me feel like an albatross. It's as if there's something basically wrong with me. Funny thing is maybe I'll miss not coming in tomorrow, when I go to New Haven. At the same time I'm afraid that at the end of the analysis I'll be like a vegetable, without feelings and too relaxed. I keep thinking you don't help me when I need it.

8   Mother used to tell me she almost died when I was six or seven years old. She had something wrong with her throat, her thyroid gland, I believe. They had to operate on her. I remember now the sight of her with those bandages around her throat for weeks and weeks. I might have become afraid to be angry at people; I might cause them to die. How powerful can I get? Yet I'm angry so often in some way and I want help that I can't seem to get. I remember that I was threatened with being sent away to reform school if I misbehaved as a kid.

10/19

       [No collar!]
1   The weekend was very enjoyable. When I left here on Friday, you smiled, a warm smile. I felt a great relief that you cared and were interested. Yes, after I had left, I had a lingering feeling that there was tenderness in that smile. I felt lonely that I wouldn't be here. I could like you and nothing bad would happen to me. The pain and heaviness disappeared from my neck except for a little spasm and twinge that I get—but not often.

2   Now I feel sad. Maybe I hurt you with this bombastic, vituperative flow of
3   words the other day. This weekend, visiting with my family, they told me I'm nicer to get along with. They don't know I'm in analysis. I find I'm not too interested any more in going down to New Haven and perambulating around.

4   I heard over the weekend that my best friend Morgan's got a girl and is in a whirlwind romance. You know that smile you gave me last Friday, I have another idea about it. Maybe there was something sexual in that smile. On the train ride back I had the fantasy that Ginny was Morgan and I was Cindy [Morgan's girl]. Ginny feels that Morgan and I had some kind of sublimated sexual affair and also that she has been terribly attracted to Morgan. Anyway, I now think such thoughts won't be severely judged, or judged at all. The treatment is to understand myself better. I felt very warm towards you and very sad, as if I couldn't tolerate any anger, but I also realized the anger was related to my babyish thoughts and wishes.

       Sometimes I wish I could have Ginny in my hip pocket—she's so intuitive.

5   I'm afraid of getting too involved here, telling you exactly how I feel about everything and about you. I'm concerned about deception. I want to leave before the opposite feelings get out from under the soft, tender, girl-like sentiments. Maybe I'm afraid you'll retaliate and be as sadistic to me as I used to be to them at home. Still I'm not as anxious thinking about homosexuality as I used to be, as if I'm becoming used to analyzing, not judging it.

MARGINAL NOTES

9/4

1. Transference: mounting frustration of dependency needs with reactive anger expressed through teasing.
2. Dream: fear of exposure of feminine impulses; castration anxiety. Transference implications. Affect, however, is insufficiently expressed.
3. Specific anatomic anal-genital references, and vivid visual and olfactory sensory percepts. An expulsive-retentive conflict expressed both ideationally and somatically—specifically anal.
4. Curiosity about a hidden penis. Attempts to minimize underlying guilt and to reassure himself that the analyst will not be punitive (transference concern). Castration anxiety chronically associated with anal sphincter spasm.

9/8

1. Preoccupation with bowel activity, retentive spasm, unrelieved as before by masturbation, painful somatic manifestation: anus. Proctoscopic examination activates severe anxiety—an indirect and incomplete fulfillment of infantile sexual impulses, penis in rectum.
2. Superego aspects, guilt, punishment for perverse wishes, expectation of the worst.

9/9

1. Persistent expectations of the worst linked with heredity.
2. Rising secondary superego tensions.
3. Castration anxiety linked with past head trauma, reflected in nightmare.
4. Attempts to cope with anxiety through sexual fantasies in which he appears in the feminine role and in which site of lesion becomes site of sexual gratification. Displacement to nose.
5. Increase in guilt.

9/10

1. Slip of tongue reveals repressed wish for masochistic gratification—at site of lesion. Sexualization of procedure with the patient in feminine role.
2. Activated recollections of phallic mother and her sexualized role in giving him enemas—retrospective but also suggestive that the anus has been an early sensitized bodily area. Identification with phallic mother.
3. More retrospective fantasies of childhood castration fears: somatic identification with man, cardiac death following intense hostility to and from wife. Guilt theme.
4. Dream associations: escape through sexual fantasies and masturbation— an early way of coping with anxiety and other unpleasant affects. Transference implications.

9/11-9/18 Summarized in text with dynamic formulations.

9/21

1. Hostility toward brother expressed in somatic terms and linked with negative transference. Fear of retaliation: in analysis and at work. Another somatic expression of hostility.
2. Confronted with absence of references to somatic condition in preceding hours. Coping mechanisms of avoidance, denial, joking to deal with secondary anxiety and guilt about impending operation.

9/22

1. Retrospective associations to operation: hospital and personnel coldly clinical. Regressive needs.
2. Preoccupation with castration anxiety supersedes awareness of physical sensations.
3. Again activation of related feminine sexual fantasies.
4. Sexualized transference: patient identifying with previous female patient.
5. Anticipatory anxiety about possible exposure of his defects.

9/24-10/4 Summarized in text with dynamic formulations.

10/5

1. Mounting hostility, with some affective discharge. Increased use of projection as defense. Regressive sexual outlet and fantasies of feminine identification, transvestitism.
2. Recollections of somatic dysfunction and identity problems.
3. Further regressive manifestations: pregnancy fantasies following planning for wife's having a baby.
4. Continuing focus on defects.
5. More references to nose, displacement from anus. Retrospective recollections. Fear of exposure of anal interests then, and currently in the transference. Cognitive reference to being trapped.
6. Expectation of injury to head and neck body areas but in reference to the woman.

10/6

1. Further references to head-neck-throat areas, both sexualized and linked with sadistic impulses.
2. Regressive hostile behavior.
3. Head-neck area seen as powerful and without defect, linked to boyhood compensatory fantasies. Competitive envy of both men and women.
4. Need for avoidance and denial.
5. More references to early injury and castration anxiety.
6. Envy of phallic women.

10/9

1. New somatic dysfunction; pain percepts.
2. Much passivity: looking as escapism.
3. Negative transference: envy, projection.
4. Neck symptoms follow sexual rejection, anger, masturbation, guilt. Preceding dream expresses physical splinting.
5. New painful area: right costovertebral angle. Somatic identification with father's urologic condition, linked with masturbation. Marked secondary anxiety about possible surgical intervention. Further somatic identification: labor pains.
6. Teasing: transference hostility.

10/14

1. Fear of exposure. Dreams of inadequate virility in Oedipal situation.
2. Sexualization of hospital environment.
3. Intellectualization.
4. Shift in somatic site.
5. Transference dream: hostility, withholding, teasing for not having repaired anal defect.
6. Regressive fantasies of change to female identity, then to being an infant.
7. Hostile transference without affect.
8. Defensive concealment of castration anxiety and hostility.

10/15

1. Concealment of hostility affectively; somatic reference to it in content; teasing.
2. Interpretation about missing affect triggers off explosive outburst of intense affect, principally transference hostility. Personification: pain in neck is analyst. Murderous rage at being frustrated and deprived. Projection. Predominance of anal terminology. Pain and plaster collar as punishment, superego aspects. Fantasies of retaliatory, murderous hostility, especially strangling.
3. Retrospective memories of similar childhood rages with threats of having neck broken by father. Actual punishment by an uncle ended these outbursts.
4. Interpretation of sibling rivalry and competition with father as reflected in transference.
5. Stress with wife and escape into passive-feminine attitudes and fantasies.
6. Masculine men seen as rapists.

10/16

1. Visual percepts.
2. Secondary reactions of helplessness and self-pity.
3. Development of insight. Improvement of torticollis.
4. Continued secondary reactions to somatic condition.
5. Fantasy of sexualized transference: fellatio. Projection, followed by shifting positive and negative transference associations.

6. Recollections of guilt over infantile death wishes. Long-standing inhibition of hostility.

7. Further ambivalence in transference.

8. Somatic identification with mother retrospectively recalled; associated guilt and threats of punishment.

10/19

1. Positive transference response mobilized, relieving guilt and influencing subsidence of physical symptoms.

2. Secondary concern about explosive hostile outburst in previous hour.

3. More detached from family ties.

4. Sexualization of transference and change in identity.

5. Concern about overinvolvement. Ultratenderness a reaction formation against sadism. Lessening superego-ego tensions.

COMMENT

Although this patient has had a longstanding character neurosis of moderate severity, there is no history of its having decompensated significantly. However, he has been troubled by frequent minor physical ailments, beginning with constipation in early childhood and frequent colds later on. A parasitic anal infestation became chronic for several years prepuberty, and during that time he was given frequent enemas by his mother. Though the somatic illness finally subsided, its psychologic consequences have lingered on.

In the first eight months of analysis, the patient's preoccupation with his masculinity, his competitiveness, and his fear of retaliation (expressed in fantasies of castration) were more prominent than his dependency needs. Intellectualization, projective tendencies, and reaction formation appeared as habitual defenses. Except for teasing and his sarcastic type of humor, affects were not easily or openly expressed. Intermittently the patient was preoccupied with various areas of his body: his genitals, anus, and nose. The latter two were often mentioned in highly sexualized terms. Anality was strongly evident in his associations and behavior. There was occasional reference to headache, a conversion type of somatic manifestation especially after masturbation. Two brief, mild upper respiratory infections during this period were related to sharp transference reactions anticipating cricism and rejection for his competitive strivings.

On return from the summer interruption, the patient's mounting, frustrated dependency needs begin to appear more prominently, accompanied by a deepening, negative transference. Blocking of both thought and affect increase and represent an attempt to ward off sadomasochistic impulses. However, under the impact of continuing unsatisfactory sexual relationships with his wife and difficulties with some of his colleagues at work, his passive-feminine fantasies begin to break into awareness. He becomes more and more preoccupied with wanting to find out what it is like to be a woman. A reflection of these trends can be noted in the dream which he reports on 9/4 when the detailed account of analytic interviews begins. The associations to it refer to curiosity about a hidden phallus in a passageway which is displaced from genital to anal area in the female and these are further linked with the possibility of injury occurring there. The dream is preceded by repeated *soixante-neuf* with his wife, during which he experiences especially vivid visual and olfactory percepts. For several weeks the patient also has been aware of sensations specifically localized to the anal area. The perceptions appear to be related to intermittent muscle spasm and, perhaps, vascular spasm, which may be the earliest manifestations of local physical dysfunction. The increase in physical sensations and the dream presage further instability in an already shifting psychophysical equilibrium. Though the patient's perceptual awareness of the anorectal area has steadily increased, the significance of the sensory impressions is as yet unknown to him.

On 9/8 after several days of constipation and a compulsion to strain at stool, the patient reports that he feels a lump protruding from his anus. Examination by a consulting surgeon reveals the presence of a small rectal polyp. Obviously a longer period of time than four days was involved in the polyp formation. But the lesion may have been silent until manifestations of its presence became so gross that they could no longer be kept out of direct awareness or disregarded. During the silent phase there may have occurred various subliminal or even stronger sensory perceptions from the malfunctioning area which escaped attention. In any event, increasing references to physical manifestations in the patient's associations, sometimes quite specific, or dreams which on analysis reveal disguised preoccupation with physical dysfunction, especially in the presence of an unstable, regressively shifting psychophysical equilibrium, are all too often disregarded, or their significance is insufficiently understood as cues of developing somatic illness.

Once the presence of the physical dysfunction has been established in the individual's awareness, many different *secondary* psychologic responses may occur. In this instance, the content of the patient's associations suggest an intensification of anxiety and guilt, but there are also more sexual fantasies involving feminine identification accompanied by activation of related memories. The impending surgery quickly comes to represent symbolic castration which activates the defense of denial so effectively that for a number of interviews there is no direct mention of the physical symptoms. The defense proves insufficient a few hours before the operation, and the patient is flooded with anxious feelings, so much so that the perception of actual physical sensations during surgery is considerably blunted (as reported on 9/22).

After a period of about ten days, during which postoperative convalescence is uneventful and preoccupation with physical symptoms and associated fantasies referable to the anus subside, new external psychologic stresses appear

(10/5). There is postponement of a decision about the patient's promotion at work. He reacts to this as if it were a critical rejection of his capabilities and a judgment that he is defective as a man. A retreat into passive-feminine fantasies occurs. In turn, this activates a surge of heterosexual interest which is, however, an insufficient defensive response. Meanwhile, hostility is mobilized, partly manifested in a disguised, affectless way in the transference, and partly displaced with some affect discharge onto his wife whom he accuses of frustrating his sexual desires. Avoidance of painful thoughts and feelings again appears in the form of blocking, but is insufficient and temporary. Projection now becomes more prominent in the alignment of defenses. However, feminine-oriented sexual fantasies and acting out continue, along with fear of exposure. There are increasing references to injury involving the head and neck areas. The quarreling with his wife extends into disagreement about plans for children, and this becomes an additional stress. Details of physical ailments, symptoms, and sensations, some with links to his sexual identity problem, are once more appearing in his associations. Especially prominent are specific sites: head and neck. They are also present in dreams: in one instance there are compensatory references to the powerful neck and shoulders of an athlete; in another, there is expression of physical splinting. Meanwhile, the defense of avoidance-denial is mobilized again. The psychophysical equilibrium is shifting rapidly. Some actual somatic dysfunction occurs after his wife's refusal to have sexual intercourse. She permitted only mutual masturbation which he recalls involved considerable muscular exertion, specifically bending his head to look at his wife's genitals during her orgasm. There may have been some muscle strain at this time, an ordinarily minor physical trauma. Then, recollections of his father's urologic condition break into the patient's awareness and are linked with consequences of masturbation. A transient, somatic identification is activated involving another body site, most likely ureter. Manifestations of actual dysfunction there are brief, and the prevailing physical disturbance turns out to be a severe torticollis. It should be noted that, preceding this illness, head and neck have a strongly symbolized sexual significance as upward displacement of genitals, and that some actual muscle strain occurs in that area. This combination of psychologic sensitization and minor somatic trauma or other malfunction in a particular region of the body may localize it as the site of physical illness when the psychophysical equilibrium becomes unstable.

On 10/15 an abreaction occurs which indicates the intensity of affect that has been blocked off. This massive discharge certainly lowers the total potential aggressiveness and consequently lessens its impact on the musculoskeletal system, specifically the neck muscles. However, simple abreaction with accompanying insight is limited in its therapeutic effect. The process of "working through" the insight developed is necessary for a significant modification of the psychologic conflicts involved in the development of somatic dysfunction and, in turn, the physical illness itself. It may be noted here that the shift in the patient's transference, at first oscillating from a chiefly negative state and then stabilizing in a more positive direction, is also a factor which favors discharge of emotions, lessening guilt and anxiety and, thus, the intensity of the total affect potential. Although the patient's somatic identification with his mother is retrospectively recalled a week after the onset of neck symptoms (10/16), her illness, requiring a thyroidectomy, was, nevertheless, an actual and emotionally significant event in his childhood. It appears then to have reinforced his infantile misinterpretation that the wish equals the deed, particularly in connection with hostile fantasies toward his parents; concomitantly his expectations of punishment became greatly exaggerated. It well could have been a powerful psychologic force acting as a deterrent to the discharge of feelings through emotional expression and at the same time a factor in sensitizing his neck area for the discharge of guilt.

K. L.

Passion Symbols

INTRODUCTION

K. L. is a married, 34-year-old physicist who entered treatment because of recurrent episodes of anxiety which had been increasingly hampering his research work. He is the older of two siblings by three years. His brother, of whom he was always very jealous, is a prosperous farmer, married, with two children. Father, a traveling salesman, was frequently away from the family as the patient was growing up. Both brother and father have enjoyed generally good health. Mother, though she never had a major illness, has always been troubled with many different physical symptoms.

K. L. had severe respiratory illness at age three, requiring hospitalization and surgical intervention. He received much attention at this time from his overanxious mother who tended to keep him close to her and, subsequently, as he was growing up, treated him as if he were a girl, teaching him household skills, especially cooking. When he finally left home to go to college, he had a long period of difficult adjustment to the separation from his mother. His father's absence he resented particularly, feeling deprived of a steady masculine figure with whom he could identify.

The patient has been married for ten years to a woman who is an overanxious person herself, socially quite shy and intermittently depressed. Both he and his wife are cultured people, with many esthetic interests in art, music, and drama. They have two children, a boy of eight and a girl of six. Marital life has been marked by fluctuating good and bad periods, but no major incompatibility is evident.

The preliminary clinical impression was that of a moderately severe character neurosis, with marked passive-feminine traits and obsessional features, decompensating episodically with resultant periods of severe anxiety and mild depression.

Since childhood, the patient has not had any serious physical illness.

The detailed account of the interviews begins with the first four analytic hours and then resumes after an eight-month interval.

CASE MATERIAL

3/6

1   It's important to be on one's back and not stomach. I'm not quite sure why I said that, but it did come to mind. Maybe it's so I can see what's happening and
2   not be taken by surprise. I came in today in a calm mood and wonder why I'm feeling so well. Perhaps it's because the agony of decision-making about starting
3   the analysis is over. Yet I expect it won't be all smooth sailing either. There'll be rough spots. I just hope I won't be bored with my words because I can talk quickly and fluently. I'm going to have to get used to the sound of my own
4   voice. I recently took my family on a long trip down South to visit relatives. I like to drive long distances and wonder if it has anything to do with a need to take on burdensome tasks. My wife and I found it hard to leave my brother and his family, and our daughter sobbed, but we all recovered more quickly than on
5   previous leavetakings. My brother asked why I was undertaking an analysis, and I said I had ambitions. That's not really the answer, and it's one I don't usually use. I want to better myself but not necessarily to get ahead of my relatives.
6   Memories of my relationship with brother are mostly good, but my wife says I tend to forget the bad parts [Low tone of voice and rapid, jerky speech.]
7   I'm disturbed by the gap between the wall and ceiling of your office. I hope that it's not rickety construction. I don't want things coming down on my head. It's a nice molding though. When I work with my hands I can see stresses in the machinery, judge the strength of a structure by the way it looks. My wife can't understand my intense mechanical interest; her interest is in ideas. My kind of thinking got me through an Air Force radar course quite easily. I have a high I.Q. and can work out things mechanically and mathematically in my mind, but am embarrassed to talk about it. Another thing I'm embarrassed to talk about is my musical ability; I play the violin, though not much in recent years, and I think I'm pretty good. Sometimes I think that my interest in such things will make others think of me as a sissy and not the rugged he-man I want them to see.

3/7

1   I've just had a haircut and hope I don't leave any hairs on the couch. I don't want to dirty it up. Today I'm anxious; my hands are cold. That's why they're in

my pocket. My heart is beating fast and hard. It seems as if my head would like to ache a bit. I feel the pounding of my heart will make me bounce on the couch.

I was awakened in the middle of the night by my little daughter coming into my—our—room to announce that her older brother had vomited. I got up grouchily and went to see what had happened and found him lying in a puddle of vomitus with some chocolate he had had for supper. Marion didn't join me, and I had to clean up the mess by myself. He's fine today, though he stayed home from school. I swallow a great deal in trying to maintain a stable home life. There are times when I suffer such frustration and anger as to be practically paralyzed for a short time. My wife, Marion, did something that if I were open and honest about it, I'd be terribly angry. She panicked at our son's getting sick after we had all been so well [pause]. Most of my feelings about my wife are well known to her. I love and hate her, but I can't get down to cases. It's as if I'm hovering like a bird over juicy meat, this hate-love business, then veer away from it. It's difficult to go after tiny tidbits of thought; I'd rather come up with something dramatic that I can show off. 2 3 4

When Marion became my wife, I knew what I was getting into. Several years before our marriage I had been aware that she was capable of deep rages or depressions, lasting from a short time to longer. This kind of reaction disappeared for the most part after she had some therapy. Shortly after we were married, living conditions were difficult and Marion found it hard to take. Sometimes it seems as if any little thing will set her off. I remember last spring we had angry interchanges. One of them occurred the night before our arrival home from a month-long trip. She got panicked about the way I was driving. We both blew up, unable to speak to each other for hours. I broke down into tears, stalked outside the motel we were staying at, and took a long walk by myself. Later she wanted me to apologize for my behavior. I finally made her see she was wrong. Actually there was no real substance to the whole argument. The next day I felt better about it. But it was frightening at the time it actually happened. My mouth was dry and my stomach was gurgling. We've also had arguments over sex. I think that this past year we settled some of them, but there are still plenty of difficulties between us on that score. 5

When we were married, Marion didn't know anything about housework except how to make a toasted cheese sandwich and hot cocoa. I, on the other hand, was a relatively accomplished cook; I had learned by helping mother when I was a youngster, and then later, living alone, I had to make my own meals. We were differently prepared for these domestic matters, and when I lectured her about them, she blew up so hard I never did that again. Since then, she's learned a tremendous amount about housework and cooking, but her unwillingness to clean the house still bothers me. However, right now, other things like poor leadership in government and an impression that we've lost the cold war seem more disturbing to me than family troubles. 6

7   A year before marriage I had told mother about my plans and her reaction was positive. I was hesitant about leaving home and when mother said I was a big boy and could leave, I actually was disappointed and hurt. I felt that mother had rejected me. That's hard for me to stand—the thought of rejection. I wonder why I'm thinking of blowups and rejection now. ["Could it be related to anxiety about what might happen here?"]

3/8

1   If my appointment had been later in the afternoon, I wouldn't have come
2   because the weather forecast is for more snow. I noticed that I felt more anxious
3   than usual as I entered the waiting room. My mouth again began to feel very dry.
      Getting here was no fun, what with slipping and skidding on ice. I had to be very
4   careful. My car was almost bashed in. I'm reminded of the state of tension I get
      into over family troubles. When we visited my brother, he and his wife verbally
      attacked Marion's sister, Eloise, which upset us. Marion began to accuse me of
      going along with my brother. I had to make the choice. If there was an
      argument, I had to make a choice on whose side I was. I finally sided with my
5   wife. Eloise had been working for a research group run by a man of doubtful
      reputation and probable brilliance. There was a question of whether she and her
      boss were involved in an affair. This fellow turned up at a party we all attended
      and took Eloise home. He's a balding, stooped, wise-cracking guy who feels
6   socially inferior. At another party, Marion got engaged in conversation with him.
      In a few seconds he had suggested he would like to go to bed with her, that he
      was a misunderstood genius, and made a great play for her interest. I could never
      do that with a woman. The remarks left her angry, and she cut him down. For a
      while, afterwards, he was quite sheepish. Marion, in evaluating what kind of
      person he was, said he was fascinating and dangerous. My God! Suppose she
      were interested in him. Actually in my marriage I've never had more than a few
      moments of jealousy. Does she think *I'm* promiscuous? All this leaves me still
      tense, with my mouth awfully dry.
7   I'm afraid of what will happen to Marion when she gets old and loses her
      good looks. She'll fly into a terrible rage at any criticism—it's one of those
      prospects that leaves me shaking. If something happened to her, I'd survive, but
      she wouldn't if something happened to me. It makes me think of the possibility
      of something happening to me.
8   I've been considering leaving my job. Marion wants me to leave because she
      feels I'm ready for a better position and because my relationship with my boss is
      strained. She dislikes him a lot; she thinks he's a pompous windbag who pretends
      to be an intellectual. Socially he's been difficult. It's necessary to be one up on
9   him, or he will try to make you look foolish at parties. Marion also wants to
      leave our present house. Once there last year I struggled with a burglar, a young
      punk, who drew a knife when I tried to detain him for the police, and he got

away before they came. I wasn't strong enough to pin him down. Another reason for leaving my job is that a boss in a different firm is trying to lure me away. I have some ideas for doing research but hesitate. I lack confidence in myself; it's like showing myself undressed. My present boss is a terribly ambitious, driving person; these are traits which bother me very much. Yet I really don't see him as unreasonable. These older men, bosses, can be unreasonable or nice. How can one tell in advance? More often I tend to think they'll be tough with me, and I won't be able to stand my ground. [There is anxiety also about how the analyst will behave toward you.] I certainly feel tense here. 10

3/9

My reaction to your interpretations yesterday makes me wonder if I'm suggestible because I so quickly agreed. Now I've had people, competent people, shoot explanations at me and they were often right. But I have a tendency to turn myself around too easily to fit what other people say. I seem to ask for these comments. There is an overtone of criticism or punishment that I detect in many of them. Some of the things I've told you so far are to make you think: He's an interesting guy, I'll keep on analyzing him. That was an admission. I shouldn't have said that because I revealed something of myself which isn't nice, that I'm trying awfully hard to impress you. 1 2

Why do I feel dizzy at the end of the hour? For a couple of minutes afterwards, I'm embarrassed to walk by any people who might be waiting or near me. I feel dizzy like I've just been awakened. My tension is high. Lying down and associating is like going to sleep. Now I'm beginning to feel nauseous. My mouth is very dry again. My anxiety is way up. I can feel a pulse in my neck beating like mad. 3 4

I keep thinking of losing control. The last fistfight I had as a youngster was when I was eight years old in the third grade. It was with a bully. Mother told brother and me it was much braver not to fight—to be a pacifist; in domestic life, too. With my wife, I've kept my anger under control. Once at work I got furious and had a nosebleed. I know now when I'm angry, but I don't know what to do with it. Anger at my boss paralyzes me. My wife won't stand for me to be so reasonable and controlled when I'm angry. I get anxious about pleasing some of my superiors and periodically I go through spells of feeling incompetent professionally. Once Marion beat me in an achievement test. I know in school when I was a kid, I never wanted to cheat, though I have a vague recollection that I did, though rarely. I vaguely expect you to disapprove just as something in me does. If I wanted to, I could dredge up a whole mess of things for which I could be judged. Yet I've never cheated on my wife, though I've had such fantasies. Again, when I was a kid, I remember I used to go to a little candy store, and on one occasion I pocketed a chocolate bar. I think I walked out of 5 6 7 the store sideways. I have an image of climbing up a narrow walk in front of a billboard and then crossing it sideways, afraid I might fall at any moment. I'm feeling dizzy now as I realize that the hour is up.

3/10-11/2 Interim Summary

The first four analytic hours have been presented to illustrate the frequency and nature of the patient's somatic complaints from the very beginning of the analysis. During subsequent months these symptoms often appeared as physical expressions of his anxiety and, at times, depression. The feelings were closely linked to a strong sense of inferiority and compensatory competition focused particularly on his relationship with his boss and also evident in the transference. His overemphasis on his sexual exploits with his wife, and his hypersensitivity to her not always acceding to his approaches indicated an underlying concern about his potency. When he had had one of his frequent run-ins with his boss or when, on his own, he felt a sense of dissatisfaction with his work or his family life, he took refuge in fantasies involving his feminine identifications and interests. Anger at feeling rejected or frustrated tended to be suppressed or diluted although actually it was strong and accompanied by guilt. There is again a breakthrough of homosexual fantasies as the detailed reporting resumes after an interim of eight months.

11/3

1   I seem to have a jumble of sensations. The weekend has left me up and down, uncertain of myself. There are three sick people at home. One kid has fever and sore throat; the other has a cough that brings on vomiting. Marion has developed sudden, severe cold symptoms. I became the chief cook and bottlewasher, burned leaves, supported one kid's head while she vomited, and

2   fed the other one aspirin. Sunday morning I masturbated for the first time in months. I didn't feel so horribly guilty. I put analysis out of mind. I had fantasies of the usual sexual activities with Marion. It's been almost two weeks since I've had any sexual outlet. There are almost irresistible surges of sexual feeling. After almost two weeks of abstinence, I wonder how I'll do. There's also a sense of pressure building up about my responsibilities, without any prospect of relief. I feel quite depressed right now, though I'm getting so much done. I've arranged two interviews with the dentist, finished up some reading, and got a lot of bills paid.

3   Maybe it's got something to do with the treatment. Last week I felt I was getting far more deeply involved than I ever felt possible. I'm more and more aware of the relationship here: I have mixed feelings, but I strongly want to

4   come and continue. I can't get rid of the feeling that Marion's getting sick was to frustrate me. I didn't snap at her, though I did at the kids. One is doing very well in reading, but the other is bored and somewhat slow in school [pause].

["Two interviews with the dentist?"] That wasn't a slip. The two sessions 5
with the dentist were both gratifying and uncomfortable. I got two important
fillings done. I had been putting this off. Pulling ideas out of me is like
tooth-pulling, but no teeth were pulled. On my second visit there I felt quite
anxious until the drilling was well under way. My teeth used to be a matter of
concern to mother. She took care of the dental appointments and paid for them
just as she took charge of so many other things. I've never felt comfortable
about taking this responsibility on. An adolescent daughter of one of our friends
was recently in a panic over having to have some complicated dental work. I
myself object to the drilling away at a small hole in my teeth. I find the
vibration bothersome. Maybe this all has some other meaning—like the dentist is
a man with his tool in my mouth. I remember that earlier in the analysis I had
strange feelings in my mouth—dryness—that came on when I had sexual
thoughts. Then there have been these references to cocksucking that I've
brought up in recent hours. Yesterday in the morning I got sexually stood up. I
woke up aroused with an erection. I asked Marion if she would kiss such a big,
solid penis. She did and that got me more excited, but then she didn't feel like
continuing and I was left high and dry.

11/4

[Puts check on desk.] 1
This morning I'm on time. I didn't get much sleep last night. This prompt
payment means I fought off not wanting to pay or come. It's bribe money,
making sure I don't stop now. Yesterday, for the first time since I was in my 2
teens, I was aware of a frank, open sexual feeling about males. I've known about
this aspect of my sexuality, but in a dim way. I recall when I was a student
undressing with others that I allowed my eyes to wander to their genitals, and
there was a surge of sexual feeling. I'm not comfortable with this awareness of
homosexual traits. My mind now is filled with images of male genitals; it's both
foreign and exciting. I expect to be understood here, but I'm also afraid I'll be
looked down on. Now for some reason I have a vague recollection of an early
illness, being in a hospital with mother. I think of being in trouble and having an
older woman around. This anxiety I'm experiencing makes me wonder if I've
turned up something. Visual images: I smoke a pipe, and I get pleasure in 3
stopping up the smoke hole. When Marion kisses my penis, sometimes she
manipulates her tongue in the opening there. Again these visual images keep
coming into my mind: dangling, fullgrown male genitals, darkened with hair,
some circumcised and some not. Father had a small one. Brother had the biggest.
Mine is in between. Now suddenly I expect to be struck with a bolt of lightning.
I never knew what mother's pubic hair looked like. The only time I saw her
naked was from the rear, her buttocks, but not what she had between her legs in
front. I don't have any memory of a direct sexual feeling about mother. I recall
sometimes hearing her urinate in the toilet with the door partly open. I also

4   remember seeing the big box of Kotex in the corner of her closet. All this reminds me that I have a strong sexual desire for Marion, but she isn't well, not yet over her sore throat. She's very upset that some of her P.T.A. plans aren't running smoothly [clears throat several times]. Something seems to be coming
5   up into my larynx [pause]. Last night I felt anxious but not paralyzed. All those sexual feelings keep surging up. Mixed images. Intrustions into my rear by a male. Marion's tonguing the opening of my penis. My own desire to penetrate Marion.

11/5

1   I feel more rested today. I developed a slight soreness in my left eye late yesterday. It's a little swelling or something which occasionally forms there but
2   quickly goes away. Today there's a meeting of my literary club, and I am giving a paper. That's a good place for me to look stupid. Anyway, things are better at home. The kids seemed healthier this morning. My desire for sexual activity continues to be urgent, but it was not possible to satisfy it last night. I talked briefly with Marion about it. She was kind and listened considerately, but was not feeling well enough to go ahead, so we both fell asleep. Now I'm thinking about angry women who leave their husbands. But I have a friend who locks his wife out when she's away too long [pause].

3   Here's an echo of yesterday's hour: fantasies about penises, their size, shape, appearance are flooding my mind. It's distasteful to me. Again I think of being pierced from the rear by this chum of mine, being corn-holed. I was about 12 or 13 years old then, and I recall a guilty kind of enjoyment of this experience. It happened before I began to masturbate. Last summer when I was ill and constipated, I dug it out with my fingers. Apart from the great discomfort I had in being so blocked up, there was something sexually exciting about having that big lump in me and finally delivering it. Despite all these homo fantasies, I feel more tender and less angry with Marion. Furthermore, today I didn't experience the slight unwillingness to come to the analytic hour that I've had in the past few days [pause].

I have a fantasy of a power plant. I can see the shiny, smooth, steel pistons moving in and out. That makes me think of the shiny head of my chum's penis. I think it was uncircumcised. I was fascinated by it and tried to look at the action going on from behind as he buggered me [pause].

My work seems to be going alright, no special situations recently. I'm again aware of this thing on my eye. It's still sore and seems to be worse than earlier. If it doesn't get any better, I'll call my doctor and ask him what to do about it. So far I've treated it with neglect.

11/6, Excerpt

[Late 15 minutes.]   1

I'm tired, worn out, ashamed. I feel too close in some ways to my   2
weaknesses. I feel shame because I have to show off the unpleasant side. Last
night I was in a thoroughgoing stew, frustrated, angry, and upset, both for
feeling too much—especially in a sexual way—and for feeling too little beyond
that. When Marion got into bed she developed, anyway she said she had, a
stomachache and a headache. Consequently there was no sex once again. I just
didn't sleep well. That insistent sexual urge woke me at dawn. I wanted to get
out and puncture somebody. I had a terrific flurry of fantasies—all sexual. I did   3
and didn't want to come here today. It's as if I have to go screaming to you after
my difficulties with Marion. It's like going home and tattling on a friend who's
tossed a rock at you. I don't want to share this with you and don't want you to
judge it. But I'm trying to speak and act in a civilized way and understand what's
going on. The next few days I've got things to be taken care of, and I've got to
control myself. That's the problem with me, either too much or too little
control, and when it's the latter, things could get out of hand.

11/10

There's been so much internal pressure in the last few days that I feel a   1
leaking out is occurring at the seams. I had several dreams. In one a man—I don't   2
know who—was about to suck on me as I lay in bed. In another the scene was in   3
several rooms of an apartment with lots of people around. I was trying to do
something sexual with a female friend of ours who's been involved with another
man. She was resisting and trying to ask questions about my family life. When I
parried them, she got angry. We were sitting on reclining chairs in a side room
connected with the rest of the apartment. I ended up in another room where
food in dishes that were already dirty was being put on a clean tablecloth.

Yesterday I just had to talk to someone. I blurted out my sexual frustration   4
to Marion and told her how upset I was and that it was all giving me a pain in the
neck. She asked, "You haven't been thinking of Mrs. L, have you? Is that what's
getting you all hot and bothered?" Mrs. L is the wife of one of my bosses. Well,
this morning I woke up and actually had a terrible spasm of my back between
my shoulder blades. I did see Mrs. L two days ago at work. She's a very
attractive, middle-aged woman whom Marion and I have met on several social
occasions.

Here's another dream I just recalled: I'm playing on a giant pipe organ and   5
trying to get just the right kind of tone, deep and sonorous. Nothing comes out

but a feeble, flabby tone. It makes me think I can't produce, no matter how hard I try. Saturday night I tried to interest Marion once again in sex, but without any success, and the next morning she had her period, so that was that. I felt dreadfully put off and frustrated. So now I'm thinking of the organ with the flat, flabby tone. The organ is the king of instruments, and in playing it one would have a great feeling of control. I've felt terribly let down, not a man, not wanted, little.

6   Yesterday all day I kept having and fighting off thoughts of masturbating. As the day progressed, I developed a severe headache. The dreams and sensations seem to confirm my needs, my frustration, my low feelings. The organ fizzled. I fizzled. Today I've got a stiff neck. Last Friday I had my jaw mangled again by the dentist. Yesterday I wrote a letter to my parents. My thoughts are jumping around [pause].

7   Saturday an urge of months culminated in action. I wanted a pair of shoes for tramping in the yard in the winter. There's something fascinating in getting a stout pair of masculine shoes. Well, I bought them Saturday together with socks and underwear. I find myself over-pleased with the purchase. I remember wearing father's tweeds and feeling like a rugged guy. A tuxedo is for high society and weak men [pause].

8   ["Any further thoughts about the dreams?"] The organ. I'm reluctant to look back at previous material, like Eurydice looking back and turning to stone. An aria from *Orfeo and Eurydice* by Monteverdi comes to mind. It's about betrothal and early love before she died. Maybe those dreams have something to do with who I think I am and what's going on here.

11/11

1   While waiting to come in, all I could think of was the pain. The severe pain left me late yesterday and then came back this morning. It reached its peak while I was driving over here and when I got into the waiting room, I almost screamed. The spasm in my back was terrific, even with the three aspirins I took. It's most annoying. I can't stand up straight, and right now I'm not interested at all in symbolic meanings, just in getting some relief. After I left your office yesterday, the pain went away very rapidly by noon. But last night, without understanding why, I couldn't fall asleep until 1:30 A.M. A while ago I was

2   feeling pain severe enough to make me grit my teeth and fight off tears. Now that it's sort of letting up, I feel empty and depressed and foolish. I look crazy

3   when I have this thing. I haven't suffered so much for a long time. What kept me awake was worrying about Marion whose sore throat and stomachache continue. I haven't had so much pain for years, when on one occasion I had to turn myself

4   into a hospital for three days. Today I have no chance to be sick in bed, just when I would like to be taken care of. Well, the couch is horizontal—a place for relief. Maybe there's something wrong with my spine. I mean something really

serious. This pain is so distressing I find it hard to endure. Now I'm empty of thoughts [pause].

You know, if I were walking out of hell now, I couldn't look back, I couldn't twist my neck. Maybe I'm really walking into it. Yesterday things were getting hot. Thoughts of walking into strange, overheated rooms. The dreams of the weekend—a man almost sucking on me. In describing it I feel squeamish about using any common or vulgar terms. Who are these unknown men entering my dreams? One of my friends told me he had disturbing dreams about someone resembling his father, no, it was his father, bending over him presenting his rear end.

The word has come into my mind again—cocksucking. It's become part of our more intimate marital life. Marion and I find it enjoyable, stimulating, but not the ultimate. I have a reaction of disgust—not strong—about men engaging in this activity, especially if I picture it as something that can be observed and watched. Also, I keep thinking how the teeth can do injury; the penis can be clipped off in the mouth [pause].

Today with all my pain, I feel like telling everyone to go to hell. To you I'd like to say, "Take care of me. Dammit, I want you to take care of me in a special way." I realize more than I ever did before how much that's what I expect from analysis, especially under these conditions. Yet you've been decent to me, haven't kicked me out for my sexual dirtiness.

11/12, Excerpt

I'm somewhat more human today. All my pain left me one hour after I left here yesterday. It seems as if the whole thing just poured out of my mind. I have an unwelcome feeling about the previous patient. I keep thinking: what's he doing in there, does he bore you as much as I do? What kind of a jerk is he?

It's embarrassing to admit that I masturbated yesterday. Marion was still sick in bed and the kids were outside. I have been accusing myself of perversions, but my fantasies yesterday while I was masturbating were about women. When I was at the newsstand, I wanted to buy some girlie magazines. The body culture magazines—those for men—seemed less attractive to me. In the last few weeks sex has been on my mind a lot, more than it usually is, with the desire to look at undressed women uppermost.

I find myself continuing to be jealous of the people who come in here. At the same time I'm afraid that saying crazy thoughts which come into my mind is sure to get me rejected. While the perverse side of sex is actually distasteful to me, I still have the urge to buy sex pictures and masturbate. At the same time I want to make love to Marion but can't because she's still sick. I get my brother and my son all mixed up in my mind. When my brother had that bicycle accident, I remember how frightened everyone was that he'd be a cripple. Mother took such good care of him and tutored him for a long, long time. I sure didn't like that, and I still don't. I wanted to be the only one with her as I do with you.

11/13, Excerpt

1 I find it hard to start this morning. If I missed the hour today, would it
2 signify a possible change for the worse in me? I used to be distrustful of you. Crazy notion. I used to have the fantasy that, when you realized how inept and inferior I am, you would somehow communicate this to my boss and thus influence his attitude toward me. But you don't even know him. Furthermore, I've said a lot of crazy things here without incurring any punishment or criticism from you.

3 The feeling inside me right now is as if I had something there to be vomited up. That would be smelly and have to be washed down the drain. Suppose they discovered at work I was in treatment and then you would be asked how suitable
4 I was. You might stand between me and success, if I don't live up to certain standards. Yet how do I look? At worst I appear as a dishonest, perverted, creepy character. It's as if I'm afraid you'll be like the father who says his son is a homosexual and shouldn't teach. There I go again, putting you in the role of a father. I guess I expect you to judge and make known my interest in girlie magazines and my curiosity about other patients—my peeping tendencies. It brings to mind a girl I once knew who described how she sucked off her boyfriends. I've always had this interest in what girls are like, how they think, feel, what they wear. I'm thinking of my intimate contact with Marion, her genitals in my mouth, the taste of her secretions, the smell [pause]. How close I have to get to her and this part of her body, almost as if it has to be taken in.

5 Now I'm feeling hunger pangs in the upper portion of my stomach. I want something to eat.

11/14, Excerpt

1 Today I'm dressed in all clean clothes. Fantasies of female genitals are running through my mind, the pink vulva with sawteeth, changing to a hard, horny beak. Now I have fantasies of giant mollusks catching pearl divers; the hard central mouth, destructive, between the legs, drawing everything in. My earliest memory of the female body is mother from behind. Again I have sexual fantasies, this time about things going in and out of anuses. Remember playing as a kid with the little girl next door. Her vagina was hidden and the anus seemed like the opening. I keep wanting to see what the vulva is doing during sexual activity. In sixty-nine Marion applies her mouth and teeth to my penis, but at the same time I am looking to see if there are also teeth in her vulva.

11/17

I feel as though I had recovered from something. The weekend was busy and   1
happy. I was thinking about the analysis—wouldn't it be nice to stop here? I've
accomplished a lot. I want to avoid any further discomfort and censure. Actually   2
it all emanates from my conscience. Last Saturday I kicked my conscience in the
teeth and got angry with it. Marion had a sore throat on Saturday. She's had a   3
lot of them. We played around. That titillated me, and I went off and
masturbated, couldn't hold off any longer. However, that evening Marion felt
better, and we had intercourse. It was most enjoyable. The stimulus for jerking
off earlier was Marion's playfulness which can be quite overpowering. Now I feel
as if the need to peep is all gone.

On Friday I got involved in a small obsession about buying a compass for the   4
car. I want to know where I'm going. The obsession became strongest
immediately after I left the house on Thursday. Well, I finally got it installed on
Saturday. ["Wanting to know where you're going has something to do with the
analysis."]

I had a dream over the weekend. One of my friends and I were driving   5
around the snow in our foreign cars. I stopped at a nearby college to look it
over. We had to duck through a low window with a bar across it, as though it
had been wrecked. People were coming through. We got into a basement, the
lower section, and there was a girl in charge. Someone called on the phone to say
that thugs were after me. This dream reminds me of the other dream of the
house whose ventilating and duct systems I was so interested in, crawling
through them. I remember at the age of six or seven that secret passageways
fascinated me. I would imagine all kinds of intricate ones. In the dream the   6
window with a bar makes me think of a guarded opening. My next thought is
that of the lower rear deep portion of the body, the rectum. Now I can feel a
peculiar sensation in my own rectum. Why the thugs? In the dream it's as if I'm   7
being chased out of these places by punitive, dark-cloaked, eerie people—the
thugs. The college must be this building, your office. The bar across the window
is the bar seen in old-fashioned elevators. There is one in the elevator in this
building. There are often people coming out. ["There is considerable curiosity
about me who sits behind you and what I do, as well as about many sexual
matters. At the same time you're afraid you'll be punished for this curiosity."]

11/18

Today the horizontal position suits me. I'm tired. There was too much   1
excitement last night: music, good food, wines. I felt stimulated and excited by
the concert. The violinist was a cold, mechanical player, playing down to the   2

audience, but technically he's brilliant. Marion is finally feeling much better so that we were able to go out. We were with some friends who enjoy music. The soloist seemed to have no concern about the audience. I, on the other hand, would not want to expose myself by performing in front of an audience.

3   One of my friends at work seemed depressed and yet tried to joke about it, about getting to a couch and getting brainwashed. I told him I didn't know where I was in my analysis, but that I did feel more comfortable in my work than ever before. At least here my fear of being perverted is out in the open.

4   I had a dream in which you were the helmsman, steering a boat I was on. Somehow I expected you to have superman powers, which you would use for my benefit. Instead you led me through my twisted thoughts about femininity and homosexuality. Marriage, that is, home and sex life, and being here represent two poles. There are certain similarities: I feel somewhat loosened up both at

5   home and here. But there's a space between the poles. I had cold feet and hands 15 minutes before Marion came to bed last night anticipating intercourse. Then she suddenly was very mad at me because of my cold feet and what she claimed was my bad breath. She had a full bladder and went to the toilet. When she came back, all her anger had been drained out. I know my cold hands and feet were accompanied by frank feelings of anxiety. One of the children had a bad cough that kept awakening me and added to my tension.

11/19

1   Had an interview with my boss yesterday, and we just don't seem to get along. Afterwards I kept having persistent fantasies of men injuring me. To top it off, Marion didn't like the way I handled myself with him and got me mad. She had another one of her bellyaches and that means no sex. I had a restless night and dreamt that I had an electric shaver with three heads. There was also a thin, long brush which was bent in half and utterly useless. The brush was inserted into the head of the shaver and then pulled out, like a piston movement which was repeated. In this way the bristles were shaved off the brush. That dream sure indicates the way I feel. As if my balls had been cut off. And not just by Marion,

2   but by my boss too. Afterwards I masturbated. I noticed that I began to itch all over. In the last few weeks when I'm excited I break out with something that looks like hives and it's very itchy. Maybe there is more pleasure to be had from masturbation than with a female of the opposite sex. Anal stimulation seems to give even greater pleasure when it's combined with ordinary, straightforward masturbation. But I feel uneasy about it.

3   Over the weekend and yesterday I felt I was about to enter a painful and unpleasant part of analysis. Maybe I'll function rather badly. I suppose that's a possibility I have to face, but I can't allow anything to interfere with my ability to work. I have a feeling that coming here is like coming to a prostitute. You see,

a prostitute is a person with whom one works out the problems of being masculine and those are my problems. Sunday night I had a cold nose, cold hands and feet. I was anxious and unsure of myself. I think of another analyst—a small man who cuts his big analysands down to size. You're small. My wife's small. It seems strange to include her in this group.

11/20

I have a slight amount of muscle soreness around my neck. Last night I sat   1
around late talking to people. Makes me think of teeth, jaws that bite and claws that scratch. All kinds of crazy thoughts are flashing through my mind. A devouring vulva. A volcanic hole. Danger there. I can't go through life thinking this.

I've had a painless redness of the eye. Could it be what's called "iriteness"   2
[iritis and irateness!]? I'm sure mad at you for planning to be away at those meetings next week. I haven't done anything for the eye condition because it doesn't hurt and maybe it'll go away by itself. You can see there's only slight redness now. I'm reminded of hunting for Dad's hidden, powerful telescope. When I was a kid, I did a lot of looking—trying to see into other people's houses, what they were doing, especially if they were undressing. I was particularly fascinated by rear ends, women's behinds. The next-door neighbor, a middle-aged widow, never pulled her blinds down, and many times I'd get an erection or come off as I watched her strip.

Last night I dreamt that I had Marion put mucilage on my rear end. That's   3
all I can remember about it. I think of mucilage looking like urine, but it's also gooey and sticky unlike urine, more like feces, maybe semen, having an odd smell. The tip of the mucilage bottle reminds me of a penis. Mucilage is for paper, and I think now of paper genitals. That has an unmanly ring to it. Images of half-men-half-women pass through my mind. I wonder how would it feel to be penetrated like a woman; that's one of my masturbation fantasies. Another is having the woman on top. Then, it's as if she's like the man, doing all the work and I'm just lying back. These ideas, like visual images, have been cluttering up my mind more than usual in recent days. It's hard to think about other things then.

11/21 - 2/9, Interim Summary

In the next few months the patient continued to have transient somatic dysfunction but no major physical illness. Inferiority feelings evoked grandiose power fantasies. Passive-feminine tendencies remained prominent especially in his sexual thoughts and activities. More hostility appeared, not only in relation to his competitiveness with other men, but also in connection with frustrated needs to be mothered by his wife.

2/10, Excerpt

1   I seem to have an urge to confess. I felt silly speaking up at a recent PTA meeting. I didn't think much of what I had to say and I was afraid of being
2   ignored or considered incompetent. With the bad weather I felt like staying in bed all day and having dreams of glory. In trying to overcome my inferiority feelings, I keep having an image of myself as a genius who knows everything about everything. In that way I avoid the opposite dreadful, unbearable thought of myself as the ineffective individual who puts his foot in his mouth and is
3   always awkward. I heard recently that a relative of father's, who was supposed to be a lady's man, has cancer of the prostate. It's dangerous to be a swordsman—a Don Juan. If you knock up a girl, there's danger in proving your manliness that way. I keep accusing myself of having a high, boyish voice and that means I'm not a man. But my being in analysis has benefited Marion; she seems stronger in the past year. I hope that I am, too.
4   Now my muscles are tight and uncomfortable. I feel like stretching. I keep thinking that through it all Marion has been warm and understanding—critical but not cruel.

2/13

1   [Late 5 minutes.]
2, 3   My left hip felt stiff on awakening this morning. I don't imagine I'll develop arthritis though. Think of struggling through traffic on my way to work or here [constant throat clearing].
4   I had a dream in which I'm driving along some place south of Boston. Some guy in a panel truck cut in front of me. I plowed right into him and scrunched the side of his truck. We stopped. I tried to find who was right and wrong. Then the truck disappeared. I came back to my car and saw the right front fender ripped.
    My first association is about plowing into the truck. The steel in my car seems as strong as the steel in the panel truck. It's a way of expressing anger. I keep in mind the possibility of trouble with father. Turning around to punch a guy in the rear while driving is what I fear most. My Dad used to criticize my driving and would give me the car only with great reluctance. I remember being angry at him for being away so much from home and for mistreating mother. I used to argue with him about his bigoted remarks about Negroes and Jews. Mother hated fights—would get terrible headaches. I'm very proud of my little car in the dream. I remember something else now—father's financial troubles, his being pushed too far by a creditor, and his being hurt deeply and at one time having to give up his own car.

The dent in the right front fender was just superficial. It's like somebody 5
with bloody knuckles or nose; they would quickly heal. The steel behind the
fender prevented any further damage. When I looked at the fender afterwards, it
seemed that nothing had happened to it, although I remember I felt the buckling
when the two vehicles rammed in the dream [pause].

I'm thinking of my sore hip—not sure now which side; the left, I believe. 6
There's something hippy about a fender. Now my thoughts are concerned with
what happens to a penis, what can happen to it in intercourse. That's bothered
me for a long time.

One of the main things in the dream was anger. I've been angry with my boss 7
at work on and off, but more recently, I've given more thought to my future
career. It seems I've been dangling like a fish on a hook, with my boss holding
the rod, and I don't want to be in that position. On one occasion the other day I
went dashing into his office and had it out with him. It was a bruising
experience, and I'm not sure who came out best. I guess I took a chance and
showed my steel. Thinking again of the dream, I see the panel truck as your car.
I recall that there is a panel on your car. [Discussion of transference aspects.]

2/14

It's good that I managed to get in here without any brushes with the law. 1
Five years ago tonight I got my first ticket for speeding. Yesterday I felt relieved 2
and bright-eyed. Something valuable had come up: your explanations about my
wanting to be like father and you, envying him, concerned I cannot be like him,
wishing him gone so I can have mother to myself. A part of me gibes that the
way to get through analysis is to agree with everything, but I can laugh at that
and disregard it. But I wonder why I've been thinking so much about the law.
["There is guilt over persisting, forbidden sexual wishes and also over 3
competition with authority figures. This guilt may influence you to act out in
such a way that you get into trouble with the authorities and then get punished
or threatened with punishment."] I feel more guilty right now about what you'll
think than about what my parents may have thought [pause].

Some childhood memories are coming back. Mother padding around the 4
house in her nightgown at night. I have recollections of sleeping with Dad. A few
times when mother was gone, I slept with him. Had a mixed sensation about it. I
felt I was replacing her. I remember occasionally his turning over at night and
landing with his arm on top of me. It was uncomfortable—almost too warm.
Mother never did this with me. Any naps I took with mother were on top of the
bed. But there must have been times when I crawled into bed with both of them.
I remember mother's softness, but there was something unpleasant about Dad's
whiskers. I know I've been aware of mother's breasts over the years; she had
rather long ones. The description of Lady Chatterley's breasts was that they

were long. When I was 11 years old and in the sixth grade, I was acutely aware at moments of other people's dirty minds from their remarks and jokes. I remember a girl cousin a little older than me, with developing breasts and big nipples. I remember also Dad's developing a little pot; this made him seem fairly old and womanish.

2/17

1   It's too nice a day to be emotionally disturbed. I feel pretty well held together today even though a hose in the car blew out, and the engine almost
2   burnt over the weekend. Marion has been rather happy, even though she's premenstrual. In a short time it'll be our ten-year anniversary. I recall when we were planning marriage. Marion's father was cooperative but not really enthusiastic about it. We got a whole bunch of useless wedding gifts. Before we got married, Marion and I had a hard time keeping our hands off each other. But both of us had a strong sense of guilt, and we didn't get really intimate. Last
3   night we made satisfactory love and were late getting to sleep. Then our daughter, Lorna, woke up several times during the night complaining of not feeling well. She's just come down with the nastiest case of chickenpox, so itchy, with sores on her eyelids, mouth, and throat. But I was sore at having to get up each time to tend to her. This morning the alarm didn't go off, and I almost got up late [pause].
4   I have a tiny bit of resentment toward you, that you enter in my personal feelings. If you should talk about my parents here, it irritates me. I think, irrationally, what right do you have to say these things about them. I keep fighting off the impulse to refer to father as daddy, like a little kid.
5   My thoughts go back to making love with Marion. I wouldn't mind if a new baby arrived. The house is big enough. I have a more benign feeling toward women now than I had a few days ago, when I felt like strangling Marion because
6   she was being so bitchy and cutting. Actually I've been afraid of having intercourse, concerned about the possibility of being impotent. But last night things were fine, and I'm not afraid now that I'll be unable to act like a man sexually—at least for the time being.

2/18

1   I had a long dream last night. There was a birthday party at the house of one of our friends. Toward the end of it, there was a movement toward the door. The atmosphere seemed odd. Several people were going to bathrooms; one was marked *women*, on the left, and *men* on the right. Lorna, my daughter, went to the toilet on the left. I opened the door of the bathroom on the left, glanced in, discovered it was the wrong one. So I went into the one on the right. It, in turn, was divided into several rooms. There was a small bathroom leading to a large

one with various, odd-looking gadgets for crapping into without partitions for privacy. I was hunting for the proper bowl, for the proper toilet. At first, there seemed to be only porcelain tops, some being square. I found a toilet, had to sit on the edge; it was uncomfortable and not clean. I dropped my pants and found my underwear smeared. I didn't take a crap, then wondered what to do with my underwear, whether to wash it. That was the end of the dream.

I haven't washed my hair for several weeks. I bring in a dirty head and drop   2
it on your pillow. Over the weekend, I lined the toilet tank with insulating material, so it wouldn't sweat and drip on the floor, leaving puddles. It was a messy job doing it. The mastic I used to bond the insulation looks like clay-colored stool. A wonderful mess. I couldn't clean it off easily. Reminds me of not being able to clean off my behind easily, always being unsure whether I've gotten it all with the toilet paper. Another messy place that comes to mind is the   3
smelly men's locker room at the public golf course. It's for men only—a kind of homosexual setting. An old memory comes up of being buggered when I was a youngster by an older boy. Last Friday I made love to Marion from behind. I   4
completed the act in this position for the first time. Marion likes the penis in her no matter from what position [pause].

Some unpleasant thoughts are forcing their way in [pause]. Why prefer   5
daddy in intercourse? Daddy is cleaner; it's part of a limerick. Wanting to be stabbed in the rear end—by you. Crazy stuff. Something's brewing, and I don't know what.

2/19

Today I'm uncomfortable—anxious, irritable, restless, and tired. A little   1
unzipped. Masturbated yesterday. It was anything but a satisfying experience.   2
The thoughts immediately preceding it have to do with dirty, childhood play: this older boy and I defecating in front of each other, examining our behinds, inserting objects into the rectum among other happenings. Before masturbating,   3
somewhat earlier, my abdomen began to feel awfully gripey, and I finally had to rush and have a bowel movement which for the first time in months was sticky. An hour later I was back in the toilet masturbating. I have fantasies during   4
intercourse of how it would be fun if it were possible to enjoy some anal sensation at the same time. I would like to have something stuck in, stuck up my rectum. Early in the marriage, using finger cots, both Marion and I went through a brief period of just this kind of exploration, stimulating each other. Smelly business.

I noticed yesterday afternoon that the back of my seat in the car needs   5
repair. It irritated me all the way home.

When my friend and I played around with sticks up our behinds, it ended   6
with a kind of ejaculation, actually defecation. I have memories of outhouses for workers in the fields; there were no seats there [as in the dream related the

previous day]. When I was a youngster, I kept worrying about getting the last bit of fecal material out of the syringe of mother's douche tube that I used to play with. I was afraid that if I left something dirty, it would hurt mother who used

7

8 that apparatus. The previous patient, after leaving your office, entered the bathroom in a rush and made noises as if he had diarrhea. I have crazy fantasies now of ejaculating through my real penis, and one I have somewhere in my rectum.

9 I keep wondering and am confused. Where does a bobcat keep his penis? Why do spider monkeys have crazy penises, hanging so far behind? With dogs there seems to be a posterior connection. Animals backing up to each other and copulating in a posterior way. Birds copulate by a cloacal kiss. I keep having persistent thoughts of anal masturbation. During adolescence the picture that particularly inflamed me was that of a very nubile female dressed only in a few grapes. I keep thinking of some of the girls I knew when I was a kid, fooling around. One in particular I recall let me play with her behind and stick my finger into her rectum. I used to picture these activities over and over again in my old masturbation fantasies.

2/20

1 I forgot to shave this morning. I started last night to cut my fingernails and didn't finish. Though I bathed, I still feel sloppy. I don't like myself this way.

2 My nose is sore. On one side is a large point of a pimple about to bust loose. When I touched it a while ago, it began to bleed; pus and matter came out. There's something sloppy about it and me. It makes me think back to the stuff I was talking about yesterday. All that crap and smell.

3 Lorna has an inflammation of her eyes. They call it conjunctivitis, I guess. It's a messy business, too. Her eyes are all matted together with this sticky discharge. It has something to do with her chickenpox. She still has some sores on her face. But I guess she'll be alright.

4 I had a dream I was in bed with another woman—a pretty secretary at work. It reminds me of a very attractive, pleasant lady amateur tennis champ I met recently. She's the sort of person everyone could fall in love with. She's gone back to California, her home state. In the last 24 hours I've had a crude realization that I may at some time in my analysis fall out of love with Marion, even turn on her. There's something very bigamous about me right now. It's possible between two people, working together, for something sexual to develop. I would very much have liked to have made love to that tennis player. If I were studying for some kind of priesthood, then I would have to remain celibate.

5 I keep having an image of dad working, and a wild impulse to rush out after the hour and look for the things he has done. In his own way he may have

6 accomplished something. I keep fondling and feeding myself with images of

conquering all women when I was a youngster, yet at a ninth-grade dance I was afraid to touch a girl.

2/21

I had two dreams. One was odd and the other was disturbing.

In the first dream, I was driving a car, going to LaGuardia Airfield which [1] appeared small, postage-stamp size, 100 yards or so, surrounded by high trees, rundown buildings, and a few aircraft. It was closed down to the biggest planes, only for small, private planes. There was a takeoff by a small plane which shot up vertically in the air. Then there was a young man on a modified motorcycle which gave a leap and flew up in the air. It also went straight up, began to hover, came down with a bang on the rear tire, bounced up, but didn't lose balance, and the young man landed smiling and in perfect control. I asked him how he did it and looked over his cycle. There was a wooden cover over the frame. He couldn't explain and I was baffled. Marion also had a dream—a nightmare from which she awoke crying something about a lover who cut off her head.

In the second dream I was going to or actually performed in a concert with [2] professional or semiprofessional musicians. At the end of the concert, I was handed a strange instrument with a burlap bag over it and vents. I was told it was an English horn with a reed in it. I made a few sounds. Although Marion was around, I volunteered to take a widow we know—a lady musician—home, and did. She became very affectionate and I very warm. We were arm-in-arm. I was with her in the back seat of a car. I knew in the dream that something was up. She was going to ask me to make love and I would accept. This, however, didn't come to pass. I went back and found Marion.

I feel shocked at this second dream, making love to an older woman. She knew people of the Old World and has adolescent children. She's a maternal person, yet in many ways unlike my own mother. It seems as though I'm adding every woman I can find to my list to screw.

In the first dream I was reminded of airmen whose training program was [See 1] discontinued, and then they were sent to boot camp. They felt so screwed. They devised a symbol of a screw with wings, a flying screw, painted black, on the backs of their dungarees, on their behinds. I realize I'm afraid of getting screwed at my job.

Marion has been crampy. She's two weeks overdue for her period. We were [3] talking in bed about pain, pregnancy, bringing up new children. Marion said she couldn't stand children going through illnesses. Our son's early illnesses contributed to her irritable temper, she thought, and wondered if his accidentally getting burned when he was younger made him feel afraid to be like other boys. He has an ear infection now and is getting an antibiotic for it which may be giving him diarrhea and a rash on the bottom. Pain, guilt, helplessness all seem to have been mixed up in her thoughts. Our little girl still has some skin sores which seem to be complicated by poison ivy.

4   I now recall my own childhood toys. I had a bicycle and a toy plane. It was quite large and could make smooth landings. It gave me much pleasure. It was painted silver and I had it when I was eight or nine years old. It made me feel big and strong when I imagined I was like those hero aviators.

2/24

1   Riding in the elevator today I felt nervous, as though it were not going to go straight up but might act crazy. This morning I was unwilling to wake up. I was standing in front of the mirror naked, and noticed the jouncing of my penis. Then I wondered about you and yours.

2   I've gone so far in not finding out anything about you. If I discovered that you had or had not written anything worthwhile, it would affect how I feel about your accomplishments and about my own. I've heard some psychiatrist friends talk about your teaching sessions on several social occasions and I felt I was listening to something I shouldn't hear. I noticed myself looking at all black cars that resemble yours [pause].

[Noise outside office.] That sound is annoying. It sounds like someone walking in the attic.

Back to you again. I feel pretty sure of one thing—that you're circumcised. It makes me feel quite anxious [pause].

3   I was kidding all weekend about how policemen are out after me. I guess I feel guilty about the way I handle my car, the way I ride around in my slightly injured car.

4   Our sexual activity at home has been cut down lately, including this weekend. Marion seems distant sexually, not interested.

5   Early in the analysis I had funny mouth sensations, and I wondered if this had to do with the desire to suck on a penis. Now my mind is flooded with such thoughts. Handling and mouthing someone's erect penis. The older fellow who showed me his when I was a kid, erect, so huge, thickened, circumcised, clean. The thought comes that I would have liked to have taken it into my body one

6   way or another. All this is making me feel hot and bothered. When I was eight years old, I remember trying to put my own penis in my mouth. As hard as I

7   tried, twisting and turning, I could never do it. The only penis that I can't visualize putting into my mouth is dad's. I can see only the brownish fur—the essential part is obliterated. I saw mother naked only once and that was from the

8   rear. There's something grand and eloquent about an erect penis. There's a dark woman in my past and in me somewhere, and she would be interested in a penis this way. When Marion sucks on my cock, I get pleasure as if I were doing it. At times I have a wish to ejaculate into her mouth. My own desire is to be filled with semen. I envy her ability to take things in, yet at the same time I look

down on her. A woman has advantages: breasts, a slim waistline, skin without a beard, a legitimate interest in a penis, nice underthings. Yet I'm very reluctant talking about this. When she was pregnant, Marion wanted me to know what her milk tasted like. I recall my embarrassment when my little boy or girl would turn toward me while I was holding them, each trying to find my nipple. I felt disgusted with my atrophied nipple. This dark woman who has been slumbering in me, is now waking up. The idea occurs to me of seducing one's lady analyst if   9 a male and the same idea in reverse. If I were only a woman, I could do it to my male analyst.

2/25

[Throws check on desk.]   1

I feel like myself today. Wouldn't it be nice if the analysis were all over? Then there'd be no traveling. But I have another thought—wouldn't I miss coming here? I've been having fantasies of when it's going to be over. I expected   2 that the outburst of homosexual thoughts last time would shake me up terribly. I did have an anxiety attack lasting half an hour afterwards. If Marion gets really   3 mad at me, I'll be deprived of sexual pleasure and of feeling that I'm wanted and needed. Then I'll have thoughts of undressing and exhibiting myself. I arrived home yesterday afternoon with a headache. Later in the evening I had sexual   4 relations and my headache was gone. However, shortly thereafter, I noticed a swelling on my forehead. It was painless. Later still, I began to feel increasingly anxious because I hadn't paid your bill and also that the mortgage payment was due. I was wondering whether my income would be insufficient to take care of my expenses for the rest of the year. I noticed that my discomfort, my tension, stopped shortly after I had written out your check. Then the swelling went down slowly [pause].

Today I'm just reporting. I don't feel very naked—that is, exposed, so   5 far—but now that I've said that, I have a compelling thought to tell you something I left out. I have avoided talking about a small variation in sexual intercourse yesterday. We ended up on a rug on the floor in front of the mirror. Isn't it strange that I would rather talk about sucking cocks in fantasy than about this way I made love to my wife which is so current and warm? I search for things that will heighten pleasure and excitement. This variation I mentioned is like looking at pornographic pictures. It's a little less civilized than the usual way—like not always being on the usual bed when having intercourse. This desire to look has been with me a very long time. When I was a kid, I would take a small hand mirror to the bathroom to watch myself defecate. I used the mirror to see what it looked like when I stuck the rectal syringe up my behind. That's something I don't do now. I've graduated to looking to see how intercourse goes on, the sticking of the penis into the vagina. My reluctance to tell you is still there because, I guess, I don't want you to take away my childish interest. I don't yet seem able to give it up.

2/27

1   I went to bed at 2 A.M. But I feel wide awake and alive this morning. It was an exciting night, but what little sleep I had was solid. There was a lot of good music, beer, cheese, and crackers. I was sweating but felt just fine. It was certainly a successful evening and a successful party. Marion was lovely, effective as a hostess, bright-eyed.

2   I had a dream that we were at a beach and I found myself without pants. Marion was there. I felt mildly embarrassed. Then I was driving home and passed two spots where there was a little bit of smoke. I called the fire department to report a possible fire. I was again concerned that I would be attracting a lot of attention.

3   Yesterday, a friend of mine told me a story how his family lost some beachfront property because of unusually high tides. Several weeks ago I almost crashed into a dangerously parked truck on one of the nearby highways. I reported it to the police. I'm stuck now. I keep wondering what the dream means. What the fire means. Yesterday afternoon as we were about to go home from a restaurant, someone parked in front—in back—of me, blocking my car. I was trying to push this blocking car back when suddenly it began to roll and crushed up against the front of another car, the side of its bumper locked into the bumper of that other car. A policeman was standing across the road, not helping, not observing. I found the two cars, locked but not damaged. Marion told me to just leave, and off we went leaving a messy situation behind us. It was something that got out of control briefly and was a frightening experience. Later that afternoon I was alone in the house and had the old urge to do something sexual, because there was no one around. I found myself struggling with fantasies of anal titillation, of wanting to watch myself sexually in the big bathroom mirror. For a while I felt helpless under the onslaught of these fantasies. It was as if I had not gotten anything from the analysis to help me, but the whole thing passed without my actually doing anything. [Interpretation: "Feeling the pressure of sexual thoughts and impulses in the presence of the policeman-analyst who is indifferent or potentially punitive."] My heart is thumping and I feel anxious, but what you said sounds right.

2/28

          [Five minutes late.] I was delayed by heavy traffic coming here.
1   The fear I experienced in the last part of yesterday's hour disappeared
2   rapidly, and for a while thereafter I was quite relaxed. I still have a bump on my forehead. I wonder if it's an insect bite. Might have gotten it during intercourse the other night and not paid too much attention to it. Maybe I put my head down on the floor and picked up a splinter. Or maybe when I penetrated

Marion, some insect penetrated me. That brings up thoughts about poison snake bites. I remember when I was six years old, looking at a tarantula in the zoo. I found it fascinating. I believe the fangs are of small diameter. Now my thoughts are about black widow spiders in outhouses and how they could bite tender genitals.

I just got a griping sensation in my colon—suddenly—as if I were going to   3
develop a case of diarrhea. It's going away. It's gone. It was like a wave
sensation, very unpleasant and sort of threatening. Now I'm reminded of a friend   4
who had ulcerative colitis. Every time he had an emotional crisis, he'd shit blood
and pus. Usually it was someone leaving him that brought it on. Maybe I'm
reacting to an expectation of being terminated here. I have notions of rushing
through to the end of my analysis, but then I'll miss it. If I talk too much about
crazy inner things, I'll disturb everything and end up getting rejected by you.
Yet if I don't say everything on my mind I'll also be subject to rejection.
Ulcerative colitis sounds like a perfectly dreadful disease to have, and I sure
wouldn't like to get it. I wouldn't like to show my feeling by tooting with my
rectum. This friend had his removed, and he can't do it any more. His blasts, the
verbal ones, that is, were rarely violent, but sharp and sudden.

I just had the fantasy of suddenly getting so angry that I would have to aim a   5
salvo of angry words and phrases at you. That gripe in my abdomen is gone,
completely. I used to think that my gut would react to anxiety not to anger, for
example, when I was taking a test. But now I think that may be because I'm not
aware of anger at the time. Again I wonder if I'll have to get up quickly to go to
bathroom, forced by my gut to spend the rest of a valuable hour on the pot.
Now I feel my heart beating away. It's causing pulsations in my abdomen and
chest, a pounding.

3/1

[Clearing throat] It seems some spit went down the wrong passage as I was   1
going into the office. I've done this more often in the past few weeks, stumbling
over my own spit. My head's been hurting since I got up this morning.

I had a dream in which there was one other person beside me. It was   2
someone I had known back in grade school—a very strong, powerfully built boy
who never did anything with his muscles. It seems I went to him with a problem
of dandruff. I brought along some kind of medication and applicators. The
applicators gave me a sense of embarrassment. There seemed to be a case filled
with rectal syringe nozzles to be used to squirt dandruff medication on the head.
There was a question about which one to use. There was also one long douche
nozzle for feminine hygiene in another case. That's the dream.

I've had fantasies of wanting to buy one of these syringes, fill it with water
and squirt it up my behind. There seem to be connections between you and the
fellow in the dream, though it's so improbable because he didn't wear glasses and

was very big. His voice may have been somewhat similar. The more I think about it, the more his voice and yours seem to gibe. His, your voice is not low, it's sort of tenor.

3   Marion was feeling quite ill Friday night with an upset stomach. She was also depressed part of the weekend. I was mad at the weather, felt generally irritable. There wasn't much lovemaking till last night.

4   My stomach suddenly feels a little upset now. I have an ache there, a griping pain. I might want to pass wind. I cannot allow myself to do that. It might go too far. I can crap all over the analyst verbally, but not actually. Right now I think of the smell of butter. Stuff coming out of large churns. Fresh dairy smell. Huge chunks freshly churned. A lot of salt and a little bit of coloring matter is usually added.

5   I'm about to yawn [and he does]. That was a great, big yawn. It's easier to yawn than to fart. That douche thing in the dream seems to be related somehow to a musical instrument—a black clarinet. It looked different from the rest of the equipment.

6   I've put away all the anxiety I felt at the beginning of the hour. My physical symptoms are gone. My headache's gone. The headache makes me think of the dandruff in the dream. Being able to express all these thoughts, even though it's embarrassing, is a relief when I get them out.

7   New ideas are coming into my mind. Society with a capital "S" fascinates me. I've been reading an article about people who are in and people who are out. A short time before I came to the hour I was talking with a friend who mentioned that he had heard of an analyst who was paranoid. I began to wonder if more analysts are like that and yet, when I thought about you, I rejected that possibility. I even thought that we're both quite sane. ["It's a comforting thought to you, in view of what you've been bringing up."]

8   That gets me right back to the dream. The dandruff and the dirt. There were anal instruments to remove it. Marion recently shaved off her pubic hair but it's growing back. I'm reminded of a joke about scratching the pubic hair because of the dandruff there. ["Having to bring up feminine impulses and connecting anal activities with sexual activities made you feel anxious."] It's true. As soon as this began to be explored, I felt physical sensations, unzipped, as if I were being opened. This stuff is not a bunch of crap but real.

3/3

1   I was in the bathroom here voiding, peeing, before coming in for the hour. I'm on a no-shampooing binge. I thought of it in the bathroom. I'm anxious, remembering the dream of the other night. Grim humor. I chuckled. It's good stuff to bring into the hour. It's better than falling asleep. That's the thing I'm most afraid of.

Looks like I equate my head of hair with the female organ and don't wash it. I come in with a greasy head of hair and lie down on the couch. I recall previously seeing you pick up the napkin on which my head rested to replace it for the next patient. I'll bet you want to get rid of it as quickly as possible. Now I'm thinking of boils, holes, insertion of a wick into them.

I just remembered a dream I had last night. I was driving a truck, going back   2
from the top of the hill. I had driven up there in a black car. At the bottom of the hill, I looked up, craning my neck to see if my car was still there. Then I decided to go back and get it. I thought it was a dangerous height in the dream, and I was afraid of it.

I want to use my head to write, to read, to be smart, to accomplish things, to be as good or better than other men.

Last night Marion and I felt tired after we bathed though we wanted to have intercourse. Because of our fatigue we were both almost unable to feel any excitement. At first, we were going through the motions which finally caused us to get excited, though it seemed like an interminable time. That gets me back to the dream. Am I manly or is there that damn feminine streak in me? It's embarrassing to talk about using your toilet. [Continued anxiety about sexual identity.]

This morning I woke up with a slight hint of a stiff neck. It looks like my old   3
problem's back. There's something dangerous in having a penis and using it. It might get hurt or ache. Now I'm feeling uncomfortably hot. My neck itches. I feel flushed. I seem to have dried up, shriveled back after coming in with a certain amount of thrust. ["Sounds sexual."] I think of the sound of an organ; church organs have such long pipes.

Feel sleepy now. Have the fantasy of a very small, old man being wrapped in cotton and placed in a ward for the senile.

I remember when I got mad and tense as a youngster, I used to have   4
nosebleeds. My mother would make me bend my head back until the bleeding stopped.

I think now how my son likes to make loud noises so my daughter can't be   5
heard. One part of my mind seems to be blocking off another. ["The feminine impulses and thoughts."]

That woke me up. I better go home and shampoo my head tonight, get the   6
dandruff out of it, stop scratching it, and then go get a haircut.

I'm reminded of sexual activity, French-kissing, contact between mouth and genitals. When I take Marion's nipple or clitoris in my mouth, I have the momentary fantasy of being penetrated. To have feminine impulses and desires seems fruitless and silly, but I'm beginning to have a better understanding of why they exist in me.

MARGINAL NOTES

3/6

1. Concern about treatment as possible attack.
2. Self-reassurance.
3. Anticipation of difficulties in analysis.
4. Reference to masochistic tendencies.
5. Denial of competitive strivings.
6. Repression of sibling rivalry.
7. More concern about treatment and whether masculinity will be noted.

3/7

1. Anxiety about treatment: anal elements and physical manifestations.
2. Further somatic references (gastrointestinal) involving son and himself, linked with suppressed feelings.
3. Ambivalence.
4. Oral references; indecision; exhibitionism.
5. Shift to wife's emotional problems and stressful interaction with her; physical manifestations (gastrointestinal).
6. Wife's lack of certain feminine accomplishments contrasted with his expertise in these areas.
7. Mother's loosening of dependency ties seen as rejection. Blowups and rejection linked with concern about treatment.

3/8

1. Resistance indirectly indicated.
2. Somatic manifestations: xerostomia.
3. Symbolic reference to castration anxiety.
4. Anxiety over family hostilities.
5. Illicit heterosexual activities in others.
6. Oedipal comparisons: inferiority feelings; wife's devaluating power; jealousy, anxiety with somatic manifestation—xerostomia.
7. Wife's narcissistic vulnerability, probably projection of such traits in himself.
8. Competitive relationship with father figure; wife's devaluating tendencies.
9. Attack, feelings of inferiority, exhibitionistic traits.
10. Concern over comparison and competition with older men, authority figures, including analyst.

3/9

1. Compliance and passivity.
2. Confessions about attempts to avoid rejection by analyst.

3. Somatic equivalent of anxiety: involvement of equilibratory apparatus.

4. Further somatic discharge: spreading autonomic nervous system over-activity.

5. Childhood recollections: maternal warning about control of anger; consequences: epistaxis; paralysis.

6. Excessive need to please, a defense against rejection.

7. Superego aspects: confessional; expectation of punishment linked with visual imagery and physical manifestations of anxiety.

3/10-11/2, Summarized in text with dynamic formulations.

11/3

1. Increased lack of confidence activated by external stress and linked with assumption of maternal role.

2. Attempted relief of sexual tension. Rationalizations. Activity a defense against passivity.

3. Deepening transference.

4. Projection.

5. Transference implications: repair of defects, ambivalently reacted to, linked with a phallic mother, castration anxiety, fellatio fantasies, xerostomia, frustration.

11/4

1. Ambivalent transference.

2. Clear emergence of homosexual ideation, accompanying erotic feeling, visual recollections, superego aspects, linked with mother-figures.

3. Upsurge of many visual sexual images of male and female family figures. Castration anxiety.

4. Somatic symptom and identification.

5. Multiple references to penetration of orifices, passive and active.

11/5

1. Somatic manifestation: note sexual visual imagery and accompanying guilt of previous hour (though patient unaware of connection).

2. Exhibitionistic anxiety, physical and intellectual. Heterosexual frustration continues, linked with hostility.

3. Another upsurge of homosexual fantasies and recollections, including disguised anal masturbation linked with voyeurism.

4. Eye, a part-object, substitute for self, linked with neglect and rejection.

11/6

1. Resistance.

2. Cognitive, affective, and somatic reactions to sexual frustration.

3. Ambivalent transference; superego aspects; concern about control of rapidly escalating hostility.

11/10

1. Reference to bodily integrity.
2. Homosexual orality, passivity.
3. Incestuous heterosexual dream with oral-anal elements and transference implications.
4. Ideational reference to physical pain, which turns out to be predictive: followed the next day by the actual somatic manifestation in awareness.
5. Concern about virility: anal elements related to further sexual frustration with Marion.
6. Conflict followed by development of physical symptoms. Stiff neck has multiple determinants: symbolic phallus, superego-punishment, castration anxiety.
7. Defensive masculine activity.
8. Feminine identification elements, with transference implications.

11/11

1. Transference aspects of pain.
2. Shifts between pain and depressive affect.
3. Punitive superego aspects of physical symptoms.
4. Analytic couch seen as a regressive haven. Hypochondriacal concern.
5. Pregenital sexual remainders, linked with father-figures.
6. Fellatio as heterosexual forepleasure but defended against in its homosexual aspects. Voyeurism, oral aggression, and castration anxiety.
7. Secondary reaction to pain: increased awareness of dependency needs in the transference. Reassurance.

11/12

1. Subsidence of somatic manifestations.
2. Sibling-surrogate devaluation and rivalry.
3. Confessional about infantile sexual behavior.
4. Sibling jealousy and fear of rejection with transference implications.

11/13

1. Resistance.
2. Projection tempered by reality and therapeutic alliance.
3. Reference to somatic dysfunction with oral, anal implications.
4. More projection with negative transference elements. Fear of exposure of curiosity about and identification with women, linked to vivid gustatory, olfactory percepts and incorporative elements.
5. Somatic manifestations of oral surge.

11/14

1. Fantasy of vagina dentata with oral, sadistic, and incorporative elements,

linked with childhood recollections. Further infantile sexual fantasies: genital displacement to rear. Continued voyeurism.

11/17

1. Resistance.
2. Rebelliousness. Personification of conscience.
3. Subsidence of voyeuristic impulses as libido is temporarily discharged.
4. Transference implications.
5. Dream: sexual symbolism, infantile curiosity about orifices and passageways.
6. Visual imagery about anal area followed immediately by interoceptive sensations: rectum.
7. Dream further linked with attack, punishment, and transference.

11/18

1. Overstimulation: oral, auditory, esthetic gratifications.
2. Envious and devaluating thoughts; need to avoid his own exhibitionistic tendencies.
3. Positive references to the transference.
4. Transference dream: analyst as guide through tortuous psychologic tangle.
5. Anxiety about potency: somatic equivalent.

11/19

1. Castration fantasies; devaluation by wife; sexual frustration; castration dream.
2. Previously unmentioned somatic manifestations. Anal infantile sexual practices more stimulating but guilt-laden.
3. Transference aspects: sexualized and devaluating. Somatic and ideational aspects of castration anxiety.

11/20

1. Return of physical symptoms in neck linked with fantasies of female genital-oral sadism.
2. Eye manifestations and retrospective recollections of voyeuristic activity.
3. Dreams of anal passive manipulation and penetration. Activated visual imagery and fantasies of the feminine sexual role.

2/10

1. Anxiety over public exposure of possible defects.
2. Overcompensatory grandiose fantasies.
3. Dangers associated with manliness. Persisting doubts about his virility.
4. Somatic manifestation of tension, but more positive feelings about wife.

2/13

1. Resistance.
2. and 3. Somatic manifestation linked with denial of serious illness.
4. An angry dream of conflict with father and the consequences. Maternal reaction to violence: headache, avoidance. Paternal vulnerability.
5. Denial of castration anxiety.
6. Fender, hip symbolic of genital displacement.
7. Angry conflict with boss (analyst), possible consequences, and reassurance about own manliness.

2/14

1. Anniversary of traffic violation; underlying superego tension.
2. Ambivalence about accepting interpretations.
3. Interpretation: guilt leading to acting out and then punishment.
4. Recollections indicate shifts from incestuous, voyeuristic thoughts about mother to passive, homosexual wishes about father.

2/17

1. Denial of tension.
2. Sexual guilt and inhibition.
3. Reference to daughter's somatic illness, which evokes anxiety-hostility.
4. Negative transference; childish feelings.
5. Lessening of hostility toward women and wife particularly.
6. Fear of impotence recently, now lessened.

2/18

1. Dream: confusion about sexual identity in anal setting.
2. Further elaboration of anal themes with transference aspects.
3. Anal homosexual associations.
4. Heterosexual activity *a tergo*.
5. Further homosexual references to father and interference. Anxious expectation.

2/19

1. Anxiety with physical concomitants.
2. Breakthrough of libidinal drives in masturbatory activity, unsatisfactory and guilt-producing. Content: anal.
3. Somatic reactivity.
4. More passive, anal homosexual fantasies, feminine identification.
5. Auto: extension (anal) of self.
6. More anal recollections: use of artificial phallus; guilt over consequences to mother.
7. Another patient's anality.

8. Multiple penises.
9. Looking for hidden and out-of-the-way penises; more anal associations.

2/20

1. More anality and guilt.
2. Somatic manifestations linked with previous anal references.
3. Somatic identification with sick daughter.
4. Heterosexual upsurge defensive against homosexual tendencies.
5. Need to identify with father's masculine accomplishments.
6. Defensive grandiose fantasies.

2/21

1. Concern about potency and being taken advantage of.
2. Continued curiosity about analyst, including his genitals.
3. Focus on wife's anxieties and guilt.
4. Recollection of childhood phallic symbols; transference expectations of being made a man.

2/24

1. Comparison of genitals in self and analyst.
2. Continued curiosity about analyst.
3. Fantasies of being sought by authorities for symbolic sexual wrongdoing.
4. Heterosexual frustration.
5. Shift toward homosexual impulses: incorporation of penis through various orifices.
6. Childhood narcissistic fantasy—own penis *in ore*.
7. Repression of visual imagery of father's penis and mother's vulva.
8. Narcissistic identification with, and envy of women; incorporative wishes.
9. Upsurge of feminine interests and impulses, with transference aspects.

2/25

1. Ambivalent transference.
2. Anxiety affect breakthrough following upsurge of homosexual ideation.
3. Exhibitionistic fantasies.
4. Varying somatic manifestations before and after sexual relations.
5. Confession about voyeurism: shift from narcissistic interest in defecation and anal masturbation with artificial phallus to interest in voyeuristic heterosexual activity. Transference fears.

2/27

1. Oral, auditory, esthetic gratifications with lingering excitation.
2. Exhibitionistic dream.
3. Dangerous situations with sexual implications, including loss of control.

Unhelpful, unobserving authority figure (analyst). Voyeuristic anal titillation impulse, finally avoided. Interpretation followed by marked anxiety: both affect and somatic equivalents.

2/28

    1. Rapid decrease in anxiety.
    2. Persisting somatic manifestation linked sexual activity and castration anxiety, current and past.
    3. Sudden interoceptive percepts.
    4. Somatic identification with sick friend. Loss linked with physical exacerbation; transference aspects. Fear of inevitable rejection. Gastrointestinal illness associated with hostility.
    5. Shift from somatic to ideational expression and back—but to another organ system.

3/1

    1. Somatic manifestations, sexually symbolic.
    2. Transference dream: feminine identification, highly sexualized and symbolized. Associated fantasies of acting out anal intercourse in the feminine role.
    3. Sexual frustration, wife's gastrointestinal illness.
    4. Somatic identification, linked with transference hostility. Related visual-olfactory percepts.
    5. Oral-anal symbolic displacements.
    6. Temporary subsidence of somatic anxiety equivalents, probably due to transference effect.
    7. Rationalizations and reassurance.
    8. Further dream associations: anal-genital displacement to head. Defense: joking. Interpretation. Recurrent somatic equivalents of anxiety.

3/3

    1. Toilet activities and references to hair linked with female genitals seen as dirty (anal). Transference aspects.
    2. Dream: continued anxiety about sexual identity.
    3. Somatic manifestation forecast in dream: neck representing a phallic symbol. Temperature percepts, castration fantasies, auditory symbolism.
    4. Hostility associated with epistaxis.
    5. Blocking of feminine impulses and ideation.
    6. Need to defend against anal interests. Oral-sexual fantasies, feminine identification better understood.

COMMENT

This patient had a major illness when he was three years old. At that time he developed a severe lung infection which required hospitalization and surgery.

Since then he has not had any major somatic illness. On the other hand, his psychologic difficulties have been lifelong and principally in the form of a moderately severe character neurosis, with periodic decompensation leading to intervals of severe anxiety with somatic equivalents and mild depression. These episodes have followed unusual stress. The physical symptoms—headache, tachycardia, nausea, vertigo, and dryness of the mouth—were not due to any discrete disease entity, but rather appeared to be expressions of autonomic nervous system overactivity, involving a number of different organs and organ systems.

On 11/3 there are indications of mounting stress: the patient's wife and children are sick, and he has to assume the maternal role. At the same time, he experiences an almost irresistible increase in sexual drives which cannot be fulfilled through intercourse. Masturbation affords no relief, only secondary guilt. The patient attempts to rationalize away these findings as well as to fend off an increase in passive tendencies by considerable activity. Projective thinking appears more frequently and in part is directed toward his wife. Dental work which is being done currently assumes transference significance and is also associated with fellatio fantasies, symbolic castration fears, and the physical symptom of dryness of the mouth.

With continued heterosexual frustration, there is a further upsurge of both homosexual and fellatio fantasies as well as curiosity about genitalia, especially male, accompanied by considerable castration anxiety. Against this background on 11/4, associations appear which focus on the physical symptom of sore throat which his wife has had for several days. These are followed by interoceptive percepts in the patient's identical body area. This appears to be a conversion manifestation, probably a somatic expression of forbidden fellatio wishes in which he identifies with the woman, his wife in this instance. The somatic form of identification is a variation of this important psychologic mechanism which is frequently overlooked. It may have either a transient or longer lasting influence in determining the site of physical dysfunction.

On 11/5 another physical symptom is reported. This time the eye is involved. It, too, is probably a conversion manifestation and most likely a somatic expression of forbidden voyeuristic impulses and associated guilt. However, the patient is as yet unaware of these connections or their significance. The neglect of the eye condition causes it to worsen and become more strikingly a punishment symbol. Here the eye represents a part-object, a substitute for the self.

As intercourse with his wife continues to be unavailable, the patient is flooded with sexual urges and fantasies, both homosexual and heterosexual. Under the pressures of these libidinal drives, his psychologic defensives of intellectualization, reaction formation, and projective tendencies become insufficient. Hostility is on the increase and though there is some outward expression of irritability, most of the emotion is turned inward. The continuing, forbidden, sexual impulses have also activated superego-ego tensions. On 11/10 the patient shows concern about his bodily integrity and reports that he awoke with severe upper back pain. The day before he described his reaction to sexual frustration as a "pain in the neck" while talking to his wife. That night there were dreams involving both incestuous and homosexual wishes. These are linked with associations of being found out and punished for his sexual desires, and in turn have transference implications. The next day, that is, on 11/10, both the site and principal symptom as previously verbalized reappear in awareness as a manifestation of physical dysfunction. The latter most likely has already been ongoing the previous 24 hours, but at that time is still out of perceptual awareness. It should be noted that additional stresses, occurring over the preceding weekend, but not reported then, include the conflict the patient has over masturbation which he finally handles by controlling himself, although he is left with a sense of frustration and of continued tension. He has also had some further dental work done which has been psychologically as well as physically very uncomfortable. A new attempt at coping with all these stresses has involved buying masculine apparel, but this defensive effort is not altogether successful in staving off the somatic dysfunction which finally results in back and neck pain.

Awareness of pain—or other physical symptoms—may be especially influenced by shifts in the intensity of transference. Both an increase and decrease in severity of pain intensity appear closely though not exclusively correlated with proximity to the analytic hour of 11/11. The inability to look back, to bend his back or twist his neck is related to voyeuristic, homosexual impulses and related guilt—all of which are involved in his transference responses. A secondary gain factor is also evident.

On 11/12 the patient reports that his pain subsided shortly after the previous day's analytic interview, when his superego-ego tensions appear to also have lessened under the favoring influence of a shift toward a more positive transference. The symptom of pain in the neck appears to have been a conversion manifestation related to repressed sexual conflicts, largely Oedipal, with some pregenital elements, but aggressiveness here plays a less important role compared with the libidinal drives in influencing physical dysfunction.

After an interval in which polymorphous, perverse, infantile fantasies continue to appear together with expectations of punishment and in anticipation of an interruption during which the analyst will be away, the patient reports (on 11/19) difficulties with his boss and subsequent masturbation. Associations follow in which there appear vivid castration fantasies. Then he reveals that he has had urticaria for the past two weeks. This condition has not been brought up before. Often such unmentioned physical sensations and symptoms may be within awareness but are overlooked or considered unimportant or irrelevant. In such instances varying degrees of denial are operating defensively, usually because the somatic manifestations would cause too much anxiety if their presence were acknowledged. The urticaria (i.e., the itching) seems more a sexualized manifestation rather than a progressive one with "weeping lesions," and the scratching is most likely a masturbatory equivalent. On 11/20 another physical condition, similarly unmentioned, is reported by the patient. He has had an eye inflammation. This, too, seems to be related to the continuing upsurge of and as yet insufficiently discharged voyeuristic impulses.

On 2/13 the patient complains of stiffness of the left hip after awakening. This is preceded by a dream which refers to the somatic dysfunction. The patient has been preoccupied with thoughts of both inferiority and compensatory grandeur. Competition with father-figures has been a prominent theme. The dream concerns an angry conflict with such figures and the consequences thereof, symbolically expressed in damage to the patient's car, an extension of himself. It is likely that the somatic dysfunction was already ongoing when the dream occurred.

On 2/18 the anxious expectation referred to by the patient at the end of the analytic hour signals a shift in psychologic equilibrium. It follows a period of steadily increasing homosexual and anally oriented libidinal drives which have become so intense that they have broken through the patient's psychologic defenses and have begun to appear in less and less distorted ideational form. There have also been indications of a shift toward the negative polarity in the transference and evidence of heightened ego-superego tensions, moderate in degree. The change in psychophysical equilibrium is evident after the interview in the onset of severe abdominal pain, rush peristalsis, and explosive, sticky evacuation. This somatic expression of psychologic tensions is followed by a behavioral discharge, that of masturbation, which then secondarily evokes guilt. There appears to be no evidence of significant diminution in the intensity of the activated anally oriented libidinal drives. This portends a continued instability of the psychophysical equilibrium. A large, painful furuncle of the nose is reported by the patient on 2/20. Retrospectively in this analytic hour, but prospectively in the preceding hours, especially the last one, possible sites of physical dysfunction have been indicated by anal and olfactory associations. Included is also a strong somatic identification with his daughter who has an infection (of the eyes) but who recently has had severe chickenpox lesions, involving large areas of the body, including the nose.

Subsequently (2/24) there is a comparison of himself and the analyst in terms of appearance and potency. Further heterosexual frustration leads to another upsurge in homosexual fantasies focused on incorporation of a penis through various body orifices. There is also narcissistic identification with and envy of women. A brief period of anxious feeling and then headache follow, subsiding after sexual relations with his wife. However, a new somatic manifestation appears: a painless swelling on the forehead. This is most likely still another conversion symptom, linked with activation of multiple infantile sexual remainders, some of which break through into awareness, although their meaning still is repressed. On 2/27 an interpretation about the patient's concern that exposure of his sexual fantasies will lead to punishment by the analyst is followed by marked anxiety including both affect discharge and somatic equivalents, but the episode is short-lived. The swelling on his forehead persists and is secondarily linked with sexualized fantasies of being penetrated and castrated by a phallic woman. On 2/28 there are rapid shifts back and forth from ideational to somatic channels of expression and also from gastrointestinal to cardiovascular systems. The physical manifestations again appear to be related to increased autonomic nervous system activity.

The patient continues to be preoccupied with sexual fantasies which have strong feminine and anal components. He reports a severe headache on 3/1 following a transference dream in which these sexual elements appear. The physical symptom is a conversion manifestation. Later in that hour, following reference to his wife's gastrointestinal upset, he develops briefly similar symptoms which have in them elements of somatic identification and links with repressed hostility.

On 3/3 a dream refers to the dangers of manliness, especially the possibilities of castration and indirectly presents a wish-fulfillment of continued feminine tendencies. Subsequently the patient develops neck pain. The dream thus indicates the possibility of physical dysfunction.

The data from four patients presented thus far have been studied in great detail, and over periods ranging from one to one and one-half years for psychologic cues signaling the development of physical dysfunction before it reaches awareness through gross physical symptoms and signs. A survey of the material reveals that such indicators in various groupings do appear recurrently in each case and can be specified as follows: (1) exposure to psychologic stress which has critical symbolic significance for the individual and is inadequately compensated for by other environmental factors of a favorable nature; (2) some degree of physical dysfunction as part of a general style of adaptation to psychologic stress in the past, with previously sensitized body areas representing potential current target organs; (3) evidence of increasing instability in psychologic equilibrium, especially regressive shifts in ego mechanisms of defense, with specific activation of the process of denial; (4) blocking of affects from adequate emotional discharge or insufficient awareness by the patient of their significance if they are being so expressed; (5) existence of a high degree of ego-superego tensions despite lessening psychologic manifestations; (6) build-up of unmodified aggressiveness which is internalized; (7) persistent increase in physical sensations and perceptions compared with previous levels; (8) recurrent dreams whose latent content contains prominent physical references, especially to some form of dysfunction; (9) somatic identification expressed verbally which, when similar to actual organ dysfunction in key objects, may be a clue to the site or type of the developing disease. The larger the number of these manifestations, the greater the likelihood of impending physical illness.

No comparable clinical research has appeared in the literature, but there are a few references which deal with the predictive approach to physical illness. Knapp (1962) has postulated two necessary basic conditions for the occurrence of bronchial asthma in an adult. The first is a "sensitized pathway" similar to Deutsch's concept of the "psychosomatic unit." The second condition is activation of a process of pulmonary intake and expulsion effort triggered by physical or psychologic (symbolic) stimuli. In connection with the latter, two other supplementary prerequisites must also be present, namely, a disruption of habitual defenses and a displacement of emotional conflict into the respiratory sphere. The approach is one of partial specificity. Knapp believes that the psychiatric data need to be assessed in terms of the patient's defensive structure. This would include both long-term or strategic defensive and adaptive patterns and immediate short-term or tactical defenses against emergent impulses. In addition, an assessment of the degree to which the primitive drives are activated is necessary.

Alexander and his associates have done extensive and intensive investigations of seven so-called psychosomatic diseases: bronchial asthma, rheumatoid arthritis, ulcerative colitis, essential hypertension, neurodermatitis, thyrotoxicosis, and duodenal peptic ulcer. Most recently (Alexander et al., 1968) these illnesses have been studied in patients in whom *they were already established,* by a "blind diagnosis" type of team investigation. Primary clinical psychiatric data were obtained from the patients. From this was abstracted a psychologic configuration which could be compared with previously stated disease formulations. Then a somatic diagnosis was derived from the psychologic data. The objective diagnosis made by internists was used as a validity check. The findings indicated that the percentage of correct diagnoses was much better than what might have been anticipated on the basis of chance alone and that differentiation between the diseases was possible. It was emphasized that the psychologic pattern was not unique to the patients with the particular disease. Other conditions for its occurrence are necessary: (1) innate or constitutional predisposition and sensitivity; (2) early life situation in which the basic psychologic pattern is developed rendering the individual particularly vulnerable to certain types of conflicts; (3) a disease onset situation activating the basic conflict to which the person is susceptible. If any of these factors is absent, the disease may not appear.

Bahnson and Bahnson (1964), without presenting any clinical material attempted to develop a hypothesis for predicting whether a disease process would be somatic or psychologic. They considered the type of ego mechanism of defense used to cope with activated conflict to be crucial: repression and denial will result in somatization of drive potentials bound up in conflictual impulse or emotion; projection and displacement will lead to neurotic and ultimately psychotic behavior. Such a hypothesis disregards the complexity of disease processes.

Four more analytic cases will now be presented in accordance with the format used for the first group. However, the discussion following each of the new cases will focus on the testing and validating of the predictive factors outlined earlier in this resume.

VALIDATION OF PREDICTIVE CUES

T. U.

Bend/Not Bend; See/Not See

INTRODUCTION

T. U. is a 33-year-old manager of research in a large industrial plant. He has been married for ten years to a woman his own age. They have two children, a boy of eight and a girl of four. The patient entered analysis because increased indecisiveness and rumination were interfering significantly with his work.

His parents are both living: the mother, a quiet housewife, is in good health; the father, a passive, obsessive, somewhat paranoid man, now retired from running a small business, has recently recovered from chest surgery. There is an older brother, 37, in good health; he is a successful internist, married, but without children.

Preliminary clinical evaluation suggested a longstanding obsessional character neurosis with several previous decompensations in the form of brief depressive episodes. The first occurred when the patient left home for the first time to attend college, the second when he finished graduate school and was looking for his first job. Physically his health had always been good except for upper respiratory infections, several a year since childhood. He had had measles at age three and mumps at five, without apparent sequelae.

The first six months of analysis confirmed the initial clinical impression and the severity of the disorder. From the beginning, the patient exhibited marked intellectualizing tendencies and considerable affect blocks except for infrequent eruptions of anger at home toward his wife or children. Other obsessional defenses were present to a marked degree: reaction formation, isolation, doing and undoing, and to a lesser extent projection. His incestuous attachment to his mother, competition with father and particularly brother, voyeuristic and exhibitionistic tendency, considerable orality, especially expressed in the need to be given to and looked after, and hard-core rage at frustration were all hidden behind these rigid defenses. His efforts to present himself as shy, nice, and inconspicuous in all situations including the analysis were impressive. The patient revealed in almost every hour a pervasive pattern of doubt, vacillation, and ambivalence: practically everything said was qualified by such expressions as perhaps, maybe, I guess, it's possible, almost as if, etc. Definite statements were rare; decisions rarer. Greediness was defended against by massive reaction formations of austerity and altruism, here an evident identification with his father. It was clear that ego-superego tensions were marked and that the patient was guilt-ridden, but not manifesting this affectively. There were urgent sexual drives which were generally blocked from discharge, except for occasional unsatisfactory intercourse with his wife and infrequent voyeuristic impulses.

During the first six months of analysis, references to physical symptoms and bodily sensations were rare. On the couch the patient exhibited a stiff restlessness, the amplitude of his movements being small. There was a deluge of words and minutiae, repetitive, boring, and affectless for the most part. The patient attempted to present himself as the "good boy," to appease and to please in the parental transference.

Thus matters stood as the first major interruption of the analytic work, the summer vacation, approached and as the patient was about to begin a new job.

CASE MATERIAL

7/14

1   I'm thinking about how to start talking. I haven't had this concern for some time. I keep glancing at the papers on your desk. I'm going up to the mountains this afternoon. Now I'm aware of feeling anxious. About what? About what I should bring along for the weekend. That's silly. It's just a couple of days. I picked up some stuff for the kids who're up there with my wife. The weather reports had said it might be a rainy weekend. I guess I should bring weekend stuff for the indoors, too. I get to worrying about what to bring, practically obsessed about it. I'm overcautious. I need to be sure, to be prepared for all eventualities. Almost as if it were to be some kind of battle, and I were arriving armed to the teeth. Even such a little thing as books. If I finish one, should I bring another? It's as if I'm on guard against having nothing to do.

2   As I tell you this, I'm aware that I had been feeling self-conscious, but I was hesitant to say so. I've been having images of naked women. There were some girly magazines lying around the yard. My kids had picked them up from a neighbor's trash barrels. I got terribly self-conscious about putting them in my barrel. What if somebody would pick them out of there and then think they belonged to me. I stuck them into a drawer where the cleaning lady couldn't

find them. Consciously I try to be correct and moralistic. It may be a tendency to deny my own enjoyment at looking at these pictures which, to a certain extent, were lurid. The main emphasis was on breast size, but they didn't show the genital area. This is where I want to look and see what's there. I don't find extra large breasts particularly attractive. Anyway I felt and feel self-conscious about such things. That word has a particular meaning for me: it characterizes my adolescence. I was just tremendously self-conscious then, so much so that I was thinking about myself and my reactions all the time, especially when I was with people. Dale Carnegie's *How to Win Friends and Influence People* became a bible, a guide book for me. I was grasping for something so I wouldn't be uncomfortable with people.

Maybe there's something I'm avoiding. I thought of Ralph who for quite a while was the closest friend I had until he got sick. I hero-worshipped him. He was a few years older and good at things I was awkward at, such as athletics. He also was socially aggressive and successful with girls which, again, I couldn't seem to be. I remember Ralph would have violent outbursts of rage toward his mother. He sure was able to express his angry feelings. I equated that with strength, but later he became terribly depressed. When he was well, I admired his ability to tell people off. I connected masculinity with aggression. I wanted to be like him. As time went on and I got more mature, he no longer remained the dashing figure. He became more and more anxious, undecided, and began to lose one job after another. Then he became very sick and had to be hospitalized. I realized he was not the strong person I thought he was. I was just like the kid who worships his father and then discovers his father's faults as he grows older. This applies really to me and my own father. He worked with his hands, outdoors. I must have equated that with masculinity. Then that awe, too, was punctured. I learned in time that he wasn't so tough, but more a shy guy.

There were a number of episodes that changed my concept of my father that now come into mind. Once, in a movie, the *Star Spangled Banner* was being played before the picture started. It's as if I can hear the music now, played on a scratchy record. My father was preoccupied, I guess, but anyway he didn't notice it and didn't stand up. A man in back of us threatened to punch him. Actually father wasn't unpatriotic. He just wasn't with it for the moment, simple inattention. This was very disturbing to me—to see him threatened and respond by simply getting up, as if he were intimidated by the other man. In another incident father was in an argument with a bunch of kids who were fooling around our house. There was a lot of yelling. He had to chase them away. It wasn't a case where father was being intimidated. I remember that I was the one who got anxious about it, with a strong feeling that father couldn't control the kids. It seemed like a threatening situation, at least to me.

Some years ago when MacArthur was fired by Truman, there was a big parade for MacArthur. I remember that day very well. I had tickets for a play and went downtown, unaware of what was taking place. When I saw the big crowds and traffic blocked off, I asked a man what was happening. He turned around and said angrily, "It's for MacArthur." He was so disdainful; I can still see his scornful face as if I should have known this. Otherwise I'm stupid and unpatriotic—that was the implication. I was impressed by the emotional quality of this man's reaction. It was close to hate. It must get back to the incident in the movies with father. People get angry at father and me for not being patriotic. Now I wonder if there's something going on here that I'm missing and you'll be angry and critical of me.

7/17

1   I've had several dreams that are puzzling. One, which escapes me partly, involved you: As if I were having another analyst in an entirely different setting, perhaps another country, with the realization I was somehow also in analysis with you. You were in the background. Perhaps you were on vacation. [Summer interruption actually to begin in two weeks.]

2   I went to the mountains this past weekend. The first night the cabin where my family stayed wasn't crowded. The next night it was—with visitors and relatives. My wife and I had a downstairs room, and we made love. It was satisfying to make love, and it was like a reunion after a week of separation. Things seemed to be going better. My wife appeared more relaxed and affectionate. It's as if the trouble between us started for no apparent reason and may go away for no apparent reason. It gives me some hope that I'm not as unworthy as I think, that someone cares about me, and maybe prolonged treatment won't be necessary.

3   On the second night of my visit, I had another dream. It was about a colleague of mine whose wife had developed a brain tumor and though still alive was very ill. I knew somebody—not well—who died of a brain tumor; he made the diagnosis himself and refused surgery. He might have been more frightened of the results of surgery than of the advanced illness itself. When I heard—in the dream—that my colleague's wife had a brain tumor, I thought that she would have trouble studying for her Ph.D. exams. In reality she had flunked those exams the first time she took them. Anyway, this was used in the dream as proof that she had a brain tumor. My own wife is in the process of writing a novel. I was bothered by the possibility that the dream reflected a hostile wish toward her. My colleague and I have both studied together. His having a more prestigious job than I, even though he's a little older than me, makes me feel inferior in professional competition and professional success.

4   These dreams occurred Saturday night, but I wasn't in a bad state of mind, though not as relaxed as Friday. Saturday I had had good luck fishing in a nearby lake, coming up with a fine catch of perch. Finally, I tore myself away and went back to the cabin for supper. Things had become crowded with the arrival of my brother-in-law and his boy. When I got there, I found they hadn't

waited for me but had had their meal, even though I had been summoned back for that purpose. For me, eating is a special ritual. It has to be quiet, carefully prepared, all eating together and without distraction. Sunday meal-time was also a disturbed occasion. It got me so depressed, I didn't feel like reading afterwards.

Father once yelled at me for hammering at the table during a meal. Everyone   5
had their own seat. I follow this in my own house. My mother's attitude about eating bothered me. She was not a good cook generally or naturally. She had limited recipes with few innovations, related to father's being a conservative eater. Mother was a slave in the kitchen, serving at all hours. She was sloppy too; the drinking glasses were always filmy. I don't have many negative feelings about mother, but this is one of the things that bothers me about her, that she wasn't a good housekeeper. She wouldn't keep a salt shaker on the table usually, never a pepper mill. It was the taste that was lacking. I like food that's properly seasoned. She seemed to lack organization for doing such work or respect for food and the process of eating. Up in the mountains yesterday the lack of focus on food bothered me, and I connected it with these recollections and experiences. Food becomes very important. Eating and what you eat have great significance for me. In fact, eating a good meal has a tranquilizing effect on me. I have a gourmet attitude toward food, though I'm not strictly a gourmet.

I remember the first time I ate non-Kosher food in father's presence. We had   6
gone for an interview at one of the colleges. We stopped in the cafeteria, and they made my tongue sandwich with butter. Afterwards I felt nauseous. That was quite an emotional reaction. It seemed distasteful and revolting. I have prejudices about food in advance even now, for example, brains.

7/19

The friend I talked to just before coming here reminds me of my own wife   1
and marriage. Last week his wife was thinking of divorce and was very depressed. This week things underwent a melodramatic change for her. Things were never better. She had had an orgasm for the first time in her marriage. The reason I related this to my own marriage was that after a huge fight, things get a lot better for a while. I keep wondering what there is in anger that doesn't get expressed that has such an inhibiting effect. I apply this to myself. The new car I bought needs adjustment, and I've had a lot of trouble getting that done at the dealer's. It gets me angry, and I tend to avoid it [much obsessional detail about the car repairs.] I feel guilty so easily, especially when I may not feel fully   2
justified. I need to always be the good guy. I keep wondering if I can be or if I should be aggressive, now and in the future. What's bothering me most is this inability to show my anger—and also the need to justify it. Anger evokes in me the image of Moshe Dayan, the Israeli defense minister. I want to identify with him—the Jew who fights back, wins wars, a powerful figure who doesn't make excuses for showing anger. I wish I could be like those blunt-speaking, direct

Israelis. I admire this in a sense. I'd like to take on such attributes. It's the positive aspect of Jewishness. The opposite stereotype of a Jew is that of a miser, greedy and squeezing money out of people. Now I'm thinking of doctors who must spend their time spending—no, counting—their money. I have a great fear of conforming to the image of the miser. My discomfort must have something to do with you. You're leaving on vacation next week, yet you were willing to let me start mine earlier, and I had been casting you in an authoritarian role. You're more flexible than I had expected. I'm pleased. It's an attitude I approve of—consideration for others. It punctured the fantasy that you would not permit me to take time out earlier and punish me if I tried to.

7/20, Excerpt

1   I spent most of the day at my new assignment in the firm I work for. It looks good and should be quite interesting. Lots of people in that department. I'm assuming I'm going to be anxious. I usually am in any new situation. My anxiety is focused on looking for structure: what is expected of me and how to go about getting it done. Working a lot seems to reduce this anxious feeling, and I expect to have plenty to do now. I feel better than if I were sitting around with nothing to do. Some years ago when I applied for work at this place, I didn't get the job. But I'm still willing to work hard. Father used to work 12 hours or more a day. One of my acquaintances has the most exaggerated work involvement imaginable—he's never home. Actually I have a lot of difficulty about work. I try to justify long hours, but, on the other hand, I have the wish not to work altogether. Whenever anything unusual comes up at the job, I get anxious in advance, but once I get into the work I find it absorbing, interesting, as well as exciting.

2   I've been asked to give a talk to a bunch of industrialists in Providence and find it hard to accept the role of expert. While the fee isn't lucrative, I need to make some extra money. Anyhow, I'll go there, though I don't feel too comfortable about it. I've been talking myself into having greater confidence, and I feel I've matured to some extent. As I deal with some of these situations, I get a feeling of my own power. There is a conscious joy at having mastered something.

7/21

1   I'm tired. I was up late painting louvres, and that's not so easy. My muscles ache. It's tedious while you're doing it, but it's worth the effort. It gets your mind off your worries. You don't have a chance to get preoccupied with them. Then I stayed up late watching TV. On one show there was a very hostile guy, interviewing an applicant for a job. Those guys who speak in a direct, blunt, iconoclastic way fascinate me—I suppose because it's impossible for me to.

Dylan Thomas was like that, but he was also an alcoholic. I recall Alec Guinness' portrayal of Dylan Thomas. There was an impressive scene which I visualize where he had sworn off drinking and was sober for a while. Then he was tempted to take a drink again and couldn't stop until he was so sick he couldn't move and finally died. I wonder if all alcoholics are that sick. I was trying to justify making behavior which is unacceptable into behavior which is acceptable. I had a German professor at college who was a marvelous translator, and he was an alcoholic. Several times he was woozy in class. One of my classmates became director of the alcoholic clinic in a New York hospital; the last time I saw him was at his house about a year ago, and he served drinks from an excellent supply of liquor. He knows how to enjoy the good stuff. That's more than others can do.

My thoughts are switching to the analysis, even though I want to avoid   2
talking about it. I keep wondering if it'll do me any good. A fellow I knew started an analysis a year or so ago and then developed a terrible illness. He became totally paralyzed—flat on his back. I feel restless now. I think I'm criticizing you and the analysis. As if you're superior and I've got to cut you down. Guess I'm afraid to be found defective. Father comes to mind. Makes me think he found lots of things wrong with me and rejected me. It's vague in terms of concrete recollections. It's just the impression that's specific. I remember more clearly his positive attitudes toward me and want to blank out the negatives. My father spanked me only once in my life. I was a kid then and had run out into traffic. He was terribly upset and warned me that I had to be careful or I would get killed. I remember being paddled as a pledgee in a fraternity at college, but that was in a spirit of adolescent fun, so-called. My father's warning must have had a lot to do with my becoming so careful and particular about doing anything, especially if it was something that could be considered bad.

7/24

[Walks in stiffly and lowers self to couch in a guarded way.]   1
I have had lower back pain that came on suddenly Saturday night (7/22). My family doctor had to tape my back up and give me medicine for the pain. I got an attack while bending over. It was almost impossible to straighten out. Then I got another smaller attack last night. I've been lying down a good deal since then. I find it very difficult to get up. I made a remark to my wife: I might have trouble getting off the couch on Monday. She didn't realize all this, the analysis, takes place on a couch. Right now my back isn't aching so much—as long as I'm lying flat. I have the fantasy that you'll be gentler with me now and more considerate. My wife's mother went into the hospital because of a nerve problem she's had for a few years, with pain from her back going down her leg. Her family doctor called it sciatica. They're doing some kind of special tests today. My wife has been at the hospital frequently since her mother was admitted.

2   I've had a fairly uncomfortable time over the weekend due to this and a number of other things. Most bothersome to me is that I've been sort of annoyed at my wife. I asked her to type up some additional information needed by the home office in connection with my new job, and she dilly-dallied until late last night when she finally got it done. This morning I brought the letter along, and I put it in the mailbox near your office. I went by your driveway and noticed two cars there. I saw one had an M.D. plate and the other didn't—maybe it was your wife's. I started to think of how you and she get along, but didn't get anywhere with that. My wife has been more relaxed and affectionate recently until the last few days when she got bitchy, moody—on and off. She pays more attention to her mother than to me. This disappointed me, especially after two weeks of separation when she was up in the mountains with the kids. This goes along with her increased irritability to the children. My back was hurting too much for me to finish the louvre painting. I guess I had kind of idealized expectations about this reunion with my family. Realistically it was just pleasant to have them back, but the kids were ill over the weekend with strep throats, and I had to get the pediatrician for them and give them the medicine he prescribed. They required a lot of attention.

3   I got this letter from my new boss on Saturday. It was short, and not exactly peremptory. My reaction was a little bit of annoyance to the "quickly" in it. It's been several months, and no one asked me for that curriculum vitae. It didn't strike me as so urgent. I also block against preparing written reports. The letter itself was botched up. I'm compulsive. My wife at times is careless. I fuss over things to be done by a certain time, and she'll let it go. It bothers me. She misplaced sending out the first payment of the loan on our car, and it was delayed. I'm aware I'm belaboring this point, but I can't help it.

4   I'm skirting around the question of discomfort related indirectly to you. My new boss, you—it's as if you're both judging me. I was watching a TV movie about a haunted house. Very spooky. And in here I'm talking about the past and rattling the skeletons in the closet. I had the fantasy that I would be told I couldn't be kept in the new job because my qualifications were not up to requirements, and I would say, "That's fine by me!"—as if I wanted an out—"So what! The hell with you! I don't need your job." [Leaves couch slowly and stiffly.]

7/26

1   [Walks in stiffly and lowers self carefully to the couch.]
    My wife's mother, who's been in the hospital, has cancer. That's very upsetting news. She had back and leg pain for a long time without having had a definite diagnosis made, though she was followed by her family physician. The pain recently got very much worse. A short time ago a good neurologist went over the case and though he too wasn't sure, he found some wasting of the leg

muscles. Now after putting her through all the tests and x-rays they've discovered a bone cancer and she's going to have one of her legs amputated. It's terribly upsetting to all of us. I feel horror-struck. It's so bad, I have a very strong wish to just avoid thinking about it. I don't understand why I'm reacting so strongly. It isn't *my* mother. After I heard the news I said to one of my friends, "Death is easier than this." He replied, "No, there's some hope here, but death is hopeless."

I guess I'm also being affected by the situation here. It's our last week of meeting before the summer interruption, and I guess I'm already feeling left behind. My conscience has been bothering me about my neglect of religion. I feel tense. You're going away, and I don't like it. It gives me a feeling of helplessness. Death looms large, what with my wife's mother having such a terrible disease. I lost an uncle from cancer, but I wasn't so upset then. I guess I just didn't like him and maybe that interfered with my grief. My wife's mother is a singular person. She's been strong, the backbone of the family—a warm, giving person, spending her life as a martyr, helping others all the time. My wife keeps asking, "She's done such good things in her life. Why does she get punished?" There's no answer one can give to such a question. As for my uncle, on the other hand, he just was not liked, and it seemed no great loss when he died. [Interpretation of relationship between summer interruption, other stresses, and increased hostile dependency and guilt somatically expressed.] 2

7/27

After I left here yesterday, I went down to the place where I bought my new car to try to get some things fixed on it that they've been stalling off for months. While I was there, I blew my stack at the service manager. I had been building up resentment toward this place. They're very unpleasant to deal with, being obsequiously polite but basically inconsiderate. There've been a number of incidents at this place with poor service. The last one was yesterday morning before I went down there. My wife brought the new car in to be fixed, and the guy yelled at her, and she yelled at him. Finally, he apologized and got her a ride home. That incensed me. It was the last straw, especially since there had been this altercation with my wife. When I got there, I decided to let him have it. But I had mixed feelings about it. I get shaky, struggling to control my anger. I really exploded more than I expected. I began to shout. Then I was upset at losing control. I was going to tell him off in a calmer way, but I said all I had to say at the top of my voice. He was backing down, but argued that I didn't realize how busy they were. I guess it was better to have expressed it in a screaming, ranting way, rather than not at all. 1

Now I think of your mentioning yesterday that some of this upset of mine about my wife's mother's illness might be related to your leaving and at a time when I'm starting a new job. I said to myself afterwards that indeed I felt very 2 threatened by this job, but I had thought that was months ago when I was first considering it, not now. Yet that's how I'm dealing with it now. Still I got some satisfaction from the outburst, that I didn't have to be scared all the time. I see a little more clearly that I've had a lot more resentment about this summer interruption than I realized. It's as if I were a helpless kid who was being abandoned by his parent just when he needed him most.

[In the next few hours before vacation, the backache, though referred to very little, showed definite improvement.]

7/28-4/14, Brief Interim Summary

Eight months have passed. The treatment progresses very slowly. The rumination, doubting, affect block, intellectualization, reaction formations, and other obsessional defenses persist with only slight modifications. There have been no further physical illnesses. The patient has become settled in his new work assignment. However, shortly before the detailed reporting of interviews is resumed, a masked competition with his boss linked with an upsurge in Oedipal conflict material begins to emerge. The patient has to conduct several discussion groups, and these are very stressful experiences. He has also just returned from an upsetting visit to his parents. It is during this visit that he notes incestuous fantasies about his mother breaking through into awareness. He reacts to this with self-accusatory, condemnatory thoughts.

4/15

1   I had a very severe headache all day yesterday. I notice I'm more prone to developing them in the past few days. I haven't had a physical examination recently, and I should have one. I'm beginning to show some gray hairs around the temples. My wife's been turning gray in the past six months. I have an image of the park where we were Saturday on our visit to my relatives. There's a concession where you can make your own pictures. The kids made some. You drop paints on cardboard which then spins. There were a lot of hippies there. We took some photographs. Yesterday we got home and I was going around in bare feet and chinos. Hippies go around in sandals or some comfortable footwear. Anyway I've had chronic athlete's foot for years on and off, and it's good for my feet to be exposed to the air. If I went around with bare feet or sandals, it would look funny. Besides people would notice that I've got athlete's foot. I've heard disparaging remarks about this condition. I've tried various ointments. Once I tried a medicine you take by mouth. Then a few days later I developed pneumonia. I stopped taking that medicine before the full course was completed. The doctors gave me antibiotics then, and I got over the pneumonia quickly.

My cousin has been trying to make some property changes that would have   2
been to his advantage but to my father's disadvantage. My father was telling me
about it during my visit. I guess I repressed or at least held my anger in at my
cousin, trying to overlook his greedy, opportunistic tendencies. He's like a
carbon copy of my uncle—a sadistic guy at heart.

[Notices that he's playing with wedding ring and pushes it down on his   3
finger.] My tendencies to try to figure things out come to mind again. I had a
couple of very disturbing sexual thoughts over the weekend—an awareness of the
physical qualities of my mother and a sexual attraction to her. I had taken a
shower in my parents' house and had used some of my mother's shampoo which
spilled as I used it. I forgot to mention that to her and felt guilty about that.
Then I had an association of mother's taking a shower and what she would look
like nude. I think of my son at times barging into the bedroom while my wife is
getting dressed. I get very annoyed at these intrusions. I'm concerned about my
looking and his looking.

One of my friends mentioned some special business opportunities out West. I   4
said apologetically that I couldn't move out of this area because I'd likely be in
analysis for several years. It's as if I expected some criticism from certain of my
friends because I'm being analyzed so long. Now I'm again aware of trying to
figure out what this means: is it that I'm expressing a negative attitude toward
analysis indirectly?

After having thoughts of sex, anger follows. When I left here last time and   5
was driving away, one of the cars in your driveway had backed out and gone just
ahead of me. I had the fantasy that as I followed this car—your wife's car, I
assume—if she stopped short, my car would hit hers. Again I thought: what if
there were an accident and some other car hit your wife? I'd be right behind,
and I'd stop and possibly lend assistance. All this occurred right after the session
when you pointed out some of my resistances, and I felt very defensive about
that. Running those conferences and my new job—I recognize that I'm anxious
about them. Yet I have the impression that things are going better.

4/16

I saw a brochure on the grass of your lawn about TWA airline flights. I   1
wondered if you were going abroad. I saw a tall girl walking down the street and
speculated as to whether she were coming out of your house and was a member
of your family. I also saw one of your cars pulling away from the house again.

When I woke up today, my left eye felt sticky. I didn't notice until I looked   2
in the mirror, and then I saw it was red and appeared to be inflamed. I started to
worry about it. My initial reaction was to feel distress and helplessness. I
hesitated to call a doctor. About ten years ago I had an inflammation there—it
was called conjunctivitis. My wife and I had just been married, and we were on a
sightseeing trip out West. We ran into an old girlfriend of mine who was also on

her honeymoon. One of those country doctors gave me an ointment for the eyes which made the condition much worse. I must have been sensitive to whatever it was he prescribed. I saw another doctor—an eye specialist—who told me to leave the eyes alone. They got better that way. I'm distressed because this upsets my plans to get some extra work done. Now I'll have to make an appointment with the eye doctor. I'll need to work it in somehow. I also worry a little about it. Why is it in one eye? Well, maybe there was a hair in it. It's not serious, I guess, but it's an annoyance, and I feel helpless at the upset to my routine.

3   If anything goes wrong unexpectedly, such as a medical problem I may have, or there's something wrong with a mechanical object, I overreact, worry about it. For some reason, the idea of calling a repair man makes me overanxious. If I can't fix it, then I keep wondering if I'll be able to get the right person for the job. What happened last night may have had something to do with the way I feel this morning. We stopped at my wife's relatives' house. When we got there, we discovered my wife's cousin had been ill the night before, vomiting, unable to sleep. She was sleeping when we got there. The question came up who should be called to see her. She lives in a small town where the medical standards, I suppose, aren't high. My wife feels that the doctors there are either incompetent or not in touch with the latest methods. Her cousin was scared about going to the hospital for a checkup, afraid she wouldn't leave there alive, and insisted she wanted to die at home. My wife has been up in the air, terribly excited about this whole thing. All that makes me feel confused and frustrated, terribly tense. What specialist should be called? It's the same indecision about my eye trouble. I wish someone else would take over.

4   The first time I saw anybody for my emotional problems, I went on the recommendation of a classmate whose father was an ophthalmologist and who himself later became an ophthalmologist. I wish he were here in Boston.

5   I thought of a joke earlier. Why should I have an eye infection? After all, I've led a clean life. How can I explain it? I've read that one source of eye infection comes from gonorrhea and is found in newborn infants. My initial reaction when I looked in the mirror at my red eye was: Oh, no! How can I go to work like this? There's something sick, something wrong, how can you hide it? I thought of, but rejected the idea of wearing dark glasses. It's like it exposes the feeling of being bad. When I have a cold and my nose is runny, I'm constantly preoccupied with it, that it'll be seen. It's as if anything amiss that shows externally makes me extraordinarily self-conscious about it. An acquaintance of mine saw me once running into my office building and said she had a negative reaction—that I looked silly running. The question has come to mind before, as well as now—do I look silly? When we first got married, I slipped, fell, and bruised my ankle painfully. My wife laughed, saying I looked comical all sprawled out. I felt angry at the remark and at her not being more sympathetic to me [pause]. I feel blocked now. Earlier I had a sexual sensation in my genitalia. I think of my fly being open, being self-conscious about things that show, that I don't want to be

seen. [Reminded of his voyeuristic incestuous fantasies and guilt activated by visit to his parents.]

4/17

[Wears dark glasses which he takes off the moment he lies down.]   1

I'm self-conscious about wearing sunglasses. My eye is red and swollen and painful. The ophthalmologist yesterday prescribed an antibiotic. He said I had a bacterial conjunctivitis. It's been worse since, maybe it's an allergic response to the medicine. The eye sticks out and looks scary in the mirror. It might be disturbing to others. It certainly makes me self-conscious. I put on an eye-patch this morning but couldn't see well. So I decided to put on dark glasses instead. I'm self-conscious about self-consciousness. That red eye must mean that something bad in me is showing on the outside. Then there's your question about seeing things I wasn't supposed to see—nude mother. Someone else made a joke about the eye. I had some theatre tickets last night, but my wife didn't want to interrupt her work. I agreed not to go because my eye was bothering me anyway. I asked one of our acquaintances if he could use them. He said my wife must have had something to do with the eye getting this way so she wouldn't have to go.

A few minutes ago the word injustice flashed into my mind together with   2
associations about civil rights and Negro racial problems. Also, when I went into the drug store to pick up eye drops, I noticed a report on the subject out in paperback and I bought it [pause]. Now I feel blocked.

I was discussing my research seminar with a friend of mine who's a doctor.   3
He talked about my having to establish my authority in the group. I'm supposed to be the leader of the research effort we're engaged in, but he pointed out that I'm too timid and when I'm pressured by the higher-ups, I tend to let my group down. He was in the last war as a medical officer. He was threatened with a court-martial because he had refused to obey an order from a line officer to send his medics to the front line and certain death. It seemed entirely mad. However, the other officer finally rescinded the threat. I have an involved, concerned feeling about these seminars. The way I'm handling them is lousing things up. I can verbalize the problem, but I can't control it; can't control my feelings. I have the desperate feeling I have to do something in the group which I can't do. My colleague pointed out that my group is quite angry at me because I'm not firm enough with them or the top executives. I agree but have to qualify it. Their behavior is provocative. They know I'm a newcomer in the company. I wonder about my ability to maintain firm control. I walk into the conference with anxiety and expectation, and the group senses it. I then go to a kind of wariness, holding back from being firm, being permissive until things build up and then having to step down hard. [Interpretation: shifting attitudes—their defensive aspects— swinging from too nice to too tough.] That is just how I react all over

the place. My usual demeanor is to be nice and easygoing. I hold off the angry reaction. Then, when I have to be firm, I lose control. I get terribly anxious. My disagreement with the discussion or arguments comes out in a flood. I have the expectation in advance that I'll be ineffective. It's enough to bring me to tears at times.

4   I remember that one summer I stayed the whole season in camp because my brother was sick at home. Toward the end of the season I became increasingly unhappy. I missed my family. Besides I was so poor at sports, which were highlighted. I was frightened of getting hurt. I think of my eye. What I disliked most about the camp was feeling left out. I couldn't compete with the other kids. Several kids used to pick on me. Then they acted as hypocrites on visiting day. I just now thought of my counsellor. My next thought is of you—and a possibly angry feeling toward you. Am I applying the word hypocrite to you? Now I feel blocked. I see a pattern on the ceiling as if in the shape of a sea-monster. Am I thinking of you? Am I getting brainwashed here?

5   When I came home my wife hadn't known my eye was infected. She asked me about it. I said I didn't know what caused it, but that some people have theories about it—including you. My wife said, "I'm sure he did." There were sarcastic implications to her remarks. I said then humorously, "I've been living a clean life, so why should this happen to me?"

6   On Monday I had to work with a new group of junior employees. I was a bit anxious about them. I'm so self-conscious when I'm observed by others. But it went quite smoothly.

4/18

1   [Analyst late five minutes.]
        I came home very early. My wife and I went to a restaurant for supper since the kids weren't home. I had a free evening. Before I could get started on some work, my wife's cousin called. She was still feeling sick with pain in her stomach. We finally made arrangements for her to be seen by an internist recommended by my company doctor. She'll be hospitalized although she was reluctant to go. She had a great fear of being cared for by an incompetent doctor. I felt somehow on the spot [much obsessive detail about this matter.]

2   I noticed you were late coming out of the office. There must be some reason for the delay, I thought. If I mentioned it to you, I would have to admit annoyance which I was working hard to deny. While I was waiting, I noticed a man across the street putting out trash barrels, together with his wife. He was wearing athletic clothes. I was speculating: how come on a weekday? Then I noticed him doing something funny—calisthenics in his back yard. After that he set out down the street, jogging. I had parked my car in front of his house. I had a feeling it shouldn't be parked at the house I'm not going into. I'm a worrywart.

3   ["But you have not said anything about your eye."] I had thought about it

at the very beginning of the hour—your looking at it as I came in, but then I shoved it out of mind. I still am concerned about it, though it's better today. Yesterday I believe I had some kind of reaction to the medicine the doctor prescribed for it. I have been thinking about it, looking at it, putting ointment on, though it feels much better today [pause]. I don't want to talk about the sexual implications—the looking business.

I'm buying a basketball—no, a baseball glove for my son today. I spent time   4
over the weekend playing catch with him and his chums. I'm getting more proficient in throwing and catching a baseball. I used to be so awkward at sports when I was a youngster.

4/22

[Five minutes late.]   1
I'm thinking about my eye. Tomorrow is a week since it first started to bother me. Today is the last day for putting drops into it. It's better. I was five minutes late because I think my watch was not correctly adjusted [pause]. ["Could there have been another reason?"] Getting even with you.

Now I'm suddenly aware of my genitals—penis. It's a peculiar sensation of   2
the weight and pressure of my clothing. I frequently still have brief thoughts about the physical attractiveness of my daughter, and these thoughts still tend to go in a sexual direction. They're mixed up, with regular affectionate thoughts. They're similar to the sexual fantasies and guilty feelings I've had about my mother [pause]. I've been to some company meetings when I've felt bored, uninterested, with no desire to attend subsequent meetings.

The weekend was pretty good. The Friday off gave me a chance to relax. My   3
wife went Thursday to visit her relatives and stayed over with the kids. I was alone Thursday night and Friday. There were a couple of incidents when I got angry at the kids on their return, because they were so rambunctious. My wife and I had very satisfactory lovemaking one evening over the weekend. I realize I'm very reluctant to elaborate further in this direction. It's still very difficult for me to let my thoughts come freely on sexual matters. I expect your disapproval.

Now I have thoughts about criminals. Bonnie and Clyde. I read a newspaper   4
article that criminal types are supposed to have an abnormal chromosome. I've been feeling unpleasant at having gotten angry at my son. I keep worrying about control over my feelings—my anger particularly. How can I control my feeling and convey a sense of my authority? I'm concerned about how I speak. Sometimes I speak low, tend to mumble. I get embarrassed and annoyed if I'm asked to speak louder. [Obsessional detail about this matter.] [Pause.] I guess I don't want to be conspicuous.

I don't know why I stopped thinking about my eye. I have the vague   5
thought—an eye for an eye. There I go again intellectualizing. I suppose the eye could have a symbolic meaning—like everything else. One of my friends tells

about how his little boy has trouble seeing the blackboard and won't wear glasses. He also likes to use his father's fishing pole which is much larger than his. I worry a lot about how I compare with other men.

4/23

1   I had a rather long dream last night. I was sitting either in a train or a boat, an ocean-liner. Many people were seated as passengers. I was rubbing my eye—the eye that was inflamed, but is now almost cleared up, though it's still itchy and I shouldn't rub it. I think of your pointing out that I had not been mentioning it. While sitting in your waiting room, I caught a glimpse of the *Saturday Review*. It looked like an old magazine, but the date was April 13. That's puzzling, if it's that recent. I couldn't believe what I observed. Anyway back to the dream: I was sitting there with my kids. Some people were selling sundry articles. Teenagers were selling hot stuff. It seemed like a situation that I had to do something about. I had to tell others to look after my kids while I went out. It was dark and I cursed for lack of a flashlight.

This morning my wife was very irritable and attacking, for no apparent reason. I tend to react defensively. She attacked my son for being so literal and compulsively honest about a matter he was involved in. I told her, "You're being nasty, cut it out." I feel she doesn't really understand him and suggested she ought to think over her impulsive behavior. She was instantly defensive and let me have it. I keep thinking of myself as not being masculine enough and not providing the best sort of figure for my boy to identify with.

I feel anxious, anticipating that conference I'm to lead this afternoon. I have another meeting at home tonight. I'm not too nervous about that. But if I have a bad time this afternoon, it may spill over to the evening meeting. As I was talking just now, I squeezed my eyes, closing them and was aware of pressure and pain in my left eye. It's still a little sore, irritable, and itchy. I squeezed my eyes just now because I was thinking of that afternoon conference, which makes me feel tensed up with my fists clenched and a lot of body movement. It's an expression of physical tightness. It reminds me of gesticulating to reinforce or emphasize something I'm saying. Though I felt so tensed up, I talked to one of the executives about my job and repeated my question whether any decisions had been made about an increase in my salary.

After the blowup with my wife, I became concerned over my loss of control. I feel as if I'm in a High Noon situation. I and those conferences. I'm pitted against a group. That's the way it seems—life or death. I realize it's exaggerated and see it as a fight, an ultimate showdown. I seem to have enormous difficulty in keeping cool. ["Why are you so angry?"] I don't know. There must be some reason why I'm blanking out things we've talked about before. It's like a helpless paralysis. Like my being anxious in front of people when I have to speak to them and blank out instead. I keep expecting that maybe you're annoyed with me and that might make me feel I'm being tested. While I want help from you, I'm also angry at the person who helps. ["Things should go your way in all respects."] I guess it's like saying let me have what I want and don't expect anything from me, else there's tremendous anger waiting in the wings to be unleashed. It's all so true it makes me speechless. I guess I can appreciate it intellectually and even with some emotional satisfaction. But there's still another feeling—that of being criticized by your pointing out my selfishness.

MARGINAL NOTES

7/14

1. Obsessive rumination, need to be in full control.
2. Voyeuristic tendencies, fear of exposure. Superego aspects. Preoccupation with appearance of female genitalia. Adolescent shyness and secretiveness, especially about sex. Search for parental guidance.
3. Avoidance of transference implications. Displacement of references to disappointment and loss onto idealized figure of boyhood friend. Masculinity equated with aggressivity which may backfire. Devaluation of hero-father.
4. Childhood recollections: auditory percepts, father's timidity, dangers of noncomformity. Identification with father's weakness.
5. Unawareness, inattention evoking criticism, with transference implications.

7/17

1. Transference dream of loss and denial of loss.
2. Reunion and reconciliation with mother-figure, temporarily lessening infantile needs.
3. Dream of competitive hostility toward wife and colleagues. Intellectualization.
4. Oral frustration, anger turned inward, little affect expressed.
5. Cognitive recollections of childhood orality and its persistence, frustrations and disappointments linked with mother, gustatory references. Good food equated with tranquilizer.
6. Oral sadism expressed by somatic equivalent.

7/19

1. Intellectualization. Hostility: its modification, avoidance, escalation, release, and varying consequences.
2. Severe ego-superego tensions. Identification with aggressive Minister of Defense (!) to compensate for inferior, bad (anal) image of self. Transference temporarily positive.

7/20

1. Major stress and anticipated anxiety. Overactivity both a coping mechanism and aspect of identification with father. Self-reassurance, another defense against anxiety.
2. Anxiety not experienced affectively during hour, but has been troublesome during public appearances. Rationalizations.

7/21

1. Unusual muscular exertion, a form of defensive overactivity. Curiosity about and envy of aggressive men. Oral aspects of aggression. Possible fatal consequences a powerful reason for its repression. Envy of successful sublimation of orality.
2. Transference doubts, intellectualized without affect. Treatment linked with harmful effects. Competitive, defensive, hostile thoughts about analyst associated with ambivalent recollections about father and his warnings that lack of control could lead to death. Punitive experiences referable to backside.

7/24

1. Onset of somatic dysfunction two days previously. Transference implications. Somatic identification with mother-in-law.
2. Hostility toward wife, largely suppressed. Further transference implications. Frustrated expectations linked with physical symptoms.
3. More suppressed hostility, toward boss and his demands. Obsessiveness and rumination.
4. Superego aspects of the transference. Expectation of the worst consequences. Fantasies of defiance.

7/26

1. Further somatic identification linked with intense castration anxiety. Avoidance an attempted defense.
2. Feelings of rejection in the transference. Implied hostility and indirect cognitive expression of guilt. Further references to loss. Mixed image of maternal figure—seemingly strong and giving, yet masochistic. Physical illness as punishment: superego aspects. Interpretation.

7/27

1. Eruption of intense hostility displaced from other sources, particularly the transference. Fears of retaliation. Concern about loss of control.
2. Stress of mother-in-law's illness and new job adjustment. Self-reassurance. Increased insight.

7/28-4/14, Summarized in text with dynamic formulations.

4/15

1. Physical symptom evokes secondary anxiety about health. Further concern about bodily defects being exposed. Complications of physical treatment in the past.
2. Hostility at oral-sadistic relative.
3. Competitive intellectualizing. Incestuous and voyeuristic thoughts about mother. Guilt.
4. Intellectualization about negative transference.
5. Thinly disguised, sexualized anal-sadistic fantasies: a defensive transference reaction.

4/16

1. Visual percepts linked with curiosity: transference aspects.
2. First reference to physical condition later diagnosed as acute bacterial conjunctivitis. Recollection of similar illness under possibly similar circumstances: activated voyeuristic, incestuous fantasies linked with guilt. Concern about inadequate treatment and interference with rigid schedule.
3. Over-anxiety, obsessive rumination under stress. Somatic identification. Dependency wishes.
4. Psychiatric referral from an ophthalmologist (!).
5. Joking—an attempt to cope with anxiety. Eye condition linked with sexual misconduct, dirty mother infecting child: displacement and projection. Fear of exposure of defects and consequent ridicule. Sexual sensory percepts. Exhibitionistic fantasies and fears. Interpretation.

4/17

1. Elaboration of physical symptoms. Possible phallic symbolism. Need to cover the conspicuous organ and voyeuristic impulses. Reference to woman's role in causing the eye condition.
2. Association of eye condition with violence and rights of individuals.
3. References to his adequacy as a leader. Defiance of unjust authority. Rumination about ability to control. Ultra-permissiveness an insufficient defense against sadistic, controlling impulses which then break through at times. Associative connection with eye.
4. Unhappy childhood recollections: homesickness, physical inferiority, fear of injury, feelings of rejection, and hypocrisy. Transference implications. Related visual percept.
5. Wife's devaluating innuendos evoke defensive denial.
6. Further concern about exposure of defects seemingly unwarranted.

4/18

1. Obsessional concern about relative's illness; somatic identification;

questioning competency of medical help an indirect allusion to hostile transference.

2. Direct reference to hostility with partial affect discharge. Devaluating thoughts and guilt.

3. Confrontation. Suppression of associations about physical condition linked with avoidance of sexual fantasies.

4. Increasing self-confidence.

4/22

1. Acting out in the transference.

2. Sensory sexual percepts precede incestuous thoughts and related guilt. Shift from changed associations.

3. Expectation of disapproval in transference—projection of own superego attitudes.

4. Concern about criminality and self-control, linked with hostile impulses. Need to be inconspicuous a defense against grandiose, exhibitionistic tendencies.

5. Intellectualization. Revenge. Eye a phallic symbol. Comparisons of phallus in child and parent. Concern about manliness.

4/23

1. Dream a secondary psychologic response to improving eye condition. Not believing what he may see in the analysis. Repressed impulses to steal what men have. Needing more light (analytic help). Attack and counterattack involving castrating maternal figure and honest child. Concern about being an adequate masculine figure.

2. Further concern about masculinity; defensive avoidance somatically expressed through eyes and body musculature.

3. Developing insight.

COMMENT

The patient's basic mode of response to stress has been through psychologic mechanisms. He has a longstanding obsessional character neurosis which decompensated twice during his late adolescence and early adult years. On both occasions he responded with brief depressive episodes to situations which represented critical separations for him. Except for upper respiratory infections his physical health has always been good.

The detailed reporting of his analytic hours begins two weeks before the summer interruption of treatment. On 7/14 the patient is his boring, wordy, ruminative self—this time about a trip to see his wife and children who are on vacation. He has found some girlie magazines and is concerned about exposure of his voyeuristic tendencies which are carefully concealed; he has always been shy and secretive about sexual matters. The impending summer interruption which represents a highly stressful event for this loss-sensitive patient is being avoided largely through the mechanism of displacement. The hostility which separation evokes is concealed in affectless transference responses. Following a three-day interval (including weekend) the patient on 7/17 reports dreams which refer to loss and denial of loss with transference implications. But there is further avoidance of this issue by a quick compensatory defensive shift to the theme of reunion and reconciliation with his family which has been on vacation. Another dream clearly reveals the presence of hostility and its preponderant position in the patient's marked ambivalence. Both dreams were preceded by an evening of oral frustration and anger turned inward. Many references to orality follow, particularly the rage when these infantile needs are frustrated, but its links with the transference and the pending summer interruption are concealed behind many defensive layers.

On 7/19 the patient's intellectual defenses appear prominently as he talks about hostility, its modification, suppression, repression, increase, discharge, and possible consequences. There are detailed references, displaced from the transference, about not getting satisfaction after a large expenditure of money for a car. In this hour the patient comes up with a compensatory wish for identification with the Israeli Minister of Defense, an interesting choice in light of his own rigid obsessional defenses and guilt-ridden voyeurism. The extent of the patient's hostility can be estimated from the number of defensive mechanisms which are being activated to contain it. A major external stress—starting a new assignment at his job—has been unmentioned recently until the patient refers to it on 7/20. He expects to cope with it by overactivity, a defense against facing his problems. Self-reassurance appears as another way of dealing with anxiety, which is not expressed as affect during the analytic hour. On the other hand, in actual public performances, the anxiety is often experienced directly in what appears as a breakthrough of feelings. An additional stress is pending: he has to give a talk to a group of industrialists. Related but not appearing in the associations at this time are grandiose, exhibitionistic, controlling impulses. They are defended against by the reaction formation of extreme shyness. Thus we note the piling on of stresses. Will a critical point be reached when psychologic coping mechanisms will no longer be sufficient to contain the tensions?

On 7/21 it is evident that the defense of hyperactivity has been carried over into unusual muscular exertion. References to this evoke ruminations about watching aggressive men to learn their secrets, interspersed with concern that aggression may lead to an inability to move, and even fatal consequences—a powerful reason for it to be held in check and not expressed. Another series of associations involving physical illness now appears, again with paralysis as chief symptom (opposite of hyperactivity) and with specific reference to the back. Closely linked are seemingly daring direct references to the treatment, especially doubts about it and the competence of the analyst, but these are intellectualized and without affect. They are linked with ambivalent recollections about father.

There are still further associations involving the back and related to punishment and sadism. The references to physical symptoms and illnesses are unusual and impressive. It could be a portent of things to come.

To recapitulate: under the doubly stressful impact of starting a new assignment at work and the pending interruption of the analysis with its transference implications, there has been an intensification of longstanding oral needs and fears of inadequate manliness. Concomitantly, hostility related to frustration and competition has been escalating. Coping mechanisms of a basically psychologic nature and part of the patient's life-long mode of response to stress have been activated: intellectualization, displacement, isolation, reaction formation, and hyperactivity in particular. The potential for affect discharge has surged up significantly, with the hostile side of the patient's ambivalence preponderant, but blocking is still very evident. However, increasing references to physical perceptions have begun to appear—linked with the powerful, hostile, competitive man (father) and the orally frustrating woman (mother). Defensive hyperactivity has culminated in muscular overexertion. Finally, references to a specific body area—the back—in others and himself have become conspicuous in the patient's associations. The psychophysical equilibrium is shifting, and the psychologic cues specified above suggest an impending somatic dysfunction involving back muscles.

On 7/24 the patient is in considerable physical distress from severe, low back pain (diagnosed as moderately severe sacro-iliac strain). There has been a three-day interruption (including weekend). The potential for increased regression during such interruptions is known and has undoubtedly been operative here. However, as listed below, a large number of new stresses also have developed in this three-day period and exerted their effect on the highly unstable psychophysical equilibrium. Consequently, the critical point where ideational, affective, and behavioral outlets become insufficient is reached over the weekend. Then the organ system, musculoskeletal, and the anatomic site, the back, both of which have come up in the material of the previous interviews, actually become physically involved. A secondary gain aspect appears in this hour, when the patient alludes to his inability to get off the couch and in this way could continue in analysis without interruption. Somatic identification with his wife's mother, hitherto unmentioned, also can be noted in the associations. Such information may not be available in interviews prior to the onset of physical dysfunction. The additional stresses that the patient has been exposed to consisted of: reactive hostility to wife's hostility, the children's illnesses, and the peremptory request from his new boss. At the very end of this hour, there is an actual brief affect discharge.

In the next interview (7/26) the patient reveals that his mother-in-law's back pain is due to cancer and an amputation will be necessary. This represents for him a symbolic castration and enhances his concern about his own physical illness, though the connecting identification with this mother-figure is outside the patient's awareness. However, there is a loosening of the affect block, and references to the transference are accompanied by some affect discharge. There is retrospective recollection of other losses. In this hour, the patient has not made a single reference to his own back, though the splinting continues to be quite evident. An interpretation is made about the relationship between summer interruption, other stresses, frustration of increased dependency and escalating hostility.

On 7/27 the patient reports an eruption of violently angry affect occurring right after the previous interview. This was displaced from other sources, particularly the transference, breaking through all the blocking and was directed at an auto service manager who himself was provocative. While the patient was able to discharge considerable affect, it was not without considerable fear of retaliation and concern that he had temporarily lost control. The previous day's interpretation may have lessened his fear of retaliation.

The backache, in the remaining hours before the summer interruption, begins to improve, and one week later has completely subsided.

During the next eight months, progress is impeded by the persistence of marked obsessional defences, ambivalence and negative transference. The patient remains free of physical illness. His new job presents problems: he finds himself competing with his boss, and disliking an assignment to conduct discussion groups. A visit to his parents upsets him.

On 4/15 the patient refers to headache—the first somatic manifestation in a month. His visit to his parents over the past weekend was stressful because voyeuristic, incestuous fantasies broke through into his awareness. There has been antecedent exhibitionistic anxiety linked with speaking in public. In the hour, the patient introduces the theme of concern about his general physical integrity, absent from his associations for several months. Prominent visual percepts reappear. He intellectualizes about his sexual fantasies, hostility, and guilt—all have transference implications. A shift in psychophysical equilibrium appears to be developing again in the direction of physical dysfunction, but this time the site most likely will be the eyes.

The patient opens the next hour (4/16) with more references to visual percepts and voyeuristic activity, again extending to the transference. Then he mentions the pain in his left eye which he first noticed on awakening. (It is later diagnosed as acute bacterial conjunctivitis.) He verbalizes concern that the new physical symptoms portend something serious and that medical treatment will make the condition worse. An additional stressful experience occurs the previous night: demands testing his manliness have been made on him by his wife, activating considerable hostility. What psychologic factors are involved in the development of the new physical illness? The emergence of Oedipal material, masked competition with his boss, and several public appearances precede his visit to his parents. The last two events prove to be especially stressful. They activate longstanding exhibitionistic-voyeuristic conflicts and, in turn, anxiety and guilt which are verbalized but not affectively expressed. The habitual obsessional defenses rapidly become insufficient and the psychophysical equilibrium unstable. Hostility is not markedly increased and remains concealed behind a many-layered defense and affect block. The eye, symbolically appropriate, and a previous target organ, becomes the site of physical dysfunction once again.

Secondary elaboration of physical symptoms continue on 4/17. The eye represents a phallic symbol, swollen, red and conspicuous, which evokes defensive needs for its concealment. Similarly voyeuristic impulses need to be hidden. Associated with the physical symptoms are conflicts over authority: the patient's bending over backward to be permissive is actually a defense against sadistic, controlling, phallic impulses which break through at times. Further associations concerning physical inferiority in childhood are retrospectively recalled. In subsequent interviews there is evidence of a favorable shift in psychophysical equilibrium, both affectively and behaviorally. Concomittantly the eye condition is improving. The stresses that preceded it have lessened. Intellectualizing tendencies have been reestablished, but the patient is more aware of their presence. On 4/23, the last hour reported, there is also evidence that the patient is developing insight into his hypersensitivity and potential for intense hostility.

N. P.

Infections, Inc.

INTRODUCTION

N. P. is a 44-year-old businessman who had been advised to seek treatment because of a longstanding problem with tardiness, especially in handing in reports at work. This had made it necessary for him to change jobs a number of times, though he was a skilled personnel manager. He had also been increasingly dissatisfied with his bachelor status and finally decided to find out why he could not form a lasting and satisfying relationship with a woman.

Both parents are dead, having passed away when the patient was in his twenties. Both had been in ill health for years during the patient's adolescence. Mother had suffered from chronic respiratory disease to which she finally succumbed. Father, an inveterate smoker, had died suddenly of a coronary thrombosis. Both had been somewhat distant figures: mother busy with her social activities, father frequently away on business trips. Gradually, because of her invalidism, mother had become isolated from her friends and even more from her family. After being cared for by a succession of maids, the patient was sent to a boarding school and from early adolescence on saw little of his family except on vacation. He went through college and business school with high marks, making a number of male friendships, only a few of which he kept up later on. He also developed a pattern of frequently changing girlfriends; usually he was the one who broke up the relationship. A younger brother, of whom the patient had always been jealous because he had received more attention from the mother, had achieved a brilliant record as a surgeon but was having marital difficulties. The patient had had a bout of pneumonia when he was in boarding school, and an undiagnosed febrile illness of two weeks' duration without sequelae shortly thereafter. Otherwise, he had enjoyed excellent physical health.

The initial clinical impression was that the patient had a severe obsessive-compulsive character structure. He was unaware of any ego-alien symptoms though he acknowledged his tardiness at work and his dissatisfaction with his bachelor status.

As the analytic treatment proceeded, it became quite clear that there was a rigidity of obsessional defenses and a walling off of affect that was very marked. Intellectualization, isolation, and affect block were joined, however, with a subtle form of suspiciousness which the patient would support with relatively calm, stubbornly persisted in rationalizations. Severe superego-ego tensions were present but masked. Hostility was hidden behind a bland but tenacious resistance to clarification and interpretation. The pattern of coming late had been manifest in the analytic hours intermittently since the beginning of the treatment and usually followed interviews in which the patient felt he had been criticized, rejected, forced to adhere to analytic procedure. It represented a defiance of parental rule. Confrontation with and interpretation of the lateness had not resulted in any significant modification of this resistance. Though the patient spoke of the many women with whom he had had contact, sexual details were conspicuous by their absence. Blocking was frequently present. There had been no mention of physical symptoms or dysfunction before the time the reporting begins, the eighth month of analysis.

CASE MATERIAL

6/6

1   I recall a dream fragment that occurred earlier in the week. I was discussing a medical problem with a man. He was describing what seemed to be difficulty in urinating. I told him he ought to see someone about it [pause].

Yesterday I was going to see Joanne; I'd met her last fall, but we had stopped going out together around New Year's. She's a teacher. She seemed hurt that business had required my breaking a date—in fact, didn't believe me. I saw her at a party two weeks ago and called her last week. She said she had a kidney-bladder infection which was being treated without much result. I advised her to try another doctor. I called her yesterday for dinner, and then at the last minute she called back and said she had developed symptoms again—so that date was off. There's another girl, Sally, whom I'm going to see tonight, for the first time since we had our big blowup a month ago.

In the dream it was the man who had the urinary problems; I'm thinking now of myself. There's only one time I can recall having urinary trouble as a
2   child. It's the time I had to be circumcised. All I remember is great fear. My aunt Flora recently had some kind of accident. A maid found her on the floor of her bedroom, unable to get up. She was seen by a doctor, but not hospitalized.

Instead a practical nurse was hired to take care of her. I'm not sure whether she had a stroke or not. About six years ago she had to be hospitalized for kidney problems. There was some obstruction. Come to think of it, I'm often blocked in here. I don't recall my dreams too well. I also have trouble writing things down—an expressive problem. The business of my being late—again I don't know—it's not blocking. But the reasons for my coming late so much aren't clear; they are blocked off. ["In the dream, you're discussing the situation with a man."] Yes, in the dream, the man is having a problem. Well, if you were bored with me, it would be a kind of blocking—you wouldn't be listening to what I had to say. I think you're not active enough. Maybe it would help me to have thoughts more readily, if you were more active. In the dream I was giving a man advice. It certainly sounds as if I'm doing that now to you. If a therapist gets bored, it probably means anxiety or frustration on his part. One of my fantasies is that before the hour with me, you should take some kind of pep pill.

6/8

[20 minutes late.]   1

I'm not feeling well. I got a typhoid shot Tuesday after I left the hour. Part   2
of my getting ready for that trip to Europe. My head aches badly; it feels stuffy in here [he opens nearby window]. I had only a mild reaction in the past when I was immunized for typhoid. I was feeling so bad yesterday that I cancelled all my appointments. Today, just before the headache began, I was at lunch in a delicatessen. It was very smoky there, a lot of food smells. That's when I started feeling nauseous and headachey. I took a nap and overslept, that's why I'm late today. I really don't feel well [Sits up briefly, obviously in considerable distress, pale and silent. Finally, after a few minutes, lies down on couch again]. I don't remember feeling this rotten in a long time. [Somatic complaints have been absent in the analytic hours.] Maybe if I lie quietly for a little while, I'll be able to go on [pause].

I had a dream last night. I was in a theatre with Betty [a girl he's currently   3
interested in]. I was trying to get backstage to see my friend Richard. I climbed to the top of the stage and was looking down, but I couldn't get there. Then I was in a car, drove out to the country and Richard was there. He went off with two fellows, one a homosexual. Richard had been drinking too much. That's the dream, but I haven't seen Richard since Sunday. We were at a nightclub. He was with a girl who was pretty drunk. She invited him to her apartment, but it was very late then, and he said he had other matters to attend to [pause]. He also didn't pick up my offer for the two of us to get together soon. I wondered if he were going to drop me as a friend. Maybe he's found more interesting companionship.

My brother's coming in tonight for our school reunion.

6/9

1   [25 minutes late.]

2   After I left here yesterday, I went home and slept most of the time. I was awakened once early in the evening when my brother called me from out-of-town to tell me he'd be delayed getting here until this afternoon. He was telling me about his marital troubles, and the sicknesses they've gone through. He's finally gotten a good family doctor. The one he had before wasn't doing a good job [Pause—continues. His attention is called to it]. I can't figure out why I was late again. I remember now that I didn't set my alarm and my TV set was on all night. This morning I have an appointment with one of my bosses which I'm looking forward to with some anxiety, because I still have some work outstanding that should have been in some time ago. It makes today a difficult one—lots of tension. I started off on the wrong foot. I could have set the alarm, but didn't. The TV was on, but that didn't wake me on time. That issue of having a good doctor would apply to you. But it sounds like I'm straining to pull things together. My thoughts just don't seem to come easily at all.

6/13

[Did not come previous hour, unable to get back from out-of-state trip in time because of poor weather conditions.]

1   We haven't met in four days. Lots has happened. My brother got here for the reunion. We met late yesterday on my return. We had planned to have dinner Sunday night, but I got weathered in and I left a message for him which he didn't get. He seems more relaxed than when I saw him last. Now that he's divorced, he's been looking around and has met a girl he likes very much; she's a divorcee. She was with him. So here's my brother, who's younger than I, thinking about another marriage, and I am still single.

2   The school reunion is this coming weekend. Afterwards we're going off into the country, Betty and I together with my friend John and his date. It'll be a time of recalling the past, of people who were in your life, then left it.

3   I've talked some more with Betty, and I don't feel comfortable about continuing with her. She's extremely anxious about her sexual response to me. She kisses warmly, but has a trigger mechanism if I begin to caress her. Her hand whips up and holds mine. It's as if she's startled. She's never told me how old she is. I keep wondering why she's so sensitive. Maybe her anxiety is due to her ethical position. It's disappointing to see how rigid she is. She also claimed she didn't know what my intentions were—where the embracing would lead to. My guess is she's in her early thirties, yet I wonder what her sexual experience has been. The whole matter gets me frustrated. I asked her to think more about it—about our relationship to each other. It would be too bad if it didn't work

out because I like her in a lot of ways. She hinted that her home life was all mixed up, that she had a lot of trouble communicating there. Well, I'm no paragon of communication myself. I guess I'll just have to keep looking. I want to be a tolerant person, but I find myself quickly intolerant of Betty. If I didn't have this problem in communication, I might not have noticed it in others to the extent I do now. I keep wondering how much is defensive and how much of my observations are appropriate.

6/16

[20 minutes late.]   1

I'll not be here Monday because of the reunion. I know I'm late again. What is it about Friday morning, the last interview of the week? It's also the day before the weekend, and now it'll be three days' absence [pause]. ["What are your thoughts?"] Reasonably it shouldn't make any difference. But it's reunion time—a time of meeting and of parting. That's the issue, and it's more intense now than at other times of the year. Maybe that's got something to do with my coming late—I don't know. I can't even identify any feelings which I know must be there [pause].

There are several girls I've been seeing recently. Had a date with Joanne last   2
night. Met her last fall. We dated for about six weeks, but then on one occasion I had to break a date with her at the end of December. She wasn't interested thereafter. But several weeks ago I saw her again at a party. She's the one who's been ill with some kind of bladder infection and also had had family emergencies. She was out of circulation for a while. I've liked Joanne since I first met her.

But I've got a lot to learn about girls, even though I'm not a young man any   3
more. I'm learning painfully that my early impressions are pretty good, but I often ignore certain things that are there because I feel I shouldn't jump to conclusions. This other girl—Martha—she's an airline stewardess. I don't usually date them. Many run to a type: they're superficial, party-girls. This one lied about our last date, wasn't there when I called, didn't get in touch with me. She said she couldn't remember my name. But there were ways she could have found it. But worst of all, she twisted things around to try to make it look as if I stood her up. It's as if she had no obligations. So I broke off with her. As I think of it now, there were signals from way back about the kind of person she was.

6/21

[Missed previous appointment. Five-day interval since last interview.]   1

My brother and I were at his summer home yesterday. I had planned to come back yesterday in the morning, but again the weather was poor and the planes weren't flying, and I couldn't get here on time any other way. It was a hectic weekend, what with the reunion and everything. There just wasn't enough time. People were coming and going. Old memories and experiences got revived. People I know here are leaving. I met some more girls—one an authoress, Eve, a sister of the wife of one of my classmates. She joined our party. She's an authoress by avocation, the family black sheep. She comes from an upper middle-class, suburban family whose views on life are so utterly different from hers. She goes on peace marches and is interested in politics of the left. She doesn't really make any money from her writings.

2   I met some of my other male relatives at the reunion. We all went to the same university. I heard about all the family troubles there: people in accidents, having operations—gloomy news. Also there was a lot of sadness at the reunion: people who have died and can't come back. There were some people whom I was very close to at school who didn't attend the reunion. There were so many things going on: sights and sounds, people coming and going, drinking, eating, talking. All these things are flashing through my mind.

3   Now I have an image of a ship I saw Sunday. It was a Danish square rigger, almost 200 years old. It had been rebuilt by a wealthy Scandinavian who wanted to make a trip around the Horn with it [pause]. For some reason I'm comparing the ship with myself. The ship was actually wrecked going around the Cape of Good Hope—that is, Cape Horn. It lost the top of its foremast in a storm around the Horn. The hull itself is 200 years old, but the furbishings, the upper part, were redone just last year. I'm now thinking that I've been in analysis about a year. Back to the ship: the interior was modified, but the exterior looked old-fashioned. I wear old-fashioned clothes; well, not really, but I'm no fashion plate when it comes to dressing. This ship had a long voyage and was in trouble, but is doing O.K. now. Thinking about all this has made me very sad. Somehow I feel very touched [voice is low and tears are visible in the patient's eyes]. Very touched [pause]. The ship had been to a lot of ports and now was heading home. I wonder why I have this feeling now and not when I was looking at the ship. [Interpretation: A time of reunion, of partings, of loss, activating recollection of the old days, and memories of a difficult journey through life, including the analytic experience, accompanied by a longing for home and parents—both of whom are dead.]

6/23

1   [15 minutes late.]
Perhaps it might work out to make the Friday hour 15 minutes later. Anyway I forgot to set the alarm clock yesterday.

2   Eve is still staying with me. It's beginning to appear that she's a pretty troubled girl. She's very bright, has warmth, but is very unhappy. She's an outsider, doesn't fit in with most groups, has left her upper middle-class,

suburban environment and yet doesn't really feel or act like a beatnik or hippie type. Some months ago she had a serious depression, from which she's not altogether recovered. Her interests now are focused on peace—against any war anywhere. She's had arguments with her relatives who disapprove of her stand. She's dating some people, particularly one older person, a teacher, who sounds as if he might be crazy. Her ideas about him also sound far out to me. He has such a block when she argues with him about war that she wonders if he isn't a government agent. What am I doing seeing a girl like that, so depressed, and who's discouraged about treatment and seems to have such a negative view of it? ["Your associations are exclusively concerned with her and her attitudes toward treatment. What about your attitudes and feelings? Last hour you were tearful."] Perhaps I'm trying to forget about myself. Wednesday night I was talking with Eve while we were lying in bed, very intense talk. Within an hour I had five phone calls from different people. That was a strange coincidence of calls, from people I hadn't spoken to in some time. Here is Eve who is very lonely and sees herself out of everything right now. Our being together is interrupted by all these calls, representing different people in my life. These calls underscored her loneliness. It's terrible because this girl needs help and yet may be arranging things that will prevent her from getting it. [pause].

Now I'm reminded of a film I saw on TV last night. It was on the life—on a   3
segment of the life—of William Halsey with Cagney playing the part. It dealt with his Pacific command in World War II. I was very moved by the film. It brought across the loneliness of Halsey, the man in command, having to make decisions, sending people he liked and knew into dangerous situations where many were killed. I think of Eve who's about to leave and go back to her hometown. At the end of the film there's a scene showing Halsey retiring. He's in civilian clothes, leaves his ship for the last time, and says goodbye. As he's being rowed to shore, a song is sung. I got very sad. I was thinking of this just after I left here last time, after I had said goodbye. That song—I wonder if the words had been written by Masefield. Some time ago I had read a poem of Masefield's—a moving poem about youthful hopes and aspirations which may be dashed against life's hard realities. I feel sad now just thinking about it. These lines are very moving:

There was a boy who went to sea and left the shore behind him,
I know that boy, that boy was me, and now I cannot find him.

I was and am very moved by recalling that scene and hearing those words. I'm sad right now, in tears [pause]. It's a time of leavetaking [pause]. After I   4
left here the last hour, I was sad. I've always been interested in the sea. Before I was born, my father sailed the high seas. What adventures he must have had! When I was a youngster, I had an uncle who was in the Navy, and he would tell such exciting stories. One of our early homes was on the seacoast. When I was four or five, a picture of me and my dog was taken in front of that house. The dog was killed shortly afterwards. I still have that picture [tears].

6/26-7/5, Summary

The affect that had clearly broken through in the preceding few hours again becomes blocked off. Coming late to the analytic hours continues intermittently. The patient is preoccupied with the weekend holiday which he considers to be a big and significant occasion. He is getting together with one very close male friend who recently has married. However, he has difficulty in finding an appropriate girl for the occasion. The one he asked has not given a definite answer; he and she have reciprocally broken dates in the recent past. Involved in her excuses has been the sickness of her mother. The whole issue underlines for him the fact that he does not have a steady girlfriend. Eve, the sad and angry girl, leaves. During her stay the whole matter of treatment and its efficacy is activated in his thinking. His concern about his own treatment is then verbalized, but with little affect.

He will soon change jobs. This brings up associations about his earlier experiences at work. He felt lonely, knew few people, had much trouble getting dates. He is now preoccupied with being stood up at the last minute for the big weekend and holiday date. The verbal content contains many hostile references, but there is no accompanying affect. The problem of communication between himself and others continues to be a major difficulty for him. He feels himself caught in a dilemma between precipitous action and doing nothing in his relationships with girls. Ambivalence remains a barrier to the development of lasting relationships with them. Additionally, there is the incompletely understood need to have immediate sexual relations with girls. He rationalizes it as an operational test indicating whether he and the girl would continue in their relationship. However, having sexual relations quickly with a girl is a way to prove that he is adequately masculine and a defense against feelings of unmanliness.

Meanwhile there are more leave-takings and going-away parties. He has a dream in which curiosity about father's previous marriage is revealed. One of his friends who is leaving the area is quite depressed. References are made by this friend to being single, in his thirties, and having his mother hovering over him. The patient is reminded of himself, although his own mother is dead. He finally invites Ellen—a colleague of his—to be with him and his friends on the holiday weekend, and she accepts, although they have not dated previously. On the third night of the long weekend they begin to sleep together, although Ellen is uncomfortable because of the presence of others in the house they have rented.

7/6

1   [Fifteen minutes late.]
     I just had lunch with a friend. He's moved into a new apartment in the

middle of town. I've never been in that area at noon. Lots of traffic. I missed the right turn-off and had to make a big circle to get back in the right direction. Joe has a great apartment with a wonderful view. I keep thinking about when I first came to Boston. It was a most unrewarding couple of months. So much work to do, keeping me busy evenings and no suitable place to live. I didn't know anybody then. The rental agents I contacted just weren't paying attention to what I was asking them to find for me. Then I started hunting more actively on my own. Finally, I saw the place I'm in now and took it.

[Long pause.] ["What are you thinking now?"] I was somewhat distracted   2
by the noise outside just now, and partially I was thinking about this matter of apartments. The kind of place I had been looking for, you don't get on the real estate market. It's something that's passed along from person to person. I guess I'm thinking of something special. How does one get something special? ["What are your associations about that?"] Maybe I'm looking for something special here though I don't know exactly what, and I don't understand why I should keep coming late, even though we've talked about that before [pause].

That sexual intimacy with Ellen. You noted yesterday that it was quick—on   3
the second, the third day we had been together. I was thinking about that, too, but I'm not sure what I can make of it. Last night Ellen brought this up herself—that we had become so intimate after a very short time. It reminded me of the conditions of stress in wartime. People might meet and have intercourse within an hour, wanting to be close while they still had the opportunity. ["Do you feel under comparable stress, though for other reasons?"] Must be so, but the stress I'm under isn't clear to me. It seems to me that I have nothing against early intimacy as long as contraception is reliable.

7/7

[Five minutes late.]

I've been thinking about the question of my sexual activity, what goals do I   1
have. It's not very clear. What does early intimacy mean in terms of the staying power of a relationship? My friends, John and Marge, were apparently intimate the second week they were going together; now they're married and things seem to be going well. I think intimacy these days may be more common than it was 20 or 30 years ago. Once a girl's been intimate, not promiscuous, if she's able to feel comfortable with it as part of her social life, it doesn't seem to be much of a strain for her, especially if she uses contraception effectively. But my motivations aren't clear. ["We have spoken of the need to prove manliness, to show conquests. How much then is the girl liked for her own sake?"]

Ellen—she has a definite *gestalt*. Some girls please me, others don't. What is   2
there about her? First of all, her physical appearance. I find her very attractive: features, eyes, figure. A part of the physical *gestalt* is movement, the way a girl carries herself, moves, sits. How does she relate? Is she pleasant? Do I attract

her? Does she seem to like me? That's important. Getting to know each other—that's the crucial area; the other things are introductory. I like a certain amount of openness, a girl who's honest, and yet flexible and curious about things. One who responds sexually. That's the issue—how does the sexual part of the relationship tie in with the rest? I could be interested in a girl sexually very early, though she may turn out to be uninteresting in other ways later on. It doesn't seem to go in the other order: not being attracted physically to a girl at the outset, but as I grow to know her, becoming more attracted that way. I have to have an outlet for sex. However, I rarely approach a girl, pick her up, have intercourse, and not see her again. There have been several exceptions: one was a girl, apparently engaged and mixed up; the other, a divorcee who was garrulous and gross. Those were instances of early intimacy and then retreat. I once met a graduate school student with whom I was intimate on our first date, and as I got to know her, I became increasingly upset by what I found out. After not seeing her for a while, I had called her and she was out. She called me back quite a bit later, and we almost immediately got into an argument in which she brought up that I expected more of her than she was willing to give. She didn't want a sexual relationship, just friendship. I found it difficult to tolerate this *post facto* splitting—sex and friendship. It seemed we were both uncertain of our feelings. I felt it would be difficult for us to be just friends. We didn't get together again.

3   Now, as for Ellen, I felt attracted to her since I first saw her and talked with her.

7/10

1   [12 minutes late.] I can't explain why I'm late [pause]. I just feel blocked on that.

2   Ellen and I spent the weekend together. There were numerous plans to include other people which didn't work out. Last night she went to join a girlfriend in the country; she had promised to stay with her a couple of days. My work has slackened off, so that I have a lot of leisure time. I miss Ellen.

3   I had a dream in which I made a call to a girl named Sophia. She was in Montreal in a rooming house, it seemed. I called her person-to-person. When she came to the phone, we exchanged greetings. I can't recall exactly what I said—something about whether she was still living there. Her answer was, "I'd rather not go into this, I'd rather not talk on the phone. I'm busy, and it's a bad time to talk." I was put out. Here I was calling, and she didn't want to talk even for a few minutes, and I told her how I felt. Our conversation went on as a low key argument, and it wasn't decided what we would do. That's how the dream ended.

Sophia is a girl I took out about ten years ago, through a friend of mother's, who was very taken by her. She's a lovely girl who seemed mature for her age—honest, perceptive, and poised. I stopped seeing her when I had to be out of the country for a while, and then I heard that she had married. The weekend was pretty lonely. Several of my male friends called me then. One of them had been South and had seen Sophia recently.

[Pause.] Now I'm thinking of the weather and how hot and sultry it has been. The weathermen say a cold front is coming. Anyone flying in a small plane would have to get over the top of this front, and if not, would have to turn back and find a passage through the clouds. [Interpretation: "In the dream you met a cold front of a different kind."] That reminds me how Sylvia stood me up the previous weekend, preferring to meet with a girlfriend. Now Ellen has gone off to stay with her girlfriend for a while. I don't think I had the same feeling about Ellen's going. She was really more apologetic than she needed to be. I must be awfully sensitive to people leaving me [no affect].   4

An acquaintance of mine, an older woman, recently went to join her brother in Montreal. She was unmarried and chronically ill. I learned she had been hospitalized. Shortly after that she left for Canada. She had heart trouble—like my mother. One demerit about Ellen is that she's a little overweight. Mother was overweight—a characteristic I found offensive. She never tried to keep her weight down. She didn't wear her overweight gracefully. I used to think mother ate too much. Then she used to talk about a gland problem. For some reason I related that to glands being out of order in her mouth. Much later I understood that she had been terribly unhappy when younger, especially after the death of her own mother. She married in a rush the first time, and her first husband left her, and shortly after she married my father, he began to drink heavily. For years that was a big problem for him until he was finally able to give it up, with the help of treatment.   5

7/11

It feels good to lie down today. I feel as if I'm coming down with the flu [pause]. I've been feeling feverish and achy, and I have a sore throat. It probably is related to my falling asleep on the couch in my living room with the air conditioner on. It got too chilly. I was just in my shorts, not covered otherwise. I think of a friend's father who I was told earlier today had had to be hospitalized with a toe infection. He had been picking at it, and it got infected. Then the toe had to be amputated. He isn't doing well and is reacting to the whole thing in a depressed way.   1

Last summer my friend John talked of strongly considering marriage, but at first wanted to defer the decision until his analyst got back from vacation. In fact, he finally decided to get married while the analyst was away. I don't think I'm that close to getting married, but I wish I were.   2

Keep thinking of other girls I've met in the last year or so. One who never called me, after leaving town for a month and returning, although we left it that way. There was something musty about her—a quality of old-maidism.   3

4   John and his wife may move. He's considering jobs in several cities. He wants a position where he can really begin a career, and where he locates will depend on this. I wish I were in his boots.

5   All the girls I've gone with I've left, except for Millie. With her it was a draw. Two weeks ago when I was in bed with Eve, I got a call from Millie. I hadn't heard from her in eight months. After a moment, she got the idea that I couldn't really talk with her then, so she just asked what my plans were for the immediate future. The pattern with the girls is that I leave them. Here I go again, thinking about leaving and being left [without affect]. I seem to do most of the leaving. It's more comfortable for me that way. I think of the girl that never called me when she was supposed to. I felt put out about that. She has never mentioned me to our mutual friends. I had some irritated feelings about that. I wondered why, when I've been told she hasn't been seen with another date. I have the impression that she doesn't date much, if at all.

6   Lucy is the first girl I remember having a romantic interest in at age nine or eleven. She showed me she had a picture of me in a locket around her neck. She was a very pretty girl. Ten years later I saw her at a party at college which she attended with another fellow. I didn't go up to her. It was in one of the fraternity houses, and I wasn't a member. I felt ill at ease about socializing, since I hadn't been invited to the party, just let in to look for somebody. I remember when we were youngsters, I played doctor and she was the patient. The treatment had something to do with using my penis which I exposed to her. She ran away, didn't even want to look. I recall another sex encounter, my cousin who used to sit on me a lot up to the time I entered high school. That's when I first started dating. The first girl I dated regularly left me for another fellow. The next girl was terribly sensuous—way ahead of me, who felt like a bumpkin. She left me too, for another fellow. After her there was a series of girls I dated once or twice, and then finally there was a girl whom I saw for some time, but I left her.

7   I next had this girl Penny. That turned out to be a big mistake. She caused me a lot of grief and pain. Penny was the first girl I had sexual intercourse with. She had two sick parents. Her father was an alcoholic who just about managed to hang on to his job. I wouldn't usually see him in action because he'd be closeted away, so it was some time before I discovered what was going on with him. There were other difficulties too. Her mother kept interfering with our going out. Penny was trapped by a pair of vicious parents and couldn't extricate herself. It was a mistake getting involved with her. In retrospect, I might have seen some signals earlier, if I had been more experienced. Penny's father discouraged any fellow who tried to see his daughter and while the mother seemed on our side at first, this was deceptive. She reversed herself. There were some big scenes when they tried to prevent me from taking Penny out. Shortly after that I left her.

8   My thoughts turn to mother. She was always big on demonstrating affection,

kissing me in an overdone way—almost maudlin. It expressed her need for closeness, I tolerated her kisses, though many times I didn't want them. I feel that physical intimacy is an important issue with me. Maybe it's related to this business of losing. When some of these girls had the hots for me, I was all thumbs, but the fellows they turned to were tuned in and apparently knew what to give them and how to communicate with them. So my hesitancy resulted in my losing out. ["Quick physical intimacy is seen as a means of guarding against quick rejection."]

7/13

I have fever and a sore throat. It's been a long time since I've had a sore throat; when I was a kid I had sore throats and ear infections. I had a strange sensation last night. My fever was up and I had a very loud buzzing in my ears. I kept wondering what caused it. I recall having had that before when I had a fever. I had a date for dinner last night, a date that had been made and postponed several times before. I didn't want to postpone it again, so we went out, but I had to go home early because I was really ill.

I had some dreams last night, but they're fragmented and not clear. The dreams had to do with Mike, a friend of mine at college. I was dreaming about New Hampshire. Mike is from a small town there. It was discovered while he was in college that he had kidney disease, when they took a urine specimen during a routine physical exam. I guess he had it pretty bad. He had had lots of ear infections as a child. He went sour awfully fast. In his junior year at college he was to be sent to Boston for a kidney operation, but the night he was to come up here, he died. It was just this time of year, a long time ago. It certainly looks as if all the bad memories are coming back to haunt me.

When I was nine years old, I had a lot of sore throats. I was taken for radium treatments of some kind. This was for trouble I had with my Eustachian tube. I believe that's what it's called. Apparently the treatment was successful because I didn't have any more ear troubles. When I was two years old, I had my tonsils and adenoids out by the doctor who delivered me; no, that's not correct, it was done by an ear, nose, and throat specialist. Nowadays I wonder if they would have done such an operation. I recall the ride home in the car from the hospital. I asked for orange juice and drank it. Last night I tried some wine and wow! It hurt! My throat is really sensitive. Now orange juice after a tonsil operation is supposed to be noxious, but apparently I drank it right down [pause.]

Just now I recall another fragment of a dream I had some days ago. It was terribly sadistic. There was a prisoner, surrounded by his captors, both of whom are unidentified, but it's like a public spectacle. There are two stakes in the ground, with pointed ends. The prisoner was hoisted on these stakes, dropped down, and the stakes catch him under the arm pits. This dream was about a week ago. What comes to mind is that during some fraternity initiations, I had my arms tied to my sides after glue had been put between them and my chest. Later my arms were forcibly pulled up. That was dreadfully painful. Part of the time I was blindfolded. There was one fellow I suspected of planning the whole thing because he was a sadist. I really felt ill that night.

5   I was ill at boarding school twice. Shortly after I got there, I had pneumonia with a high fever and was getting penicillin by injection every few hours. Then, a few months later, it was time for me to go on vacation, and my parents were in Texas. So I had to get down there, and it was an arduous trip in those days. I had to carry a bag almost as big as myself. I can remember how heavy that was and how painful to carry from one railroad station to another. I finally got on a plane that took 12 hours to get to Texas with many stops on the way. When I finally arrived, I had a terrific fever. I spent the entire two weeks in bed. I was delirious at times. I never knew what that illness was. I can't be sure if it came after that attack of pneumonia. I guess it did come afterwards. I had pneumonia during one of the school terms, not during any vacation.

7/14

1   [Ten minutes late.]

[Silence.] ["Why are you silent?"] I don't know. Just thinking of not feeling well, which I—most people don't like to hear about.

2   Wednesday night I called Ellen. She had said she would call me on her return from her visit out-of-town. I thought she might have called in my absence. She hadn't, and I wondered if she had lost interest. I told her I had been sick and didn't know how I would feel the next night. She called again yesterday afternoon. I was still feeling sick, so she came over to my place and made dinner [pause].

3   This illness really bothers me. I'm terribly uncomfortable. I have a continuing sore throat, fever, and general feeling of weakness. For some strange reason my gums are getting very painful. It's ironic that I have parties to go to tonight and tomorrow night. I've had fevers lasting 24 to 48 hours, but this fever has already lasted four days. Ellen came through with a cheery note. She'd been reading about fatal blood diseases in a magazine article, where it was stated that painful, bleeding gums are often a first indication of the illness. Ellen and I didn't seem to be on the same wave length most of the evening. I had wanted to see her but wasn't feeling well, and she knew that. After dinner she came over and sat down beside me. It was obvious she wanted to make love. I did sort of half-heartedly, but I really wasn't feeling well. It was a very uncomfortable evening. It was hard for me to distract myself from my bodily discomfort, and my mind kept returning to it over and over again.

4   I thought this thing would go away if I just took it easy. I haven't called a doctor for that reason. But I'd better do so now. The thing that bothers me most is the pain and soreness in my gums. I can't imagine why I would have that.

Last night I somehow felt uneasy with Ellen. Maybe being ill had something   5
to do with it. She obviously wanted to have intercourse, but at the same time
had to allow for the fact that I wasn't feeling well. There's a preoccupied quality
about her. I keep wondering what my being ill stirs up in her.

7/17

Well, a diagnosis has finally been made. I've got what the doctor called acute   1
herpetic stomatitis. I must have picked it up from Ellen who had a cold sore on
her lip a week ago. The doctor told me that's how one gets the disease. I got
sunburned one day later and that blistered. Then a day after that I felt sick. I
didn't connect those blisters on my face and back, and the sore throat, with
having kissed Ellen while she had this cold sore. The doctor said that when I
shaved, it spread the sores. I have it in my throat—many white patches—and I
have these cold sores on my face and shoulders where I was sunburned.

Last Friday I went to see a doctor who examined me and couldn't tell what I   2
had without blood tests. But he was leaving for the weekend. He sent me to the
hospital emergency room to get these and called the doctor there who was
covering for him. He said he thought I had a virus but wasn't sure. I already had
these sores on my face, and I mentioned that I had been with my girlfriend who
had a sore on her lip, but it's amazing how it went unheeded. At the hospital
there was a long delay. The first blood they drew wasn't a good sample. When
they finally got the first blood tests done, they at first thought I had infectious
mononucleosis. They sent me home, told me to take aspirins, force fluids, and
come in today for a special blood test. But over the weekend I called another
doctor, and he made the diagnosis of acute herpetic stomatitis and said there was
no doubt in his mind about it.

Anyway it's a debilitating, painful illness. I haven't been so sick in a long,   3
long time [pause]. The doctor said if I hadn't gotten sunburned and blistered, I
wouldn't have had what he called a systemic reaction. It's practically laid me out
for a week, and I haven't been able to get anything done. There was a dinner
Saturday night which I didn't go to. Tomorrow I have some business to attend
to which I'll have to postpone till later in the week.

Ellen came over Saturday night, made dinner in my apartment, and stayed   4
overnight. I got to know her better. I had an opportunity to talk with her about
many different things: family, childhood, illnesses, growing up, painful
experiences of various kinds. It was a very quiet, relaxed time.

I've been sleeping a great deal. One gets so many thoughts while half-asleep. I   5
guess I was feverish a great deal of the time. I kept thinking about Mike and his
illness which so rapidly killed him. Until the last doctor made the diagnosis on
me and reassured me that I would soon be better, I had thoughts that some
mysterious disease which the doctors couldn't discover had attacked me and I
was terribly concerned about the outcome. Some vague story about two

brothers—one a robber and the other a clergyman—was floating through my mind. The robber donated a large sum of money to a charitable institution with one condition—that clergymen would not be welcome. I wondered if that had anything to do with me and my relations. The bad and the good—seems all mixed up. I'm reminded of several appointments I've had set up with my boss at work, which he didn't keep and didn't leave any word so that I would know that he wasn't going to be there.

6   I've had difficulty recalling all the things that went through my mind in the past week. The illness literally took a week out of my summer—a rather important week because there was work I had to finish. I had planned a trip afterwards. Now I don't know where I stand. My plans will have to be changed.

7/18

1   [15 minutes late. Silence. No association to lateness.]

2   I see you have the air conditioner on. It feels rather cold in here. I recall that a week ago Monday I got a sunburn. That night I fell asleep with the air conditioner on in the living room. I was exposed. I just had a pair of shorts on and slept all night that way. It was the next morning that I began to feel sick. It's eight days now. There are no new skin sores. The last ones were a couple of days ago. I still have a sore throat and sore gums which are very troublesome and hurt. I guess it will take a while for all this to go away. I still don't have much appetite and have been sleeping a great deal. The doctor told me it would take over a week anyhow to begin to clear up [pause].

3   I've had to postpone some work [pause]. I'm very annoyed by the occurrence of the illness at this time. I wouldn't exactly welcome it any time, but when does it appear—right at the first period in years when I've had some free time to make plans. Well, it's fouled up my plans. I wanted to visit with some friends in Europe, but now it's not going to be possible. A large part of being over there would be with people like these friends who know the places I want to go to and whose company I enjoy very much. I guess I don't live right.

4   I had a dream last night. There were several parts. It had to do again with flying. I'm developing a headache. It's been coming on for the last half hour. I have a sensation—it's in my left eye; it's one-sided. I don't remember the dream clearly. Another dream I had a long time ago occurred to me just now: it had to do with a landing field in a jungle some place. Anyway, the dream I had last night also concerned a landing field somewhere. I was on the ground and there were people around. I'm trying to recall if there was a flying sequence—if I'd first landed there. A plane that belonged to me was there. A group of people was standing around and looking the plane over. I was explaining something to them. One fellow, looking like a military man, became agitated, climbed up on a wing of the plane, tramping on it where he wasn't supposed to walk, and damaged it. It broke in several places. He grabbed hold of a tube and broke it off. It reminds

me of damaged goods, of myself. I guess I've been quite concerned about my health during the past week, much more than I had realized. [No further associations to the dream].

7/21

I had another dream last night. A group, including my brother and myself, are on a street, on a lawn, like a shaded, city street at night. A table was set out. My brother was sitting near a house and I near a sidewalk. Something was going on down the street; I don't know what it was. My brother was talking to me, saying: Guess you're right. It had to do with the business that was going on down the street. Then the dream shifted to another time, but it was the same place. We had been eating; my brother and I were sitting next to each other. He made a comment about the stainless steel table, saying it was a good table. I told him I bought it at a mail order house. It was a joke between us. He buys lots of stuff there, but I don't because of their inefficient delivery. We were being looked at in the dream from the side, and I thought they can't see my bald spot—it's as if it isn't visible at all.

I can't identify the place. I had a letter from my brother a few days ago—the first since he was here last month. I think back to a time when we were vacationing with our parents. I was 15 years old then. It was a rare occasion because all of us were together. We stayed part of the time at a pleasant inn near the ocean. It was on a hill overlooking the water. In the dream there was a view from a hill [pause].

To a certain extent I still feel blocked. Yesterday I felt very much that way. As I look back over the past week, I guess I've been more blocked than usual. Concentration is difficult, but I'm not sure what interferes. I seem to be thinking of my physical sensations and discomfort to an extent that usurps other thoughts. Often when I've been silent this past week, my illness, the symptoms, have been on my mind. Actually, though, I'm feeling better today than I have for the last ten days.

My thoughts now go back to the dream. My brother has been long aware that I think he got the wrong girl to be his wife. We disagreed on lots of other things, too. There's always been a rivalry between us, even when we were kids. I had the thought often of being the only child, even after he came. All this week I've been feeling I want someone to look after me but couldn't say it. It would sound as if I couldn't take care of myself.

7/24

[15 minutes late.]
I'm still coming late. Don't leave enough time to get here. It's as if I figure how much time is necessary under conditions where there'll be no hitch, and

often there is. Today, someone blocked my car in the parking lot, and it took all that extra time before I could get out. As I try to explore this lateness now, I run into a blank wall.

2   Physically, I'm finally feeling back to normal after about two weeks. I spent most of the weekend with Ellen. She has a propensity to name-drop and gossip. I finally mentioned this to her because it was bothering me. It's part of her style, which is to have a lot of superficial facts, and this may include information on people, but she doesn't tie it together in any meaningful way. There were several articles in a current magazine related to peace and war. She hadn't read these, had just quickly glanced over them, yet she talked with an authoritative air. She had assumed certain things about war on the basis of what she had picked up in some recent conversations. She attributes this style of hers to her education. She says she went to a school where she wasn't required to question or investigate for herself. She's a pleasant person but puts together some outlandish propositions. It's difficult to allow for this. I wonder why she behaves this way? ["You continue to focus on her, what about your own feelings and reactions?"] It makes me think of my brother [pause]. I seem to have trouble focusing. My thoughts seem to drift in and out, nothing stays [pause].

3   It's a complicated business, how feelings between two people, father and mother, affect their children. Sometimes I wish I had read less about psychology. It's a fascinating thing, but when it comes to the matter of the personal choice of a woman for a wife and thinking about having a family, it raises a number of questions which otherwise would not be raised if I had no knowledge of psychology. I go about trying to figure other people out in an amateurish sort of way. As you put it, to avoid facing my own problems.

7/25

1   I've been trying to figure out what's been happening, especially in the past two or three weeks. It's been a very bad time in different ways, including my experience here. I seem to have come to a halt. The month started out badly. The holiday weekend, lots of bad weather. Then a few days later I got this illness. I haven't been this sick in many years. In the early part of the summer I had so many plans, I was going to catch up on my work, fix up a summer place, go to Europe. In fact, I did none of these things. In a sense, I relied on Ellen. ["For what?"] For companionship mainly, friendship, a sexual outlet.

2   Now I feel disenchanted. It's a combination of many things: my present job is coming to an end. I've been saying goodbye to a lot of people who've left town. I'm also leaving a lot of people whom I've known. While I'm looking forward to my new position and new contacts, the interim period is not what I planned at all. The relationship with Ellen hasn't turned out well. What I had hoped for the summer is not materializing. That's a big, big disappointment.

3   Last night Ellen came over for dinner. She dropped a number of remarks

indicating that she, too, is discontent with our relationship. She wanted to get out more and do things with other people. Well, I frequently do things with other people, but while I was ill, I didn't feel like socializing. Her remarks didn't sit well with me because she didn't allow for the fact that I was sick. She also remarked that I sometimes call her rather late, but she has called me rather late on a number of occasions. Her complaint was that she didn't know what to expect, and why didn't I call her earlier. I can understand that, but it was hooked up with her not going out with other people. After all, she has options. If she gets another date, and I haven't been in touch, she can go out. Another thing about her—she seems too preoccupied with gossip. A child of one of the people at work is seriously ill and may die. The comments she made about it had a morbid quality, and I had no interest in pursuing it. Her seeming relish, her enjoyment in discussing the subject, bothered me. Then she asked an unanswerable question—how do parents feel who have a child that's dying? So we had a lapse of conversation. She asked if she should go home. I simply said, if she wished. However, she didn't. She stayed all night.

I was struck by the reaction I had to her remarks. I was annoyed. I was also 4 upset and depressed by other things—the way the month has gone. But it was all emphasized by the things she said—they had a marked lack of understanding for the condition I was in. She was steering the conversation into every area that was unpleasant [pause]. She does something very irritating, related to something my mother did. She'll ask a question and won't listen to the answer. My mother would say she hadn't heard the answer, but that would beg the question because there were plenty of times when she heard very well. Ellen doesn't have a hearing deficit, but some other kind of process must be at work. When I mentioned this to her, she smiled. I'm wrestling with what I should do about Ellen. Should I continue on and try to work it out, or should I see less of her and more of someone else? I'm undecided.

Anyway, I had a dream which I remember. It was about a boy. He had 5 something, some magic power, about finding water—a diviner. He would go over the countryside, locate water with his fingers, and make a well.

Now I'm reminded that Ellen is left-handed. In grammar school she says a teacher would beat her left hand with a stick to discourage her from using it. Then one day the principal came into the classroom while this was going on, took Ellen and the teacher to the school nurse who said Ellen could write with her left hand. So she continued to do so afterwards, but it's not very legible. I recall that when I was little I used my left hand. I'm told that I was ordered to change it by my mother, but I don't recall this. When I got to school, I was using my right hand and writing very well.

I'm looking for some answers to my problems. I suppose I hope for some 6 magic solutions. When will I find the right girl? I seem to be looking for perfection, because I manage to find fault with so many different girls ["Looking for an ideal mother."]

7/27

1   I'm not having clearer associations. I relate it to being ill. During this period I've had more difficulty in recalling things. I don't feel ill now, yet some of this has persisted. One part of it is not remembering things as clearly as I might, e.g., dreams. I know I dreamt a lot last night, but now I can't recall any of the specifics. Recall is a problem. Then it's difficult getting some meaning out of what does occur. It's also difficult to make connections. There's a kind of scattering of my thoughts. I haven't been tying much together recently. I feel discontent, restlessness, and annoyance [blandly said]. Things aren't going well, and it seems to parallel this month when my plans didn't materialize. ["The separations, leavetakings, disappointments culminated in the physical sickness. The preoccupation with it and then the persistence of anger turned in and not felt much, if at all, could slow down and block thinking processes. All of this has to be considered, especially against the background of the forthcoming interruption in the treatment."]

2   This past month I felt I wasn't getting much done here. I wish that hadn't been so. Just before this past month, lots of things were coming up which would have been useful, but then it didn't continue. It's a disappointment, but I don't mind so much because it hasn't been a productive time in general. I'm wondering if there's a rhythm about this business, even allowing for the illness. I still wonder about the blocking—what that's all about. There seems to be a rhythm or cycles of how things go: periods of relatively free thinking alternating with periods of blocking. I'm thinking of several comments you made recently. I wouldn't have any associations at the time and later I would wonder what associations were you trying to develop. While I was ill, you would say something, indicating you recognized how I felt. But at the time it didn't lead to anything—just seemed like repetition. On a number of occasions I've felt we weren't working together. I guess one big disappointment is that things aren't going faster [no affect]. I keep thinking of the people I know in treatment, and they've all been in a long time. I don't figure myself being in treatment that long because I hope that some of my problems could be worked out soon. If I felt I'd be in treatment five to six years, it would be a very depressing thought to me at this time, unless in the meantime I had worked through enough things to be able to get married and get going in this way. I seem to relate all this to a matter of rhythm and how we work together.

7/28

1   I'm thinking now about the year gone by. Comparing many parts of the year, particularly socially, with the previous year or two, wondering how it stacks up in terms of getting closer to finding a girl, getting married, and settling

down. All in all it was a year of a number of relationships which were not terribly long, some of which go on. That may be the most salient difference between this year and the last two. There are girls I've gone with intensely, then stopped seeing regularly, but continued to see from time to time. It's fair to say, though, there haven't been any girls this past year I was serious about in terms of marriage.

About six weeks ago I was feeling more obviously sad, both here and outside   2
the analytic hours, though I don't feel that way now. In terms of expressing my feelings, that represented a distinct difference compared with previously, when I seemed to feel nothing. I guess it was important, but I'm not sure how it came about. The issue of separation must be involved. Today is the last day before the summer interruption. June also was a month of terminations.

Thinking back a few years, I note a pattern then: when I stopped seeing a   3
girl, I wouldn't see her any more. That's changed. Parting meant really giving the person up. It's a little different now. But I'm still thinking about sadness—where that comes from. There were these earlier relationships when I first began dating. There was a whole group of girls I knew and lost. But I think it goes beyond that. ["You mean, earlier."] Yes. I'm not sure how or when. I think of mother and her problems. I lost her in an obvious way when she died. Then there's father's death, but its significance for me seems less clear. I had been home a month before he died, but not at the time he died. During that time he was very ill, not lucid, and not talking much. In fact, he was withdrawn. As I'm thinking of their deaths now—I don't feel particularly sad like I did six weeks ago [pause]. ["What are you thinking?"] Just wondering about the emergence and disappearance of feelings of sadness. My thoughts go back to the Korean war—brother's leaving and going away. The boy across the street who was killed in an accident.

Leaving is a big issue. Now I find myself feeling sadder. It has to do with the   4
war. I was very moved by the film of Halsey's story, especially the ending, when he was leaving his ship and his career. I was reading an account of Midway and was interested to know that Halsey had had an acute illness that prevented him from going to the battle, and he sent his deputy instead.

Here I am, recently recovered from an acute illness myself. My battle still goes on—with my neurosis.

7/29-12/2, Interim Summary

Following a quiet August, the patient resumed his analytic work, and during the next three months there was essentially little change in his psychophysical equilibrium. He had settled into his new job, doing good work except for the continued tendency to hand in late reports. Intermittently in the analysis he continued to come late, especially after some confrontation or interpretation which he distorted into criticism or rejection. On those occasions it became clear that the patient neurotically saw the analytic situation not as one which was therapeutic and into which he had voluntarily entered, but as a forced procedure where he would be judged and punished, arousing a rebellious and defiant attitude—a duplication of childhood experiences. All the principal defenses continued to yield only very slowly to persistent work, especially those of intellectualization and avoidance. A subtle projective trend proved most difficult to outline and bring into the patient's awareness. An affect block of considerable degree persisted with but slight modification. Superego-ego tensions remained high but masked. The pattern of temporary relationships with women continued as before, with initial interest, followed by disillusionment, and then rejection. Specific sexual fantasies or indeed most references to such activity remained conspicuous by their absence.

12/3

1   I had a very interesting time last night. I had another date with a new girl, Rachel, good-looking, a little on the large size. It was at a dinner party that two of my friends gave. Rachel is divorced and has two small children. Another divorcee. But she's quite extroverted and a good talker. We seemed to hit it off very well. I took her home, and on the way she put her hand on my knee, and it wasn't long before I had to stop the car and we did some heavy petting. I found her very passionate and myself responding in kind. She lives in a small house with an older sister, a spinster, who babysits for her and, I guess, is quite jealous of her. I'd been feeling the lack of female companionship for over a month and especially since I broke up with Ellen.

2   Now it occurs to me that in some ways Rachel reminds me of mother: she's a heavy smoker and has a bad cigarette cough, though she appears in good health. I hope to see a lot more of her. We've got a date for tomorrow night. I like pretty girls. Actually in that respect Rachel's different from mother who was never physically attractive; she let herself go and became quite obese. Anyway, prettiness isn't the answer. I really would settle for a woman who's responsive, has a sense of humor, and isn't necessarily a beauty. I guess there's a problem about my relationship with women. I'll go along a while and for some reason won't meet girls or girls I'm interested in. Then I begin to get restless. Finally an opportunity arises, and I'm in danger of getting too enthusiastic. I wonder how I can keep my perspective. I haven't been able to master that. I don't want to waste energy at the wrong time with the wrong girl. I guess that's where my neurosis gets in the way.

12/5

[Late 15 minutes.]

1   Here we go again. Rachel stayed late and by the time I got her to her home

and got back to my apartment, it was almost 3 A.M. I set the alarm radio, but I didn't have it set on a station that was on. That channel wasn't broadcasting this morning. The set went on, but there was no sound. Rachel and I are getting along very nicely. We had sexual intercourse that was very enjoyable. We have a strong physical attraction for each other that cancels out any differences we may have otherwise, at least so far. It's difficult for me to resist physical arousal; at such times, somehow, wisdom escapes me. Rachel appears to have gotten in with an activist group involved in racial problems, and some of the acquaintances she's made there seem far out, but she finds them quite acceptable.

Often, I feel as if I have problems in getting across to others. It's true at the office and in my social contacts with women. So far, at least, this hasn't come up with Rachel. Then there's the problem of lateness. So often my estimate of time I need to do something—whether it's a report I have to submit or whether it's getting here—well, it's just inadequate. I seem to have difficulty in adapting, changing, getting things done faster. Must be some kind of rigidity, a stubbornness when I feel I'm being forced to do something. This being late here. I think of it frequently and can't find a reason other than what I just said. You have called it resistance. It's hard for me to come to terms with it [laughing]. I can't figure out what I'm resisting so much. ["You resist punctuality in situations where that has the significance for you of being controlled."] I remember when I was younger coming in late for dinner. Both mother and father would comment on that and express annoyance. I know that mother was quite punctual, getting to places on time, and also in her correspondence and writing. My parents would set a dinner hour when none of the other kids would be eating. My chums would eat earlier and then be out playing. I'd be with them and have to leave in the middle of all the fun because dinner at my house was later. I'd have difficulty in leaving. I asked my parents to change the dinner hour, and they refused. They insisted that we had to eat together at night. We ate together at noon often. This was supposed to be compensation for our not doing many things together. The dinner hour was one hour we were all together. But dinner took time, and I couldn't go back out to get to play with my friends. I wasn't in any position to openly defy my parents, but I was certainly annoyed. What I got out of it was that the family was inflexible. After all, there were other ways to be together than just at dinner. So it made something unpleasant out of what was to be hopefully a pleasant sharing of time.

My parents failed to recognize my appeals, my enthusiasms, or to answer most of my questions. Then I became the observer of their thoughts and feelings. I had the impression that if I got no response from them, they must be caught up in their problems. Here in the analysis, there's little feedback from you such as one might get in normal conversation. It affects my ability to note my own feelings during the hour. One thing that occurs here that doesn't when I'm alone: you'll ask what my feelings are and that makes me temporarily uncomfortable while I try to assess them. You see, your question implies I'm not acknowledging my feelings. It comes up again and again, but I don't seem to get better in that respect. In the sense that it's something I'm asked to do, putting aside its importance, it becomes a request, an instruction from you, a chiding. I continue to react to that, though I try to become more aware. I don't learn fast in this area, and it's bothersome to me. But I rarely feel anger, though my father used to be openly and often very angry. My style has been: a soft word turneth away anger.

12/6

1   Out with Rachel again. Guess I wonder where I'm heading with her. I have a huge pile of paper work at the office, and I'm not keeping up with it. I'm taking time that should be devoted to my work, and I'm using it for my social life. I need to have this social life or I'd feel terribly lonely. But I think that my social life is getting in the way of my doing my work. I can't seem to strike a balance that's workable. Those reports have to be very detailed. I know it's necessary to keep up with the work, yet it gets very difficult for me to put in that kind of time.

2   Rachel talked about how difficult her marriage had been and how difficult it was for her now to make financial ends meet. She's been thinking about getting a part-time job to supplement her small income. She and her sister don't get along well together, and she's going to have to find a baby sitter for these two kids of hers.

3   I had a brief dream about the neighborhood I lived in as a child. All I recall of it was the house we had there and it seemed so much bigger than it actually was. My parents were not involved with the people who lived in the houses nearby. I wish they had been. I knew some of them through their kids with whom I played. But my parents kept aloof and to themselves. I guess I was sort of the family representative to the community. Earlier, when I was very little, I guess my parents had been more involved socially, but then they withdrew. They actually avoided the people whose children I played with. If my parents had been more involved, maybe things would have been a lot friendlier all around. I keep recalling how aloof and isolated they had become before they died.

4   I'm thinking now about Rachel. Is she filling some kind of vacuum? I know before I met her I had been feeling particularly lonely and out of it. I really needed some female companionship.

12/7

1   I've arranged to take a trip out into the country with Rachel. We've tentatively set a time for departure early Sunday morning, then we'll visit some

of my friends who have a farm. It's a good two-hour auto trip. I've agreed to take her two kids along. Looks like a family venture. I keep thinking of a ready-made family.

The disappointments I've had in the past are very much in my mind. The **2** things that should have been different, and weren't, and never will be. I weigh the disappointments against the current possibilities, so that for me it's become important that the woman I choose for a wife is as close to ideal as possible, and then that would make up for a lot of things. Actually I don't think that's realistic because the future will not undo the past. Now Rachel comes to mind: we like each other, but there is more to it—her children, for instance. Expecting the ideal intrudes into my reports. I want to do such a complete job, I don't get them done. I remember in school I was the teacher's deputy, but then I was rejected by the other kids in the class. I had the need to be accepted by somebody, at least by the teacher, so I did good work and handed in good work. Now it's out of hand. I want it to be so perfect, and I can't get going. ["Perfection is necessary because of the fear that otherwise defects will be found and exposed, especially if your work is on record, so to speak, and available for scrutiny by others."] Yes, deep down are, I suppose, feelings of inferiority, but I can't easily admit to them.

I want to let you know that I'm planning to take a few days off around the Christmas holiday. I need some relief from my work, haven't had any for a long time.

12/10

What a hectic weekend! Rachel really let fly at me. We had to cancel our **1** trip. My car had broken down the night before, but I thought I could get it fixed in time for our trip and told Rachel I would let her know Sunday morning what the condition of the car was. Sunday morning I was awakened by a telephone call from Rachel. She was very angry, in fact, furious with me. She practically screamed why hadn't I gotten in touch with her. I looked at the clock and realized that it was almost the time I had agreed to pick her up. I said I would go downstairs, check the car to make sure it was alright, and be over as soon as I could, trying not to be too late. Well, you guessed it. When I got down to the car, it wouldn't start again. No matter what I tried, it just wouldn't turn over. It was Sunday morning and I couldn't get anyone to come over and fix it, and so back I went to the phone to break the news to Rachel. Well, that brought on another explosion. She accused me of having no consideration for her. She had gotten up early, gotten herself and the kids dressed, and waited for my call. I didn't really care about her, she said. How could I do such a thing to her? Under this barrage, I tried to explain to her that I had had the car fixed the day before, that it seemed alright, and I had expected that it would be ready for our trip. It wasn't my fault that it had conked out again. I admitted that I had overslept a little, but I had been working late the night before, trying to get some reports ready for the office Monday, since I wouldn't have had a chance to work on them while we were on our trip. I offered to try to rent a car, but she was just beside herself. She kept saying that I just wasn't communicating with her, didn't think about her, didn't care about her. I tried to explain again, that I did like her very much, that it really was not my fault that the car had broken down again, that I would try to hire a car, but she just wasn't buying any of it. Finally, she hung up on me.

2   I've been trying to figure out just what got her so upset with me. There are things about her that have made me wonder. Her kooky friends, her impulsive attachment to me. There's something bothering her badly for her to blow up this way. ["But what about *your* reactions to this? You tend to focus on what's going on in her, trying to figure that out, but how about your own thoughts and feelings?"]

3   Well, I certainly was annoyed and irritated by her outburst [blandly said]. I wondered what was bugging her. I realize that I have some problems in communication, but as far as I can see I wasn't that remiss and didn't deserve such a blast. It's been a long time since I've been on the receiving end of something like that. It's hard to apologize under these circumstances, but I tried to. I certainly had some responsibility for what happened.

12/11

1   I got a call from Rachel today. She seems to have simmered down. So we'll get together tonight. I somehow have difficulty in seeing less of her, even though she blew her stack at me over the weekend. This time of year is a bad one for me because in the past I've broken up with a number of girls just around New Year's. It's funny, but I just thought that a number of them have been on the plump side. Reminds me of my mother who was always overweight. It's a characteristic which bothers me, especially in a woman, yet somehow I seem to wind up with a lot of girls like that. Mother's overweight restricted her activities. Now I'm wondering if I saw her undressed. It must have been extremely rare. I don't really remember when. Anyway how could I understand what I observed anyway? She had a very wide girth with a lot of weight in her stomach.

2   Rachel is still on my mind. She just wanted to dismiss that blowup altogether with a "let's not talk about it." In my family dinner conversation was often boring. The family arrangements were so damn inflexible and so annoying. There was a stock reply, "Because I said so." That would end further discussion of any issue, even though there was much left to be said. My parents were prejudiced and used to probe me about my Jewish and Roman Catholic friends. But they wouldn't listen to the things I wanted to talk about. My younger brother seemed to adapt himself much more readily to this arrangement than I

was ever able to do. That's one of the things that made me jealous of him. I guess I thought he was the favorite and best-liked.

I think of Rachel's dismissal of the telephone row as uncalled for, because it's treating me as if I were a child. My plans for going away are still indefinite, but I'm looking forward to some rest and relaxation. I really feel pooped out. I can't seem to include her in these plans. 3

12/12

When Rachel came over to my apartment, she wanted to go to bed right away. It's difficult for me to resist physical arousal. When I'm in bed beside her, somehow wisdom escapes. Although I tried later to bring up the Sunday quarrel, she just wouldn't talk about it. I'm puzzled and uneasy, trying to figure out what's going on, why she behaves that way. Why do I continue to see her? Partly, it's a matter of being lonely, especially before the holidays, not wanting to take a chance and start seeing somebody else during this period. You see, it's a problem in keeping my equanimity in this situation. My usual response is to face loneliness for a while, then go out and find some girl, settling for less than if I weren't depressed. I must have run through hundreds of girls. The pressure of work is depressing. When I run hardest looking for someone, I slip my wheels. Yet to sit back gets nothing accomplished. 1

As I was driving Rachel back to her house, she told me that one of her activist friends was in some legal trouble and needed financial assistance to fight his case. She asked me if I could contribute some money. She didn't give me many details, but the whole thing didn't sound right to me. So I refused. Well, that upset her terribly, and she said goodbye coldly and abruptly when we got to her door. Funny that she would say goodbye instead of good night. Well, maybe it isn't so funny. 2

I slept very fitfully when I got back to the apartment. I recall having a dream about Geraldine, a girl I knew years ago. There were other people in the dream. Geraldine and I seemed apart some of the time, then together some of the time. We'd split up, then come together. There was some allusion to injury. I don't remember the dream very well. Once I actually was on a motor trip with Geraldine through the Rockies. I fell asleep at the wheel just as we were approaching a motel and we banged into a tree. I awoke to find Geraldine lying on the front seat with her head in my lap. She had banged her head on the dashboard and had a minor cut in her scalp. For a while she was hysterical. I couldn't comfort her. She was screaming, yelling, wandering around. After about ten minutes she settled down. A car took us to a nearby hospital where we were attended to. That was a horrendous experience. I had never done that before. Luckily neither of us had any real injuries. I broke off the steering wheel against my chest, but there were no cracked ribs. I hurt for a couple of weeks—chest pain. 3

4   It sounds like what's going on between Rachel and me, a coming together and breaking up, getting hurt. ["But what are your feelings; you speak as if it were some other person who's involved, not you."] Well, I certainly am irritated with her [blandly], think it's strange, the way she's behaving. I wonder why I continually get hooked up with that kind of girl. I must be missing signals along the way, signals that tell me things won't work out.

12/13

1   Another mad telephone call from Rachel. Another mad outburst—and there was nothing I could do about it. She again told me off, and this time she said she was really through. I'm accused of not communicating, not really showing that I care for her. She just wouldn't listen to my reasoning, my attempts at explanation. She slammed down the receiver and it was over. As far as I'm concerned, it is over. I don't like to be alone again, but I can't take that kind of behavior any more [continued blandness and lack of affective expression]. ["But what are your feelings about this?"] I'm annoyed, yes, angry, though I realize I don't sound it.

2   At times at the office some of my colleagues walk by without looking at me. I feel bad about that. As if they were walled off. Not the slightest glimmer of recognition. I like to say hello to people when I pass them. I wonder if they don't like me, or if there's something wrong with me.

3   This has been a bad week. Rachel's comments really hurt, those references to irresponsibility and not caring. I just don't see that. My boss at work has been bothering me again about those reports. I told him I had been working pretty hard, trying to catch up. I have difficulty getting a straight answer from him. I don't know how much is my part and how much is his style. He's hard to talk to, at least for me.

12/16

1   I awoke with a cough, bringing up a lot of phlegm. I feel generally achy. I've been developing a fever and a stitch in the right side of my chest for the last half hour. It's now beginning to hurt there as I breathe. It makes me think of the time I was so sick when I was a student in boarding school. I'd been there only a few months and I got pneumonia with terrible pain in the same side as now. They told me I was delirious for a while. I seem to be getting rapidly worse by the minute [continuous coughing].

2   I remember getting sick again shortly after I had supposedly recovered from that pneumonia at boarding school. It happened during the Christmas vacation. I had this terribly long plane ride. It took so many hours to get down South to where my parents were. The plane was cold. I got chilled and developed a fever and was very ill during the entire Christmas vacation. It's the sickest I've ever

been. I don't think they knew what I had. I was just wiped out, sleeping most of the time. The only treatment I got was bed rest, aspirins, and a lot of fluids. I don't even remember seeing a doctor then, but there was a nurse who looked after me. I was very angry about that illness because I was looking forward to that vacation. I wanted to relax and get into the sun. When I had the pneumonia, I do remember being treated with penicillin. I never saw so many needles as I did then.

Sick as I feel now, a joke comes to mind. This fellow meets his former analyst on the street. They reminisce. The ex-patient says: "You really helped me a lot; I got over the mother-complex I had about my mother. But there's something I've got to tell you now; that you're a substitute for my mother."   2

Analyst: "That's not unusual."

Patient: "I was thinking about it this morning as I was having coffee and orange juice."

Analyst: *"That's* a breakfast?"

I'm very annoyed that I'm feeling ill. I was invited to a party tonight. I want to go to it very much. I would likely meet some desirable people there. I've also been invited to a party tomorrow night. These occasions don't arise very often, and I hate to miss them. No word from Rachel. I guess that's all over with. I certainly feel let down about it.   3

The heat in my apartment isn't working well. There's either no heat at all or no constant heat. I feel awfully warm here; too much heat. Maybe my sickness is due to my apartment being too hot and dry. The heat was hitting me almost in the face there, drying out my mouth and throat. I took your telephone number last time [new phone had been installed three weeks earlier and the patient informed of this change]. Just in case I had to call in the future.   4

I'm thinking of those painful sores in my mouth that weren't correctly diagnosed in the beginning despite all the evidence, when I was sick some time ago. What's wrong with doctors, anyway?   5

I had dinner with a couple of my friends last night [the ones who introduced him to Rachel]. We were talking about a fellow we all knew who was killed in Korea. Ironically he was on his way out of the area to meet his wife [blocked].   6

[Coughing.] Beautiful. That must be pneumonia I've got. I'm so annoyed by this. I have a date with a new girl. But it looks like a bust, the way I'm feeling. I want to load myself up with aspirin and go to these dates. I hate to pass up such opportunities. My friends saw Rachel the other night with one of her kooky friends. Jim says he's always found it difficult to talk to her, and he too can't understand some of things she does.   7

The holidays coming up—what to do. I got a card from my brother last night. Hadn't heard from him in quite a while. My firm will, of course, be open right through except for Christmas and New Year, but I plan to take a few days off. Maybe I'll go and visit him during the holidays [coughing]. There's nothing quite as annoying as a cough, especially when it hurts, and I've got this pain in   8 my right chest. Nuts! It sure doesn't look as if it's going to clear up tonight, so I'll be alone again.

9   I remember how my parents went on smoking two packages a day for years. They would get up in the morning and immediately reach for a cigarette. Then the coughing would begin—for the rest of the day. How could they choose to do that? I remember as a youngster I had lots of ear trouble and was advised not to smoke until I was 21. I never quite understood what the two things meant. Maybe the doctor who took care of me was impressed by my father's cough.

12/20

[Four days' absence—illness.]

1   I loathe these heavy colds. I guess I've got the flu, maybe a touch of pneumonia. I still haven't called in a doctor. I figured I'd just stay in bed and rest as much as I could. Today is the first day I've been up and out of the house since last Friday [four days]. On Friday when I was last here and for three days afterwards, I had a temperature around 102°-103° and was coughing up a lot of phlegm. I read that's what a lot of people have been having with the flu. On Saturday I coughed up a real lunger and after that my chest felt better. Something must have been stuck there. Now I feel in fairly good shape generally. That chest pain bothered me the most.

2   Two nights ago I had a dream that I remember. I was with my friend Henry and his wife, Katie. We were on a beach. There was sand and grass. From the shore there stretched out a large lake bordered by wooded land and hills. Boats were going by, including a large ocean liner and a big freighter. There were other people on the beach. The freighter came near the shore. The crew were yelling at women on the beach, and the boat went off into the distance. I think it was a German boat. At one point, I thought it might take off and fly. Some aircraft appeared over the boat. After it went by, I began to itch in the crotch. I scratched [coughs] for a while. The itching got worse. I looked and saw some insects. Some of these insects looked like crabs, some like spiders. They were all snarled up in the hair. I was struggling to get the insects off. I was trying to get Henry to help me without Katie's knowing it.

During that day I was in bed most of the time. Lily came by. I had met her through Henry. She had invited me to the two parties over the weekend that I couldn't attend. She brought over a small Christmas tree. Her parents live in Florida, on the beach. We talked a lot about Fort Lauderdale where I used to go with my folks for winter vacation. I had seen Henry and his wife last Thursday night. When I had the crabs, I had been dating a girl named Eve. Then Henry, who was single at the time, took her out for a while after I stopped seeing her. A month ago, Henry, his wife, and I went to a movie together. It was about a sailing boat, *Voyage Around the World.* Katie later gave me the name of a divorcee with one kid, not attractive. Henry said she was very obese, so I never called her. This dream has three people in it, including me. Right now I feel some pain in my scrotum. Once as a child I was on an inland lake way up in Vermont. We went around it on an excursion or was it a mail boat? It was a landlocked lake. When it got near the dock, they blew the whistle which scared the hell out of me. My mother was always telling me to watch out for the water and threatening to have father whomp me if I disobeyed.

After this hour the patient did not return for ten days. During most of this time he was ill and in bed at his brother's home. A diagnosis of lobar pneumonia was finally made after medical consultation had been insisted on by the patient's brother. This diagnosis was confirmed by x-ray. Antibiotic medication soon brought the disease process under control, and there was an uneventful convalescence except for residual tiredness.

MARGINAL NOTES

6/6

1. Dream of sick man linked with a relationship that is mutually ambivalent, involving a girl who has similar physical dysfunction. Reference to inadequate doctor. Identification with the sick person. Recollective castration anxiety.
2. Further identification with mother-figure who is physically incapacitated. Physical obstruction linked with psychologic blocking. Transference: projective and accusatory aspects.

6/8

1. Resistance.
2. Malaise ascribed to typhoid inoculation, but headache linked to oral-olfactory percepts. Rationalization of lateness. Exacerbation of physical discomfort, a rarity in the analytic hour.
3. Dream theme: difficulty in getting closer to male friend—a brother surrogate; expectation of rejection.

6/9

1. Resistance.
2. Oversleeping and tardiness linked with brother's delayed arrival and anticipatory anxiety over pending interview with a father-figure. Transference implications. Attempts at intellectualization. Blocking.

6/13

    1. Sibling rivalry.
    2. Anticipation of memories concerned with loss.
    3. Another unsatisfactory relationship with a rigid and sexually anxious woman. Difficulties in communication. Intellectualization.

6/16

    1. Continued resistance linked with reunion and separation. More blocking.
    2. Defensive focus on girls he knows, particularly their defects.
    3. Denial of negative cues; superego aspects; further concentration on girls' problems.

6/21

    1. Another missed appointment. More references to reunion and separation. A new girl under scrutiny, avoidance of his own problems.
    2. Depressive associations: various losses. Many sensory stimuli. Oral activity.
    3. Imagery of ship—extension of self. Symbolism: castration; difficult journey through life, including analytic experience; longing for parents. Affect breakthrough, first since analysis began. Interpretation.

6/23

    1. Continued resistance.
    2. Familiar defense: avoidance of own problems, here specifically tardiness, and focus on the other person's difficulties. Interpretation.
    3. Identification with the loneliness of the man in command and his leavetaking. Yearning for childhood idealism. Affect discharge.
    4. Links with high adventure through identification with paternal figures. Loss. Further affect discharge.

6/26 - 7/5, Summarized in Text with Dynamic Formulations.

7/6

    1. Resistance rationalized. Recollection of loneliness.
    2. Blocking. Distractions include auditory percepts. Entitlement: transference aspects.
    3. Quick heterosexual conquest rationalized.

7/7

    1. Rumination and rationalization. Interpretation.

2. Listing of necessary attributes in a woman, with sexual attraction most important. Recollection of several sexual acting out experiences.

3. A new relationship.

7/10

1. Resistance.
2. Reference to loss.
3. Dream of rejection and hostility linked with loneliness.
4. Symbolic expression of a foreboding change in emotional climate. Intellectualization about hypersensitivity to being left.
5. A sick mother-figure departs without his knowing. Ellen's resemblance to his mother linked with her orality and mouth dysfunction. Further references to mother's depression and losses. Father's orality linked with illness requiring therapy.

7/11

1. Prodromata of influenza. Associations about coldness and then about surgery on a father-figure—symbolic castration.
2. Envy of sibling figure.
3. Defensive devaluation.
4. More sibling jealousy.
5. Leaving girls he's known and focusing on their problems—a defense against being left by them.
6. Many recollections about relationships with girls, some from childhood with sexual exhibitionistic elements, linked with being left and leaving.
7. Recollection of a specific traumatic experience but with the focus, defensively, on the reactions of the other people involved.
8. Ambivalent response to mother's oral seductiveness. Difficulties in communication. Quick physical intimacy a defense against anticipated loss. Interpretation.

7/13

1. Continued physical symptoms with addition of tinnitus.
2. Dreams linked with anniversary of a friend's fatal illness, with history of many ear infections and severe kidney disease.
3. Recollection of body areas sensitized by physical illness during childhood. Pain linked with oral references.
4. Dream of sadistic practices associated with actual initiation tortures.
5. More retrospective associations about previous illnesses.

7/14

1. An additional resistance.
2. Concern about rejection. Need for maternal care.
3. New symptom linked to possibilities of a fatal outcome. Intense preoccupation with bodily discomfort, interfering with sexual activity.

4. Rationalizations overcome by persisting illness and increasing anxiety.
5. Again defensive focus on the other person's motivations.

7/17

1. Definite diagnosis. Transmission of illness through oral contact and prolonged actinic exposure.
2. Devaluation of doctors.
3. Severity of physical reaction, interfering with activities.
4. Longed for maternal care.
5. Regressive tendencies. Earlier preoccupation with possible fatal outcome. References to ambivalence. Verbalized resentment.
6. Difficulty in concentration. Bland affect.

7/18

1. Resistance.
2. Symbolic transference aspects: feelings of rejection associated with illness. Lingering somatic manifestations.
3. Punitive elements of illness—interference with a pleasurable time.
4. Dream linked with currently developing somatic manifestation and symbolic reference to damage, defects, and castration.

7/21

1. Dream connected with sibling rivalry, need to be superior and the favorite, and concern about physical appearance.
2. Considerable blocking. Preoccupation with bodily sensations.
3. Further reference to sibling rivalry. Awareness of regressive pull.

7/24

1. Resistance, rationalization, and blocking.
2. Physical illness in remission. Continued defensive focus on the other person's problems and avoidance of his own.
3. Awareness of this defensive tendency, combined with intellectualization.

7/25

1. Review of disappointments and losses, with Ellen an insufficient substitute source of support and gratification.
2. Further reference to separation anxiety and dissatisfactions.
3. Again a defensive focus on Ellen's defects in reaction to her discontent.
4. Growing awareness of hostile affect linked with Ellen's irritating resemblance to his mother. Ambivalence.
5. Dream of omnipotence. Defensive superiority.
6. Relationship with women influenced by search for ideal mother. Interpretation.

7/27

1. Regressive effect of physical illness. Interpretation includes reference to summer interruption which had not heretofore been brought up.
2. Ambivalent transference aspects. Somatic outlets and affect discharge replaced by defenses of isolation, displacement, and intellectualization.

7/28

1. Review by patient: improvement in relationships with women noted.
2. Greater awareness of affect linked with separations.
3. Sensitivity to loss related to death of parents, brother's leaving for military service, death of a boyhood chum—but in a seemingly intellectualized way.
4. Separation now associated with partial affect discharge, identification with paternal figure disabled by illness.

7/29-12/2, Summarized in Text with Dynamic Formulations.

12/3

1. A new relationship with quick physical intimacy. Intense object hunger.
2. Rachel compared with mother: similarities and differences. Neurotic interference with objectivity.

12/5

1. Resistance reappears. Quick sexual intimacy followed by doubts, defensive focus on possible defects in the woman.
2. Problems in communication and recurrent tardiness linked with resistance to any suggestion of force or control. Interpretation. Recollection of childhood experiences: punctuality associated with eating, parental rigidity and enforcement, deprivation of pleasures, artificial togetherness, as well as suppressed and repressed hostility toward parents.
3. Genetic origin of shift of attention from self to others. Rebelliousness. Transference aspects. Repression of anger in himself compared with father's demonstrativeness.

12/6

1. Familiar pattern: increasing doubts about Rachel. Pile-up of work neglected for physical gratifications that block off awareness of intense loneliness.
2. Continued focus on Rachel's problems—a defensive avoidance of his own.
3. Dream linked with recollections of family isolation in the past.
4. Intense object hunger.

12/7

1. Fantasies about a family of his own.
2. Past losses balanced against possible restitution. Current interference of idealistic expectations and perfectionistic tendencies. Special intellectual efforts a means of gaining acceptance, a defense against feelings of inferiority. Interpretation.

12/10

1. He becomes the object of Rachel's intense hostility. Rationalizations to explain own acting out—waiting to the last minute. Unsuccessful at rectifying the situation and warding off accusations.
2. Defensive focus on her defects. Confrontation.
3. Bland acknowledgment of anger. Continued defensiveness. Superego aspects.

12/11

1. Rachel's change of mood. Recollections of previous broken relationships with women, their identification somatically with his mother, his ambivalent reaction to these traits. Vague memories of mother's physical appearance.
2. Focus on Rachel's defensive avoidance, which only highlights his own avoidance. Recollections of parental intolerant authority and closure of discussion. Sibling rivalry and jealousy.
3. Rachel's parental-like rigidity evokes retaliatory response in him.

12/12

1. Need for sexual gratification—a defense against loneliness—overrules rationality. Rachel's continued use of avoidance. His continued use of the same type of defense as well as the defense of intellectualization.
2. Another quarrel portentuous of rejection.
3. Dreams of ambivalent relationship with a former girlfriend. Recollection of physical trauma in auto accident with residual of severe chest pain.
4. Affect block. Confrontation followed by hostility in content, but blandly expressed. Some awareness of defensive denial tendencies.

12/13

1. Shocking rejection. Affect block. Confrontation. Persistence of block.
2. Projective tendencies.
3. Accumulation of stress includes criticism from parental figure at work about tardiness.

12/16

1. Somatic manifestations begin developing shortly before the analytic hour. Pain percepts evoke recollections of pneumonia during adolescence.
2. Attempts at minimizing physical discomfort through a joke involving orality, mother-transference, and analyst's unrecognized countertransference.
3. Frustration. Reference to rejection.
4. Temperature percepts. Indirect expectation of illness.
5. Devaluation of doctors—transference implications.
6. Reference to death.
7. Further feelings of frustration. Support for negative opinion of Rachel.
8. Turning toward brother, linked with loneliness and illness.
9. Recollection of parental addiction to smoking and its somatic consequences.

12/20

1. Seeming improvement in physical condition. Preoccupation with bodily symptoms. Avoidance of medical consultation.
2. Dream of Oedipal significance, sexualized, with reference to swapping of female partners, symbolic castration anxiety, possible homosexual elements.

COMMENT

This patient's obsessive-compulsive character structure was notable for the rigidity of defenses and severity of affect block. Reference to physical discomfort, symptoms, or sensations of any kind was rare.

Consequently, the appearance of associations dealing with physical manifestations, as the reporting of analytic hours begins (6/6) is unusual. Urinary symptoms in a girlfriend evoke recollections of similar manifestations in a mother-figure and also in himself during childhood. He was treated by circumcision then, and experienced intense castration anxiety. In previous analytic interviews the references to the physical have been brief, confined to one hour, and then have not appeared again for months. It remains to be seen whether this is the way it will be again. On 6/8, however, physical malaise is ascribed to a typhoid inoculation, and headache is linked to disagreeable olfactory percepts. As the hour continues, there is exacerbation of the physical discomfort, accompanied by associations about difficulties with a brother-surrogate and the possibility of rejection. A shift in the psychophysical equilibrium is developing.

The patient now enters a period of reunions, leave-takings, and separations, involving his brother, relatives, and friends. He experiences the losses more keenly on balance, with corresponding mobilization of hostile potential without affect discharge. Acting out in the transference is manifested by persistent tardiness and missing analytic hours. The patient continues to show a readiness to argue in the most exquisite detail, using an impressive intellect for this purpose, whenever confrontations or interpretations are made. These interventions are distorted by him into criticisms, admonitions, or prohibitions. He also continues to avoid looking at himself and his problems for the most part. Instead, he focuses on others, developing explanations for their feelings, actions, and behavior. This has brought him into special difficulty with women he meets and with whom he tries to develop a relationship. These defensive structures, however, are not entirely sufficient to cope with the continued stresses consisting of largely symbolic and some real losses which the patient is experiencing. Several dates have been unfulfilling as substitute objects despite quick sexual intimacy. A further shift in the psychophysical equilibrium appears to be in the offing. After a four-day interruption which included a missed appointment, the patient on 6/21 reviews the plethora of sad news he's been exposed to at the reunions he's attended. Then he recalls the details of a ship he has seen several days before, which symbolically he percieves as an extension of himself. The imagery triggers associations of his own difficult journey through life, including the analytic experience, accompanied by a longing for his parents, both of whom are dead. This is followed by an affect discharge of tearfulness and sadness, the first since the analysis began. On 6/23, after exhibiting the familiar defenses of avoidance of his own problems, particularly his tardiness and focus on his current girlfriend's difficulties, still another confrontation about this is presented to the patient. This subsequently evokes recollection of a TV film he has seen the preceding night in which he strongly identifies with the loneliness of the hero. In turn, these thoughts are linked with youthful hopes and aspirations which may be dashed against life's hard realities, a yearning for childhood and a closeness with an adventurous father-figure, and recollections of a pet dog that was killed. Another affect discharge follows.

The affect that has clearly broken through in the preceding hours again is blocked off as superego-ego tensions and external stresses abate temporarily and the habitual defensive alignments are reestablished. After a week, however, new stresses begin to develop. He is preparing to change jobs. A steady relationship with a new girl which seemed initially to hold promise appears as elusive as ever. She has some resemblance to his mother (overweight) and, for a while, serves as a substitute object compensating in part for losses to which the patient is reacting in a hypersensitive way. Now she, too, begins to disappoint him. An unstable psychophysical equilibrium follows.

On 7/6 ideas of entitlement appear prominently. The patient also tries to explain his quick heterosexual conquests as reactions to continuing stress, the nature of which, however, is relatively unclear to him. On 7/7 there is continued rumination and rationalization about sexual intimacy, and some interpretations are made about the need to prove his manliness through this activity.

On 7/10 the patient refers to his deepening interest in his new girl and missing her when she had to leave for a few days. Work is currently not sufficiently distracting. Then, in this hour, there appears a symbolic reference to a foreboding change in emotional climate, as expressed in a dream which reveals that he is responding with feelings of rejection and ideas of hostility to his girl's departure and to unpleasant experiences with other girls. No affect is expressed, however. There are further associations about a mother-figure who is physically ill and has left the area. In turn, the patient is reminded of his new girl's resemblance to his mother, and there is a rush of associations about mother's orality and mouth dysfunction as well as father's orality. This emphasis on somatic identification in a setting of recurrent stress, together with the dream symbolically referring to an ominous emotional change, suggests that the current, unstable psychophysical equilibrium may be shifting in the direction of a physical somatic dysfunction which is not yet within the patient's awareness, probably involving the mouth. On 7/11 the patient exhibits the prodromata of an influenza-like illness.

As the patient's physical condition worsens, a new symptom—tinnitus—appears on 7/13. His prior dreams and subsequent associations reveal that an anniversary has come up—one that he might not even have recalled ordinarily. It is the anniversary of the death of a college friend who had many ear infections, developed kidney disease, and died many years ago, almost to the day. It is not clear whether the patient's otitic symptom activated these memories or whether the anniversary itself was an influential factor in evoking the tinnitus. If the former were true, then the recollections would represent a retrospective type of data. However, if the latter were true, the recollections would be prospective data. Then anniversary and the associations it evoked might be considered as psychologic factors influencing the development of further dysfunction in either of the two possible sites, namely, ear and genito-urinary tract. The symptom of severe sore throat has activated in a less ambiguous way secondary, retrospective associations in the form of memories of childhood sore throats, radium, and operative intervention. There are also other retrospective references to illnesses during adolescence: pneumonia and fever of undetermined origin.

On 7/14 there is the first mention of painful gums and mouth lesions. His girl's (Ellen's) return seems to exert no perceptible, positive effect on the course of the illness. In fact, her behavior is an additional irritant to the patient who, in his regressed state, longs for mothering and doesn't get it from her. On 7/17 a definite diagnosis is finally established: acute herpetic stomatitis with spread of lesions throughout the oropharynx to the face, chest, and back. The herpes simplex virus was transmitted by contact with Ellen through kissing; she had a cold sore on her lip at the time. There was also overexposure to the actinic rays of the sun. All this occured after the patient's psychophysical state had been shifting under continued stress—first, in the direction of temporary physical dysfunction, then temporary affective breakthrough, and then reverting to an obviously unstable type of equilibrium. Further unremitting stress again caused a shift which could have adversely affected host resistance. Exposure to viral agents under these circumstances led to the development of physical illness which had become severe and debilitating. The patient had not been so physically sick for many years. The impact of repeated separation and loss situations reached critical levels and could not be contained by the psychologic systems in the patient's obsessive-compulsive character structure, which had been only slightly modified as yet by the analytic process.

The physical illness causes a further secondary, regressive shift. The patient takes to bed, sleeps a great deal, finds himself blocked and unable to concentrate. Establishment of the diagnosis partially alleviates his earlier preoccupation with the possibility of a fatal outcome. The punitive aspects of the illness appear relatively late in the patient's associations, a seemingly secondary response. However, there has been escalating superego-ego tensions prior to the illness, and though masked, they cannot be dismissed as an influence on the shifts occurring in the patient's psychophysical state.

Blocking and resistance continue for another week. The patient is much preoccupied with bodily sensations. Then as the physical illness begins to remit, there is reestablishment of the habitual defensive constellations. Intellectualization and focus on the other person's problems while avoiding his own become prominent again, but this time the patient seems to recognize their presence more readily. There is also a brief period of partial affect discharge as he reviews current and past experiences, but more significant is the patient's growing awareness of his hypersensitivity to loss and separation. This is indicated by his last remark in the last analytic hour before the summer interruption, "Here I am, recently recovered from an acute illness myself. My battle still goes on—with my neurosis."

Following a quiet August, the patient resumes analysis, and during the next three months essentially little change occurs in his psychophysical equilibrium. His neurotic view of the analysis continues. All the principal defenses persist with only slight modification. Affect block of impressive proportion yields only very slowly. Superego-ego tensions continue to be severe. Relationships with women are characterized by initial interest with quick sexual intimacy, growing disillusionment, and, finally, rejection. Specific references to sexual fantasy or activity remain conspicuously absent.

On 12/3 when the reporting of analytic hours is resumed, the patient, feeling very lonely once again, has met and quickly become intimate with still another woman—Rachel. He notes certain features in her as in other women he has known which remind him of his mother. This time it is her heavy smoking and persistent cigarette cough. Within a week the optimistic beginning of the relationship is quickly superseded by doubts and a familiar defensive focus on Rachel's problems, thus avoiding his own. Problems in communication and punctuality are again reflected in an intensified way in the transference, at work, and in the relationship with Rachel. This is clearly a reenactment of defiance and rebellion at parental rigidity, in connection with childhood eating schedules which are recalled as depriving him of the pleasures of playing with his chums. On 12/5 the genetic origin of his persistent focus on others and avoidance of his own problems and feelings becomes more evident though these defensive patterns persist. On 12/6 the patient notes that work at his office is piling up, as he neglects it for the physical gratifications with Rachel which ward off an upsurge in loneliness. His special intellectual efforts in the past and perfectionistic tendencies, to the point at times of being inhibited, appear as a means of gaining acceptance from others and a defense against thinking of himself as inferior.

Then, on 12/10 the patient reports that reality circumstances have evoked an intensely hostile, rejecting outburst at him from Rachel. What has remained outside his awareness is the hostile significance of his acting out toward her in the trouble-making incident. He is unable to adequately cope with Rachel's hostility, is unaware of his own intense feelings other than a sense of disappointment, and can only devaluate her. The affect block is impressively present. Superego-ego tensions rise as the potential for hostility rises, but they are also outside awareness. A sudden change of mood on Rachel's part brings only slight and temporary relief from stress. The focus on her defensive avoidance only serves to highlight his own defensive avoidance, but his awareness remains limited. Rachel's rigidity is linked with recollections of his parents' intolerance and closure of discussion. He fails to see his own rigidity. His need for sexual gratification to ward off loneliness again overrules rationality. The psychophysical equilibrium becomes unstable.

On 12/12 the patient has a dream of an ambivalent relationship with a former girlfriend and in his associations recollects sustaining physical injury in an auto accident with residual of severe chest pain. A day later (12/13) the patient reports a shocking and final rejection by Rachel, yet exhibits no noticeable affect, and even when confronted, refers only to his being disappointed and upset in a bland way. At the same time he has been the recipient of sharp criticism from a parental figure at work. The stresses have become sharply overwhelming and a critical shift in psychophysical equilibrium appears to be at hand. The psychologic cues suggest somatic dysfunction involving the chest area.

Just before the next analytic interview (12/16) the patient begins to feel feverish and to experience right-sided pleuritic pain. These symptoms accompanied by cough rapidly increase during the hour. Cough and chest pain both have appeared in the patient's recent associations as the only prominent physical symptoms. They can be said to have been cues of where physical dysfunction would most likely occur. Now, in the analytic hour, the pain percepts evoke secondary or retrospective recollections of pneumonia during adolescence, following what was apparently then a prolonged period of homesickness while at boarding school. As the hour progresses, the physical symptoms continue to worsen. The patient attempts to cope with the acute discomfort by a joke involving an exchange between a patient and his analyst involving the former's insight into his orality and mother-transference, and the latter's lack of insight into his over-maternal countertransference. The pregenital components in the patient's conflicts are revealed in this associative response. Temperature percepts appear next, followed by disguised hostile references toward incompetent doctors, with transference implications. There are also feelings of frustration and references to death. Here again is masked evidence of the patient's hostility and guilt. A deepening regressive pull turns the patient's associations toward an intense longing to see his brother. The hour ends with retrospective recollections of his parents' addiction to smoking and its somatic consequences.

In the last reported interview (12/20), following a four-day interruption, there is seeming improvement in the patient's physical condition. He has been mostly confined to bed, sleeping a great deal. A dream of Oedipal significance is brought in, linking the illness with a symbolic castration. For the first time, forbidden homosexual wishes emerge. However, primarily he has been and continues to be preoccupied with bodily symptoms. After this hour the patient leaves for his brother's home where he has a severe relapse and spends most of the next ten days ill in bed with lobar pneumonia, *left* lower lung.

L. M.

A Cold Farewell

INTRODUCTION

L.M. is a 26-year-old administrative assistant to an advertising executive. She entered analysis because of recurrent concern about pleasing people and particular difficulty in relationships with men, most recently with her boss.

She is an only child. Her father, a distinguished judge, had been in good health until he became ill with a rapidly developing metastasizing cancer of the stomach from which he died three years ago. He had been married once before and had children by his first wife before divorcing her and marrying the patient's mother who was much younger than he. He was in his fifties when the patient was born and represented for her an elderly father, distant and passive. Mother is described as demanding, willfull, a charmer of men, and a free-lance writer, always physically well. The patient's contacts with her step-siblings had been infrequent as she grew up; these meetings occurred chiefly during summer months.

As a child L. M. was troubled with episodes of vomiting and was said to have been overfed by her mother who was very concerned about her thinness and her tendency to develop frequent upper respiratory infections. Otherwise she has been physically well. The patient has been in lifelong conflict with her mother, fearing her domination, her accusations of selfishness, and the possibility of becoming like her. Feelings of inferiority tended to keep the patient isolated in social situations throughout her early school years, and she was not comfortable with either girls or boys. She found that it was necessary for her to compensate by superior scholastic achievement and then later in college to gain attention from men by sexual promiscuity. This was followed by a period of avoidance of sexuality until she started her most recent job. Then she became increasingly interested in and involved with her boss. At the same time she was ambitiously planning to further her business career.

Preliminary clinical impression was that of a moderately severe character neurosis with obsessional and hysterical traits, and acting out tendencies.

During the first three months of analysis, the patient proceeded in a highly intellectualized fashion, in great descriptive detail, and with considerable reference to her extensive reading in psychology to present current and past aspects of her basic problems. There was a great need to please and, at the same time, a strong competitive push and ambition to further her career and also be very attractive to men. This was reflected in the developing transference. Behind this independent exterior were deeply dependent needs which occasionally broke through in the form of brief periods of helpless and pessimistic feelings about the future. Hostility was intense, but strongly defended against, particularly by her logical presentations and ingratiating ways. Superego-ego tensions were manifested in frequently verbalized references to guilt. A period of acting out of sexual impulses, representing both an identification with mother's seductiveness and a rebelliousness toward her domination, had abated but was in process of being revived in the growing intimacy of her relationship with her boss.

As the detailed account of the analytic interviews begins in the fourth month of treatment, the patient is confronted with her masculine strivings and a growing awareness of her confusion over sexual identity.

CASE MATERIAL

1/26

1   [Silence.]
This seems the hardest time for me [late afternoon, Friday]. It's the end of the day and the end of the week. It's more difficult than usual to dissipate the things on my mind—including Friday traffic.

2   On Wednesday night I dreamt I grew a beard and had had it for a long time. It was as if I wanted to see what it would look like. That's the standard phrase men use when they grow beards. In the dream various friends and people saw it, and some said it didn't become me. I couldn't find an outfit to go along with it. So I shaved it off without regret [pause].

["Associations?"] It's funny in a way. I just smiled when I thought of the dream. It's not my usual response to dreams. Ludicrous. I wasn't taking myself seriously. It looks like transvestite behavior, assuming a masculine role. Pardon my psychological lingo, but it sounds right.

3   Last night [Thursday] I had two seduction dreams again, both involving older men who work at the agency. These occurred in a setting where I had been

left to take care of my stepsister's baby. It's strange that she should be in the dream. I've had so few contacts with her. Once when I was younger, I did spend a vacation with her children. It was a wonderful summer—one of the best I ever had. When I was little and growing up, I thought I had a big sister by Daddy's previous marriage. The idea of having a sister was very pleasing to me. When I was very little, I went to her wedding. She seemed very beautiful. My own mother later explained that all the children of father's first wife had been by another man, including my half-sister. I felt very angry that my mother had broken the spell of my fantasies about all this. Mother kept trying to point out how terrible my father's first wife had been. Father was very angry that I had been told. Mother was really very vicious about father's first family. She would not allow him to see them. What a tremendous lot of swallowing of his own wishes he had to do because of my mother! Things between them became terrible as time went on.

When I was a junior in high school, I was under a great strain. I thought I was being excluded from the in-group of girls. My appearance, my clothing was in accordance with my mother's tastes which were just all wrong. I was too intellectual, wouldn't make small talk. I began to be bothered by persistent vomiting. I knew I had to talk to someone about it, someone other than my parents—and I finally decided on my father's sister, my favorite aunt, a very independent, straight-forward kind of person. I blurted out a lot of my problems with mother, especially her attempts to rule me and show me off to others. Later, when I was sleeping around and got pregnant, my mother said it was my fault for having talked with my aunt and having followed her advice to be independent. She insisted it was my aunt's influence that got me into a jam. My mother had eavesdropped on the whole conversation, I found out afterwards. 4

Back to the beard. Some of the people at the agency have beards, the men that is [laughs]. Pulling on the beard in the dream made it come out of my face. I guess that the most disturbing part is that I'm not sure what I want to be, even though it makes me laugh to think about it. ["One way to deal with disturbing thoughts is to laugh them off. There's a curiosity about what it's like to be masculine, but at the same time through the magic of fantasy you can be masculine or not—as you choose."] 5

1/29

I've done a lot of thinking about what you said the last time. I recognize it as a major and important problem—my masculine strivings. I guess I looked up to father much more than to mother. Much of my present problems I guess are related to that. I've had occasion to see and fill out a questionnaire from my alma mater about woman's role in society. There are such questions as whether women should work, how much, how can they manage a family and a job at the same time, and so on. I remember when I was going to grammar school with a 1 lot of children from lower middle-class families. There was a lot of feeling and emphasis regarding grades. It was like a cult of achievement. I played right into it and tried to get the highest marks. I competed with the smartest boys. I do have a certain envy of men. Their role seems more straightforward and less open to interpretation. Is my work something I want to do or is it antifeminine [tears]?

2   Just now as I was talking about this problem, I began to feel very upset inside. If things came out intellectually, that wasn't the way I was feeling about it. I thought you would say my crying was an involuntary indication of weakness. I've been concerned about how my crying would be taken here. You may not understand my frustration at not knowing what's behind my crying. Anyway, O.K., my identity is a charged subject: male or female, which direction? Maybe I've somehow kept back the origins of these troubles, but certainly not my confusion or concern about it. I just don't know what the answers are. Why do I do the work I do? Why do I enjoy it? Is enjoying it being unfeminine? Is every woman who has a job—is this open to suspicion? ["You're not under suspicion here, not on trial; we're trying only to understand the meaning of your problems. If there are neurotic elements in your having a job, that's different from saying women should or shouldn't work."]

3   I wonder if I'm making generalized value judgments when I bring up these questions about the women who are successful and who do men's kinds of things. They are regarded in a conflicting way by society. I haven't resolved this matter for myself. Besides the neurotic elements, the whole issue is a difficult and confusing one for me. All kinds of influences have affected me. Some of my most competitive years were in all-girl schools with all women teachers. If there was any competition with men involved, it was indirect. When I got so concerned about boyfriends and that kind of popularity, I guess I was reflecting the concerns and competition of the other girls at school.

1/31

1   I had an interesting experience after Monday's hour. At the office I discovered I was in the grip of an intense suspiciousness. I felt that people were talking about me, that I was incompetent, that I shouldn't be there. With it was a tight, empty-stomach feeling and a dazed sense of people around me being superior. After an hour or so there, I was bursting to get out, but I didn't. It didn't happen again the next morning. I've had such experiences before, but they haven't been so distressing. It wasn't just associated with being in the office. Wherever I would have been Monday afternoon, I would have had the same responses.

2   Driving back from here Monday I had an intense feeling of hating mother in a new and specific way. It wasn't just an intellectual disapproval of her as a person, but I felt she didn't love me at all and never had—even though she protests that I'm the *raison d'etre* of her life. Father once told me that in all the

25 years he had known her, she had not been capable of introspection or taking any blame on herself. She can't come to grips with her own faults or her inadequacies at all. Right now I don't feel consciously angry. I do have fears of becoming like my mother. I didn't know what was expected of me as a child. I was given or took upon myself so many symbolic roles, my whole personality became built up of abstract notions of what I was or should be, and whether I was right or wrong.

I feel tremendously blocked. I'm trying to get at what it was I really wanted   3
then. Did I want my mother to really love me or not want her around at all and have father to myself? ["These are large questions, the answers to which will evolve, but cannot be forced out."]

An uncle of mine made persistent attempts to seduce me for about two years   4
when I was in my teens. As this comes into my mind, I feel my adrenalin picking up, my heart pounding, my palms sweaty, my breath coming with difficulty. My aunt and uncle had come up from Florida to visit mutual friends. At dinner one evening my uncle, who was drinking but was not drunk, was feeling my leg under the dining room table. My reaction was one of horror and fascination. My uncle had always seemed so inhibited and so cold to his wife, and here he wasn't suddenly. The situation seemed to me to be one of being needed by a man, of bringing life to an insensitive person. There was also something very exciting about the immorality, with incestuous overtones to the whole thing. But my better judgment reigned—more than his did. I can't say there was no encouragement, at first at least. I rationalize by telling myself I was helping him. Later that evening he followed me around—it's a big enough house so that we could be alone—and he kissed me surreptitiously several times, saying he wanted to sleep with me. I refused. All this was taking place while just about everybody was drunk and out of it. Later that night he came into my room naked with a full erection. I kicked him out. That was the most blatant incident. Thereafter other episodes occurred for a year or so. When I told my mother about how her brother-in-law was acting, omitting the first incident, she mentioned that he had once tried to do the same thing to her. I had a dreadful feeling that I had been involved in the same kind of sick situation mother was constantly in.

2/2

[Silence. Hands on chest, then folded behind head.]   1
I half feel like continuing with what I was talking about the last time. I don't   2
know how much those experiences with my uncle affected things afterwards, because I began to become more and more promiscuous. I don't know if one led to the other [silence]. I haven't talked here about all the various affairs I've had, except in passing, because they seem so very complicated, requiring much time and less fear on my part. Lying here, trying to think about my problems in a direct way is not useful, I guess. I wonder if anything will be. There are a whole bunch of things passing through my mind and confusing me.

3   Yesterday I picked up a biography of Freud and found myself absorbed. His life seemed foreign and different, but I had a funny feeling of identification with him and an admiration and curiosity I didn't have when I read the book the first time. The first chapter dealt with his upbringing. His father was older than his mother. The person who wrote the book talked of his discovery of repression and resistance. So many of his ideas were heretical at the time. The book moved me. My own childhood events are still troubling me. I began to bog down on the whole question of why is there repression when a person seemingly doesn't feel afraid to know these things.

4   That period when I was promiscuous: I was operating under blatant delusions, since I convinced myself or tried to that I knew what love was. It was some kind of way to get recognition from men. I didn't know about love at all. I don't have any answers. What I have is so much trouble on how to organize and proceed with my day-to-day life. In the past three months I've essentially eliminated almost all romantic contacts, because I don't know how to have a good relationship. I'm too much involved in knocking things down [tears, silence]. I'm afraid I'll just become more and more dependent on the idea of waiting till I figure out things before I try them. No one's telling me what to do—to have or not have a relationship.

5   I have this terrible conflict. I'm still afraid of Joe [her boss], no matter how hard he tries to win me over. I feel so guilty about it because it's so irrational. I don't feel I love him—then start to point fingers at myself, asking: how do you know? I really knock myself all the time, even for the smallest things [tears]. Maybe this is a period when confusion and uncertainty prevail, but I hope it's not necessarily always so. I'm afraid that Joe may take advantage of me, and I resent that [gesticulating with right hand in clenched fist]. I feel bad—thinking things that aren't there. Maybe guilty isn't the right word [hands in back of head, left hand holding right, as right-hand fingers gesticulate]. I feel frustrated, confused. There must be some kind of guilt. I've invested so much in Joe. When I first met him, he seemed so overpowering [right-hand fingers curl open and shut]. My feelings about Joe were like my feelings about mother; they're both dominating people. There were feelings of fear mixed with feelings of being subordinate. Last night I dreamt I went back to my old high school and Joe was along [right-hand fingers gesticulating]. Now I'm not sure who had been to school with me—Joe or mother. Mother had taught me how to function in the world in a lot of practical ways—how to ride a bike and roller skate. There was this kind of dependency on her and at the same time resentment. It's as though I've reacted to Joe in the same way [stomach gurgles].

2/5

1   I spoke at some length with my mother yesterday. She's going away for a
2   vacation. It didn't take long for us to get into a hassle. Afterwards I had two

dreams [arms crossed on chest]. In one there was a carnival setting. An incident occurred at a cafe. A woman, a girl, was sitting at a table. She had very short hair—was boyish-looking. She looked and smiled at me, flirting with me. I felt she must think that I'm a man—incredible. I walked to a mirror and looked—I looked at myself. I wondered why the girl thought that way about me. Then I found myself walking with a friend past this same girl, and this time she realized my true sex.

The second dream I had was also bizarre. I was in a little private plane with mother. The plane seemed rocket-shaped. My mother insisted that I fly the plane. I was reluctant and scared. Then it seemed we were getting lost. I looked out of the window, and we were flying over skiing country which had many trails in the snow. Then we headed straight down to a tropical sea and in our way was an interconnected mass of ropes and buoys. I turned to mother and asked, "Could it do damage?" She said, "Yes." Then she grabbed the controls, but didn't quite avoid this mass and we fell into the water. I took off my shoes, swam to a little island and found mother there. She said that when I was in the water, I told a woman I'd pay $100 to rescue her. The woman replied, "For $100 I'll give her the last rites [silence]."   3

["What are your associations?"] That second dream of the airplane—rocket going down—seems to me to be very sexual [right hand by her side, pointing up with fingers]. Mother didn't trust me, wanted instead to take control of flying the plane from me. I had messed it up. Seems destructive. The whole thing shifts. That plane seems to be a sex symbol belonging to mother with which she was letting me experiment and play, showing me how to fly it. But then there is this great fear of the consequences of doing so. I didn't keep control [both fists clenched]. There wasn't a man in the plane. No father. Unless he's the plane. Mother had control of it, him, and she was letting me experiment with it, him. But I didn't do well. I almost, but really didn't destroy everything [hands clasped below bosom]. Then mother intervened when I lost control. By her taking over, the accident wasn't so bad. That last rites remark: listening to Joe Kennedy's being in a coma, getting last rites. Wondering what might be passing through his sons' minds. My own hostility toward mother is easily aroused and also toward Joe—my Joe. I keep thinking they don't treat me as a person in my own right.

That first dream was like the beard dream with the confusion of whether I was a woman or not. That confusion was there unless I was walking on a man's arm. This is the way I have felt a good deal of my adult life [relative quiescence of hands compared with first part of the hour]. It's the same as wanting to shave off the beard that looked so funny with the woman's clothes I wanted to wear. I'm still obviously very confused by all of this—wanting what men have and yet wanting to be a woman. I remember my favorite aunt, the independent one, arguing with my father about this matter and she would say, "Of course I wished I had a penis, etc." But one thing a woman can do that's unique, and that is to   4 have a baby. When I actually was pregnant [out of wedlock] mother couldn't face people. She was mortified. She accused me of being cruel and selfish, not thinking of others—meaning herself.

5   I've been thinking more in my waking hours about having babies [tears, hands clasped behind head]. There has been so much feeling that sexual relations outside of marriage are wrong, that I should never get knocked up because it would be the end of my life—and all this came from my parents [more tears]. My whole life has been a lot of competition, expectation, and achievement with intellectual success being held up as the worthwhile goal. ["There has been lifelong confusion and pressure about what your role in life would be."] Mother wanted to create me in her own image [arms crossed on chest]. As a child I thought father was attracted to me but mother always was interfering. I guess mother undertook to see that I wasn't in her way. I don't really remember this, but the ideas came to mind because of things I've heard or read. They do seem right and true. Maybe it's because then my conflict becomes more understandable. So there I am—both attracted to and afraid of masculinity.

2/7

1   [Silence. Hands folded on abdomen.]

2   I'm in the grip of a swirling sadness for the last couple of hours. I've finished a special assignment I've been working on for the last month or so. I no longer have that to distract me. Being absorbed in that has been a panacea. Now I can't hide behind it. I find it hard to think of tomorrow. In the past week I've been working at an exhausting level, and now I feel suddenly let down. I don't even have mother to fight with on the phone. She's gone off to Europe. I guess her plane must have landed safely or I would have heard about it now. Morbid thoughts.

3   Now that I don't have this work any more, I feel without direction. The feeling of being very lonely has been growing. There's the whole question of what my work should be anyway. It's tied up so much with my relationship with Joe. If I'm tied up in work, my problems with Joe are outweighed. When there isn't enough work, the gaps and emptiness become all too apparent. I have overwhelming urges to meet new people and develop new friends. But I may have basic problems that will not fundamentally change because of this. How do I break patterns and move out of this web, when I'm so afraid any such movements will be based on neurosis [tears]?

4   I had a dream last night. It was about sex to the point of intercourse. I was truly enjoying it with a married man. Our bodies were stark naked. His penis was vividly clear and very large. I didn't feel guilty and wanted very much to have sex with him. Funny that my first thought now should be recoiling from Joe's touch [hands behind head]. I've imposed a "no" response to his sexual

demands. I feel too confused, too guilty about it. He's married and has a wife and kids. My part formerly in the sex act was secondary to what he was thinking about and wanted. ["One-way gratification."] It's true that Joe wasn't aware of two-way gratification at all. It's an immense problem. Even though he's promised that he's going to separate from his wife, I still think the whole feeling on Joe's part in his desire for sex is to show me that he's a better lover now, that he can think about me more. I get from this a physical sense of stress. It's as though it all goes—the moment I start to talk—into the same category of sensation as when mother tried to get me to love her all the time.

2/9

[Arms crossed on chest; legs crossed.]

My mind is flitting from one thing to another. I'm thinking of a meeting earlier today. Then there was my conversation with Grant last night. He's a platonic friend of mine. An article in the *Saturday Review*. Drinking tea at work. Impressions of people. I'm wondering if I should take an evening course I signed up for last week. The work I'm doing now is with more confidence. I now have an image of Joe and think how important he is to me. Wondering what that meant. How to judge it and understand it. I was self-conscious last night. Joe had recommended some changes in an ad layout I had prepared, even though he praised it for the most part. I have a funny awareness of people—a constant observing of them which has transformed me to a point where I have less fear and more interest. Sounds contradictory. I just came from a tea. I watched people's movements, their nervous maneuvers, but also nice things about them. Now the whole question of the future keeps circulating around me like a water-jacket. I have a feeling I want to call mother, but that's foolish. It would be too expensive—an overseas call.

The most recent work assignment I've gotten isn't interesting, but maybe I ought to get started on it anyway [pause]. 2

I've received a letter from a former acquaintance. He wrote and asked if he could come and see me. I said yes and he's coming tomorrow. Up until now I had forgotten he was coming. The visit seems like an invasion, yet some years ago I was always looking for such diversions. 3

I have a dead—sad feeling. I have to keep my eyes close to the ground in front of me. If I raise them I'll look sad. It's preferable to what I used to be doing—constantly waiting for new men, activities, stimuli, seduction. This seductiveness must have been a way I had of proving myself. When I looked at my activities, it seemed like I was a little girl running around with her head chopped off. I wish I had known then how damaging all that would be to me now. How much my conscience made a big banner of it waving in my face all the time. It was like a disease that took hold of me for three years and then went away. But it left me still with a great sense of inadequacy.

4   I had had a delusion that I had tried to maintain, that my parents were happy together. My father had told me that when my mother learned that I was pregnant, she was furious at my father because he had been so lenient with me, then refused to have anything to do with him sexually for many weeks. About three weeks before father died, he blurted out, "I don't know anything about psychological causes of illness, but this growth in me started when your mother rejected me sexually and in effect left me." He was dead in three months. But I had the thought that their marriage broke up on account of me and that it was I who had killed father. [Tears. No change in posture during entire analytic hour, legs crossed, arms crossed on chest].

2/12

1   I have a very bad cold. It began late Saturday night after my date with Dick. I was terribly restless that night and feverish all of yesterday. Now it's gone into my chest. Last night I had a dream about the analysis. I was doing some special work and realized I had forgotten to come 20 minutes after the hour I should have been here. I had mixed feelings—that I ought to come, yet if I went I'd be very late. There was a question of calling you. I was aware more and more time was elapsing. The dream ended with the issue unresolved.

2   Today I had a great deal to do at the office, but I felt too sick and weak to go to work. I really didn't want to come here either, but was concerned that my absence would not be tolerated by you. ["Just as mother didn't tolerate illness."] Yes, that's what I expected.

3   I also had a seduction dream about an older man, but he wasn't interested [gesticulating hands]. My cousin and I and his girlfriend offered to drive him home. The man lived in Montreal, and in the dream there seemed to be canals there, frozen over, with us skating. Everything seemed to be made of ice. He then went about showing us, actually my cousin, the extraordinary sights of this fantastic ice city. After I awoke the realization persisted that the man didn't have my name and wasn't interested in seeing me again. That was shortly before I was due to come here and made me feel I had to make it no matter how I felt.

4   Over the weekend Dick came to see me. He's about ten years older than me. We had a good time, though I think I was beginning to come down with the cold. I was aware of the game to play to cause him to be interested in me. I stopped doing it after a while. It was a game to show I knew how to get a man interested in me. I finally realized it was indispensable, that it was a situation that was controllable. Actually I never would marry him or have an affair with him. It was instructive, though. He was playing the game but unaware of my knowing it. It was like watching a movie where people don't know they're being filmed. I was breathless, waiting, wondering whether it was going to materialize

into something. My attention wasn't on the man or myself, but how things were going [thumbs now hidden in clenched fists]. I had the feeling of failure and of envy afterwards when we went to a party where there were some beautiful girls, and I heard one tell another what gorgeous red hair she had. I was sad at that because I'm still not able to say something like that to a girl [hands gesticulating]. It's a big problem area—my fear of women and awkwardness with them—especially women I admire. It goes back to grade school when one of my best girlfriends said she was afraid of me. I remember back in the seventh grade in a new school I had no friends. I kept wondering why I wasn't accepted. I guess I used to overrespond. I gradually learned the art of seeming callousness.

Sex was *verboten* at the schools [loud coughing, arms crossed on stomach].   5
The bad reputation idea haunted and plagued me. I had the ancient desire to please a man [stomach grumble]. To make him like me, yet I had a fear then of a bad reputation [cough, right hand clenched to mouth, frequent hacking cough]. The second feeling—the suspiciousness of men—won out for a long time [more coughing, unable to catch breath, has to sit up. Leaves briefly to get drink of water and puts cup by the couch]. Until the spring of my sophomore year, I didn't do anything more than kiss my boyfriend [hands folded on stomach]. One night after a dance we were sitting in front of the house, and I leaned over to kiss him, when he put his hands on my breasts. I was thrown into great conflict. I was terrified that somehow this would be talked about. Yet I was overwhelmed by the physical reaction. I got gooseflesh and became short of breath. I was so overcome by the physical feelings that they won out. He felt my breasts for five minutes. Then the fear got the better of me and I stopped him. I went to my room, threw myself on the bed, trembling. I finally fell asleep, awaking about three or four in the morning, with all my party clothes on. When I awoke, I felt a blush of embarrassment. I wondered if mother had seen me lying on the bed that way. From that time on, at least with this boyfriend, the conflict began to take hold. I enjoyed the physical feeling of petting, and at the same time I was terribly concerned about other people knowing. Then, after other dates, when we returned home, my boyfriend wanted to pet. It appeared as if it was a tariff to be paid in return for being taken to a dance. The physical aspects began to be lost in the fear of becoming known as a fast date. At one point he took my hand and put it on his very erect and large penis. I was frightened [left hand gesticulating]. It had something to do with babies, and I felt then it was something to be reserved for marriage. As soon as I could, I pulled my hand away [fingertips touching]. I remember being amazed at how big it was. I'm sure I saw my father with an erection, but I don't recall it. My recollection of father was that he had a small penis which didn't appear as if it could get hard. I was very confused, but also afraid of the whole thing. My fear was more important to control than my curiosity. That summer, when I was 16, I went to camp where there wasn't anyone to talk to about all of this.

2/14

1   The most immediate influence over my thoughts at the moment is my cold. I've really been having a rough time. My chest ached terribly until today. While my fever went down, I've had this hacking cough which hangs on and on. In the midst of this misery, my cousin called to say her mother, my aunt, is dying of heart failure. My reactions are mixed. Alright, she's 77 and it's bound to happen, yet it shouldn't. She'd been carrying on full time at her work until last week. I have guilt feelings that I haven't seen more of her. I feel a sense of fierce loyalty to her because she was somebody I could turn to when I was upset as a youngster, and she helped me through a lot of turmoil then. Maybe it's melodramatic on my part—that I should immediately go to be with her. Actually she's on the intensive care service and can't see anybody. What comes naturally is to be somewhat remote from it all. I was in awe of her in the past. She was so efficient and seemed as strong as any man. I remember once when I was a little girl visiting with her. A bunch of Negroes had been in a fight nearby and had come into her house for assistance. There was so much noise; women were wailing and men were shouting. I was terribly frightened. The police came. But my aunt was busy, calmly bandaging the injured people and removing any possible weapons from their reach. I was scared that one of the men might be hiding under the sofa. I recall that, once, the house next door caught fire and a man was burned, asphyxiated, smoking in bed [left hand holding right, then both to nose, snuffling; then arms crossed on chest and silence].

2   I recall my aunt's first husband was a great disappointment to her. He was impotent and she wanted children. So he told her to find someone who would make her pregnant and she proceeded to do so. Well, this second husband turned out to be a worthless character. But my aunt focused her full attention on her two children. But my cousins didn't benefit from this, and they haven't gotten anywhere as they grew up [coughing, hands over mouth, then to sides of face]. I guess this business of unhappy families doesn't sit well with me. Can it be that my past has so badly affected me that I will get nowhere in the future? That makes me furious [coughing, left first over mouth].

3   [Patient is reminded of the present.] I'm still in great confusion about Joe. I've had a feeling of heightened sexuality in the last four or five days, wanting to make love, wishing my emotional problems were not there, so I could go to bed with someone. The sexual sensations have been very strong. I spent most of today in bed, trying to get over my cold. I watched a movie on television last night. It got me to thinking of what love is anyway. This was a strongly romantic story of separated people [coughing; arms crossed on chest]. I find that when I get involved in such romances, I get carried away by them. Great love seems to be the main theme in movies, plays, and novels. It's so confusing. Often, during my chronologically adult years, I've tried to create such love, but it's turned out

a sham. So I'm still asking—what is love? I recall my parents used to talk about how much they were in love all the time. Really?

2/15

I feel confused about my attitude to men. On the one hand, I seem to have 1 fears of men and yet act as if I'm not afraid of them—or at times as if I want to be one of them. That I have a fear of men I don't deny. A lot of the men I was exposed to, when little, were frightening men and presented themselves as such to me. Some of my male relatives were loud, pushy, alcoholic, and I often wanted to be protected from them. Once one of them, who had high blood pressure, became enraged in my presence and had a dramatic nosebleed. There was blood over everything. All these men seemed so threatening and, by comparison, my father seemed so gentle. But that led to my confusion about whether father was masculine or not.

I recall two sex experiences when I was in grammar school. The first 2 occurred when I was eight years old. Some boys in the neighborhood whom I didn't know asked me if I'd "show," meaning that I should lift my skirt and drop my pants. Well, I did this because I had no understanding of why they wanted this. Then, when they returned with others all giggly, I refused to repeat it. I guess I sensed it was bad. Then, at age 11, I had a brutal experience. We had a cottage on the seashore. I had a little motor boat of my own. A new yachtsman asked me to board his big boat. He was a movie producer and about 45. He asked me if I wanted to see his thing and I said, "No!" He asked, "Why not?" I felt frightened but in a strange way. I was interested in his boat and his being a big shot in Hollywood. I told him I'd seen my father naked and also my male cousins. He said, "You can play with mine, put it in your mouth and see stuff come out." I bolted from him. I never told anybody about it. I just swallowed it down and kept it in.

The major reason my life began to break down when it did in my teens was 3 that the men in my life were interested in other women, not their own, not me. My confidence in myself has always been shaky [hands behind head; crying]. These tears are an attempt to make it clear to you and myself that some of the things I've been afraid of I haven't made up. ["Do you feel accused?"] I accuse myself of that. In the past three or four weeks I've been having more and more panicky feelings that everything I thought I represented might be illusory [violent crying]. The people that say they like, love me are those that I think I've deluded—when they find out what I really am, I'll lose them.

I slept about 12 hours last night. I had a long talk with my cousin who's very 4 upset about my aunt's dying. I was very good and comforting to her. When I woke this morning, I wondered if this emotional upset of mine was real or was I just putting on a show and aggrandizing myself. I realize I haven't said a good or positive thing about myself since I've been in analysis [violent crying]. ["We began the analysis with the understanding that you had a neurosis, but not that you were all neurotic."] Part of the trouble is that I do feel all neurotic. This aspect is such a devastating one. It feeds on itself. Hypersensitivity and hyperconscience are the two words that describe me best [crying less violent]. There's this constant questioning and devaluation of myself. It's not always as severe as now, but I never know when it'll take over. I really know that I'm not as bad as my conscience pictures me.

2/18, Summary

1   Crying and jumpy over the weekend. Another cousin, her favorite one, has announced wedding plans. Feelings of intense jealousy and of being left out and abandoned. Increasing hostility, especially toward the analysis, "If I weren't in it, I could compensate somehow and do what other people are doing, just get along with arbitrary answers—though I know that that's illogical and irrational." Expectation that analyst will be angry and react unfavorably because of such wishes.

2/19

1   I had a dream last night. I went with my favorite cousin to a store, trying to get a check cashed. I had an idea I would withhold the check from the income tax people because it was too big. Then I came to an unexpected, very steep bridge covered with snow. That seemed strange. Maybe it was so because the bridge was over a river which cools it and the snow doesn't melt. The bridge went into the door of the shop—a bakery. I asked how to get out and they said I couldn't. The door was locked. Then there was an Alice-in-Wonderland thing with all sorts of rooms. I became more and more of a child—until I was a little girl. There were all sorts of things to play with. One room had modern furnishings, and a man was trying to entice me to stay, but I wanted out. Finally, a dog, a golden retriever, got past the door and allowed me to escape with it to the woods. A man collecting children who were cutting down trees with hatchets saw the dog and me, recaptured me, and brought me into the house again. Suddenly I seemed to be making love with an older man in the middle of a room. Then I woke up, very much turned on sexually.

2   I first think of the bridge to the house. There's a European overtone to the whole scene. It has something to do with Joe's trip and my doubts about accompanying him. Now I have thoughts of going up the hayloft into the barn, being afraid and wanting to. I'm reminded of an older boy saying he was a big, bad wolf and would eat me up—it scared me. I hated being called ridiculing nicknames. I wonder if that had anything to do with my feeling insecure.

3   The dream seemed to be a surrealistic impression of my childhood. One of my uncles who died when I was five—how much he scared me! He died of drink

and high blood pressure. I see him in the kitchen sink with blood gushing out of his nose. Those feelings of unfamiliarity—not knowing what I was supposed to do and how I was supposed to act in the presence of the older boys, my cousins. They were just three or four years older but they seemed terribly old and threatening.

Now I recall another part of the dream: when it was clear that the man knew where the dog and I were hidden, we jumped up and ran—through a maze of houses. I saw a woman in a kitchen of one house, ran in, and then realized I had been tricked, that the house was the same one the man was trying to get me into.

I've had a bad stomachache since last night. The pain is beginning to bother   4 me again. Joe and I went out to dinner and had much food and wine. I felt troubled about my relationship with Joe: my conscience bothered me. When I finally got to my apartment, I was very tired and went right to bed. I awoke at 5 A.M., feeling awful, full of gas, burping, threw up a bit, and had these horrible pains. I was awake from 5 to 7 A.M. and then fell asleep and had this dream. I wasn't aware of the pain until I started talking about the dream. I have a sense of great pressure and heartburn now.

I'm reminded of another dream, earlier in the night, before I woke up with   5 all this stomach distress. It was about my cousin and her fiance. I was going to a concert with them and Joe. The concert was by a Negro soul singer. At the concert hall I realized I had told another friend of mine, Bill, that I would have dinner with him. I then got out, met Bill at a bus terminal, and got a cherry drink which tasted awful. I was edgy to go back to the concert. There was a new transit system, fancy, like at these expositions. There were a lot of women with packages in the car. One of them put a clip on the hair curler in my hair, but I took the clip out. Then I was back at the concert. On the stage Negro girls were singing a Bach cantata, dressed in dance hall costumes. I noticed one girl had only a veil on, and I could see her breasts through the veil. In the next scene my cousin, her fiance, and I get ready to take the local train to their apartment in the suburbs. Tickets were $25 each and obtained by putting money into a machine. I thought that $25 was quite expensive. Then we were on the train, and it was time to get off. I couldn't get my sandals on because of my stockings. I finally got off the train and into a taxi where my cousin was very angry at the driver.

My cousin is very anxious about tipping, afraid that people won't like her. It's like buying their approval. She'll give money to beggars. In the dream she was acting opposite to what I know of her by berating the driver for the high charge [pause]. I had the feeling during the train ride that I was tagging along with my cousin and her fiance, being looked after by them. As a child I traveled a great deal on a bus. I also guess I needed or wanted a lot of attention. But being sick was a frowned on activity in the family. Mother had no sympathy or paid no attention to stomachache or headache or colds that didn't involve fever. I never got attention for feeling ill. Mother was so terribly healthy, she never stayed in bed and insisted this was the way to be. I do know there was a stomach pattern of vomiting. It happened when I was a baby, I'm told, and again only when I was well along in high school.

6   Last night I did a lot of thinking and talked to Joe about some aspects of the analysis. It was an uncomfortable subject. As the evening went on, I had the feeling that to thrash around against analysis while here was wasting my time. Two paths were open—one to keep upset and crying, the other to try to put myself into the work as much as I could. Now that part of the dream with the man after me, trapping me, comes to mind. I guess I'm more afraid of the analysis than I realized. Maybe what I'm getting here or expect to get is not to my taste, neurotically speaking. ["It's giving you a stomachache."]

MARGINAL NOTES

1/26

1. Resistance.
2. Dream: masculine strivings wished for, tried, and denied.
3. Seductive dream—to prove femininity. Linked with Oedipal associations, mother's jealous, devaluating attitudes, and conflict with father.
4. Social tensions, conflicts with mother exacerbated during adolescence and linked with somatic manifestations. Supportive mother-surrogate. Independent strivings and pregnancy condemned by own mother.
5. Symbolic, part-object masculine representation. Humor a defense. Ambivalence. Interpretation.

1/29

1. Masculine strivings. Seemingly greater identification with father. Questions about woman's role. Penis envy. Conflict about work.
2. Defensive about tearfulness as a possible indicator of defect. Confusion about identity. Clarification.
3. Continued conflict over woman's role. Early competition with women (principally mother).

1/31

1. Upsurge of projection as defense against inferiority feelings, linked with interoceptive percepts.
2. Hostility associated with rejection by mother and devaluation of mother, without currently expressed affect. Concern about identification with her. Confusion about roles during childhood.
3. Attempts to force answers to Oedipal riddle. Clarification.

4. Breakthrough of traumatic sexual memories with current physical equivalents of anxiety. Elements of excitement, seduction, incest, superego prohibition, rationalization, and identification with mother.

2/2

1. Resistance.
2. Ambivalence about revealing further aspects of sexual problems and experiences.
3. Identification with father-figure. Intellectualization mixed with naivete.
4. Promiscuity, a defense against being rejected by men. Interference of sadistic impulses. Self-pity. Fear of procrastination.
5. Conflicted about father-figure. Guilt. Affect discharge. Self-reassurance. Hostile-dependent reaction to Joe compared with that to mother. Physical manifestation follows cognitive reference.

2/5

1. Hostility to mother and impending separation.
2. First dream: shifting sexual identity.
3. Second dream: sexualized. Involved are control, trust, envy of and attempts to imitate mother's phallic behavior and dealings with men, fear of near-fatal consequences with necessary intervention by mother, and defensive hostility toward her and Joe.
4. Further associations to first dream: confusion over sexual identity. Penis envy. Compensatory reference to woman's unique ability: child-bearing, which evoked mother's hostility.
5. Pregnancy a defense against masculine strivings. Affect discharge linked with parental (and superego) disapproval of pregnancy out of wedlock. Conditioning toward intellectual achievement and competition. Interpretation. Hostile mother in Oedipal situation: an intellectualization. Ambivalence about masculine strivings.

2/7

1. Resistance.
2. Affect breakthrough. Defense of overactivity unavailable. Reference to mother's leaving linked with ambivalence toward her.
3. Feelings of loneliness and aimlessness. Ambivalent relationship with Joe. Need for other object relationships. Fear of basic defects.
4. Dream of incestuous sexual relationship, linked with Joe. Imposed abstinence related to guilt. Joe's selfishness identified with mother's.

2/9

1. Defensive posture. Rambling associations. Attempts at extroversion defensive against hypersensitivity. Longing for mother.
2. Ambivalence about former boyfriend's visit.
3. Further references to depressive affect replacing defensive adventures

with men: seductiveness to disprove inferiority. Castration image. Superego aspects.

4. Myth of parental happiness. Reactivation of Oedipal conflicts. Mother's rejection of father linked to his fatal illness. Guilt with affect discharge.

2/12

1. Severe upper respiratory illness. Ambivalent transference dream.
2. Mother transference: negative expectations.
3. Second dream: attempted seduction and cold rejection linked with transference and illness.
4. Real but partial acting out of seduction. Voyeuristic and exhibitionistic aspects. Comparison with beautiful women: envy and hostility; latent homosexual attraction. Recollections of awkward childhood relationships with girls.
5. Memory of sex impulse and taboo linked with activated physical symptoms. Superego aspects, masochistic fears. Vivid recollection of being seduced: physical concomitants, fears of discovery, fears of consequences, activated curiosity. Devaluated sexual image of father.

2/14

1. Preoccupied with symptoms of illness. Guilt activated by mother-figure's illness. Ambivalence and avoidance. Imagery of a phallic woman. Recollections of frightening and stimulating sights and sounds involving injured men.
2. Further comparison of the phallic woman and impotent men: traumatic effect on children. Identification.
3. Ambivalence. Upsurge of libido linked with defensive avoidance of problems and probably heightened masochism. Intellectualizing and romanticizing about love and separation. Disillusionment with parents.

2/15

1. Ambivalence toward men: fear of and wish to be identified with them. Memories of violent men. Doubts about father's masculinity.
2. Recollections of traumatic childhood sexual experiences.
3. Adolescent disturbance linked to rejecting men. Chronic lack of self-confidence. Self-pity, self-accusation.
4. Temporary shift in role. Question of secondary gain. More self-devaluation, affect discharge. Clarification and reassurance. Superego aspects.

2/18 Summary.

1. Increased tensions, triggered by feelings of envy and rejection. Increasing transference hostility and fears of retaliation.

2/19

1. Transference dream: hostile, erotic, masochistic elements.
2. Ambivalence about relationships with older men. Recollections of childhood insecurity.

3. Further memories of violent men, feelings of inferiority with boys.

4. Recurrence of physical symptoms, originally preceded by over-indulgence in oral gratification and superego tension, activated by recollection of dream.

5. Another dream, actually preceding first: manifestations of physical dysfunction with Oedipal and transference aspects. Associations include attempts at buying of approval, unsatisfied need for maternal affection, lack of secondary gain from illness, references to childhood gastrointestinal upsets, probably linked to tension.

6. Transference aspects: ambivalence and activated physical manifestations.

COMMENT

Except for episodes of vomiting during childhood and adolescence and a tendency to get frequent upper respiratory infections, this patient has enjoyed good physical health. Generally she has responded to stress with psychologic manifestations, occasionally with minor physical dysfunction. Her neurotic traits had become more severe at the time she entered analysis, being activated by a deepening conflict between her feminine and masculine strivings. Her career aspirations impelled her to work especially hard at her job in an advertising agency. At the same time she found herself becoming more and more deeply involved with one of the executives whose administrative assistant she was.

The first reported hour (1/26) reflects this conflict. Dreams are reported to which there are many Oedipal associations. At the same time her mother appears as a phallic woman whose devaluating attitudes toward, and conflict with the patient's father are vividly recalled. The focus on mother continues with recollections of the patient's own conflicts with her during adolescence marked by attempts to escape her dominance, instances of defiant acting out, and episodes of gastrointestinal dysfunction, principally vomiting. This image of mother is followed by memories of a supportive, kindly mother-surrogate who, however, is also seen as having phallic qualities. In the next hour (1/29) there are continued, indirect references to competition with mother and confusion about sexual identity. Penis envy is clearly evident. Intellectualization is a front-line defense.

On 1/31 there can be noted an increase in ideas of being inferior and unwanted which are defended against by an upsurge of projection and the appearance of interoceptive percepts referable to the stomach. There are more references to hostility directed at mother because of her rejecting ways, despite her protests to the contrary. Again father is described as a witness to and victim of mother's intense narcissism. The patient voices the concern that she has taken on mother's undesirable attributes and attitudes, including her seductiveness. Behind this concern are the wishes to outdo her and to win the man—father—and father-figures away from her. Very little affect has been expressed up to this point, when there is a sudden breakthrough of physical anxiety equivalents, as she recalls traumatic sexual experiences during adolescence, involving an uncle. It is clear that these experiences originally had elements of intense excitement linked with forbidden incestuous wishes stimulated by the uncle's approaches; the seductive actions were not one-sided. Also associated with these recollections were superego prohibitions, rationalizations, and identification with the mother.

Following the last hour resistance has developed (2/2) about revealing further details of her sexual problems and experience. This is related to transference expectations of being judged and condemned. Promiscuity appears in part as a defense to ward off rejection by men. Repeated references to guilt, especially involving her affair with her boss, a married man, can be noted alongside her concern that men will take advantage of her and her competitiveness with both men and women. The hostile-competitive-dependent responses to her lover resemble the ones experienced with her mother. These associations are accompanied by stomach hyperperistalsis which often signals or appears simultaneously with activated oral needs. But affect is minimally expressed.

In the interview of 2/5 can be noted how an external event acts as a stress and causes a shift in the existing psychophysical equilibrium. The patient has a hostile exchange with her mother who announces that she is leaving by plane on an extended European trip. The intensification of the patient's conflicts follows immediately, and that night is reflected in several dreams. In one, the theme of confused sexual identity is repeated with shifts from penis envy to emphasis on woman's unique child-bearing ability. In the second dream there are references to coldness and warmth, followed by symbolism of a highly sexualized and ambivalent relationship with mother. Elements of control and trust are involved. There is envy of and attempts to imitate mother's phallic behavior and sexual dealings with men. Fear of near-fatal consequences (plane crash) and hostile dependency toward parental figures also are represented. References to guilt over extramarital sex relationships again reflect parent and superego disapproval. The death wish toward mother is an additional guilt-activating factor.

Further regressive shifts in the psychologic equilibrium can be noted during the 2/7 hour. The defense of overactivity to ward off awareness of affect is no longer available because of reality circumstances, and the patient is experiencing sadness. This affect is linked with mother's departure and the ambivalent response which this has activated in the patient as reflected in the dream of the plane crash and references to coldness and warmth (rejection vs. acceptance; anger vs. love). All this occurs following an upsurge of Oedipal and pre-Oedipal conflicts involving mother principally and the patient's boss, a father-figure, secondarily. A state of loneliness and aimlessness is developing. There is insufficient gratification currently from the ambivalent relationship with her boss. The net result is a continued sense of loss, an intensified but as yet frustrated need for other object relationships, insufficient psychologic mechanisms of defense, and an increasing potential for hostile affect which is not being discharged externally. At this point, the psychologic cues suggest that continuation of these shifts in equilibrium will lead to involvement of somatic systems and that physical dysfunction in the near future is very likely.

In the hour of 2/9, the patient's posture reflects her general defensiveness. Her reporting of extroverted behavior indicates a further attempt to contain her hypersensitivity, but further references to depressive affect indicate insufficiency of her defensive adventures with men, designed to disprove her inferiority as a woman. There are signs of increased superego-ego tensions. Toward the end of this hour, another signal appears which further suggests impending physical dysfunction. There is a recollection linking mother's rejection of father to his fatal physical illness. The patient has felt involved because mother's behavior was due to father's refusal to punish her for becoming illegitimately pregnant. The formula now seems to be: Mother left father because he disagreed with her; father became ill physically. Mother left the patient because of disagreement; patient becomes ill physically. The patient's guilt currently has multiple links. There is hostility to mother for her dominating ways and for her leaving the patient. There is competitive hostility with her lover's wife and less prominently with her lover. Finally, the patient has become again preoccupied with the thought that her parents' marriage broke up because of her and that it was she who ultimately had caused father's death. Some affect—sadness—is apparent, but appears as an insufficient discharge compared with the intensity of the conflicts now surging up in the patient.

The next hour (2/12) is after a three-day interruption. The patient has developed an acute, upper respiratory illness during this interval. Prior to its onset she has a date with a former acquaintance and begins the old, defensive game of seduction, but does not follow it through. At a party later she compares herself with some beautiful women who are present, feels envious of and hostile toward them. The experience evokes recollections of awkward childhood relationships with girls and their seeming rejection of her. The result of her total experiences that evening is a further increase in her sense of loneliness and bitterness. The following night, with the respiratory infection fully established, there are dreams that indicate a secondary reaction to the illness: The patient is becoming concerned that her being sick will not be tolerated by the analyst as prior illnesses have not been tolerated by her mother. She fears she will be coldly rejected and forces herself to come to the analytic hour. Her physical symptoms are intensified repeatedly as various associations emerge: References to the need to prove her femininity are linked with audible stomach hyperperistalsis. Recollections of sex taboos in school and superego responses are associated with frequent loud coughing. Vivid memories of seduction by a boyfriend the accompanying sexual excitement and fear of discovery by mother as he manipulated her breasts evoke marked dyspnea. There is further recall of sexual curiosity involving father. Of interest is the sequence of activated cough reflex leading to dyspnea and then recollection of the seduction scene and its physiologic concomitants.

Why was the chief symptom of the respiratory infection a persistent cough? Was this purely due to a particular viral agent that specifically attacked larynx, trachea, bronchi, and thus permitted secondary invaders in these tissues to become activated? Not necessarily. Psychologic factors may also be involved, e.g., possibly the particular area becomes more susceptible because it has been sensitized in the past as a target organ for psychologic tensions. On the other hand, when symptoms of a physical illness become established, do they secondarily determine and trigger the release of particular associations from past and present into awareness? Such secondary psychologic responses can be frequently noted. In any event, to answer these questions more fully will require further research with particular focus on such problems.

The pressure of acute physical symptoms will provide a focal point for the patient's attention, especially if the multiple forms of the psychologic defense of denial are not utilized or ineffective. Then it may be difficult for the patient to think of anything else more than briefly, if at all. This can be noted in analytic hours where the patient has acute physical symptoms. The interview of 2/14 begins this way. However, further external events of stressful magnitude have been occurring and competing for the patient's attention. Her favorite aunt, who represents a benevolent mother-figure, has become gravely ill. The prospect of further loss evokes an ambivalent response and guilty thoughts which the patient tries to cope with by avoidance, but this defense is insufficient, and there is a flood of recollections about this aunt, who determinedly carried on her life despite many vicissitudes. These memories are linked with unhappy families, unhappy future, and hostility, and are accompanied by fits of coughing. It should also be noted that there has been an upsurge of sexual impulses during the course of the illness, which in part represent an attempted escape from troublesome thoughts and in part have an exciting, masochistic basis related to the physical discomfort.

In the interview of 2/15, the patient has shifted her focus from women to men, and reveals her continued ambivalence toward them, her fear of and wish to be identified with them. There are many recollections of childhood contacts with frightening, angry, bleeding men contrasted with her father seen as gentle and passive, thus questioning his masculinity. Two traumatic sexual experiences are also recalled. She links her adolescent difficulties to rejecting experiences, especially at the hands of men. Here a shift can be noted: affect is beginning to break through, but there are large secondary gain aspects to it. There is further evidence of continued superego-ego tensions. As the physical illness abates, tearfulness and hostility increase, further activated by envy of a favorite cousin, a sibling figure, who is about to get married. On 2/20, the final interview reported, the respiratory illness has completely subsided, but the patient complains of a gastrointestinal upset since the previous night. She spent the early part of the evening with her boss and they mutually overindulged in oral gratifications. Afterwards the patient's conscience kept troubling her about her relationship with a married man. Her sleep was troubled and she had several dreams. The first one preceded her waking with a stomachache. The associations to this dream recall past needs for attention which could not be obtained from her mother who never paid attention to the patient's physical ills, including colds and gastrointestinal upsets. The dream and the somatic response reflect the patient's ambivalent transference attitudes, her hostile dependency, her frustration in trying to gain support and sympathy, and also a less influential desire to work at her problems in the analysis. In effect, the neurotic distortion has it that what she is getting from analysis is giving her a stomachache, but even that will not get her any sympathy.

Q. R.

A Malignant Identity Crisis

INTRODUCTION

Q.R. is a 35-year-old graduate student in physics who entered treatment because of recurrent dissatisfaction with her role as a woman. She is married to a younger man, a biologist, who recently received his Ph.D. in that field. They have two children, four and two and one-half years old.

The patient's mother had been a sickly woman with various indeterminate physical ailments which required frequent hospitalization. She died of pneumonia during the patient's early adolescence, and a paternal aunt took over the care of the patient and her siblings. Father, who was often jobless, was and has continued to be distant and frequently unavailable to the family, having left them often in difficult financial straits. There are three younger sisters, all married now and with small families. Their health has been variable. The youngest sister has has fibroids of the uterus, but no surgical intervention. The next in age has had a recurrent benign tumor of the breast, surgically removed without sequelae. The patient's rivalry with her siblings has always been intense.

The patient's premarital relationships with men had been relatively limited, and she found herself unable to achieve orgasm except rarely. The tendency toward frigidity persisted after marriage. There was infrequent recourse to masturbation which was invariably followed by a rise in guilt feelings. She had a serious affair with a very sadistic man who left her after a year of repeated quarreling and incompatibility. Shortly thereafter, on the rebound, she met and after a brief courtship married her present husband, a bright but very passive man with whom there has also been continued difficulty. A compulsive need to have babies resulted in the birth of two boys in quick succession. The combination of being a mother and continuing with her graduate studies made her feel under almost constant tension and subject to easy fatigue. She felt cyclically depressed and mildly euphoric. She had always been thin as a child and now found herself underweight again. During adolescence she began to have frequent sinus headaches which had continued intermittently since. When she was 19 she became pregnant and had an abortion, without apparent complications. At age 28 she had an acute kidney infection. There have been three operations: the first was for biopsy and removal of a benign cyst of the left breast in her early twenties; a saphenous ligation was done several years later, and an emergency appendectomy was performed a short time after she had her last child.

On preliminary examination this patient's character neurosis appeared to be of mixed type, with obsessional, depressive, and hysterical features.

As the analysis began, it became quickly evident that the patient had been concerned for years with the idea that she was defective. Each physical illness and each operation intensified this concern. Now she feared that treatment also would reveal serious mental illness and the need for electroshock, or that she would be ridiculed and then rejected. She had also been troubled for a long time by fantasies that she would be taken advantage of and that there were powerful, aggressive men who would attack her. These masochistic trends became more and more sharply defined as the analysis progressed. Still other fears involved her ability to control her own hostile impulses and also her flirtatious tendencies, with terrible consequences anticipated. Father was seen as powerfully sadistic, unpredictable, and distant, but also devaluated as an alcoholic incapable of holding a steady job. Transference attitudes reflected this mixed image. There was an intense need to be loved, frustrated and unfulfilled, not only by father, but expecially by the sickly mother who had devoted her attention to the siblings that rapidly followed one another. This need became quickly evident in the patient's associations and again was reflected in the transference. There was marked penis envy and persistent, unsettled conflict between desire for a career and wish to be attractively feminine. An extreme degree of ego-superego tension could be noted early as depression alternated with mild euphoria. Intellectualization was present from the beginning as a notable defense structure. Moderate projective tendencies also were apparent.

A continuing stress from the onset of the analysis was the patient's largely realistic concern that her husband would leave her, and this became a practically intolerable expectation. In addition, impending academic examinations that would either permit her to go to thesis preparation for her Ph.D. or block this finally, became an additional, increasingly severe stress. Competitive tensions increased between the patient and her fellow students and professors as the exams approached. Although she had been carefully checked over, with negative findings during an annual checkup two months ago, the patient began to experience intermittent frequency of urination and a vague, generalized malaise. Her concern about her bodily integrity intensified, and scattered references to having a serious illness began to appear. Preoccupation with the size of her abdomen also could be noted. It is at this point, after one year of analysis, that the detailed reporting begins.

CASE MATERIAL

2/18

My friend Miriam says I look thin. I didn't like to hear that. It seemed to me that she meant the remark to be critical, so I said some things to make her wince. I talked to her about her father's coarse behavior. When I told her I needed a certain book to study for my exams and was going to the library for it, she turned around and told me she had taken the book out and was waiting to see how hard it would be for me to get a copy. That burns me up—to think of all the waiting on her that I've done, only to have her play tricks like that on me. She's like her mother in some ways. Miriam's mother is so stingy, she never puts herself out for others. Miriam also told me she has neuralgia in her right hand, from doing lots of housework. She's been taking hot packs for it and carries her arm in a sling. I wonder what her husband thinks about that? For Miriam to be sick is unusual, but I've been sick so often in the past, it seems to be all the time. Yesterday I had to start myself on aspirins. The headache that I get so often with tension was back. I've begun to think of the possibility of cancer. Another of my friends, Carol, had fibroids in her uterus, but, after her last baby was born a short time ago, they disappeared. Now she looks quite nice, especially her hair. Somehow I connect bad-looking hair with tumors. I looked in the mirror, and I do look poorly. My hair seems so lifeless. Several times yesterday I felt my abdomen, and I thought I could feel a great big lump. But it disappeared. It was my bladder, I guess, that must have been full and taut. Miriam was supposed to visit today. In the past couple of days, I've had to urinate frequently. I wonder if it has anything to do with competition. I think of my sisters and how I used to be so jealous of them. Miriam's health is generally good while mine isn't. My son Richard's cough kept him up all night.

I arrived here early today and noticed the fellow who came out, the one who has the hour before me. I guess I'm jealous of all the people who come here. I want to beat them all at being the best patient. Now I feel full and have a great urge to urinate just like the time I had kidney trouble.

There must be something terribly wrong with me. I can't get along with Miriam or with my sisters. My parents thought it was awful that we couldn't get along; we were the biggest fighters. How angry that book incident with Miriam made me feel! I'll wait till I die before I ask her for that book. I recall saying, "You stinker" after learning she had it. I thought of telling her that I've been a babysitter for her a number of times and she hasn't returned the favor. Yet she calls me ungenerous. I remember mother saying there were so many things I didn't do to help her out and that she might die of overwork. She also kept warning me that my temper and rambunctiousness would be the death of her. That's troubled me on and off ever since.

4   Some of my other friends haven't been to see me for some time. It annoys me to have them think of me as a burden. I don't think I ask very much of them. I do have something to contribute to these relationships. They enjoy talking with me about academic subjects as well as home things. But I can't visit them now because of the attention my children need from me. Clara said she wouldn't come to see me because I don't visit her. She made an unreasonable demand that I come over, spend the night with her, and just leave my husband and kids. If that's a sign that I'm interested in our friendship, that's too much. I remember my sisters asked all sorts of favors of me which they never repaid. I keep thinking of Miriam's reluctance to loan me that book. She's funny about money and other things too. Why shouldn't she loan me the book? I continue to do things for her and others. I try awfully hard in here, but is it appreciated? What do I get in return?

5   My husband, Steve, is still sending out applications for jobs to different universities. He has one firm offer so far. We just can't seem to regulate our sex life. He's so passive, and I just don't get any satisfaction in sex, especially after we disagree about so many things. I guess I'm envious of him—that he's got the degree and I haven't.

2/19

1   My friend, Elsie, tells me she's changing from psychotherapy to analysis and how much she likes her doctor. She has nothing but good things to say about him, and that's quite different from the way I feel in here. I guess you could call it a mixed reaction; sometimes more positive, often not.

2   John, a fellow student, helped me to review some work in preparation for the general exams. It's the way I answer questions, not what I really know, that makes me flunk. I get so anxious, such stage fright! Then I can't think straight.

3   I had two dreams: In the first, Steve is talking to John who is trying to decide about having an affair with a girl they both know. Steve is telling him not to. The girl calls Steve by another name, Juan, and seduces him. He has the affair with her and then leaves, uninterested in her even though she's pregnant. All he seems to be interested in are his books and his research. I call him Don Juan and he doesn't like it. That girl looked a little like me. How I'm preoccupied with being left! In the second dream I'm at a formal gathering at my mother-in-law's. There is an older man, a doctor, it must be you, though I don't recognize you. I want to impress this man with my charm. A little girl wants to march around with me. I say, "No. Little girls should march with little boys. I'm grown up." I

then go upstairs to change into a formal, two-piece gown with bare midriff. My sister helps, but I can't seem to hide the scar that's there.

The dreams are typical of what I've been talking about yesterday and today. Yesterday Steve asked, "What is that delicious dinner I smell?" I felt I was being flattered in an unreal way. I was tired and irritable and thought he was pulling my leg. The dream is stupid because it's so far from the way Steve acts with girls. He's not interested in them. I sometimes suspect him of just not liking people. I feel so childish at times, worrying about my health. My friend Germaine said it took her a year to recover from her operation. Still, some people say I'm looking well.

You probably answer questions for other patients, but not for me. I'd like to 4 ask you about an offer of a fellowship that I'm not decided about, but I won't be told what to do. Other offers are available also, I understand. How light-hearted my friend Elsie is about her treatment! Here I'm worried about things not coming out in mine. Part of it is in speaking—just as in an exam: something restrains me. Elsie always says what's on top of her mind. I feel constrained, tight. I'm bitter about people who are able to speak fluently but know less than I do. I have a headache now and am feeling kind of blocked. I have a feeling of frustration at not being able to hide that scar in the dream—it's like hiding my inadequate knowledge in the exam. Things fly out of my mind under pressure and then I have trouble talking. I get these shut-down feelings not only here but also in exams. When I talk with people, I tend to feel uninvolved. My talk in here is mostly about other people, not about myself. ["You are greatly concerned about how to avoid exposing your physical and emotional problems which you see as defects. If you don't think, and don't talk, you don't expose yourself, but then there is the danger of failing. So a compromise is to go through the motions. In here you try to associate, but these interferences cause you to block and the associations become scattered."]

2/23

I feel uneasy. I'm so mad at Professor X and his son Fred. When Fred heard 1 me take off on his father, he seemed quite troubled, yet he offered to babysit whenever we needed someone. Now he's the last person I'd want. I don't like his leaving his girl, throwing her over when she was so much in love with him. I think there's something amoral about him. He lies about his research. For that matter you can't be sure of anything he says. This kind of behavior is what my father showed: he was a liar and a philanderer. Fred surprised me when he said he wanted to study with me. I feel he knows more than I do. He has a need to know everything awfully well. But I think he wants to find out what I know and not tell me what he knows. Yet he's told me a few answers to tricky questions we might expect in the exams. One of them was wrong, so again I'm leary of working with him.

2   I keep thinking of myself as a person who gets things wrong. Shall I concentrate on the exam and neglect my other work, then make it up later? I think I may misjudge people at times. Yet I know Fred and my father are both liars. Fred—that poor son-of-a-gun—he's got lots of personal problems. How's he going to get a job? Do I need to torture him? He's tortured enough. Why do I have such thoughts?

3   I keep thinking of my operation—the defects—the scars. But things with my husband Steve seem better recently. He isn't interfering or criticizing me so much when I have something to say. Joan, a fellow student, was at our seminar yesterday with her thumb bandaged up. One of the other girls related a dream about a psychology teacher who hit her thumb with a hammer. I pointed out Joan's thumb. Later in referring to a psychology teaching assistant who seems to have sex on his mind, I said, "Thumb teacher"—and tried to pass it off as a joke. ["Thumb teacher?"] Someone concerned with penises. It's embarrassing in that sense. I'm afraid that he wants to cut people down like I do. When I talk about Fred, I guess that's what I want to do to him.

4   When Steve kidded me yesterday about his being attracted to another woman I had the thought: I'm not dead yet. But I have these fears of cancer. I know somebody who's dying of cancer. Steve's aunt has cancer. Professor Y had a slow death from cancer, but his mother succumbed in two weeks from it. It runs in families. I think of various sore spots in my body. I remember the sore throats and hoarseness I had last year. Those are the symptoms Steve's aunt is suffering from. Some years ago I had a little mole under my right arm which swelled up and dropped off. I was told by a doctor then that the danger was over, but that mole could have become cancerous.

5   I keep thinking that I can't be or don't dare to be at all aggressive as a true female, but I don't feel sure about that. Another thing I'm not sure of is whether my husband cares for me or not. It's unusual for me to feel like a wanted wife. Well, when I think of myself as defective and not wanted, I try to fight it, but I can't seem to win. It's hard to forget I've had previous operations and have been left with real scars and that real parts of me have been cut out.

2/24

1   I've had sexual thoughts coming in here. When I looked at you, I remembered a time when I felt I was flirtatious toward you. Was I trying to get control over you?

2   I have an appointment to see this man about the fellowship. What's the best way to get the job? Should I play up or play down the way I look? Should I look plain or fancy? He sounded nice on the telephone, though Miriam said she doesn't like him. I don't always agree with Miriam. That's an understatement.

3   I dreamt of my former husband's best friend to whom I had an attraction but felt he detested me. In the dream he comes to visit me because of my cancer.

In reality he wouldn't come, doesn't like me. In the dream he's coming to Boston to get a medical checkup at the Lahey Clinic, near Dr. R's office (her surgeon). He asks me subtly if I'm going to the Clinic. It appears to be a way of finding out if I'm dying or not dying. In the other dream I'm very irritated with my son, Rick, who seems to want so much. Actually he's settled down some since his grandmother (patient's mother-in-law) left. When I awoke after that dream I was astonished that I had such aggression, when I don't really feel it toward my sons. There seems to be a split in my personality.

Last week I went to lunch at the school cafeteria and Prof. M was there. I sat next to him and introduced myself in a low voice, but he heard me. He looked at me through great big, thick glasses; his eyes were so big. Betty, another graduate student, came over. She's a floozy. I saw her 3 to 4 years ago when she did a sexy dance at a party. I was amazed at her abandon. I first saw her again at this luncheon. She did a lot of talking to Prof. M very dramatically. I was envying her this facility. I was thinking of my upcoming exam, wishing I could formulate things so people could understand me. When I told Prof. M I was looking for some academic work, he was apologetic and said his funds had not come in yet. I then said I wasn't definite either. ["There are two types of girl in you: one is quiet and reserved, the other is bold and angry."] To tell you the truth I'm not happy with either. I feel Betty's behavior is not quite in good taste. She has robustness, but she isn't a big girl. I find her brash sexiness frightening and feel she would frighten others. They wouldn't want to be friendly with her. **4**

My favorite aunt used to warn me that I shouldn't tell my husband about my previous sexual life, especially about my experiences when I was a teenager. She said he wouldn't understand. I never told Steve. I never intend to. ["Haven't you also been reluctant and frightened to talk about sexual fantasies here?"] I feel a buzzing in my ear. My sexual fantasies are not in good control. I'm afraid they'll come out when I don't want them to. In here especially I have to force myself to talk. [Reassurance.] It's alright for men to be abandoned, sexy, but not for women. I've had the fantasy of having an affair with you without anyone knowing about it. I never get close to Steve or touch him unless I'm going to have sexual intercourse; it's almost like a formality. With my last boyfriend I was very easily aroused sexually, but he was no good for me in every other way. He was absolutely neglectful. We had no future together. **5**

2/25

I keep thinking of my body. It's difficult to get on the couch the way I used to. I can't get on from the bottom. I would have to pull myself up, and it would be a strain on my abdomen. Last night it hurt all over. I decided to follow your advice to call Dr. R, and I made an appointment to be checked over by him in a few days, even though my dread of what he would find makes me reluctant to see him. I feel especially crummy today. I'm going for that interview about the **1** fellowship, but I feel unlucky. I've been sniping away at Steve because I've been so irritable. I finally studied with Fred last night. He seems to know a lot, but he talks all the time. I recognized I was going to be competitive, trying to catch him, but he knew too much and I grew more admiring and envious of his ability.

2   About the analysis, I feel as if I don't want to continue. I enjoyed my three-day holiday last week. Yesterday I discussed sex here—maybe that's why I think of vacations. I want to get away. That competition with Fred got me tense, and I noticed that my urination became more frequent. It makes me angry that he knows so much. Yet, when it comes to reducing—he's overweight—he's a fake; he needs to eat and eat. [Anger is defensive.] Oh, well, it doesn't make any difference. I'm going to die anyway. Last night I thought I had lumps in my bladder that were making me urinate so often. I thought of my abdominal scar and wondered if I had another lump there.

3   I often feel you're trying to stop me from criticizing people. Well, I don't really believe that. It came out of nowhere. ["Nowhere?"] It seems that you're trying to make me think I'm more defective. Well, actually I'm concentrating on my scar, which is a symbol of my defectiveness. It's just that I feel I'm bad. You must think so—you must make judgments. I feel gloomy. It's the wrong day to look for a job. I can't cover my inadequacies. It's the tension of the job interview. I guess I'm even uncertain whether I want it or not. I get terribly anxious when I don't know everything by heart. [Needs to be perfect.]

2/26

1   [Much throat clearing.]

When I do this I'm reminded of my husband's aunt who has throat cancer.

2   All I can think of are my ailments. There's certainly something wrong with me. I have to urinate all the time. My bladder is so big and hard. Besides that my feet swell up. Maybe it's some kind of poisoning. I think there's something wrong with my urinary system. However, my feet have been swelling for years—so that's nothing new. And I've had to go to the toilet frequently when I've been nervous—so that also is nothing new. Last night when I went to see Fred to review some questions with him, my legs felt sore. I spent an uncomfortable night, feeling that soreness in my legs and in my bladder. Maybe it's all nerves. I'm so competitive, wanting to get the highest possible marks in the exams, trying to get that job. But, at the same time, I have the conviction there's something wrong physiologically. The job I inquired about has to do with people in crisis, like diabetics. I may have diabetes. I drink a lot of water. The job wasn't a very exciting one. I don't need the fellowship to teach me how to do research. I met Thelma when I was on my way to the job interview. She's had a divorce; she's a bold, forward type of girl. I remember once at a party her trying to get this fellow we both knew to dance with her instead of with me. She

seemed quite disturbed to me. When she saw me, she asked if I were making the trip to the hospital for treatment. I said no. She said she was being analyzed by one of the doctors there and was tired of going to the same old place every day for so many months.

I find myself very undecided about getting a job. My aches and pains are in my mind so much. I keep thinking I won't have enough energy. I'm going to see Dr. R today for that physical checkup. It seems no sooner is one crisis over than I'm involved in another. After I had the interview about the job, I felt a great release of tension. I bought some flowers and felt quite happy, but it lasted only a short time. ["That test is over with, without your having failed, but a bigger one is at hand."] Still I'm not sure about getting the job. If I give them my curriculum vitae, I somehow feel they'll find out my shortcomings. But I think my professors will give me a good recommendation [sneezes]. These special exams I'm to take are a screening device to see if I'm really involved in physics. I keep wondering whether I am. That's another big, big test.   3

I feel tension all over—from the tension in my bladder. It makes my stomach puff up. What I seem to be concentrating on is that my parts are running down, giving out. Here I am, hardly 35 and I feel my body's giving out. I compare myself with my old car which has had so many troubles and breakdowns. I'm different, though. I've got a mind, but my car hasn't. So what good does it do to take things out or fix them mechanically, if my mind continues to be upset. I wonder if analysis makes the process of growing things in yourself much more rapid, stimulating it. ["Analysis tries to undo the repression which causes the conflicts to operate harmfully."]   4

Mother was always complaining of having tumors within her—tumors as big as an orange. It makes me think of fruit of the womb instead of fruit of the loom. She used to take various douches, mashing up red stuff in water. I had to help her put it into herself when I was a youngster. It was awful, her making me do that. I don't know if it was medication of some kind or birth control. At the time, I wasn't clear where it was going, maybe her anus because that's where she would give me the enemas, although I didn't get many. I kept thinking that she had a tumor somewhere low in the abdomen. But nobody else believed she had it. However, one thing she did have was a hernia. It was impossible not to notice that. She always had it, sticking out like a big, big lump. I was told that one of my aunts wore some things to reduce her own hernia, but my mother didn't wear them. She often complained of shortness of breath because of the hernia. She was also supposed to have heart trouble and tuberculosis, though people didn't believe she was sick from these illnesses.   5

2/27

Did Dr. R call you? ["Yes."] [The surgeon was pessimistic in his estimate of the patient's physical state, bringing up the possibility of metastases to the   1 posterior pituitary from a malignant ovarian tumor. An exploratory laparotomy is to be done.]

I'm exhausted. I didn't sleep well last night and had to take a sleeping pill. I've been feeling sore down below. The examination made me worse, I guess. I called my friend Lucy and told her about my condition. She came to visit me. I was so tired I could hardly talk to her and wished she'd go. I feel the same way now, as if I haven't got anything to say. I told Lucy that Dr. R wanted me to be hospitalized. My son Richard has had a bad night; he's had a cold for three weeks, with a bad cough. I called my pediatrician and told him also about my sickness. He thought I didn't have cancer. Dr. R seemed more pessimistic—maybe because he has to send me to the hospital. He told me, though, it might be a cyst on one of my ovaries. I think of the unpleasantness of having to go to the hospital. It's not so much whether the tumor is benign or malignant, but rather that I can't stand the operation. I have the fantasy of never waking up from it because I feel so weak. I remember the last one—waking up and seeing gloomy people around me. Steve's cousin died a couple of days ago; she had multiple sclerosis.

2   I just had the thought that you're disgusted with me. My husband yelled at me yesterday very angrily. I told him he was angry at me because I was sick again and had to have an operation. I called his mother about coming back. I felt she didn't want to return. I keep thinking I've got cancer. You must be disgusted with hearing the same dreadful expections. ["I am not disgusted with you. I know that this is a very difficult time for you."]

3   I must have had this thing for a while, though it's begun to bother me only in the last week or so. I have a tendency not to consult doctors. I'm afraid of what they'll find. But you know I went for my annual physical two months ago and was given a clean bill of health. Dr. R said he wanted to take out both ovaries, so I wouldn't have a recurrence. I protested that I didn't want to have to take pills and become masculinized and lose my sexual interest. Dr. R said there may be something else wrong: this business of drinking lots of water and the feet swelling. I'm thirsty all the time. I've been a heavy drinker of water in the last couple of years, but worse in the last few weeks. What's odd is that it stops—it did for a couple of days—this urinary frequency. My irritation and competition with Miriam and Fred seemed to bring it on. Anyway, the fact that I drink so much water—it has to come out. Also, my feet have been swelling on and off for many years. Somehow I associate the drinking with my tensions. I get a feeling of annoyance in restaurants because no waitress gives me enough water. I wonder if this need for water has a physiological basis. Ten years ago I had a kidney infection and had to force fluids for a long time because of the doctor's orders. Whenever I feel a slight irritation in the bladder I start drinking water again. I had a lot of guilt feelings about having that affair when I was in my teens. What was I trying to do? Buy attention with sex? Then I had to have an

abortion. What a terribly difficult time that was for me. It was a punishment for my sins. I wonder if that had anything to do with my urinary trouble.

I'm so tired that if it weren't for the operation, I'd be happy to go into the hospital and rest. I think of goofing off in my studies and in the analysis. But this morning I did quite a bit of reading for the exams and maybe this time I'll keep up what little I have in my head already. I have a sick feeling when I think of discussing that other ovary with Dr. R. Part of the gloom is that I'm preparing myself for the worst. Now that I've been told I may have a cyst, I'm afraid it'll burst. I have a tremendous amount of gas in my stomach now. There's nothing more miserable than gas after one of those operations. Everything they do to me makes something else worse in my body. A rectal examination makes me bleed. I can feel an irritation right there now. My rectum is too tender an institution. I have to put oil in to defecate.

3/2

Over the weekend I got worried about cancer again. I felt along the scar where Dr. R had examined me. I recalled his talking with his secretary behind a closed door and his gloomy face. I look at myself, and the moles on my body seem to be getting encrusted; that's a sign of cancer. My thoughts are muddled. I had a slight headache but it's going away. Either Dr. R did something about the pressure on my bladder or it's what he said, but anyway it's quieted down. My mother-in-law came back to take care of the kids. Now I have a better idea of what hurts. Dr. R said a cyst on the ovary could be pressing on my bladder. I guess urinating was an attempt to get rid of the pain by relieving the pressure.

My defects: I think of Steve knowing about my defects. Saturday night a practical joke of Steve's threw me into a gloomy state. He showed Fred a copy of a letter to Prof. B. In it Fred was described as having made slurring remarks about Prof. B, and these were attributed to Fred's alleged instability and drunkenness. It turned out to be a hoax. I thought: here I'm going into the hospital, and Steve is going nuts writing a letter like that. But the hoax isn't going to teach Fred to keep his mouth shut. Maybe Steve's getting ready to walk out on me and can't tell me directly. I don't learn anything unless I ask straight out what's going on. But I don't want to provoke Steve.

My children don't know yet about my going back into the hospital. They're both pleased to have their grandma return. I'm reading a book, *The Will to Live*, which I'll take to the hospital with me. Why don't I have such a strong urge to live as some people do? This is a failing which could keep me from conquering my illness. I don't want to lose that second ovary. One of my friends was saying I'd have to resign myself to having tumors. Maybe they've been causing the maladjustments of my sex life. I thought it was getting better, and now all my libido is residing in this tumor. Do I have to have it out? I must go on living for the sake of my children.

3/3

1   I'm still around. Maybe I won't have to go to the hospital; that fantasy makes me feel better. I remember a dream fragment about traveling to London where I felt very lonely and had to find people whom I could visit. It reminds me of actually being in London some years ago. Steve wanted to stay and visit people on business, but I expected we'd have a miserable time. I asked, "Why couldn't we just pass through?" Actually we did stay two days at a friend's house and that turned out to be quite enjoyable. Last night Steve took me and his mother out to dinner, and then we went to a movie—about van Gogh. His loneliness and his great needs were very frightening to me. I have these contradictory feelings about my friends. I want them all to come and see me, but then I feel the opposite way. I want to be self-sufficient and not catered to by anybody. Prof. X, the head of my department, has been notified about my illness, according to Fred. Mrs. X called to inquire how I was. Meanwhile I keep thinking I have to pass those exams. This doesn't seem to be the time to get chummy with Mrs. X, yet we have some things in common. I told her that the exact nature of the condition wasn't known yet. She offered to take care of the kids and help out my mother-in-law. All this trouble she'd go to for me, and I hardly know her. My mother-in-law was very enthusiastic and invited her over for tea.

2   I have a conflict about my thesis. If I quit, the conflict isn't solved. My own husband said I really didn't want an advanced degree. Yet the graduate studies have broadened my outlook. Can I also be a good mother and wife?

3   My illness is a way of getting attention. Yet I really don't want to be sick. There's a certain freedom in not caring about living or dying. How I envy those people who have it.

4   The advanced degree seems an insoluble problem. It involves missing the pleasures of the children. Yet when they grow up, I want to have other interests. How could I solve things by not getting the degree? The kids wouldn't be enough. I could take courses and piddle around, but how happy would I be with purposeless activity? It would be like an act. The advanced degree means I am somebody. This is what I can do—a specialty. If I can't do that, what am I? All my life I've been a bookworm, always liked intellectual things. After this operation, will it mean I can't have any more sex life? That would be a death blow to my instinct for being more feminine. Are my children better off, if I'm not building my life around them? Maybe it's all rationalization.

5   I told my mother-in-law I don't feel tired now that I know I can rest some. I feel I need a breather from responsibility. My illness is a way of escaping from

responsibilities, from my children, from finishing the requirements for my degree. Well, I'm going to complete the requirements; but after I get my degree, I'll still have a conflict about whether to get a job or not.

The tumor—it feels like I'm pregnant. I remember when I was 18, I was **6** pregnant but didn't know it at first. I had the same sensation of fullness in the abdomen.

I think of fear, yet I have a lot of control over myself and believe I can make **7** myself feel the way I want to. I have been working on the requirements for the degree with as much energy as I can. I spend some time with the children. Then when I work on the degree, it seems more legitimate to cut off my contact with the children. I feel angry, though, that I have all this work to do. My conflicts appear as insoluble at times. Will I be a despised type of woman or a successful, aggressive, achieving kind of person?

3/4

My terrible temper forced my mother-in-law to go to a lecture with Miriam **1** who was visiting with us. I had a nasty feeling about Miriam's coming and then staying on for dinner at her convenience. I felt depressed about being so aggressive. Miriam is so selfish and domineering, you have to be blunt with her. Words I regretted popped out of me before I could control myself. I act like a disciplinarian. I didn't get along with Miriam in college, but I thought I was getting to tolerate her a little more, even though she still reminds me so much of my next older sister.

I had a dream: I was looking at a map, some place down South. The state of **2** Texas had to be reduced in size to get it on the map. I said to Steve, "Why don't we go where it's sunny and warm?" I thought he'd refuse but he agreed. On awakening, a line from Poe occurred to me. "Quoth the raven never more." The raven is a symbol of death. I keep thinking of my prospective operation. I called Dr. R's office about the arrangements for hospitalization. They're so slow. I'm afraid if I don't go tomorrow it'll be the weekend again. I can't put my whole mind on my work with this hanging over me. There are lots of things my mother-in-law wants me to tell her about so she can take care of things when I'm away. But I have little patience for that.

Then there's my dilemma about the degree. I'm reminded of the dilemma I **3** had about my parents: how badly I felt as a child about them. Full of guilt. I had the thought I'll never be able to make up for hating my parents so much. A feeling of criminality is associated with this hatred. My temper bursting out as it did still seems criminal. I remember having such violent and uncontrolled behavior as a youngster. My rationalization then was that, if I acted this way, mother would stop trying to dominate me. Now I feel easily criticized by my mother-in-law. Does Steve think I should die and get it over with since I'm so chopped up? I just want to hold on until the children grow up. Steve doesn't say he cares for me though he makes certain gestures that he does. My father showed so little affection toward us. I feel very bad about this dilemma of what I should do—live or die? Steve's the person I have to live with—and my children. Regardless of what he thinks of me, I should stay alive for the children. I feel that I would be punishing him by staying alive, if indeed he prefers that I die. He probably doesn't know what he wants. Steve is so emotionally unstable; it makes him terribly nervous to have people just stand and talk with him. I'm concerned about how he'd manage if I wasn't around. Why, just the other day he lost his address book and felt helpless until I found it. If there weren't the kids to look after, I'd have no good reason to remain alive. I resent Steve's mother looking after them while I'm in the hospital. For the sake of the kids and because there are certain things of the mind I enjoy; I want to stay alive.

Hospitalization and convalescence of three and one-half weeks. Bilateral salpingo-oophorectomy performed. Right ovary: moderately large cyst with a few suspicious areas suggestive of earliest carcinomatous change found on microscopic section. Left ovary: several small cysts, benign.

3/29

1   The third night after the operation, I couldn't fall asleep; thoughts kept crowding into my head. I seemed to be repeating my A, B, C's in my sleep and that would wake me up. My mother-in-law had told me she didn't know whether her ovaries were removed when she had her uterus out. On this particular night I kept thinking for some reason that ovaries are not connected with the uterus. Dr. R took out the tubes as well as the ovaries. I feel depressed, like weeping, like before my other operation, when I thought I would never come out of it. That feeling has only recently begun to let up. My thoughts have been mostly about being cut to pieces, and about unnecessary and exaggerated cruelties being inflicted in hospitals.

2   Several days before I left the hospital, Dr. R had been in. My intestinal muscles hadn't been working well, so I had to defecate frequently, but not much at a time. He said I had to have a rectal exam. The first time I accepted it. The next day he came in and found a hot water bottle on me. I said I had gas. He said he had to examine me internally. He gave me a vaginal. I said, "O.K., but I don't like the rectal exam." He insisted that I had to have another rectal. It exhausted and hurt me. I've always been sensitive there, from way back when mother gave me those damn enemas. Then, when he changed bandages, the pubic hair was growing back so that when he pulled the adhesive off the hair he almost killed me. He looked annoyed at my reaction. The next day he was exaggeratedly kind.

3   The night before the operation I got two sleeping pills, but I had read an article that you can't lose both ovaries and keep your youth and vitality. I

couldn't sleep. I felt I hadn't emphasized to Dr. R that I didn't want the other ovary removed. I got up and the nurse wrote such a note for me. I also went and telephoned him. He reassured me that he wouldn't take it out unless it was diseased. Then an intern later said I didn't need the other ovary. Such talk—such philosophy alarmed me. What a state to be in before an operation!

The cruelties come really when you can't help yourself. Several people tried **4** to punch my veins and couldn't do it in one arm, so they worked on the other. This happened while I was drugged and couldn't protect myself. I told off the girl who kept punching me in the arm with a needle. I told her off—that she wasn't the best one for intravenous work. There was a sadistic night nurse who insisted on giving me an enema right after a castor oil movement. Then there was this old woman who couldn't help herself and the nurses picked on her particularly. A practical nurse came in one night when I had a coughing fit and simply turned off my light and left. When you get better, then nobody appears even this way any more. I'm still quite leary of Dr. R. I finally asked him what was the purpose of the rectal exam. He said he wanted to see how the healing was coming along.

Two days after the operation seemed the worst. I went to pieces, couldn't do **5** anything for myself, felt there wasn't anyone to do anything for me. Dr. R said there weren't enough nurses. He gave me tranquilizers which I thought was hardly a way to solve the nursing shortage. They made me feel depressed. Interestingly, the nursing shortage didn't occur again. It was just when I needed them most that I felt it wasn't the shortage but the cruelty of the nurses.

I feel angry toward Prof. X. He had recommended Steve for a university **6** appointment, but with reservations. That's no good, because I don't think Steve will get the job with such a recommendation.

I've been studying because otherwise I'll just sleep all the time. I seem to **7** have made some progress in my preparations for the exam.

My affection for Steve has grown. His inability to get a job makes me feel **8** terrible. When he finally got the letter from the university turning him down for the appointment, I was upset because of what I'd heard about Prof. X's doing. I told Steve part of the story. Later I told his mother about it. She lectured me about not standing up for him and that got me angry.

3/30

I read the newspaper account of the kidnapping of Mrs. E in Africa. She's **1** the wife of the colonial administrator who was killed by bandits. He was hated, a fellow who thought he knew what was best for everybody and never took advice. I had some personal contacts with him once when he was in the United States and found him mighty unpleasant. He got what he deserved.

My thoughts turn to my own inferiority feelings, to my troubles. So many **2** people are sympathetic. I have other thoughts: about victims and being a victim.

I read the book, *Compulsion*—about Leopold and Loeb. There is some reason why these families became victims of tragedy. I think of the arrogance and infinite superiority of Mr. E, which led people to wish something bad would happen to him. Now it's happened. I have my own fears that even worse things would happen to me. If I let myself think farther in this way, it will happen. I keep having thoughts that people are not listening to me, especially at the hospital. I have so many things wrong that if I mention more I wouldn't be believed. The idea of not being listened to comes from the idea that I'm not saying anything worthwhile, that I'm boring. ["Did you get the impression that I was bored, not listening, because I didn't say much?"] I'm not sure. But I equate my hospital experience with being captured by bandits. I have this terrible feeling of inferiority. Now I remember again how much I've devaluated my father. It's my punishment now for having had such thoughts about him.

3/31

1   I decided to look and see who the artist is in the picture on the wall of the waiting room. There was a sale of prints at the college store, and I bought one by an artist with that name.

2   I'm not feeling very well. I have a headache, my neck is sore, and I feel sick to my stomach. It's been happening the last three days, late in the afternoon. Am I having any symptoms as a result of the operation? I wonder if I'm getting hot flashes, because I notice I'm warmer than usual. I'm afraid I'll age as a result of the operation. I looked at myself carefully in the mirror, and I look unhealthy. My mother-in-law had an upset stomach a few days ago, and I might have caught something from her. I wrote a letter about not being entitled to indefinite sick leave from my position as graduate assistant, but that I needed the money badly and would like to make up the time I have to miss now by working during the summer term. I keep having these critical thoughts about Prof. X who'll have a lot to say about this. I think he's effeminate; even his wife says so, but then she's so masculine herself. I keep thinking of these awfully hostile thoughts that make me feel guilty. Then I feel I need to be punished.

3   I'm so angry at Miriam; she could help me get a job and hasn't done so. That's really a distortion; she's actually helped me. I have the fantasy that she favors young, good-looking men whom she might meet at a party, but me she doesn't get a job. My feelings of inferiority lead to my talking down other people. I think of myself as a hated person. My arrogant thought: people should get me a job whether they want to or not. Prof. X is not coming to see me. He doesn't like my mother-in-law. This annoys me further. I want to bat him on the head. I wish I didn't have such hostile thoughts.

4   I think of workmen digging into the street to get at a gas main. They dug a hole as big as the couch. They kept digging, digging as if into my insides. What would you do if I can't pay you? But I don't anticipate this, though.

The urinating isn't so frequent any more. It was the tumor squeezing on my bladder. The idea of giving up analysis occurred because it didn't help my symptoms. But Fred said I was one of the few people improved by analysis. That made me feel like laughing. I really don't feel hostile to analysis. I'd like to continue it for many years if I had the money. I have no desire to work now, though. Well, I do have hostility to analysis. It's driving me to work which I don't want to do. I want a lot of things: analysis, my children to go to a private school, time for leisure. But when I think of what an angry person I am, I feel I don't deserve to have these things.

4/3

I'm jealous of my son Rick's calling out for his grandmother—not me—in his sleep. My thoughts are muddled. If I go into the exams that way, they'll jump on me. Fred's a competitor of mine in the exams, so there are no holds barred between us. On the one hand, I'm afraid of the analysis not being over, yet also wanting to go on for five years because I think I need the support. I'm feeling angry toward my mother-in-law for going away on the weekend to visit some of her other relatives.

I really feel I haven't got anything to say. I've been picking up books for the exams in the library. I got a cold but continued in spite of it. I don't want to sit and do nothing; neither do I want to sit and think. I go over and over the material I'm preparing for my exam. I feel guilty for having those bitter thoughts about Mrs. E. now. She was neither pretty nor sexual. I wonder if the dead are aware of hostility. Mother used to warn me about mean deeds or criticism of her—that I'd be sorry for them. Rationally, I don't think there's particular harm in bad thoughts. Neurotically, I see the cold I'm getting as more punishment for having had such thoughts. Generally, except for the cold, I feel somewhat free from physical ailments, now that these terrible tumors are out. Yet I keep thinking the cancer might pop up somewhere else. I've often had the fantasy that I'm going to die from cancer, and Dr. R won't tell me anything definite. I heard there's a rumor around that I had gone back into the hospital because of a recurrence of cancer.

My husband Steve has been terribly grouchy. Yesterday I was thinking: to hell with him. He just doesn't talk much. I need to talk to somebody. When Fred came over, even though he talked a blue streak, I felt relieved. Steve is angry about my operations. It's as if I'm not a person any more. I sometimes think I'm trying to neutralize myself into something neither male nor female. You haven't had any operations, but there's a psychiatrist, I hear, who is a eunuch and impotent. He's become a prominent person despite this, but I tend to belittle him as I do myself. Those fears that I'll get real old quickly still bother me. I'm worried about taking hormones, but Dr. R didn't give me any, saying to wait and see what symptoms I may get. I've been feeling very hot suddenly during the night, then feeling very cold again. I believe my mother-in-law is going through a late menopause; she complains of hot flashes.

4   I have the dilemma, as I had before hospitalization. Am I going to have a cancer or not? Will I be more like a man now?

5   I hear you moving around. I'm angry that you're restless. It's as if you're accusing me of not saying anything worthwhile. I can't help it.

4/4

1   I still feel blocked. My head is stuffed up. I'm slightly off my feet. I seem to react to everything physically. I envy the good health of other women. I'm irritated with all the material things being brought into the house that can't be used. My mother-in-law and Steve bring such things in.

2   I suppose anger at you could block me. I hate to mention it. When I was in the hospital, I hoped you would see me before the operation and you didn't come. I was left on my own about the other ovary, and panicky. I guess I thought you were going to protect me from Dr. R; I thought I should take matters into my own hands which I finally did. But I should have notified you that I had gone into the hospital and would be operated on the next morning. This I failed to do.

3   I still feel blocked. I think of Steve's long silences.

4   My lop-sided figure, my defects, my operations, preoccupy me. My defective memory, maybe it's a fungus growing in my brain. All the antibiotics I've had, and my memory being cloudy, make me have that fantasy. It's typical of my family to be foggy and crazy in their thinking. Maybe the effects of drugs continue long afterward, making things hazy.

4/5

    My cold continues, but it's getting better.

1   I had a startling dream. It indicates tremendous passion which I must be blocking. There's a long street, has two rows of trees, far apart, with a greensward. Toward the end is a row of houses. Wounded people are lined up. I'm one, though I'm looking at these people. There are Russian Cossacks on horses. One sees me and puts his horse's hoof in the middle of my stomach, making a hole. Someone is trying to sew me up and I have a look of infinite patience. I recall feeling as if I'd been run over by a train after my operation. Then, in the dream, I'm changed. I'm a young girl unemotionally observing myself and others. I'm in a two-level house. The first floor is the basement with a big door, the garage door. These Russians ride right into the basement and say they're going to take all the things. The girl, who is clever, says, "Go ahead and take them." So they leave only one man, the one who thrust his horse's hoof at

me. As he climbs on some boxes, the girl—I, murder him. Then I run and find a Cossack chieftain, saying a terrible accident happened to this fellow, and the explanation is accepted.

I'm reminded of an Ojibway Indian with a stubborn lack of emotional expression, like the girl in the dream who shows no emotions but has terrible anger inside. I realize now how the operations aroused my hatred; I'm astonished that I could have so much hate that I would murder somebody. It's nutty, psychotic.

I used to be deceitful when my mother would give me laxatives, pretend I'd take them. My mother-in-law is deceitful in telling me I'm cute, attractive, smart, etc. I'm worried that the dream means that I'm so mad at all men that I could commit murder. The trouble is that I don't feel angry. I just know I am, from the dream. It's as if my sex has been taken from me by a brutal man, something I've always been afraid of. In the dream another person who got stepped on by the horse was my mother. I remember she used to complain all the time about hurting and being sick. Mother used to sleep a lot because she felt so tired all the time.

I'm conscious so much of the time that I've got defects: a sore in my nose right away makes me think of possible cancer. I keep feeling my scars; they feel tight and sore. I thought this morning of saying to Dr. R, "How will I know if the cancer is back?" I keep looking at myself now, though I never did before. I have fantasies of having had this ovarian tumor many years before. I keep wondering if my intestines are healthy, if there are any more tumors there. I've recently been constipated.

I'm astonished that I still have fears of analysis. They're the fears of talking about murder and murderers.

Last night I began to think of intercourse, but decided to wait for one month after the operation. I keep thinking of Steve's excited little boyish appearance after so much abstinence.

On awakening from the dream last night, I was aware of emotions stirring in me. In the dream the person lying down [on the couch] showed no emotion at all about what was going on, and I wondered how that could be. On awakening, I had a sense of fear that I would have to tell you about the dream. ["What about the girl who showed no emotion?"] It must be I and I must be afraid of you. ["Must?"] Yes. I still don't really feel it. I have background fear. I know somehow I have it. ["The forces of repression make these attitudes and thoughts sound strange."] I can't see why I should want to murder you—or even some casual person on the street. But that, of course, is a rational point of view. ["In first consideration these thoughts about me may seem strange, but there is a concealed meaning involving infantile needs and wishes."] I guess I consider these murderous thoughts as actions—which they're really not.

Brief followup:

The patient's convalescence was slow but without physical sequelae. She was able to successfully complete the requirements for her advanced degree. Her analysis continued for several years more with significant modification of her neurosis and no recurrence of tumors or any major physical illness.

MARGINAL NOTES

2/18

1. Hypersensitivity evokes hostility to a teasing, selfish sister-figure. Somatic dysfunction linked with femininity. Recurrence of physical manifestation of tension. Expectation of the worst. Preoccupation with physical integrity. Intellectualization.
2. Sibling rivalry associated with interoceptive percepts.
3. More bodily concern. Recollections of sibling rivalry and hostility. Mother's accusations and warnings. Superego aspects.
4. References to rejection and denial of dependency. Justification for attitudes. Unrewarded generosity and goodness. Transference implications.
5. Coexistent devaluation of husband and penis envy.

2/19

1. Ambivalent transference.
2. Exhibitionistic anxiety.
3. First dream: devaluation and teasing of husband; masochistic associations of abandonment. Second dream: incestuous transference aspects, denial of infantile tendencies, need to hide physical defects.
4. Hostile and anxious aspects of the transference. Blocking linked with somatic dysfunction. Fear of exposure of inadequacies. Pseudocompliance. Interpretation.

2/23

1. Hostility toward men linked with mistreatment of women: an aspect of father-daughter relationship. Distrust.
2. Self-doubts, guilt.
3. Associations about castration.
4. Concern about husband's infidelity linked with fears of having cancer. Somatic identification.
5. Inhibition of hostility. Uncertainty about husband's love linked with anticipation of rejection because of bodily defect. Reinforcement of fears because of previous surgical intervention.

2/24

1. Transference: erotic and controlling aspects.
2. Anxiety and indecision about job interview.
3. First dream: secondary gain from physical illness; preoccupation with death. Second dream: hostility toward demanding child (self); guilt.
4. Rivalry with sexy sister-figure; envy and devaluation. Uncertainty about feminine role: demure or bold. Transference implications.
5. Maternal warning about keeping sexual secrets. Interpretation of transference aspects followed by tinnitus. Fear of losing control over sexual impulses; guilt. Incestuous transference fantasies. Mechanical versus exciting (masochistic) sexuality.

2/25

1. Anxious preoccupation with bodily integrity, especially abdomen. Concomitant anticipatory anxiety about job interview. Competitiveness with and envy of men.
2. Transference resistance. Defenses of avoidance, intellectualization, and devaluation. Expectation of the worst. Self-diagnosis and localization of physical dysfunction.
3. Projective tendencies in the transference. Self-devaluation. Defensive perfectionism.

2/26

1. Somatic identification.
2. Continued preoccupation with physical symptoms. Attempts at self-reassurance. Rationalizations unconvincing. Somatic identification. Defensive downplaying of job and devaluation of sibling figure.
3. Ambivalence. Successive crises. Concern about being exposed as defective physically or mentally.
4. Interoceptive percepts. Sense of progressive bodily deterioration. Intellectualization. Projective tendencies. Clarification.
5. Critical somatic identification.

2/27

1. Increased secondary anxiety and preoccupation with body, reinforced by surgeon's pessimism (realistic). Focus on operative procedures, their highly unpleasant, real, and symbolic significance. Preoccupation with death.
2. Marked expectancy of rejection. Reassurance.
3. Avoidance. Further loss of body parts and of femininity anticipated. Attempts at intellectualization and rationalization. Oral elements. Recollection of genitourinary infection linked with guilt over sexual experiences during adolescence.

4. Exhaustion, probably a somatic manifestation of underlying depression. Compensatory activity. Interoceptive percepts.

3/2

1. Secondary reinforcement of anxiety about bodily integrity. Remission of some physical symptoms.
2. Concern over husband's trickiness and possible rejection.
3. Rumination about seeming insufficiency of self-preservative instincts. Intellectualization about physical state. Intensified narcissism. Children as motivating forces for living.

3/3

1. Self-reassurance. Fear of loneliness. Conflict between dependency and self-sufficiency. Ambivalence about maternal figures.
2. Conflict between career and femininity.
3. Secondary gain. Envy of those who use massive denial.
4. Ph.D. a proof of adequacy, a masculine symbol. Concern about possible loss of libido and femininity. Intellectualization.
5. Further reference to secondary gain from physical illness.
6. Tumor linked with pregnancy.
7. Further conflict between femininity and masculinity.

3/4

1. Outburst of hostile affect. Guilt. Superego aspects. Sibling rivalry.
2. Dream: wishful escape to happier surroundings. Preoccupation with fatal outcome of surgery. Interfering anxiety.
3. Conflict over identity. Recollection of violent hostility toward parents, linked with intense guilt. Defiance rationalized as a means toward independence. Children rather than husband a basic motivation for living.

Interim 3 1/2 weeks: Hospitalization and convalescence.

3/29

1. Depressive reaction secondary to operation, linked with masochistic fantasies.
2. Anal hypersensitivity. References to surgeon's sadism.
3. Preoperative anxieties about total castration.
4. More associations about sadism with symbolic sexual meanings.
5. Postoperative feelings of helplessness and abandonment.
6. Hostility toward powerful father-figure.
7. Attempts to counteract regressive trends.
8. Less hostility toward ineffectual male (husband) and more toward critical mother-figure.

3/30

1. Revengeful thoughts about a disliked father-figure.
2. Preoccupation with defects. Masochistic fantasies. Defensive arrogance, suppressed and repressed, linked with expectations of retaliation. Fear of being ignored and disbelieved. Transference implications. Guilt over devaluating tendencies.

3/31

1. Transference manifestation.
2. More preoccupation with physical symptoms. Menopause linked with sequelae of operation. Defensive devaluation of authority figure followed by guilt.
3. Hostility toward sibling figure linked with possible homosexual jealousy. Narcissism activated. More hostile thoughts.
4. Transference resistance with symbolic sadistic elements.
5. Transference ambivalence. Oral needs. Guilt.

4/3

1. Inferiority feelings. Expectation of attack. Competition. Ambivalence in the transference and toward mother-figure.
2. Conflict between passivity and activity. Guilt over hostility linked with recollection of maternal warning about retaliation and with current respiratory infection. Continued fear of cancer.
3. Further devaluation of uncommunicative husband. Mutual hostility. Concern about loss of sexuality. Projective transference implications. More fears of aging and menopause. Somatic identification.
4. Continuing concern about sexual identity.
5. Defensive hostility in the transference.

4/4

1. Varieties of blocking. Reference to somatic hyperreactivity. Hostility linked with envy.
2. Projective and hostile aspects of the transference.
3. More blocking.
4. Preoccupation with physical and psychologic defects. Somatic identification.

4/5

1. Dream of violence. Masochistic aspects. Symbolic sexual attack (castration) linked with operation and hospitalization. Retaliatory murderous fantasies.
2. Reciprocal mother-daughter deception. Hostile affect related to long anticipated and now realized castration. Somatic identification with mother.

3. Continuing preoccupation with bodily integrity, cancer, and possible gastrointestinal involvement. Gastrointestinal links.

4. Transference fears.

5. Return of sexual desire.

6. Beginning awareness of emotional reactions, especially in the transference situation. Interpretation.

COMMENT

This patient already has had a relatively large number of physical illnesses although she is only 35 years old. These somatic disturbances have involved the genitourinary tract particularly. She had an abortion at age 19 and a kidney infection at 28. Surgery has been performed for breast cyst and appendicitis, and for painful varicosities. During the course of the analysis, retrospective material became available which indicated that each of the illnesses had been preceded by marked psychologic stress involving a crisis in her relationship with the man with whom she was currently involved. The threat was always the same: loss of the significant object without prospect of its replacement.

Since the start of the analysis, the patient had been subjected to chronic stress from two sources. One was the relationship with her husband, which had been an unstable one since they were married, with recurrent crises. The most recent crisis had lasted over a year and involved a largely realistic concern that her husband, passive and shy in the extreme and absorbed in his research and experimental work, would leave her. Another growing concern had been an impending series of academic examinations that would either permit her to go ahead with writing her thesis or else would disqualify her from further study for the Ph.D. degree, thus basically affecting her career plans.

The patient had had a thorough physical examination two months prior to the reporting of the detailed case material, during an annual physical checkup. The findings at that time had been entirely negative.

In the interview of 2/18, physical symptoms referable to the genitourinary tract appear for the first time. These include intermittent frequency of urination which the patient, while feeling herself for growths, attributes to emotional factors—ambition, competition, etc. Actually, this focus on the psychologic is an attempted defense against an intense anxiety that the symptoms might be an indication of the worst physical possibility—cancer. In this interview there is the first mention of such concern, and it is linked with appearance, specifically of the hair. The defensive need to explain physical manifestations as being due to psychologic factors can become highly dangerous to the health of an individual for it may postpone the seeking of necessary medical consultation. This patient has had the actual experience of surgery for growths. There has been some real basis, thus, for her past concern about more growths and feeling herself for them intermittently since then. Now she has resumed this activity with an accompanying rise in anxiety which, in view of the psychophysical background, cannot be considered as basically hypochondriacal.

Old hostility to a selfish mother and sibling competition, now especially manifest toward professors and fellow students, can be noted in the content of the associations, but the affect that is most evident is an anxiety evoked by the appearance of physical symptoms. The hostility is bound by projective and intellectualizing mechanisms and expressed cognitively for the most part, though there is some affect discharge in the form of low-grade irritability and annoyance. However, the significance of the current hostility in terms of frustrated oral needs, injured narcissism, and activated envy, involving family figures and their surrogates, remains largely outside of the patient's awareness. Consequently, even if the patient had expressed more anger affectively, the greatest part of it would still not have been discharged, and the internal potential to generate continued hostility, frequently actived by external events, would remain unmodified. It is this potential in the patient which has to be sufficiently modified for its impact on somatic function to be truly lessened, rather than effecting outbursts of rage which may bring only temporary relief, if any.

In this hour there are further indications of why, early in the patient's life, defensive psychologic systems developed to block off direct expression of hostility. Her sickly mother's constant admonitions and warnings about the patient's aggressiveness were important influences in inhibiting its affective expression.

On 2/19 the patient's continued preoccupation with being abandoned appears to be reaching a high point. This theme has been increasingly evident in the patient's associations during the past three months. It, together with the appearance of new physical symptoms and indications of insufficient discharge of psychologic tensions has to be considered a signal of impending or possibly already existent somatic dysfunction. Such is the patient's mode of response to continued, strong stress, as evidenced by her physical illnesses in the past. She does not respond primarily by severe anxiety or depression, nor does she cope with stress in such a way that she is able to adjust without pathologic sequelae. Her general style of adaptation is through a characterologic set which has pathologic elements: defenses of intellectualization and projection, penis envy, compensatory competition, and minor anxiety-depressive and euphoric cyclic responses. However, this mode of response becomes insufficient during critical periods of stress. The discharge of the conflictual energies is then shifted so that they exert maximum impact on target organs and organ systems.

There can be noted on 2/23 a still further preoccupation with being unwanted, particularly by men, stemming from traumatic experiences with father. A principal defense against the intense, persisting ideas of inferiority is devaluation of others. Expectation of the worst continues to be reflected in repeated references to cancer and associations about people with cancer. The question again comes up: is this hypochondriacal anxiety, or is there an actual growth present, though the physical symptoms may appear to be equivocal? The signals noted in the interview preceding cannot be disregarded. The patient's physical condition needs to be immediately and carefully checked over again, even though two months ago this had been done with completely negative findings. There is a strong possibility that between then and now somatic dysfunction has been occurring silently, that is, outside the patient's awareness insofar as physical manifestations are concerned. What has appeared is a mixture of psychologic signals that indicate a critical rise in tensions and only in the last few days some equivocal physical manifestations which suggest a site of dysfunction in the abdomen. The anxiety is secondary to the appearance of the physical symptoms. If this patient were not in analytic treatment, it is questionable whether she would have gone to be checked over within a few days after the appearance of physical symptoms, in view of her very recent clean bill of health at the time of the annual physical examination. She might have delayed doing this until the physical discomfort had become unbearable. Furthermore, despite her concern about cancer, there was a strong avoidance defense operating: she did not want to have her worst fears confirmed, which is what she anticipated hearing from the consultant. She had to be urged quite insistently to go for the physical checkup before she finally agreed to do so (2/25). Once physical symptoms enter awareness, they may activate considerable anxiety. In turn, this may evoke a corresponding degree of defensive denial, a basic reason why so many patients delay seeing a physician until a serious even fatal disease is upon them.

The physical manifestations are increasingly in the patient's awareness (2/26). Concomitantly defensive attempts at self-reassurance are activated but are minimally effective. The external stresses continue to mount: job interviews, impending physical examination, preparation for the academic examinations, and husband's rejecting behavior. In this interview there are recollections of a critical somatic identification with a sickly mother. Identification, a basic human psychologic mechanism, has been studied mostly in terms of attitude, behavior, and cognitive style—its psychologic aspects. However, physical manifestations of identification may appear in the associations during an interview. Such references have often been overlooked, but they are useful in providing clues to the site of organ dysfunction, as may be noted in this case.

A preliminary diagnosis of malignant ovarian tumor with possible metastases to the posterior pituitary is made by the consultant surgeon who advises an immediate exploratory laparotomy. With a physical diagnosis now established, though its specifics have been withheld from the patient, she enters into a new phase of coping with this most immediate and critical of all the stresses facing her. There is (2/27), at first, a preoccupation with operative procedures, the patient drawing on her unfortunately abundant past hospital experiences, mixed with fantasies in which expectation of the worst predominates. The psychologic mechanisms of avoidance, intellectualization, and rationalization which are integral parts of the patient's defense structure are again mobilized against the secondary internal tension that has been activated by the impending operation. Affect discharge now not only includes more manifest anxiety, but also a growing awareness of thoughts that link the illness with punishment for the past sexual activity and fantasy. There is little reference, however, to guilt over many hostile impulses which themselves are still not clearly within the patient's awareness.

On 3/2 the patient has become preoccupied with the seeming insufficiency o. her self-preservative instincts, a reflection of the power of the hidden, self-destructive impulses. These are countered by the motivation "to live for the sake of the children." It is as if there exists an unstable, shifting equilibrium between countervailing forces which, like icebergs, still remain largely concealed. What is now appearing in the patient's awareness is a generalized, vague, cognitive recognition of this uneasy balance, appearing alongside the relentlessly emerging physical manifestations. Self-destructive tendencies are not manifestations which are exclusive to the psychologic domain—severe depression, suicide, or self-destructive behavior—but may appear in the form of physical illness. The attitude reflecting a tendency toward recovery common to all human beings has been called by Bibring (1937) "biological sense" or "biological thinking." He considers this an illustrative rather than explanatory term: "Under this heading come a tendency to recognize the requirements of reality, a capacity for experience, a sense of what is expedient, a higher valuation of the object relationships as compared to other relationships of the libido, an inclination towards a social environment, etc."

While awaiting hospitalization and the operation, the patient continues (3/3) to be subjected to an increasing regressive pull. The activated dependency, in turn, evokes further defensive responses of self-reassurance, thoughts of independence, and compensatory activity. The illness also stimulates many associations concerned with secondary gain. There is an intensification of conflict between feminine and masculine strivings which continues alongside the more immediate and dominant issues of survival or death. The symbolic significance of the Ph.D. degree becomes more evident as a substitute for the anticipated, impending, further loss of body parts through surgery. Another attempt to compensate for this loss is through fantasies in which the illness is not an illness but a pregnancy.

Continued references (3/4) to hostility and sibling rivalry evoke superego responses expressed cognitively, but without appreciable affect. Guilt is inferred, but the affect is not discharged. Expectations of a fatal outcome to the operation continue to be verbalized and linked now with punishment for old, hateful behavior toward parents. There is still the uneasy equilibrium in which the self-destructive trends are enhanced, but the countervailing motivation to live for the sake of the children is also reciprocally increased and greater on balance. Patients awaiting operation will not respond in any uniform manner. Each person has his or her individual mode of response. Some will cope with the impending surgery by massive denial; others will become preoccupied with erotic fantasies as an escape. Still others will be flooded with anxiety, etc.

A number of the patient's pre- and postoperative responses appear in the first analytic hour (3/29) some three weeks after surgery had been performed. There is an initial depressive response with some affect breakthrough. This is linked with references to loss of sexual body parts and complicating sadomasochistic fantasies. Retrospective recollections of preoperative and postoperative anxiety, many sexualized, appear in the patient's associations, but most prominent is the need to be cared for which was greatly intensified and insufficiently gratified, leading to additional secondary hostility.

In the interviews of 3/30 and 3/31, revengeful thoughts toward father-figures who hurt and reject her are mixed with continued rumination about her defects. Hospitalization and surgery are seen repeatedly as a punishment for such hostility. The sexualized aspects fade out very quickly and the intensity of the libidinal drives continues to be far less than that of the aggressive drives.

On 4/3 and 4/5 the patient is beginning to think more about the upcoming academic examinations which she plans to take. However, the persistence of thoughts about cancer has not yet diminished. She is haunted by mother's warning that mean deeds bring consequences, and her illnesses continue to be seen as punishments for masturbation, illegitimate pregnancy, penis envy, and other hostile thoughts and activities. A possible coping device, that of being neutral—neither masculine or feminine sexually—is continually mulled over by the patient. When the operation is seen as a symbolic castration, there are reactive thoughts of retaliatory murder against the men held responsible for her condition. Concomitantly, the patient is beginning to be aware of her hostility as an affect and of its potentially great intensity, especially in the transference.

* * * *

The patient's convalescence was slow, but there were no physical sequelae. Her analysis continued with significant modification of her neurotic traits.

A different outcome was reported by Inman (1964) in a middle-aged female patient undergoing psychoanalytic treatment who developed two different types of cancer. No verbatim material is given, only a highly condensed summary. The patient was involved in a love affair with an older married man which activated emotional conflicts in her that could not be resolved, and she suffered from severe guilt. It was then discovered that she had an adenocarcinoma of the breast and a sebaceous cyst of the scalp which showed malignant epitheliomatous changes. Death from general carcinomatosis resulted one year later. Inman postulated that a conflict for which no solution can be found may turn out to be an important factor in setting the stage for development of a malignancy.

General Discussion

GENERAL DISCUSSION

The eight cases demonstrate that there are psychologic cues which signal the development of somatic dysfunction before it reaches the individual's awareness through gross physical symptoms and signs. These sensitive indicators add a new dimension to the resources of medical science already being used in the early detection of somatic disease. Hitherto, physical manifestations have been the warning signals which have influenced the individual in whom they occur to seek medical consultation. They have been highly publicized for many diseases, and information about them has been widely disseminated. The physician himself has been trained to look for the earliest manifestations of these illnesses either in the patient's physical history or physical examination, aided by x-ray and laboratory instruments and techniques which may pick up signs of actual or potential dysfunction otherwise not physically evident. On the other hand, the role of emotional factors in physical illness, though acknowledged, has tended to be simplistic and retrospective. This has been a major, though not exclusive reason, why their significance has been discounted and their usefulness limited as part of a truly comprehensive approach to the problems of somatic disease, including the predictive and preventive aspects.

It is not the basic purpose of this book to study the part psychologic factors play in the causation of physical disease. Rather, it is to point out and examine certain psychologic phenomena which have been found prospectively to be useful in forecasting somatic illness. While the focus is on the psychologic manifestations, this is not to deny in any sense their somatic origin. Furthermore, these psychologic cues are regarded as supplementing, not replacing, those physical indicators which have proved so valuable in the early detection of somatic disease.

The cues elicited in this study will be discussed now in considerable clinical and theoretical detail under the following headings: (1) Psychologic stress; (2) Life style of adaptation to stress; (3) Psychologic equilibrium—Ego aspects; (4) Superego functions; (5) Drives; (6) Dreams; (7) Somatic identification.

PSYCHOLOGIC STRESS

The relationship between psychologic stress and somatic reactions recently has been reviewed and also discussed on the basis of original work (Silverman, 1968). These stresses originate from interaction between human beings and from responses to manmade socioeconomic, political, and cultural institutions. Man is surrounded by an extraordinary array of noxious stimuli besides those from bacteria, viruses, molds, pollutants, earthquakes, hurricanes, floods, and other natural and unnatural phenomena of the physicochemical world around him. A vast variety of sources contribute to unhealthy psychologic stress, and in many instances there is a circular relationship between the two: poverty, unemployment, overcrowding, slums, population explosion, dislocation of homes, a vast variety of work tensions involving everyone from top-flight executive to menial laborer, racial differences, violence in the streets, general political and economic stresses and upheavals, the draft, the outcry of the younger generation with its demands and rebelliousness, the growing use of drugs, the increasing incidence of venereal disease, the threat or actual occurrence of war with its multiple complications, and the danger of nuclear confrontation and holocaust. These environmental factors reach down into all strata of society and affect everybody directly or indirectly. They impinge on the psychologic problems of the family unit and those of the individual. However, each human being, with his or her particular psychophysical makeup, will cope with environmental stresses in a highly individualized adaptive way. Some will react with emotional illness, some with physical illness, while others will show little or no evidence of either psychologic or somatic dysfunction.

In considering psychologic stress further, it is important to note that it is not always evident at the time it occurs. It may be sudden or cumulative, its significance often may be masked, and its presence may be first manifest through physical responses. Disguised sources of stress are often found in anniversaries of births, deaths, illnesses, marriages, divorces, holidays, promotions, failures, or other events. Many of these anniversaries are forgotten by the individual, or if recalled, their symbolic significance is not known. Everyday happenings, myriad in their manifestations, represent lesser, transient forms of stress that often elude the individual's attention altogether.

It is inaccurate to think that psychologic stress begins to exert an impact on the individual only at the moment of its actual occurrence. There is also "anticipatory stress"—the anticipation of the stress itself becomes stressful. The actual event may be preceded by news of it, allusions to it, fantasies about it, plans for it, etc. Such anticipatory stress may be quite variable in its intensity—from marked to minimal. It may in this preliminary phase activate defensive responses which in turn may be more or less successful in coping with it. The more likely or realizable the stress becomes as its actual occurrence approaches, the greater the impact on the individual and the more intensive and extensive the activation of the coping mechanisms. While this study focuses on psychologic phenomena, a few comments will be made here about somatic defense reactions. They are classified as (1) general and (2) local. The first category has been described as including flight-fight and withdrawal-conservation patterns. Major features of the former are "neuroendocrine changes concerned with both rapid and long-term activity . . . mobilization of substrata for energy." Withdrawal-conservation patterns are still poorly defined. They include decreased skeletal muscle activity, secretory and motor activity of gastrointestinal tract, and secretions of other membranes. Local biologic defenses involve body portal entries and riddance reactions to noxious agents, actual, symbolic, or anticipated (Engel, 1962).

The more the meaning of actual stress is disguised and outside the individual's awareness, the greater the resultant impact on his psychophysical equilibrium. However, even anticipation of stressful events may be sufficient to evoke a response.

Successes are a particular group of potential stresses not easily recognized. The following is a case illustration: A plant foreman, aged 42, who had been in generally good physical health except for occasional limited attacks of indigestion, was suddenly promoted to the position of plant boss. The former superintendent whose assistant he had been for several years had become increasingly irascible at work and one day had finally "cracked up." The owner of the plant immediately asked the patient to take over. The latter had secretly coveted this position and had had many fantasies of getting rid of his former superior. Outwardly he appeared very pleased with his promotion. What he did not reveal to anyone was a vague but growing sense of tension which he began to experience shortly thereafter. Although the discharged superintendent soon showed signs of improvement, he was refused any further employment at the plant by the owner. The patient now felt even more obligated to prove his worth and spent unusually long hours at work, but could not rid himself of a nagging concern about whether he would fill the position adequately. He began to experience epigastric discomfort after eating, and then suddenly had an acute attack of right upper quadrant abdominal pain which led to his hospitalization, one month after his promotion. A diagnosis of acute cholecystitis was made. His recovery from the illness was slow. Emotional factors appeared to be involved and a psychiatric consultation was requested.

It then became more evident that the patient had been suffering from an activated sense of guilt since he had taken over his new job. He also revealed that one year previously his father, whose hard-driving success as a businessman he had always envied and whom he had constantly tried to equal in this respect, had died after an operation for an obstructed common bile duct. The patient had shown little grief at the time, but had been aware of more indigestion thereafter, a mild prototype of what was to develop eventually.

Sexual impulses, which for varying reasons become associated with anxiety or guilt, may act as stressors, regardless of whether they occur in fantasy or are acted out. A patient whose voyeuristic impulses had begun to break through the defensive barriers that had long been present against them reported the following during therapy: One evening the possibility had "suddenly" occurred to him that he might be able to watch a woman neighbor undress in her apartment which was just across from his. Actually he had been aware for several weeks that this woman had not been drawing her shades at night. He had studiously avoided looking to see what was going on in her apartment. On this particular evening the idea of indulging his voyeuristic impulses became persistent. He experienced rapid and then irregular heart beat, a sensation of a knot in his stomach, and generalized tremulousness. He did not actually look, but the physical response lasted for almost an hour. On a subsequent occasion he yielded to his voyeuristic impulses and watched the woman as she took her clothes off in preparation for bed. The anxious reaction, both affectively and somatically, began the moment he decided to look and became much stronger than in the previous instance. The sight of the naked female body was also accompanied by an increasing awareness of pleasurable genital sensations such as might precede orgasm though there was no erection. The patient was on the verge of ejaculating when he interrupted his voyeuristic activity which had lasted about five minutes. A sense of guilt overwhelmed him. He also became secondarily fearful that the previously noted somatic symptoms which had returned were indicative of some form of physical damage, and he became immobilized in a chair by the hypochondriacal thought he had to conserve his bodily energy and integrity. However, he was also flooded with images of what he had seen and with further fantasy elaborations of how to get a closer look at female genitalia with the infantile expectation of finding a hidden phallus there. The anxiety, guilt, and physical symptoms persisted for several hours and interfered with his falling asleep till very late that night. During most of the next day the patient experienced severe headache and pain in his eyeballs. These represented conversion symptoms.

A particular form of stress has been the subject of much study in recent years. It is associated with the actual or threatened loss of a significant human relationship. Should substitute objects be unavailable, it is postulated that the ensuing feelings of helplessness and hopelessness may be related to "increased biological vulnerability" (Schmale, 1958). The concept of "vicarious object" was introduced by Greene (1958) in his studies on leukemia and lymphoma, though it was not considered unique for these diseases. It is suggested that many adults have adapted to loss by denying the grief and projecting the significance of the loss and the affect onto another person subjected to the same loss, and this person (usually someone in the family) is then comforted as a "vicarious object." When this adaptive mechanism becomes insufficient or no longer possible, then somatic illness may develop. In a further consideration of this mechanism of adjustment (Greene, 1959), leukemic children were found to have been vicarious objects for their mothers. When they were given up as such, the manifest illness developed. Another opinion about object loss has been advanced by Imboden et al. (1963). He and his coworkers felt that previous studies of the subject were inadequately controlled and retrospective, and that "under these circumstances studies which appear to point to an association between separation experiences and somatic disease may be merely reflecting a characteristic of the human condition rather than a characteristic unique to the clinical entity being studied . . . The criticisms implied in the discussion above do not mean that the authors have rejected the possibility that antecedent separation experiences (with their affective and possibly physiological consequences) may be importantly involved in the etiology of many diseases."

Losses of significance to the individual often do not appear in his thinking directly in terms of human relationships. Instead they may be symbolically represented by parts of the body and various physical functions (loss because of illness, operation, injury, mutilation), or by money, position, prestige, reputation, or other external factors maintaining self-esteem, including alcohol, drugs and obsessive hobbies.

One type of loss, quite common and usually unrecognized as such, that of the familiar sights and sounds of an habitual environment, especially in older people, and in those with phobic predisposition, may result in serious regression, psychologic and/or physical. The case of a 75-year-old woman, living with her spinster daughter, age 47, for the past 20 years illustrates such a response. For some years, the patient has had generalized arteriosclerosis, mild hypertension, compensated arteriosclerotic heart disease, paroxysmal auricular fibrillation, and maturity onset diabetes—all adequately treated by antitensives, quinidine, digitalis, and chlorpropamide. Occasional bouts of fibrillation and extrasystoles were the only disturbing symptoms and could be controlled by temporarily increased medication.

After much deliberation and hesitation the daughter decided that they would move to a new apartment from the flat where they had spent the last 30 years. Following the move a psychologic regression occurred in both mother and daughter. The older woman, a longstanding severe phobic who had made an adjustment in her old environment by limiting her range of activities outside the flat to a shopping center a few hundred yards away, became enormously fearful in the new milieu and unable to leave the apartment. Accompanying the fear was an intense hostility to her daughter for changing their living quarters. The anger could not find an outlet either in affective or verbal expression. The daughter also experienced increased anxiety and hostility, but of relatively lesser severity, and with some discharge in the form of open rage reactions, both directly at the mother and displaced onto other relatives. Projection was prominent in her verbal expressions. They both showed evidence, to some extent affectively, of depression which again was more intense in the mother. The latter gave up doing any housework, took to bed, became less and less responsive verbally, and showed increasing evidence of memory loss.

A set of new physical symptoms also appeared in the mother at this time and became increasingly severe and persistent. These included excessive salivation, marked difficulty in swallowing, and anorexia—so that food intake was severely limited and, at times, even fluids were refused. Weight loss of at least 20 or more pounds accompanies these symptoms. Organic causes were suspected, particularly a hidden carcinoma. Physical examination, x-rays, and laboratory studies were essentially negative except for signs indicative of the chronic diseases already mentioned; there was no evidence of carcinoma or other organ cause of weight loss.

The symptom of sialorrhea may be considered a response to stimuli which are complexly perceptual, activating complicated cognitive activity, both being related to the stress of the change. Included are the sights, sounds, and other perceptions of the new physical surroundings and neighbors, and their symbolic significance which was outside the patient's awareness. Also involved are the sights and sounds reflected in the appearance, emotional activity, remarks, and behavior of the principal and only human object in the patient's limited surroundings—her daughter. The latter is away 8 A.M. to 5:30 P.M. weekdays at work but phones in several times. Evenings and weekends she is almost exclusively with her mother, and during those occasions she exhibits highly ambivalent attitudes toward her.

Many associative chains are linked to the perceptual core. These associations in turn are connected to the presentation of food. The patient was fed almost from infancy by an older sister with whom she had had a most ambivalent relationship. For years eating occurred under emotionally charged conditions. Now she kept calling her daughter her sister. The daughter, reacting with great concern to her mother's anorexia and weight loss, hovered over her with various offerings of food, pressing her to accept these and when refused would fly into an anxious rage. The whole childhood feeding situation was being reenacted.

The complexity of object relationships influences different responses in different individuals sustaining personal loss. In some there is great relief at having a burden removed by fate. In others there is a sense of abandonment and loneliness. Varying degrees of ambivalence and, in turn, of guilt are involved in these relationships. The more narcissistic an object choice is, the more stressful the loss, the greater the impact on the individual, and the more pressing the tendency to identify with the lost object.

The basic difficulty in understanding the importance of losses or other major psychologic trauma as stresses is due to the fact that the psychologic conflicts which they activate are outside the awareness of the involved individual or are not detected by his physician. All emotional stress has unconscious as well as conscious meaning. What on the surface appears to be an ordinary or even trivial event may have great significance in the emotional life of the person who has experienced it. In addition, the intensity, frequency, accumulation, and duration of stress need to be specified in order to assess its impact on the individual's current psychophysical equilibrium. Within a given period of time, there may be a piling up of a number of different stresses which activate the same basic conflict or there may be a sudden, massive increase in a particular kind of low-grade stress which up to this point had caused only minor shifts in psychophysical equilibrium.

There are many kinds and combinations of psychologic stressors. They are signals that adaptive responses will be mobilized. It was possible to follow a large number of these variations prospectively, longitudinally and in depth in the eight subjects studied, and to derive their symbolic significance for the patient and the impact on his or her psychophysical equilibrium.

In the case of E. F., a basic longstanding source of stress is his need to search for a nurturing parent, shifting from maternal to paternal figures and back to maternal again, subject to repeated disappointment and complicated by associated infantile sexual impulses. The specter of unhappy marriage and its dissolution in his own family haunts him. Although he has had affairs with a number of girls, he cannot settle down and, in this respect, identifies with his father who, for many years now, has been unable to make up his mind about a remarriage. The patient's attempts to obtain relief from buildup of tension by masturbating produce only more stress. During the early part of his treatment, the level of stress rises and falls within a relatively uniform and moderate range. Thereafter, the patient's feelings of being deprived and deserted begin to extend deeply into the transference. The stress level increases sharply after a visit to his mother and sister. On the surface this visit appears neither unusual nor spectacular. But like so many such incidents, there is a hidden significance involved. In this instance the patient's sibling rivalry, jealousy, and infantile need to be nurtured are strongly activated. At about the same time, he engages in unusual physical exertion, mountain climbing. This often found combination of psychologic and physical stress, each reinforcing the other, is followed by a shift in psychophysical equilibrium, culminating in a recurrence of his somatic illness which is itself secondarily stressful. Physical stress, which is the kind usually focused on by patients and their doctors, can be of many different kinds: bacteria, viruses, allergens, pollutants, and all kinds of physicochemical agents, etc.

Subsequently, E. F., after remission of this illness, again enters a cycle of accumulating stress caused by a favorite uncle's death, increased work demands, further difficulties with his girlfriends, more frustration of transference expectations, and another episode of unusual muscular exertion, Then, in one evening, there occurs a series of encounters with girlfriends and his mother—all of whom disappoint his narcissistic expectations and anger him in the extreme. Once again, there is a peak rise in stress and an impact on the psychophysical equilibrium followed by somatic dysfunction with its secondary tension.

In G. H. there may be noted a series of stressful experiences which superficially seem rather ordinary but, again, have considerably more meaning. Her hostile dependency on her mother has been a longstanding, major emotional problem. Her relationships with men (starting with father) also have always been competitive and difficult, with penis envy an interfering factor. Even her closest friends are unaware of these two basic sources of stress. The patient's own understanding of her infantile impulses is minimal early in the analysis. A stress which is destined to persist with exacerbation and remission becomes evident with the return of a man-friend, seen as a last-hope marriage prospect. The summer interruption with its transference implications looms as an additional stress. Masturbation resorted to for substitute gratification turns out instead to be secondarily stressful. Still other stresses following one on the other are mother's attempted interferences in her romance, frequent competitive tiffs with the men at her place of work, stage fright while auditioning for a local amateur symphony orchestra, and belated recall of the anniversary of father's birthday. It should be noted that these stresses early in the treatment evoke mostly psychologic coping mechanisms, mixed however, with transient, minor, physical dysfunction, generally gastrointestinal.

Her visits to her man-friend become increasingly stressful. The patient is unable to experience orgasm in sexual intercourse with him and expects at any time to be rejected. Her fears about being dirty and frigid finally reach such intensity that the habitual psychologic defenses against them become insufficient and several episodes of minor physical illness occurs.

The next patient to be considered, C. D., has long experienced chronic stress associated with inferiority feelings about manliness and competitiveness with authority figures. This is reflected in the transference. His preoccupation with guilt-ridden sexual fantasies and unsatisfactory relations with his wife constitute chronic psychologic irritants. Behind these is a dependency which is activated from time to time and especially by the summer interruption of the analysis. When treatment is resumed and the detailed reporting begins, the patient continues to have difficulties with his wife at home and his colleagues at work. He wants both to get rid of his wife and hold on to her. These stresses are added to by the breakthrough of anal and feminine sexual fantasies. A rapid increase of emotional pressures can be noted and, soon thereafter, a small rectal polyp is discovered. Waiting for the recommended surgery is an additional stressful experience.

Subsequent to his convalescence from the operation, new stresses appear: there is postponement of a decision about his promotion at work, and the patient reacts to this as if it were a critical rejection of him and a judgment that he is a defective man. Further quarreling with his wife ensues; this time the disagreement is about plans for raising a family. His concern about being an adequate father and also about having rivals for his wife's attention and affection are increasingly involved. A highly unsatisfactory sexual experience with her immediately precedes the next episode of physical dysfunction.

K. L. in the early interviews reports that his wife and two children are sick. This may appear to be only superficially stressful, but the patient's assumption of the maternal role at this time activates long standing conflicts over independence-dependence and masculinity-femininity. At the same time, an almost irresistible increase in sexual needs cannot be fulfilled through relations with his wife. Masturbation affords no relief, only more stress. As sexual frustration continues, the patient finds his sexual fantasies more and more painful. The negative transference deepens. Dental work is experienced as highly stressful, both physically and psychologically. Transient physical symptoms appear in addition to the psychologic responses to these stresses, but as the tensions rise, severe upper back and neck pain develops. Subsequently more stresses accumulate: the analyst's absence symbolizes a rejection for the patient; difficulties with his boss are seen as castration threats from a paternal figure. More minor physical dysfunction is associated with these events.

The next patient to be considered, T. U., is a severely obsessional neurotic man, plagued by doubt and guilt, hiding his aggressive exhibitonistic-voyeuristic impulses behind rigid reaction formations of shyness and overpoliteness. For him, as for the other patients, the pending summer interruption in the analysis is stressful, and especially so, because he is extremely sensitive to any form of loss or separation. It is compounded by the absence of his wife and children who are themselves vacationing at this time. His discovery of and interest in girlie magazines lying around in the rubbish near his house activate anxiety that his voyeuristic interests will be discovered. Later, the reunion with his family is marred by frustrations that are specifically oral. Then, in succession, more stresses pile up. He takes on a new assignment at work and is concerned about being adequate in it. He has to give a public talk and has anticipatory stage fright. He engages in unusual muscular exertion. Hypersenisitivity to his wife's criticism activates poorly contained reactive hostility to her. The children's illnesses which come on at this time arouse concern about his body integrity through identification. Finally, there is a peremptory request from his new boss which activates his conflict with authority figures. The accumulated stresses reach critical levels and are followed by physical dysfunction.

In a later period there is continued more or less masked competition with his boss, mixed with uneasiness at having to conduct a number of discussion groups. Each experience is distorted to be an exposure of his unmanliness and reacted to as such. A visit to his parents, which on the surface seems uneventful, actually is very upsetting to the patient and is followed by somatic illness. Incestuous and voyeuristic fantasies directed toward his mother are activated during his visit, but are not known to anyone but the patient, and he has great difficulty in referring to these impulses in the analytic situation. Such secret tension is. a common occurrence, and then everyone who supposedly knows the individual is surprised to learn, if it comes out, that he has been under stress. More often these secrets remain with the individual.

N. P., a loss-sensitive patient, has been involved in a longstanding pattern of relationships with women which constitutes a recurrent form of stress. He is attracted to a particular woman and if she responds, he quickly becomes intimate with her. Following a brief period of calm, their relationship begins to deteriorate rapidly as he discovers more and more faults in the woman, and he then usually breaks off the relationship. This phase is succeeded by one in which he feels very lonely and when no other contact seems likely or possible. Usually he finds another woman before too long. This seemingly unending search for an idealized and perfect mother-figure goes on, destined only to be frustrated again and again. In this patient, an accumulation of stresses concerned with loss for which no immediate and inadequate replacement is available, can be noted prior to his coming down with a severe viral sickness. He does not appear to react emotionally as he receives a plethora of bad news about relatives and friends. He also is preparing to change jobs and wonders how he will make out in the new setting. Meanwhile he has formed a new relationship with still another woman and her leaving for a brief vacation upsets him. The anniversary of the death of a close college friend is at hand. Then he becomes physically ill. The illness itself is experienced as highly stressful with the patient's need for mothering sharply increased. Some months later, after very brief relationships with several woman and much interspersed loneliness, the patient again forms a seemingly intense attachment, this time to a divorcee who reminds him of his mother. Meanwhile stresses from being behind in his work and being critized for it by his boss are mounting. In the midst of this, his girlfriend suddenly becomes violently angry at him for what she considers his lack of consideration for her and rejects him in a shockingly final way. At the same time he is once again sharply criticized by a parental figure at work. The combination of these two events—signifying to the patient utter rejection by maternal and paternal figures simultaneously—results in a critical level of stress, followed by another episode of severe physical illness.

L. M. has had a lifelong conflict with her mother, feeling deprived by her, yet fearing her domination and the possibility of becoming like her. She also has been chronically conflicted about competition with men in terms of career aspirations, yet at the same time wanting to be attractive to them sexually. There is the growing stress of an intimate relationship with her boss, a married man, as the detailed account of her analysis begins. Shortly thereafter, the patient has an intensely hostile exchange with her mother who announces that she is leaving on an extended European trip. The patient's oral dependent needs, so tenaciously defended against, become markedly activated. There is insufficient, current gratification from the ambivalent relationship with her boss. The net result is a greatly intensified sense of loss with an upsurge of loneliness and aimlessness. All this is followed by an acute, severe, upper respiratory infection.

In the case of Q. R., a continued stress from the onset of her analysis has been a largely realistic concern that her husband would leave her. This expectation relentlessly becomes part of her everyday life and enormously intensifies fears of being abandoned and left utterly helpless—a persistent emotional remainder from childhood. Her attempts to make possible an independent life for herself through a career by getting a Ph.D. degree is interfered with by troublesome, repetitive thoughts of inferiority and inadequacy, especially in comparison with the men in her field of study. An impending series of academic examinations becomes a concurrent source of stress. Her conflict over her sexual identity, her penis envy, and her displaced hostility toward professors and fellow students are all markedly activated. These unremitting stresses precede the first physical signs of somatic dysfunction.

This detailed recapitulation illustrates both long-term and short-term varieties of stress, their superficial and symbolic meanings and their fluctuating intensities. The study further indicates that noxious psychologic stress is always present and reaches a critical level gradually or suddenly prior to the development of physical dysfunction. *However, the presence of stress is not inevitably a cue that such illness is impending. What it does signal is that the organism is being confronted by forces which may evoke an adaptive response whose manifestations will be highly variable, ranging from those of minimal, transient dysfunction to major psychologic or physical illness.* A more detailed examination of the economics of a loss-separation-disappointment situation may reveal that there are compensatory substitutes, replacements or shifts in the patient's environment externally or internally, current or future, which could be overlooked in a search for data which focuses only on the negative. The presence of such balancing elements is an important reason why not all stressful situations are necessarily productive of major pathology. The stress experienced by two persons may be quite different for each. What represents loss for one individual may be relief for another. Furthermore not all psychologic stress is unhealthy. As indicated elsewhere (Silverman, 1968), a certain degree of stimulation and excitation—of the right kind and under the right conditions—is essential for normal existence. Such may be provided by physical exercise, the challenge of complex problems, the exploration of new frontiers, etc. Experiments involving adults exposed to sensory deprivation point to harmful physiologic and psychologic affects of such an environment (Solomon et al., 1961). During early human life, many forms of sensory deprivation appear to prevent the development of basic mechanisms and response patterns necessary for adequate adaptability (Spitz, 1945; Dubos, 1965). It is interesting to note that whereas the human infant would not survive without a mothering figure, the monkey infant is able to do so, largely because of its early locomotor ability, enabling it to "reengage the environment" (Kaufman and Rosenblum, 1967).

Pathologic emotional stresses involve disturbances in human object relationships, direct or symbolic. Loss of or disappointment in an object seen basically as a source of sexual gratification appears to have less impact on physical systems than when the object provides oral, narcissistic satisfactions necessary for maintenance of self-esteem and ego intactness (Silverman, 1968). In the latter instance, the shadow of the object may fall on the ego (Freud, 1915) *or on the vulnerable organ or organ system*, i.e., psychologic or physical illness may follow. Freud (1895), referring to the origin of perception, notes that our awareness of the living objects around us is mediated by perceptions of them which are fused with perceptions of our own body. As reemphasized by Deutsch (1962), loss of human objects, especially those earliest perceived and with whom most intense sensory contact occurred, may be equated psychologically with body loss and may have somatic repercussions.

Despite its importance, psychologic stress is neither the only factor involved in physical illnesses, nor the only one available in forecasting their development. Nevertheless, a thorough search for the presence of psychologic stresses should be part of every examination of a patient who presents physical complaints or symptoms, even though somatic illness is not eventually found.

LIFE STYLE OF ADAPTATION TO PSYCHOLOGIC STRESS

Dubos (1968) has pointed out that: "The biological and psychological uniqueness of every human being generates many conceptual and practical difficulties for the study of behavior and the practice of medicine. Theoretical scientists can make generalizations about man's biological nature, but psychologists and physicians must deal with individual persons ... Early influences certainly play the most important role in converting the genetic potentialities into physical and mental attributes, but it is obvious that these attributes change continuously throughout life ... At any given time, the constitution of a particular person includes the potentialities that his experiences have made functional; its limits are determined by his genetic endowment. Since the constitution changes continuously with time, it can be defined in scientific jargon as the continuously evolving phenotype of each particular person." However, despite the modifications and fluctuations that occur in an individual's mode of adaptation to emotional stress, there is a core pattern of somatic and/or psychologic responses which can be noted. It has important roots in his genetic endowment, is influenced by his early psychophysical development and life experiences, and tends to repeat itself in successive stressful situations, and be resistive to change except under unusual conditions. It might be called life style or adaptation to psychologic stress and since it is unique for each individual, may help in predicting the likelihood of physical disease. A search was made for this cue in each of the cases under consideration. The data were derived from preliminary history and a prospective study of the ongoing analytic process.

E. F. had scarlet fever, mumps, measles, and episodes of joint pain as a child. During such times he had a great deal of attention, especially from his mother, both of a nurturing and sexually seductive nature. Except for some frightening experiences with a doctor who tried to do a venipuncture during an examination, the patient generally recalls "the pleasures of being sick and getting all the attention." The family mealtime was generally tense; anger was frequently expressed and "everyone got indigestion." The patient also remembers "having much less breath" than his boyhood friends and not having their stamina. This appears to have been related to competitive anxiety. During adolescence and into adulthood, physical health remained good while regressive shifts of small amplitude in his character neurosis occurred under minor stress. However, several years before beginning analysis, he had the first recurrence of joint pain since childhood. It could not be definitely diagnosed, although rheumatoid arthritis was suspected. This followed the breakup of a disturbed relationship with a girlfriend. During the early months of analysis, psychologic manifestations again were predominant responses to stress and somatic symptoms occurred chiefly in the form of anxiety equivalents. Then as stress escalated, he had several episodes of arthralgia when, under continued stress, psychologic coping mechanisms proved insufficient.

The responses of G. H. to stress in the past had been largely through episodes of major and minor physical illness, less so through regressive psychologic shifts in her longstanding character neurosis. Childhood feeding appears to have been a troublesome experience for the patient. Her mother was going through a period of depression and tended to be neglectful. Later the patient received overattention from her with regard to toilet training and appearance. Her rebellious reaction was manifest in her stubbornly holding in her bowel movements. During childhood, following sister's birth and activation of intense sibling rivalry, the patient was in bed for a whole summer with what was called "bronchitis." It is also evident that for many years while growing up the patient experienced frequent, but transient anxiety and somatic anxiety equivalents when exposed to father's nudity, especially in the toilet. At age ten she had warts on the fingers of her right hand. During adolescence she had severe acne. Both were associated with having "dirty sexual thoughts and masturbation." A serious case of measles was temporally connected with father's separating from the family. Vomiting and troublesome cramps accompanied the patient's periods for years after they began. During late adolescence she had anemia of undetermined origin, requiring hospitalization for some weeks and several blood transfusions. This occurred at a time of great indecision about whether to plan for career or marriage. In her early twenties she developed an acute duodenal ulcer following a job crisis. This responded to a medical regimen. There has been no recurrence. The principal manifestations of dysfunction since the ulcer episode appear to have been psychologic, with particular anxiety about her sexual identity and competitive hostility. Epigastric distress, however, was a frequent but transient symptom. This trend persisted during the early phases of analysis but was interspersed with several episodes of minor physical illness.

C.D.'s responses to stress have been marked by either minor physical illness or minor regressive shifts in his character neurosis. Early in childhood, shortly after his younger sibling's birth, which probably activated sibling rivalry, the patient began to have frequent colds, and this was the reason given for removing his tonsils and adenoids. In the fifth grade during a period of feeling physically inferior to and afraid of competing with other boys, enhanced by myopia and the need to wear glasses, he sustained a severe thigh laceration while being chased by a bully. When he was a youngster his sexual fantasies and activities included a strong anal and transvestite interest, always indulged in secret and often acted out by putting on his mother's underclothes. He developed a persistent anal itch between the ages of ten and thirteen, and his mother, who had frustrated desires to be a doctor, gave him palliative and curative enemas after finally discovering that pinworms were causing the trouble. During adolescence, the patient had frequent headaches which became worse following a car accident in which he sustained a mild concussion. This occurred during a time when the patient had been especially defiant toward his parents and also had felt especially guilty. The first phase of analysis was marked by frequent, brief, minor physical symptoms and sensations, generally conversion reactions or anxiety-depressive equivalents. The most prominent manifestations, however, were anal character traits. Subsequently he experienced several episodes of minor physical illness.

K. L. had a major physical illness when he was three years old. At that time he developed a severe lung infection which required hospitalization and surgical intervention. This apparently activated great anxiety in his mother, who overprotected and feminized him for years afterwards. However, except for an occasional cold, the patient has been in excellent physical health since childhood. On the other hand, his psychologic difficulties have been life-long and principally in the form of a moderately severe character neurosis, with periodic decompensation after unusual stress leading to severe anxiety and mild depression. At such times, the patient did experience frequent physical symptoms, many of which appeared to be expressions of autonomic nervous system overactivity involving a number of different organs and organ systems. This pattern persisted during the analysis, and the patient exhibited various conversion symptoms and manifestations of minor, transient physical dysfunction.

T. U. has a longstanding obsessional character neurosis with two previous decompensations in the form of depressive episodes (1) on leaving home for college and (2) on finishing graduate school and looking for his first job. His responses to emotional stress have been basically through psychologic systems. He had measles at age three and mumps at age five, without apparent sequelae. He has been in good physical health since childhood except for upper respiratory infections. During the first six months of analysis, references to physical symptoms and bodily sensations were rare. However, on the couch, the patient exhibited a persistent stiff restlessness. It was anticipated that his basic mode of response to stress would follow the old rigid psychologic patterns until their modification by the analytic process might render them insufficient to cope with intensification of external stress. Then physical dysfunction might occur. In fact, as the analysis continued the patient did have several episodes of minor somatic illness.

N. P. is another longstanding obsessional character whose adaptation to stress has been largely through psychologic systems, but there have been a number of notable exceptions: several childhood ailments and two self-limited episodes of physical illness early in adolescence. At age two he had tonsils and adenoids removed, though the reasons for this are unclear. At age nine he had frequent irritation of his Eustachian tubes and ear symptoms which were treated with radium "successfully." During these childhood years he felt his parents to be distant, had problems of communicating with them, and found them uninterested in and not listening to what he had to say. When he was 14 and starting at boarding school, away from home for the first time and feeling very lonely, he had pneumonia lasting a week. Several months later returning home for a vacation period, he had an undiagnosed febrile illness of two weeks' duration, requiring complete bed rest and much nursing attention. In his early twenties he fell asleep while driving a car and sustained trauma to his chest (no fractures) when it crashed into a tree. Other than these experiences, the patient has been in excellent physical health. During the first seven months of analysis, he mentioned practically no physical symptoms nor sensations. Again, the combination of analytically influenced modification of his obsessional patterns and unusual stress made it likely that physical dysfunction would occur. The patient subsequently did experience two episodes of rather severe somatic illness.

L. M.'s basic mode of response to stress has been marked by psychologic manifestations, especially an increase in self-devaluation and sexual acting out, with relatively few instances of physical dysfunction and these, in any event, were of a minor nature. They occurred mostly in childhood when there were episodes of vomiting associated with overfeeding by mother, who was much concerned about the patient's thinness. There was also a tendency to develop upper respiratory infections. Conflict with mother continued to be intense right through adolescence to the time of treatment, but in latter years was manifested by sexual acting out. In the early phases of the analysis, the patient presented no physical manifestations. It was expected that with increased stress and relative insufficienty of psychologic coping systems that she might experience minor physical illness, and this is, indeed, what happened.

Physical dysfunction is prominent in Q.R.'s responses to stress, although she has had a longstanding character neurosis. She was thin as a child, constipated, and was given enemas by a sickly mother. The patient had frequent headaches during adolescence which was a stressful period for her, especially because of sexual identity problems. When actual or impending losses became severe, they had been followed by more or less serious physical dysfunction: one episode of medical illness—an acute kidney infection at age 28 and three operations: (1) biopsy and removal of benign cyst of left breast in her early twenties; (2) saphenous ligation some years later; and (3) an emergency appendectomy nearly two years ago. At about the time of the last operation, the patient noted a mole under her right arm; it swelled up and dropped off without treatment. For years she had had intermittent swelling of feet and frequency of urination connected with forcing fluids and also linked with guilt over an earlier abortion. A year ago the patient was troubled by sore throats and hoarseness. From the beginning of the analysis, low-grade anxiety and depression were present, interspered with minor, transient aches and pains, but a physical examination was negative. Then two months later, as emotional stress built up, persistent symptoms of generalized malaise, headache, frequency of urination, and fullness in abdomen became increasingly evident. Her life style of adaptation to severe stress indicated that psychological coping mechanisms might be insufficient and that a more or less serious physical dysfunction was in the offing. This turned out to be so.

These data suggest that, although each person's life style of adaptation to emotional stress is unique, certain broad observations can be made about this factor in forecasting physical illness. Firstly, its usefulness by itself as an indicator of minor physical sickness is limited. On such occasions, it is of more value when considered in connection with other predictive factors. If the individual's response to stress in the past has been through activation of psychologic mechanisms, such will probably be the current reaction. However, should the stress become increasingly severe and persistant then the possibility of a major adaptational shift has to be considered. Here it is necessary also to have an estimate of when ideational, affective and behavioral outlets for discharge of tensions become insufficient. Should this occur, a serious physical illness may result.

If psychologic shifts and episodes of physical illness occur variably in response to stress, a careful examination of the circumstances of these adaptational shifts will be useful.

If an individual has responded to severe stress in the past by developing a major somatic illness, this may provide a clue to the vulnerable organ or organ system that again may be involved, especially if the disease process is of the "chronic" or "recurrent" type. However, another body area may become the site of dysfunction. Information about somatic identification, sensitized organs, and genetic endowment will be helpful in making a determination about site and disease.

Many individuals respond to stress with frequent somatic symptoms that are, however, self-limited and transient. These may represent anxiety, depressive equivalents, or conversion phenomena. Often they are associated with episodic dysfunction of the autonomic nervous system. Though such persons often refer to physical discomfort, they do not have organic disease and may not for very long intervals. These somatic complaints are in effect by-products of primary psychologic dysfunction. However, the need for regular physical check-ups in these individuals must not be submerged by the explanation that "it's psychosomatic or hypochondriacal," especially when there is a change in the character of the physical symptoms.

Somatic illness will evoke *secondary* psychologic responses of varying kind and degree. At times these are severe and followed by a psychotic episode. More often the many forms of secondary gain from physical illness will be present.

In any given episode of illness, major shifts in dysfunction may take place from somatic to psychologic and from psychologic to somatic. Much more often, there are minor secondary physical manifestations complicating a primary psychologic disorder, or a major physical illness with secondary psychologic reactions to it, against the background of the individual's basic personality structure.

PSYCHOLOGIC EQUILIBRIUM — EGO ASPECTS

Having considered emotional stresses and the general life style of adaptation they evoke, a more detailed study of psychologic equilibrium and its shifts is in order. Ego aspects will be given special consideration. When external emotional stresses activate already existing internal conflicts and the habitual ego coping mechanisms are unable to maintain a relatively steady state in psychologic functioning, regressive shifts of varying kind and intensity will take place. Regression is a general mechanism of primary importance at all stages of mental functioning, whether normal or disordered (Glover, 1968). Although their consequences (when not "in the service of the ego") are most often thought of in terms of more serious psychopathology, it should be emphasized that regressive shifts may lead to physical dysfunction of varying severity. In the cases studied, data about ego functions and psychologic equilibrium were derived that provided cues useful in indicating whether somatic illness was impending or developing. It also became clear that shifts in equilibrium of smaller amplitude or relatively sudden in their occurrence, ordinarily would not be detectable except by the kind of close observation possible during psychoanalysis.

E. F.'s basic infantile needs to be nurtured by women and his incestuous attachment to them, if frustrated, would generally, but not exclusively, evoke a turn toward homosexual fantasies, feminine identification, and longing for a feeding father-figure. Activation of such needs led to intensification of countervailing forces: intellectualization, rationalization, and projective tendencies—longstanding defense structures. This dynamic interaction was evident in the early phases of his analysis.

Then, as the analysis proceeds and dependency needs are activated, shifts, at first of small amplitude, begin to appear. Stress at work and in his relationship with women further intensifies his need to be nurtured and his hostility at its frustration, extending deeply into the transference. More references to the physical now appear in his associations. Transference interpretations have only a brief stabilizing effect. Continued stress evokes denial as a dramatic new but insufficient defense response. The psychologic equilibrium undergoes a sharp, regressive shift and a previously experienced physical dysfunction recurs— arthralgia. An abreactive episode of anger at his sister—a key rival for parental affection—diminishes internal psychologic tensions temporarily, and there is lessening but not cessation of physical dysfunction. Another increase in hostility again blocked from sufficient expression, the continued but unsuccessful search for a rescuing father, and acting out of sexual needs through masturbation shift the equilibrium sharply in a regressive direction again, and the arthralgia worsens. Following a confessional hour there is another shift, away from this regressed position. Subsequently the joint symptoms subside.

Later in E. F.'s analysis, minor, brief shifts occur: recollection of childhood enemas given by mother is rapidly followed by both affect discharge and perineal muscle spasm. Frustrated (oral) relations with girls precede another toothache. Then a visit to mother and sister, activating old sibling rivalry and associated hostility, results in a sharper shift in psychologic equilibrium and an upper respiratory infection. Subsequently, more frustration of dependency needs and intensified aggressiveness blocked again from sufficient discharge are regressively followed by a return of the arthralgia. Positive transference developments favoring acceptance of interpretations shift the equilibrium favorably so that there is both greater affect discharge and awareness of the repressed conflicts. The depressive mood lifts, and the joint symptoms subside.

G. H. in the early months of her analysis exhibited overpoliteness, excessive thankfulness and seeming compliance, which were massive reaction formations concealing intense rebelliousness toward both male and female authority figures. At the same time, strong dependency needs were masked by a drive to achieve great success in her career. Marked hypersensitivity led to easy tearfulness, but the patient was not in close touch with her feelings and their meaning because of marked intellectualizing tendencies. Her primary sexual outlet was masturbation, only infrequently and reluctantly referred to. During the first few months, there were no major changes in this equilibrium. However, minor shifts toward physical dysfunction had occurred frequently, though all were of short duration, involving gastrointestinal, cardiovascular, and respiratory systems. The principal target organ was the stomach, already the site of major, but circumscribed dysfunction (duodenal ulcer) years previously.

As the ambivalent relationship with her male friend continues, the patient goes on "the pill." The stomach symptoms are less troublesome. A shift from masculine, phallic strivings toward a less ambiguous, feminine identity is attempted but arouses concern about passivity, dependency, and masochism which are linked to it. The need to be looked after intensifies, especially in the transference, and its frustration is followed by a shift in psychologic equilibrium, and an upper respiratory infection with persistent postnasal drip and cough. The patient takes many cold remedies, sucks for days on cough drops, and babies herself greatly. The physical symptoms subside. Meanwhile the conflict of sexual identity continues. Dreams reflect it and there are increasing anal references in the associations and concern about control, especially loss of sphincter control and messiness. Here again the psychologic equilibrium is increasingly unstable. As negative transference deepens and psychologic defenses become insufficient, a new somatic symptom appears—vaginal pruritus and discharge. In one hour (10/27) there are rapidly shifting representations of guilt: somatic, affective—with partial discharge—and ideational (verbalization of an incestuous-like episode several nights previously). Finally (after many months), the patient confesses her last secret—masturbation with an artificial phallus. In the following weeks, as the vaginal infection subsides, a shift occurs in which dependency needs appear less frequently, being replaced by a sharpening conflict between the needs to control and to be dominated. The tendency to control and difficulty in parting with anything seen as part of her becomes increasingly prominent but remains largely out of her awareness. This shift is followed by references to very painful hemorrhoids. As the patient becomes more aware of her controlling tendencies and use of ingratiation to ward off hostile impulses, the somatic symptoms subside.

In C. D.'s character neurosis there were obsessional, depressive, sadomasochistic, and passive-feminine elements. Anality overshadowed orality. There was frequent nose-picking and expulsion of flatus during analytic hours. Teasing, flip attitudes, projective tendencies, and intellectualization were all prominent. Though the patient had a few explosive quarrels with his wife, especially over unsatisfactory sexual relations, hostility was only indirectly expressed in the transference. Anxiety was somewhat more openly evident. A marked sexualization of various body areas could be noted.

In the first eight months of analysis, this patient's concern about his masculinity and fear of retaliatory castration fantasies are more prominent in his associations than his dependency needs. Two brief upper respiratory infections during this period are related to sharp transference reactions anticipating criticism and rejection for his competitive strivings. After the summer interruption the patient's psychological equilibrium begins to show evidence of greater instability as his associations are more and more filled with references to the anal area and linked with homosexual fantasies. A sharp shift is foreshadowed by a dream of a hidden phallus in the female sexual parts. Shortly thereafter, a small polyp is discovered in the patient's rectum on physical examination. The impending surgery represents a symbolic castration which is then effectively warded off by the defense of denial so that for days, in fact up to a few hours before the operation, there is no direct mention of physical symptoms.

Subsequent to an uneventful recovery from surgery, new stresses evoke a retreat into passive-feminine fantasies and a defensive surge of homosexual interest. Growing hostility is partly manifested in a disguised affectless way in the transference, and partly expressed in quarrels with his wife. Projective tendencies become more evident. There are also increasing references to injury in the patient's associations; the neck and head area are particularly prominent. These are signals that the psychologic equilibrium is again becoming highly unstable and then physical dysfunction occurs. It improves dramatically following a massive discharge of hostile affect. The symptoms subside altogether as the transference, at first oscillating away from what had been a predominantly negative state, finally stabilizes in a more positive direction.

K. L. has experienced episodic decompensation of his character neurosis with resultant periods of mild depression and severe anxiety, accompanied by somatic equivalents and conversion symptoms. There is, thus, a long history of instability in psychologic equilibrium. The detailed reporting of analytic interviews indicates that heterosexual frustration is followed by an upsurge of homosexual fantasies and conversion symptoms. As drive pressures increase and the usual defense alignment of intellectualization, projective tendencies, and reaction formation become insufficient, the instability of psychologic equilibrium deepens, but hostility continues to be internalized. Shortly thereafter the patient develops a severe upper backache, a conversion manifestation. The physical symptoms are brief in duration. Subsequently there is a period in which polymorphous perverse infantile fantasies are prominent, treatment is temporarily interrupted by the analyst, and the patient experiences difficulties with his boss at work. During this interval he has urticaria, an eye inflammation, and stiffness of his left hip. These physical conditions are mild and brief. During a later episode of instability signaled again by activated but frustrated sexual drives and by increasing negative transference, there is severe abdominal pain, rush peristalsis, with explosive bowel movements. Still later with similar psychologic conditions prevailing, the patient develops a large, painful furuncle on his nose and a painless persistent swelling on his forehead. Toward the end of the period reported, in one hour there are rapid shifts back and forth from ideational to somatic channels of expression and from gastrointestinal to cardiovascular systems.

T. U. from the beginning of his analysis exhibited both marked intellectualization and affect block, except for infrequent eruptions of anger at home toward his wife and children, but without awareness of the significance of the affect being discharged. Other obsessional defenses were present to a marked degree: reaction formation, isolation, doing and undoing, and to a lesser extent projection. Hidden behind these rigid defenses were his incestuous attachment to his mother, competition with father and particularly brother, voyeuristic and exhibitionistic tendencies, considerable infantile orality, especially expressed in the need to be given to and looked after, and hard-core rage at frustration. His efforts to present himself as shy, nice, and inconspicuous in all situations including the analysis were impressive. Additionally in almost every hour there was a pervasive pattern of doubt and ambivalence. Sexual drives were generally inhibited voyeuristic impulses. Thus a rigid psychologic pattern, resisting change, was evident.

During the first six months of analysis, references to physical symptoms and bodily sensations are rare. This, then, is the equilibrium as the detailed reporting of treatment begins. At this time, stresses rapidly accumulate and the defenses of denial and avoidance of problems through overactivity become more prominent. Increasing references in the associations to physical illness and symptoms appear; these are unusual. These changes indicate impending physical dysfunction and are shortly followed by severe, low back pain. Subsequently, interpretations and an eruption of violently angry affect displaced from the negative transference lessen tensions and the physical condition improves after a week.

During the next eight months, the psychoanalytic treatment progresses very slowly. Rumination, doubting, affect block, and intellectualization show only slight modification. Ambivalence is heavily weighted on the negative side and is reflected in the transference. During this interval the patient remains free of physical illness. Then stresses pile up again and the patient develops headaches, the first somatic manifestation in a month. Concern about his general physical integrity, absent for many weeks, reappears. Visual percepts become prominent in his associations. Again, the shifts suggest physical dysfunction and he does, in fact, develop acute bacterial conjunctivitis. Increasing insight into his hypersensitivity, voyeuristic-exhibitionistic impulses, and potential for intense hostility is accompanied by subsidence of the eye symptoms.

N. P. with a rigid, obsessive-compulsive character structure was unaware of ego-alien symptoms at the time he started his analysis, although he acknowledged his tardiness at work and dissatisfaction with his bachelor status. Affect block was extreme. There was an avoidance of looking at himself and his problems for the most part. Instead, he focused on other people, especially the girls he met, trying to analyze them. His pattern of coming late usually followed hours in which he felt he had been criticized, rejected, or verbally coerced.

No physical symptoms or dysfunction appear until after the first seven months. Then an affect discharge of tearfulness and sadness also occurs, the first since the analysis began and soon is followed by another—an indication of temporary instability in the psychologic equilibrium. The patient finds his work no longer distracting; the defense of avoidance is becoming insufficient. Dreams indicate a foreboding change in emotional climate. A rush of associations about somatic disturbances, especially in mother with whom there is strong identification, further suggests that the current, unstable, equilibrium is shifting in the direction of somatic dysfunction. The patient develops a viral infection which causes a further secondary regressive shift: he takes to bed and is quite ill for several weeks feeling quite sad and lonely. As the sickness remits, there is reestablishment of the habitual psychologic equilibrium except that the patient has slightly increased insight into his hypersensitivity to loss and separation.

During the next three months there is essentially little change. Then an intensely hostile and rejecting outburst from a new woman-friend initially evokes little overt emotional response in him. His need for sexual gratification to ward off loneliness overrules reason, and, using denial, he acts as if nothing untoward had happened in the relationship. He dreams about an accident. The psychologic equilibrium is again under pressure. A second and final rejection by his woman-friend brings about only a mildly irritable response outwardly, but a severely regressive shift internally. Shortly thereafter, a sudden physical decompensation occurs.

L. M.'s character neurosis had been a relatively stable one with chiefly obsessional and hysterical traits, except for intermittent sexual acting out. In the early phases of analysis she remained entrenched behind a highly intellectualized defense, presenting in great descriptive detail the current and past aspects of her problems especially with her mother. The developing transference reflected her great need to please and be attractive to men as well as her strong, competitive drive to further her career. Behind this were deeply dependent needs which occasionally broke through in the form of brief periods of helpless feelings and pessimism about the future.

Shortly after the detailed reporting begins, minor shifts in the psychologic equilibrium appear: there is an increase in thoughts about inferiority, defended against by an upsurge of projective tendencies. Interoceptive percepts referable to the stomach become evident. Then there is a brief breakthrough of somatic anxiety equivalents as she recalls traumatic sexual experiences during adolescence. Following a hostile exchange with mother who announces she's leaving on an extended trip overseas, there is a sharp, regressive change in equilibrium. Her hostile dependency on and envy of mother intensifies. Overactivity and extroverted behavior, which the patient had used in the past to avoid thinking of her problems, is not effective now, and she becomes slightly depressed, but a somatic outlet appears to be in the offing and she does develop an acute upper respiratory infection. As this illness remits, greater affect discharge becomes possible, and for a while the patient is both tearful and openly hostile. Subsequently a dream and a brief somatic response (gastrointestinal) reflect the patient's continued ambivalent transference attitudes.

Q. R. has had a history of markedly unstable psychophysical equilibrium, but, in her case, the episodes of decompensation involving physical dysfunction have been severe. The defense constellations including intellectualization, reaction formation, and projective tendencies have been frequently insufficient under the impact of external stress. Masochistic fantasies then become dominant. Her striving for career success and penis envy often have fluctuated with intense needs to be taken care of and at other times with attempts to present a desirable feminine image.

Two months prior to the reporting of the detailed analytic material, the patient had undergone a thorough physical examination which was negative. Now however, threatened by the possibility that her husband will leave her and facing difficult, important academic examinations, she begins to experience frequency of urination which she explains to herself as being psychologic—in an attempt to cope with intense anxiety that the symptom might be really an indication of cancer. Hostility toward her husband, professors, fellow-students, and physicians can be noted in the content of her associations, but the affect is not expressed as such, except for some low-grade irritability and annoyance. Physical symptoms and sensations increase. Marked instability of the psychologic equilibrium indicates a severe regressive shift in the direction of physical dysfunction. Exploratory laparotomy reveals ovarian cysts, one with early malignant changes.

These eight cases illustrate the dynamic fluctuations in psychologic equilibrium accessible to psychoanalytic observation in an hour as well as from day to day, week to week, month to month, and over even longer intervals. There are shifts between dysfunction in which physical manifestations predominate and dysfunction in which psychologic symptoms are most prominent, as well as varying mixtures of both types. At times the psychologic equilibrium may be shaky, but this generally is not directly obvious to the individual. However, there may be indirect signs that this is so, e.g., persisting sleeplessness, recurrent headache, or greater than usual irritability, though again their significance is often overlooked. In this study the focus has been on the manifestations of shifts within the psychologic systems and their significance for predicting the development and occurrence of physical disease. The ego mechanisms of defense are particular and important factors in such forecasting. Their capacity to cope, either through changes in their long-term or short-term alignments with stress-activated instinctual drives, influence but do not determine whether the outcome will be in a psychologic or physical direction. A previously existing alignment of psychologic defenses may compensate with resultant new and more regressed manifestations, e.g., a person with an obsessive-compulsive character structure and defenses develops incapacitating depression; or the decompensation is in the form of a major physical illness such as pneumonia. This coping capacity has important economic aspects, but the quantity of drives activated and the quantity of psychologic defensive energies mobilized to deal with them can as yet be estimated only grossly. However, the qualitative nature of these defenses is also of significance and from a particular standpoint: how much do they interfere with perception of reality and to what extent do they block discharge of affects as such in the patient? Tendencies toward denial of certain realities associated with emotional conflicts and/or affect block if of sufficient degree, and in the face of increasing stress and expectable shifts in psychologic equilibrium, are signals that somatic dysfunction, possibly of major proportions, is impending. Denial and affect block, in effect, are indicators that psychologic pathways of perception and expression are becoming or are indeed insufficient.

There is a close relationship between perception and denial. Deutsch (1950) has noted that persons born blind have an unusual capacity for denial. They are able to give up reality and escape into fantasy very easily, because they do not have to deal with the visual stimuli which would contradict their denial. Linn (1953) states that anything which interferes with perception facilitates denial. Patients with organic brain syndromes often avoid those observations which would interfere with the denial of their illness. On the other hand, suppression of many perceptions may go on normally in order to eliminate distractions from pursuit of a central goal. However, denial may have a defensive purpose—to avoid anxiety. It should be noted that what occurs in denial "is not so much an annihilation of reality as an attenuation of reality which then facilitates repression." Linn cites a case illustrating the vital defensive function of the absence of auditory stimuli. A patient with otosclerosis had a fenestration operation, relieving his deafness. His prior adequate psychologic equilibrium broke down when this new channel of perception became available. Severe depression resulted, followed by suicide. Gifford (1957) comments on the aftereffects of interference with habitual methods of dampening perceptual stimuli. One of his patients would shut her eyes and cover her face to block out visual perceptions and in effect to hide. When this was forbidden, visual stimuli activated exhibitionistic, scoptophilic impulses, and she complained of photophobia, pain over her eyes, nausea, and vomiting. Knapp (1956) states that to be too keenly aware of our sensory impressions is to be affectively involved in a given situation. Although denial may be successful in modifying awareness of unpleasant stresses, consequent conflicts, and their associated affects, it may at the same time serve to shunt the impact of stress from psychologic expressive systems to body organs or organ systems with resultant physical dysfunction. This activity of the mechanism of denial *before* the development of somatic illness has to be differentiated from the way denial may operate *after* physical sickness has become established (Weinstein and Kahn, 1955; Titchener and Levine, 1960).

There are instances in which denial (under facilitating circumstances) may actually predict the occurrence of physical sensations or symptoms. For example, a patient during an analytic hour, while talking about a stressful home situation, suddenly had the thought, "Despite all this, I don't have a headache." His associations continued to refer to his difficult relationship with his mother-in-law and her interference in his marital life. Five minutes later he became aware of a slight frontal headache which rapidly worsened. The physiologic and biochemical reactions that had been triggered off, resulting in the pain were outside awareness in the beginning, though their representation in the form of a physical symptom would eventually enter consciousness. But preceding this was a denial, in effect, of anything at the moment associated with anxiety, whether it was the ideational reference to the stress or its somatic repercussion. Subliminal internal sensations, eventually becoming manifest as a symptom, must have activated the process of denial. While a somatic disease is developing, the affected individual may have such subliminal perceptions for a much longer period of time than in the example cited above. During this period he will have no discrete physical symptoms but may be aware only of vague differences from the "usual" perceptual patterns. At the same time there may be recurrent denial that there is anything wrong somatically. Bahnson and Bahnson (1964) refer to the mechanisms of primitive denial and secondary repression which are invoked by cancer patients to cope with their crises, but note that these defenses precede and may be potentially related to the development of malignancies.

Turning to affect block, it should first be noted that the intensity of affects can be remarkable. Anyone who has experienced or witnessed an acute anxiety reaction, an explosive outburst of rage, or an agitated depression can testify to that. If the affects, representations of the instinctual drives, are blocked from sufficient emotional discharge or if their significance has not been adequately understood and worked through by the individual, the intense energies that have been generated will exert their considerable impact on physical systems, especially on target organs. Affect block may occur as the result of marked intellectualization, reaction formation, isolation or denial, or various combinations of these defenses. The circumstances which originally led to the blocking of affective expression may be many and varied, e.g., identification with "affectless" family figures, early disturbances in communication, parental prohibitions, fear of punishment, fear of hurting others, etc. However, even if there are affect discharges, they still may be insufficient in the sense that they are simply that and their internal origins—the activated conflicts—have not been essentially modified by the development of insight. Affect block or outbursts of emotion without awareness of its meaning are signals that drive energies are exerting a possibly noxious influence on the soma.

The persistent appearance of somatic references in the associations of an individual in whom they are ordinarily absent or minimal may be a cue that psychologic equilibrium is shifting and physical dysfunction is developing, even though it is at a stage where clinical manifestations in the form of symptoms and signs are not evident either to the patient or examining physician. These early somatic references may be in the form of (1) sensory perceptions which are not necessarily a direct indication of the site of the dysfunction, (2) associations about the patient's past physical illnesses specifically linked with organs or organ systems already sensitized by them as potential target areas, or (3) associations about illness in other persons, usually emotionally significant to the patient. However, these physical references also may be forerunners of anxiety and depressive equivalents or conversion symptoms, or else may be a heightened awareness of body functioning whose meaning is distorted hypochondriacally by the individual.

The idea of the physical sensation may enter awareness before the physical sensation itself. For example, the individual may be aware of the idea of headache before experiencing the pain itself; or the idea of an irregular heartbeat before the extrasystoles or auricular fibrillation actually begin. This may occur in a matter of minutes, hours, or longer. Hypochondriacs, or those who are preoccupied with ideas about bodies, quickly perceive minimal, transient, internal, physical sensations which others do not notice because their "attention cathexes" are attached to other stimuli, especially external ones. However, in others, heightened psychologic conflict may activate associative connections with past physical illnesses, symptoms, or sensations which occurred in a generally similar emotional setting. If these internal tensions subsequently trigger dysfunction in a target organ, the idea of the particular manifestations will precede the actual symptoms in awareness. Initial somatic dysfunction may result in only subliminal internal physical stimuli which simply do not reach consciousness as such, though related cognitive representations may. However, the latter are not always direct and clearcut, but may be embedded in many other associations or appear in highly disguised form. This is due to the influence of repression. Actually, illness occurring in childhood is subject to considerable distortion. Bergmann (1965) writing about the psychologic reactions of sick children, especially those who are hospitalized, points this out in detail. Surgical intervention, whether major or minor, is apt to arouse fears of attack, mutilation, or loss of an important part of the self. Illness is seen as a punishment. Bergmann notes that the younger the child, the more closely mind and body are linked and since mental outlets through thinking, reasoning, and speech are underdeveloped as yet, physical channels are used very often for emotional discharge. She considers that emotions also play a role in major physical illness, precipitating it, delaying or speeding up recovery from it. Furthermore, somatic disease, in turn, evokes many secondary psychologic responses in children: (1) disturbance of the balance between pleasure and unpleasure influencing mental development and subsequent attitudes to life; (2) overreaction to being nursed expressed either in the form of rebelliousness or extreme passive compliance; (3) distorted interpretations of the reality: hospitalization or isolation as a rejection for unworthiness; diets as oral deprivation; medical examination as exposure of damage due to masturbation or as seduction; and painful procedures as fulfilling masochistic needs. Many years later these psychologic elements with their distortions may reappear in the adult who is developing a physical illness or in his responses to one that has already been established.

Adult patients, in whom repressing forces are very active, may have great difficulty in recalling the actual events prior to onset of somatic disease or during its progress, even shortly after recovery. A patient in psychotherapy reported that he had accidentally bitten the left side of his tongue one weekend when visiting with his girlfriend. This happened during dinner. Although the laceration was superficial, the pain was severe, and his girl was very solicitous. The patient had been preoccupied with depressive recollections all day and was verbalizing them while eating. He felt that he was overdoing it and had said at one point, "I could have bitten my tongue for saying all those things." This occurred against a background of partial sexual and oral gratification which, however, was accompanied by guilt. The pain persisted for two days, gradually subsiding.

One week later the patient suddenly became aware that the left side of his tongue was quite painful. At first he was unaware of any possible reason and began to have some concern about the significance of the pain, thinking vaguely of the possibility of cancer. Later that day, during a therapy hour, he recollected, for the first time in a week, the tongue-biting of the previous Sunday. He associated that with the promise he had made to telephone his girlfriend in the evening, his reluctance to do so because of his decreasing interest in her, and his guilt about that. Following these recollections, the pain subsided rather quickly. The original trauma had been repressed and ordinarily might not have been recalled and certainly its significance not understood.

Another psychotherapy patient, following a violent quarrel with his mother with whom he had been living, developed hematemesis and had to be hospitalized. His condition was diagnosed as a bleeding peptic ulcer which was soon controlled by a conservative medical regime. Several months after his recovery, the details of his hospitalizations had become generally blurred, but more importantly he recalled the critical events preceding his physical illness only with the greatest difficulty at first, referring to them simply as a "disagreement with my mother." Again, the forces of repression had been at work.

SUPEREGO FUNCTIONS

Disturbances in superego functions and increase in ego-superego tensions are found in the presence of either psychologic or somatic dysfunction. In the latter instance, it is common to refer to the role of the superego in terms of the physical suffering and the disruption it causes in the individual's life—both linked with guilt and seen as a punishment. But this is a secondary response, after the somatic illness has become established. Superego disturbances, however, also precede physical illness and are, thus, involved in its development in a primary way. The connections may not be obvious in the patient's associations, though involved in the internalization of unmodified aggressiveness with its resultant impact on somatic systems. This process remains generally outside of the patient's awareness but, nevertheless, proceeds in relentless fashion.

In all eight cases in the series under study, moderate to severe superego pathology was present prior to development of physical dysfunction. It was expressed indirectly through verbal references in content, through affect discharge, through disturbances in behavior, or combinations of these responses, until a variable period of time before the manifestations of the physical illness. Then, during this interval which could be days, weeks or longer, *the verbal, emotional, and behavioral expressions of superego pathology would become much less evident.*

E. F. frequently verbalized guilt, most commonly after rage at mother or mother substitutes who frustrated his infantile needs, after masturbation—especially if there were accompanying homosexual fantasies—and after strong narcissistic demands for nurture and attention. While some sadness was evident at times, tearfulness more often was associated with self-pity. At times he attempted to circumvent his guilt reactions by reference to his loneliness and the suffering already experienced because of it. The prohibitions associated with superego activity were influential in blocking a more direct expression of his hostile impulses. Shortly before the episodes of arthralgia, there were histrionic verbal references to guilt and sadness, but they seemed to be only shadowy manifestations of superego disturbance, as if they were operating from a concealed position.

Much guilt was verbally expressed by G. H. when she referred to various aspects of her sexual life, past and present, beginning with very early and prolonged exposure to her father's nudity, her longstanding, insatiable curiosity about male genitalia, frequent masturbation, and later her occasional heterosexual activity. There was, however, extreme reluctance for many months to go into the details of her masturbation, particularly her use of phallic substitutes to excite herself. This prolonged silence was an expression of the severity of her ego-superego tensions as reflected in the transference. Another such nonverbal indicator was her essentially self-destructive behavior when she had attempted some years previously to abort herself with a skewer, believing herself pregnant when she actually wasn't. Her conflicts with her mother, rage at frustrated dependency needs, and competitive hostility with men were all further sources of verbalized guilt. Frequent tearfulness, however, did not seem so much an expression of sadness as it was of her marked hypersensitivity. A very strong need to ingratiate herself with people seen as external representatives of her superego was much in evidence. Prior to the onset of physical dysfunction, there were references to her need to feel free of domination and control by superego figures, but these were indirect indicators which rapidly faded out of her associations.

Although C. D. had had no previous episodes of psychologic decompensation, he had experienced many minor, brief, depressive reactions. Both his preoccupation with sexual fantasies and activities in which polymorphous, perverse, infantile elements were prominent and his hostile competitiveness with other men which dominated much of his behavior had long been principal sources of guilt. Before his episodes of physical illness during the reported analysis, there had been an intensification of sexual and hostile tendencies, but a proportionate increase in superego activity expressed through psychologic manifestations was not evident. In any case, the patient's awareness and understanding of his superego difficulties were as yet insufficient to exert a preventive and modifying effect. However, during the period he was disabled with severe torticollis, a more positive transference shift and a massive abreaction of emotion were helpful in shortening the duration of the physical dysfunction.

There have been periodic decompensations in K. L.'s character neurosis with resultant brief intervals of severe anxiety and mild depression. His superego difficulties have been in the moderate range of severity and when not expressed in ideational, affective, or behavioral manifestations have tended to be less obviously reflected in minor physical dysfunction. These have usually followed upsurges in passive-feminine tendencies, whether sexually or otherwise exhibited. The physical symptoms themselves have become associated secondarily with punishment themes.

T. U.'s superego pathology was very severe, expressed largely in psychologic manifestations and notable in several episodes of incapacitating depression prior to analysis. His behavior in general was pervaded by a rigidly moralistic attitude. Because of his great concern that his "badness" (sexual and hostile thoughts and actions) would show, his need to present himself as the "everlasting good guy" was equally intense. Meanwhile, self-effacing, self-devaluating, and self-defeating trends exerted a powerful influence on his thinking, mood, and behavior. Tears, however, were conspicuously absent. On each occasion before the development of physical dysfunction during the reported analysis, there were some verbal indicators of increased guilt in the content of his associations, but this was not accompanied by affective or behavioral equivalents. It appeared as if the main impact of the increased ego-superego tensions was being directed internally and silently against organ systems.

N. P. also clearly had severe superego pathology, but the manifestations were masked and indirectly expressed through behavioral equivalents which caused the patient much unnecessary difficulty and misery in his relationships with people, both professionally and socially. During the early phases of analysis, tears and sadness were rare, occurring only twice in the first eight months or so. Verbal references to guilt were likewise uncommon. Consequently, on the occasions when he had been exposed to stresses of critical intensity with activation of major psychologic conflicts, including ego-superego tensions, the relative absence of affect expression and references to guilt in his associations was not impressive. However, silent but marked superego disturbance could be inferred as evidence of severe physical dysfunction developed.

L. M.'s verbal references to guilt have been frequent, especially in connection with her hostile dependency on her mother, her struggles to free herself from this ambivalent bind, and her tendencies toward promiscuity. Her awareness and understanding of her basic emotional conflicts, including her superego difficulties, were as yet undeveloped before her first episode of physical illness. There occurred at that time an upsurge of frustration and anger toward her mother, hostile competition with her lover's wife, and less prominently, with her lover. There were verbal references to guilt, but the related feelings were relatively inconspicuous.

An extreme degree of ego-superego tension has been present in Q. R. for a long time. She has been riddled by guilt manifested both psychologically and physically. Cyclic shifts between depression-anxiety and mild euphoria were principal manifestations of superego disturbance when the patient was free of physical illness. Her intense needs to be loved, originally frustrated and unfulfilled not only by a psychopathic father, but especially by a sickly mother devoting her attention to the younger siblings, have been very evident in the relationship with her husband, and, during the analysis also, were reflected in the transference. There was also marked penis envy. The hostility associated with these neurotic tendencies were impressively severe. Guilty reactions to this were reinforced by frequent recollections of masturbation and persistent frigidity. The relative subsidence of references to guilt and lessening of affective responses, which occurred as stresses intensified, suggested not that superego difficulties had abated, but rather that they had gone under cover and might be expected to exert their harmful effect more directly on physical systems.

The more severe the ego-superego tensions already present, the greater is the guilt and likelihood of its serious impact on the individual following critical stress. This effect may be exercised on psychologic systems, physical systems, or both. If, in the past, the response has been through psychologic manifestations such as depression or self-destructive behavior, it should be noted that the meaning of this is frequently not recognized by the individual. Though guilt may be directly expressed verbally or affectively, it often may appear as a generalized sense of discomfort or tension, or quite differently, disguised as a powerful need to ingratiate oneself with others, a persistent expectation of catastrophe, a sacrificial attitude, or an unnecessary involvement in situations which bring only misery and suffering. The lessening or absence of such manifestations following guilt-activating stress suggests a shift toward somatic dysfunction. The superego pathology has not abated, but has become even less obvious as it exerts its disturbing, possibly destructive influence more directly on physical systems.

INSTINCTUAL DRIVES

The varying manifestations, major dispositions and strengths of the instinctual drives, especially in relation to each other can be studied extensively and intensively during psychoanalytic treatment. Useful estimates can be made of their role in the development of physical dysfunction and, thus, provide cues in the forecasting of such disorder. Sexual drives associated with repressed conflicts seem to have a relatively less disruptive impact on somatic functions, resulting in the more transient and reversible kinds of physical manifestations, e.g., the conversion symptoms, anxiety equivalents, minor somatic illness, etc.; whereas unmodified aggressive drives blocked from psychologic expression appear to be associated with physical dysfunction of greater severity (Silverman, 1968). A recent study has noted that the majority of adolescent epileptics have a severe form of the disease together with a low I.Q. and behavior disorders which are involved with problems of aggression rather than sexuality (Pond, 1965). Under certain circumstances (important object loss, severe superego pathology, marked ambivalence, regression) a "defusion" of the drives takes place and the mitigating influence of the libido on the destructive instincts is reduced. This results in an upsurge of unmodified aggressiveness which, if there are inadequate ideational, affective, and behavioral pathways of discharge for its energies, will have a primary impact on physical systems. Thus, clinical psychologic manifestations of such a chain of events indicates that a significant shift in psychophysical equilibrium is taking place in the direction of physical illness.

In E. F. relatively direct references to both sexual and aggressive drives appear frequently in his associations. There is a histrionic quality about their presentation which, at times, makes them seem even more intense than they actually are. However, the urgency of the sexual drives is undeniable. On a number of occasions the patient refers to genital excitation during analytic hours, when his associations contain vivid sexual imagery. Homosexual fantasies with strong anal and feminine identification elements appear following heterosexual frustration and, at times, accompany rather frequent masturbation. There are no actual homosexual experiences. The aggressive drives, also urgent and pressing for discharge, are, however, not basically hard-core. Several abreactive episodes of anger are followed by limited remission of his physical dysfunction. On balance it seems that the sexual drives generally exert a modifying effect on the patient's aggressiveness. His somatic illnesses, though troublesome, are not severe.

G. H. was subject to much sexual excitation during her childhood. Thereafter, her curiosity about male genitalia has been extreme. She masturbates often and has used an artificial phallus; masochistic fantasies are prominent. Heterosexual activity is much less frequent and accompanied by frigidity. In general, sexuality is seen as both harmful and dirty, especially when masturbation or occasional homosexual fantasies are involved. Her car currently represents a clearly symbolic extension of herself. Sex and food are interrelated at times, associated with filling one orifice or another, spaces which seemed continually empty. Comparatively, however, her sexual drives appear to be less intense than her aggressiveness. A hostile dependency and stubbornness are still prominent in her relations with her mother and mother-figures, and there continues to be persistent competitive hostility toward men. Under conditions favoring extensive defusion, an impressive reservoir of aggressiveness could be released, and if shunted from sufficient discharge via psychologic pathways, the aggressiveness would have a severe impact on physical systems. This apparently occurred in her adolescence and early adulthood. However, in recent years and during her analysis this trend has not continued and somatic dysfunction is relatively minor.

In C. D., references to both sexual and aggressive drives appear directly and frequently in his associations. There are confessions about his secret transvestite behavior, his masturbation, and his passive-feminine, sadomasochistic fantasies. Some of the latter are acted out, together with other polymorphous perverse infantile sexuality, during relations with his wife. His defensive and competitive hostility is at times expressed in quarrels with his wife and difficult relationships at work. At other times it is internalized and the patient has minor episodes of depression. There is an affective discharge of hostility during the second of his episodes of physical illness which, though quite marked, is interspersed with sexual elements. In general it appears as if both basic drives are not markedly different in their intensity. In any event, defused aggressiveness has not been marked as yet and has been discharged both through somatic and psychologic pathways.

K. L. has urgent sexual drives. When these cannot find expression in sexual relations with his wife, he experiences frequent sexual fantasies in which there are some homosexual elements, and then he struggles with impulses to masturbate. Hostile expressions and actions are moderate in severity, expressed in competition with authority figures and in sibling rivalry and jealousy; there is no evidence of hard-core aggressiveness. The physical manifestations in this patient under stress turn out, to be minor and transient.

In T. U.'s associations there is sparse reference to sexuality. Intercourse with his wife is infrequent and usually unsatisfactory. Masturbation in recent years has been rare. Voyeuristic and exhibitionistic tendencies, though present, have little or no direct expression either in fantasy or in action. His aggressiveness is marked and hard-core, but except for occasional outbursts at his wife and a massive one at an auto service manager, anger is hidden behind impressively rigid obsessive-compulsive defenses. Decompensation under stress has resulted in a depressive reaction. However, with beginning modification of his habitual defensive armor by analytic work and with the continued recurrence of stress, the drives, especially unmodified aggressive ones, tend to exert a more direct effect on physical systems. Nevertheless, as expected, the somatic dysfunction turns out to be relatively minor, because the stress is not critical and psychologic systems are still bearing the brunt of the aggressive drives.

The drives appear directly only in shadowy form in N. P.'s associations. The severe obsessive-compulsive character of this patient gives him the semblance of a seemingly pleasant "mechanical man" who, at the most, shows only bland annoyance and irritation. He refers to his heterosexual contacts with many different women only in the most general terms in the first phase of analysis. It is not until months of treatment have passed that a brief episode of sadness occurs in several of the hours, but outward affective expression of hostility is minimal to absent still. Yet, while modification of the obsessive-compulsive psychologic defenses are ongoing, intense ambivalence and severe superego pathology continues. Thus, when critical stress occurs in the continued presence of an impressive affect block, the release of large quantities of "silent," unmodified aggression is expected to exert an effect on physical systems and does, followed by relatively severe somatic illness on two occasions.

Episodes of sexual trauma during childhood and early adolescence are recalled with considerable affect by L. M. Sexual acting out late in adolescence and subsequently indicates the urgency of these drives. More recently she has become involved in an affair with her boss, a married man. However, her hostile dependency and continued conflict with her mother are indicative of strong aggressive impulses. Quarrels with her mother are frequent, but their neurotic aspects are not understood by the patient during the early phases of her analysis. Following an especially severe clash between the two of them, her mother announces her departure on a long trip overseas. At the same time the patient's affair with her boss is not going well. There is an increase of aggressiveness which cannot be sufficiently discharged through the habitual psychologic pathways of overactivity and sexual acting out, both of which have been used frequently in the past, but are now unavailable. At the same time affective outlets are relatively blocked. Physical dysfunction expectably is minor.

Q. R.'s aggressive drives are proportionately far more urgent and intense than her sexual drives. She derives very little satisfaction from sexual activity, and her interest in it has been largely a defensive one as manifested in her unsustained, half-hearted flirtatiousness, and her earlier sporadic sexual acting out to prove her femininity. Masturbation is infrequent. Heterosexual relationships are accompanied generally by frigidity. On the other hand, her orality and anality, manifested in great dependency and need to control, and competitiveness with men are central features of her psychologic difficulties. Severe conflict with parents and surrogates, as well as frustration of infantile-dependent expectations, evoke intense, hard-core hostility. Marked superego pathology, ambivalence, and loss-sensitivity set the stage for critical upsurges of unmodified aggressiveness during stressful periods, and in the past when psychologic expression of this was blocked, episodes of severe physical decompensation occurred. During the analysis reality problems activate a massive upsurge of internalized aggression, again blocked from sufficient discharge through psychologic pathways. A major physical illness is likely and, in fact, does occur.

Aggressiveness is indeed a factor in the development of physical disease, but it cannot be referred to simply as a matter of "repressed hostility." The sexual instincts, and the aggressive (or destructive) instincts appear separately and in opposition during the early stages of psychologic development. Later, they form combinations with each other and become more or less fused. This union has a powerful modifying influence on the aggressive instincts but never a complete one. Consequently, a certain amount of unmodified aggressiveness may exist at all times. Regression causes an increase in defusion of the instinctual drives. Another explanation for this process is what has been referred to as impairment of the ego's capacity for neutralization (Hartmann, 1964). This results in the liberation of large quantities of unmodified aggression. These energies, turned against the self, have a disruptive effect on organismic functioning, manifested through either psychologic or physical channels of expression. If the stress causing the regression involves the loss of a narcissistic object relationship, the patient identifying with this object then sustains the sadism formerly directed against it. If this identification occurs in the ego, involving psychologic processes primarily, severe depression and possibly suicide may result. However, under certain circumstances the outcome may be physical illness: it is possible that attempts to regain the lost object occur via a different kind of identification. Instead of ideas, words, or behavior being used for this purpose, sensitized body parts are involved, i.e., parts that have been associatively linked with that object in the past, perhaps during a physical illness in the individual or the object. Concomitantly, the individual's habitual mode of discharging hostile emotions through psychologic channels—ideational, affective, or behavioral—may become insufficient, perhaps because of unusual stress—incapacity of the ego to maintain the usual psychologic equilibrium, or other factors. Then the impact will fall on the sensitized body area symbolically representing the object. Such an influx of stimulation may interfere significantly with the physical functioning of the involved part.

DREAMS

The dream has been described as a guardian of sleep through its control of unconscious wishes, but its significance as a wish-fulfillment is at first glance not clear. What is recalled after awakening, the manifest content, often appears to have no coherent and recognizable meaning. There is, however, also a concealed, latent content which can be derived through free associations, and the unconscious wish may then be uncovered. Even if the dream is an unpleasant one, it may still represent a wish fulfillment, especially in guilt-ridden individuals whose unconscious need to suffer and be punished is made possible through such a dream. On the other hand, the anxiety dream occurs when the fulfillment of the unconscious wish would be too painful; the dream interferes with this by causing the individual to wake up. In the analysis of dreams, a daily residue is found. It is derived from both external and internal experiences of the day, including not only the individual's ideas of the present and recollections of the past, but also his current sensory impressions and perceptions. The latter are probably quickly registered as memory traces (Fisher, 1957). In persons in whom somatic dysfunction is in the larval phase of development, regressive psychologic manifestations, the significance of which is outside the individual's awareness, and an increase in physical sensations, which may largely be subliminal, become part of the residue of the day. The internal stimuli from somatic dysfunction also continue during the night. They may be woven into the dream and, when its latent content is revealed, may provide cues about the physical changes that are occurring, even though the latter may not otherwise be detectable as yet.

An instance of the relationship between a dream and a subsequently perceived minor, transient, physical dysfunction follows. Immediately on awakening in the morning a patient remembered the following dream: In it a smiling former boss with whom he has had a highly ambivalent relationship for several years is out "to get" him by sending hired thugs after him. The patient tries to evade them. One catches up with him. The patient reaches desperately for a gun and finds one. They exchange shots. The thug's bullet hits him in the left side of the abdomen and he experiences a soft, painless penetration as though a stream of water were passing through. A half-hour after awakening the patient began to experience intermittent pain in the left side of the abdomen, probably associated with periodic spasm of the descending colon. The symptom persisted through the day and was still present when the patient began his analytic hour. Analysis of the dream revealed that during the preceding day he had been anxiously preoccupied about an impending interview with a senior executive of the advertising agency where he is employed. This was to be about a possible promotion, and the patient was concerned that he might be turned down because certain weaknesses or defects would be uncovered. He also felt quite ambivalent about, and competitive with, this person. He anxiously expected that the executive would find a weak spot and "bore in." His associations contained many references to authority figures. He recalled still another boss many years ago when he had first started in the advertising business. This person was a sadistic psychopath who made cutting remarks about the patient, evoking much anxiety and barely concealed hostility. He also recollected that his mother, with whom there was a very strong identification, had a barium enema ten years previously. She was very frightened by the procedure. All that was found was a small, asymptomatic diverticulum in the descending colon. About five years ago, following persistent right upper quadrant abdominal pain, the patient was examined and x-rayed. Physical examination was negative and barium enema revealed that he too had a small diverticulum in the descending colon, of no current clinical significance. Further associations revealed that behind the anxiety linked with possible frustration of oral needs and discovery of possible defects and compensatory competitive hostility was an ill-defined homosexual interest in his boss and a wish to be his "pet." While these associations were being clarified and interpreted, the patient's abdominal pain gradually subsided.

Of the eight patients in this study, seven had dreams containing cues suggestive of impending physical dysfunction.

E. F.'s dream of the sucking binge alcoholic is related to the intense oral wishes he has and the frustrations associated with them. These are linked with recollections of violence between his parents, his own physical inadequacy during childhood, his mother's attention to him when he had joint pains, and most recently the development of such somatic symptoms during a negative phase of the analytic transference. Thus, hostile dependency, physical manifestations, and secondary gain are closely linked. The arthralgia recurs soon after this dream. In another dream there are associations about a boyhood friend who had poliomyelitic paralysis from the waist down and who would ride the patient as if he were a horse. Here homosexual interests are interwoven with physical references, especially to mobility-immobility, in the associative content. Several days later the patient has another episode of joint pain.

G. H.'s preoccupation with her sexual identity, her concern about the aftereffects of masturbation, and her need to appear attractively feminine are the background of dreams linked to somatic dysfunction. One involves getting a new briefcase, symbolic of genitalia which the patient sees as defective in herself and for which she wishes a replacement. Another dream is concerned with the theme of dirtiness-cleanliness. The patient's associations go back to her struggles with her mother over toilet-training and her incontinence while hospitalized for anemia. Shortly after these dreams, she begins to have a vaginal discharge due to trichomonas infection. Later in the analysis, dreams linked with separation from her parents are associated with physical manifestations. In particular, the conflict with her mother is reflected in her ambivalence and activated loss-sensitivity. An upper respiratory infection develops soon thereafter.

During a period of intense preoccupation with sexual fantasies involving many anal, feminine, and voyeuristic elements, C. D. has a dream about an elevator shaft which is associated with looking at female genitalia and trying to find a hidden penis there. Some four days later the patient becomes aware of symptoms which turn out to be due to a rectal polyp. A few weeks later, three days before the development of severe torticollis, the patient has a compensatory dream in which he is identified with an athletic young man whose neck and shoulders are powerfully built. This occurs against a background of preoccupation with thoughts of physical inferiority and inadequacy.

In K. L., several dreams are followed in a day or two by minor, transient physical dysfunction. In one, the patient plays a giant pipe organ, but only a feeble tone comes out. He is very much concerned about his potency and struggles against anal-feminine impulses during this time. He subsequently "fizzles" (is unable to sustain an erection) in heterosexual activity with his wife, develops a spasm of the upper back and painful stiffness of the posterior neck. These areas are symbolic phallic representations which include anal elements. In another dream, the patient is in an auto crash and wrecks a fender of his car, which symbolizes an extension of himself. The next day the patient has a brief episode of pain in his hip. The symbolic significance of both dream and somatic symptom is derived from activated castration anxiety related to authority figures. A third dream is about dandruff, with rectal syringe nozzles directing medication to the head. The patient's anal impulses, conflict about cleanliness-dirtiness, and conflict about passivity-activity are involved. After reporting the dream, he has an episode of gastrointestinal pain and explosive bowel evacuation.

T. U. has a dream about physical illness—brain tumor and headache in a woman—six nights before he develops a severe backache. It reflects (1) his guilty, hostile impulses toward his wife, heightened by current oral frustrations for which he holds her responsible, and also (2) his own deeply repressed female identification.

A dream of a cold reception from a girl, tantamount to rejection, is followed a day later by manifestations of an acute viral infection in N.P. The illness then is complicated by an acute herpetic stomatitis. The background is that his most recent in a long succession of girlfriends has just left for a vacation, while he has been immersed in a welter of situations involving losses and separations. His loss-sensitivity dates back to childhood when he felt his parents, particularly his mother, to be distant, even when he was ill. Later in the analysis he has a dream referring to physical injury. It occurs at a time when he has been through another difficult relationship with a new girl, ending in her violent rejection of him. His hostility to her is hidden, but the dream brings back memories of an actual car accident some years previously in which he and a female companion of the moment sustained injuries when he fell asleep at the wheel and crashed into a tree. At that time he had severe chest contusions and considerable pain. About four days after the dream, the patient develops a severe upper respiratory infection with acute chest pain, and subsequently he is found to have lobar pneumonia.

L. M. dreams of coldness and warmth linked to her ambivalent relationship with her mother, especially her hostile dependency. This occurs when her longstanding conflicts have once again been activated by a quarrel with mother, who subsequently leaves on a long trip. Several days later the patient becomes ill with an upper respiratory infection. At another time, following an evening of overindulgence—eating and drinking—with her married lover, the patient's conscience keeps troubling her. Her sleep is disturbed, and she has several dreams. The first one precedes her waking with a stomachache which continues into the next day. The associations to this dream are concerned with the need for approval and attention which could not be obtained from her healthy mother who disregarded the patient's physical ills, including colds and gastrointestinal upsets. The dream and somatic response have transference implications: what she is getting from the analysis is giving her a stomachache, but even that will not elicit any sympathy for her.

Q. R., before her illness is diagnosed and while her developing physical discomfort is still vague and poorly defined, dreams of a scar which can't be hidden. Her preoccupation with physical defect has become intense, and the possibility of cancer is prominent in her thinking. In another dream, a visitor comes to see her because she is ill with this disease. Some weeks later, surgery reveals an ovarian cyst with very early malignant changes.

Dreams assume significance as predictors of physical illness when they occur in the presence of other such psychologic indicators. Then the latent content may provide cues about the general site and nature of developing somatic disturbance. Dreams contain early but disguised signals of such dysfunction, which has begun to develop over a variable period of time, depending on the circumstances, before the individual becomes aware of discrete physical symptoms caused by the malfunctioning organ or organ systems.

Another instance of early signaling of somatic dysfunction, before actual perception of the physical symptom itself, is the "slip of the tongue." A schoolteacher in analysis reported that he was engaged in talking with his fiancee about troubles with his headmaster, when he heard sirens blowing outside her apartment. He put his head outside the window to find out what was happening and saw fire engines passing by. When he turned back to continue talking, he picked up the thread of the conversation as follows, "And what was that you were saying about the headache—I mean the school disorders?" Ten minutes later as they continued to talk further about educational matters and school problems, the patient became aware of a rapidly developing headache. It may have been present subliminally, but this was his first actual perception of the physical symptom. The headache, probably of the tension type and related to the "headmaster (father-figure) gives me a headache" theme, persisted for several hours during the ensuing conversation. The idea of the headache had preceded the actual perception of the headache. At other times, the idea may appear "suddenly" as a seemingly isolated act of cognition. For example, during a psychotherapy hour, a patient who was anxious about his potency and had just begun to refer to his latest but unsuccessful attempt to seduce one of his girlfriends, suddenly said, "I just thought of my old friend, my heart irregularity; I haven't had that for quite some time now." Several minutes later he began to have extrasystoles, and these soon changed to a brief episode of paroxysmal auricular fibrillation. The characteristic physical sensations entered his awareness only then. The idea of the symptom was, of course, not an isolated act of cognition, but associatively linked with his problems about potency. Here the question arises whether the activated emotional conflict was being reflected more or less simultaneously in both cognitive and somatic form or whether it first triggered the dysfunction of the heart conduction mechanism with resultant subliminal sensations which immediately became linked with memories of arrhythmia during previous episodes of attempted seduction and entered awareness as such—as an idea. The physical dysfunction may have only subsequently become gross and persistent enough to produce a symptom which would command the patient's attention.

Fisher (1957), referring to subthreshold, visual stimuli, confirmed that such preconscious perception is involved in dream formation. A large quantity of complicated visual material is extracted from the perceptual field without conscious awareness and then very quickly registered as memory traces. These are then subject to the psychologic processes of the dream work and have a significant role in transforming dream thoughts into plastic visual images. Fisher then went on to show that preconscious percepts or their memory images are subjected to similar distortion and transformation, appearing in conscious imagery shortly after the subject has been exposed to tachistoscopic stimulation. He concludes: " . . . Perception is a process extended in time which can be broken down into three phases: (1) the registration of the percept; (2) contact of the percept with a preexisting memory schema; and (3) the emergence into consciousness of the percept." It was considered that the first two phases take place outside of consciousness. Internal perceptions may follow the same course.

Mason (1961) notes that, generally, the noncognitive area of inner experience is not usually in the focus of awareness, though there may be considerable difference amongst various cultures, primitive and modern, in the emphasis placed on internal and external perception. Concentration on one area of awareness is generally at the expense of other areas of experience. This principle is also operative in the area of noncognitive internal perception. For instance, if the individual is focused on hunger, other internal sensations will be less vividly perceived. "A given quantum of the mental characteristic awareness appears to exist for a given individual at a given time that limits the number of things to which he may attend, but the relative concentration of awareness on a given thing also limits its scope." Man is ordinarily not aware of most reactions occurring at lower neurologic levels within the body. Most internal physicochemical change is integrated outside of awareness. It is possible for both cognitive and noncognitive activity that has gone on unnoticed to reach awareness. Psychotherapeutic treatment increases cognitive awareness. Stress situations may increase awareness of noncognitive internal perception. Actually it is highly difficult to focus on the complex processes taking place in the internal perceptual field because awareness must be directed generally on the external environment for the organism to function adequately. When the internal milieu's physicochemical functioning is *sufficiently* disturbed, then increasing awareness may be diverted in that direction. At such a time the actual sensory perceptions and physical symptoms will be noted by the individual. However, before that point is reached, the *idea* of the perceptions or symptoms will come into awareness. The physical dysfunction may be as yet of such a low order of intensity that the internal sensations are also minimal in degree, insufficient to compete with stronger perceptions for attention. Nevertheless, these preconscious perceptions may become connected with a preexisting memory schema and emerge into awareness in a disguised cognitive form—as in dreams or parapraxia. At other times they may appear more directly as a cognitive expression, followed shortly by the actual perceptual experience itself. Thus dreams, parapraxia, and cognitive references to physical perception may indicate the presence of a degree of somatic dysfunction which is as yet not revealed by discrete signs and symptoms of illness, or even detectable by laboratory tests and instrumentation.

Dreams of patients with physical illness have been reported, but these have occurred after the sickness has become established. For example, in thyrotoxicosis, dreams about dead people in coffins are noted. Patients with arthritis commonly have dreams of paralysis, and these may also occur in hypertensives (Alexander et al., 1968).

SOMATIC IDENTIFICATION

Identification is ordinarily thought of as a mechanism by which one individual manifests basically psychologic resemblances to another. Identification is an ambivalent process from the beginning. It is important in object relationships and as a form of psychologic defense. Identification may be partial or relatively extensive: the former type is seen in individuals who form more durable object relations, and the latter is seen in those whose object relationships are unstable and highly narcissistic. However, identification also has strong physical roots, and the term somatic identification refers to resemblances between the individual and persons emotionally important to him which are expressed in physical terms—somatic symptoms, illness, or dysfunction of various body organs, systems, or areas: When a relationship undergoes regressive modification, elements of somatic as well as psychologic identification with the frustrating object will be byproducts of such a change in the affected person, but they may not become quickly apparent. As noted elsewhere (Silverman, 1968): "Somatic identification appears as a manifestation of reactions in the physical systems especially to the impact of losses, deprivations, and disappointments experienced by the individual. It represents an attempt to compensate for the loss." Such reactions may manifest themselves in the form of markedly increased sensory perceptions from a body area, organ, or organ system similar to one actually involved in the key object or fantasied by the patient as being so involved. The significant objects, mother, father, siblings, or early surrogates, may also be represented by more current substitutes. The notation of physical characteristics or illness in any of these objects, as they appear in the patient's associations, will prove to be useful in cross-checking later against his somatic responses following stress involving one or another of these figures. Such data may then provide cues about the site and type of somatic dysfunction which subsequently develops.

In E. F.'s case there are both retrospective and prospective references to somatic identification. The initial history reveals that his mother has been troubled with osteoarthritis for many years and his father had had chronic osteomyelitis of the left arm, finally cured. During the first episode of arthralgia the patient refers to a father-substitute who had become badly crippled by severe rheumatoid arthritis and confined to a wheelchair. He fears a similar outcome for himself. References to his father's osteomyelitis appear during a later period of stress, five days prior to the onset of another episode of arthralgia. Subsequently, prior to still another period of illness with joint pains, there are references to his mother's current hospitalization with acute thrombophlebitis of the leg.

The history given by G. H. indicates that her father had a duodenal ulcer with chronic symptoms. It appears quite likely that exacerbations of this condition occurred when he was under high tension. The patient, who identified with her father in many ways, particularly in her competitive strivings to become highly successful in her career (as he had become in his), also has had an acute duodenal ulcer. Though it healed with no recurrence, she experiences frequent stomach symptoms. These appear when she is exposed to more than usual stress in her work and social relationships or during periods of negative, competitive transference in the analysis.

Both of C. D.'s parents had major physical illnesses—the mother, a thyroidectomy when he was seven years old, and the father, a prostatectomy during the patient's late adolescence. C. D. had fantasies about his father's illness in which he ascribed the condition to excessive sexual tension and masturbation and thought the operation had been done through the rectum. Whenever his anxiety about his own sexual activity becomes severe, he anticipates the possibility of a similar outcome in himself. This is the case during the stressful period before his rectal polyp develops. When the patient is incapacitated with severe torticollis, he retrospectively recalls his mother's enlarged thyroid, her going to the hospital for an operation, and her neck swathed in bandages for many weeks. He has, however, known all this for many years, though he has rarely thought about it.

K. L., whose physical dysfunction during the reported analysis is recurrent but minor, shows tendencies toward feminine identification, especially in his sexual fantasies. Somatic aspects of this response are derived from his relationship with his wife who has frequent colds and gastrointestinal upsets, and from his occasional preoccupation with memories of his mother's chronic physical complaints including "women's troubles," although she never has had a serious physical illness.

In T. U.'s associations there is retrospective identification somatically with his mother-in-law. After he becomes ill with severe backache, he brings up references to her being hospitalized for diagnostic studies. Actually she has had back and leg pain for some time and this has been known to the patient, although omitted from his associations prior to his sickness. He has also been aware of his wife's marked concern over her mother's condition and has shared some of this with her, although, again, he has not referred to it previously. A diagnosis of bone cancer is finally established in her case, and amputation of the involved leg is recommended. This evokes great tension in both the patient and his wife.

N. P. has known for many years that his mother had chronic respiratory difficulty. This was complicated by her obesity and her chain-smoking of cigarettes. Shortly before the first episode of illness is reported in his case, the patient's associations contain references to an older woman, a mother-figure, hospitalized for heart trouble—her chief symptom being shortness of breath. There are also connecting recollections about his own mother. These deal with her obesity and his infantile fantasies that attribute the reason for her being so fat to the glands in her mouth being "out of order." The patient develops a severe cold the next day, and this becomes complicated by an acute herpetic infection, principally involving mouth and throat. Prior to the later episode of illness, the patient has formed a quick, intense relationship with a woman who is somewhat overweight, a heavy smoker who has a bad cough—all reminding him of his mother who has these characteristics. Following this woman's violent rejection of him, he becomes ill with an acute upper respiratory infection in which chest pain is the chief symptom.

While L. M.'s parents had been essentially healthy people during her childhood, her father later became ill with cancer of the lung from which he rapidly succumbed. A severe cough and marked weight loss were the chief outward signs of his illness, which left a deep impression on the patient. Shortly before she becomes ill with a severe upper respiratory infection during the analysis, she recalls in vivid fashion his accusation that rejection by her mother had been the psychologic trigger which led to his fatal illness. The patient's sickness occurs after a quarrel with her mother, who then immediately leaves for a long overseas trip.

There has been a high incidence of tumors in the female side of Q. R.'s family. One sister had fibroids of the uterus; another had a benign tumor of the breast, surgically removed without sequelae. Her mother was always a sickly woman. For years during the patient's childhood she had a prominent hernia. Q.R. has always been concerned with physical defects, even more so since her own recurrent ilnesses. Preceding the last episode of somatic dysfunction, this concern reaches new high levels with the focus on the possibility of cancer. There is also considerable reference to her mother's continued complaints that tumors of one kind or another are growing in her.

Somatic identification is a regressive reaction to an actual or threatened loss of a key person. It primarily involves somatic systems rather than psychologic ones. It imitates the object's physical characteristics as they were originally perceived, represented, and reacted to, i.e., not via differentiated thought processes but via sensory complexes which evoked motor or organ response. The elements identified with may be posture, gait, body build including deformities, and somatic symptoms, signs, or illness. There may or may not be *direct* verbal reference to these physical features. If there is none, the identification becomes more evident only when the individual's bodily manifestations show similarity to those of the involved object.

The development of object relationships and identifications in the infant proceeds from an oral and perceptual basis. Sensory complexes which represent key figures in the environment are fused with the infant's perceptions of its own body in terms of particular areas or functions. The modalities of perception involved, their frequency and intensity, vary from child to child. They are affected not only by hereditary factors and major stress but also by everyday responses to the environment and the objects in it. Subsequently, as thought processes become more differentiated and language facility develops, these sensory complexes are replaced but not erased by the idea of the object, and are linked with the word for the object. Later disturbances in object relationships—involving unfulfilled oral demands, issues over control, envy, competition, frustrated sexual longings, etc.—will find expression not only in psychologic manifestations, but also physically. The former will include ideational, affective, and behavioral changes; the latter will occur through identification with the object's physical characteristics as they were originally perceived, represented through fusion with particular parts of the body, and reacted to via sensory complexes which evoked abnormal activity of those body parts. The more such sensory-motor-visceral links there are between the individual and his emotionally significant objects, the greater the potential for organ or organ system sensitization. Thus, it is possible for certain body areas to become specially identified with a particular object. The existence of such sensitized organs provides targets for drive energies, if they are blocked from sufficient discharge through psychologic pathways of expression. Hereditary factors will also influence which body parts are more vulnerable to dysfunction. Psychologic reinforcement through the processes above mentioned will predispose such targets even more to the likelihood of somatic disturbance.

FURTHER CASE ILLUSTRATIONS

Great progress has been made in the early detection of physical disease, but thus far psychologic factors generally have been overlooked as useful cues in forecasting the onset or recurrence of such illness. If any attention has been paid to them, it has hitherto been productive of such simplistic and generalized concepts that their value as predictive aids has been extremely limited. However, the psychologic variables that have been presented in this study—because they are prospectively derived, extensively followed, take into account unconscious mental forces, and have been tested for validity—have considerable merit as cues useful in the earliest detection of somatic dysfunction. The results strongly suggest that such indicators may be even more sensitive for this purpose than physical data. *However, they are not intended to replace but to supplement* the physical history, examination, laboratory findings, x-rays, etc.

Some brief clinical case material is presented to illustrate how psychologic cues could have been useful in predicting and, most likely, preventing the occurrence of somatic disease, though unfortunately these indicators were not so utilized.

D. K., a 45-year-old married woman living on the West coast, had been in essentially good health for many years. All outward signs pointed to a seemingly well-adjusted, happy-go-lucky person, showing little hostility and enjoying what appeared to be a good relationship with her husband and two children, a boy of 23 who was a graduate student in a Southern university and a girl of 19 who was finishing high school. She was especially interested in her daughter's dancing talent which had won for her a scholarship in a prominent New York ballet school. At about the time this good news was received in the spring, D. K. and her husband had decided that the birth control methods they had been using should be changed, and she began to take "the pill." Several months passed without incident. As the summer drew to a close, D. K. helped her daughter prepare for the trip East and appeared to be very happy, although from time to time she spoke of the 3,000 miles that would separate them and the limited financial circumstances of the family that would make it impossible for her to visit at least in the near future. She briefly talked of missing her daughter, but then quickly put it out of mind. She felt tense and "physically not right." A week after both her son and daughter left for school, she noted that the veins in her left leg had become painful, but her general tendency to deny both unpleasant physical and emotional symptoms led her to pay no attention to what was a beginning thrombophlebitis. She continued her work as a saleslady in a department store, which involved a great deal of standing. Late one afternoon, some days later, on her return home she suddenly felt faint, experienced a sharp pain in the left side of her chest, and collapsed on the floor. Fortunately, her husband arrived shortly thereafter and rushed her to a hospital. A diagnosis of pulmonary embolism and infarction was made, and the patient was seriously ill for several weeks.

This patient had denied more than the presence of thrombophlebitis. She had not let herself think of the painful and stressful effect her daughter's leaving had had on her. She, in reality, had experienced a highly traumatic loss of an object with whom there was a strong narcissistic identification. The daughter was in effect an extension of herself, and all her own unfulfilled hopes and aspirations were being realized through this girl (in fantasy). Actually a severe regressive shift in psychophysical equilibrium had been taking place beneath the happy facade. Denial was a prominent defense mechanism, and both hostility and depression were blocked off. However, activated but internalized aggressiveness was exerting a severe impact on the patient's soma. Physical history revealed that her mother had been ill with a blood dyscrasia, and her father had had pulmonary tuberculosis when he was a young man.

If the patient had heeded the early warning signals of emotional tension and had consulted with her physician, and then, if he had recognized that the patient was reacting sharply to psychologic stress, the oral contraception would have been stopped forthwith. Also preventive measures including the use of anticoagulants would have been instituted, and the patient would have been helped through short-term psychotherapy to externalize her emotional responses, be more in contact with her feelings, and, thus, avoid the thrombophlebitis or at least the life-threatening pulmonary embolism.

Another patient, H. P. was a childless, 50-year-old, frigid, obsessional suburbanite woman whose high-pressure salesman-husband, a highly competitive man with a deep sense of inferiority, was often away and immersed in his work and golf. She developed a left breast carcinoma ten years previously, following a long period of severe marital discord. This was treated by radical mastectomy and subsequently a bilateral ovariectomy. The patient gradually recovered her strength and began a "new life." She concentrated all her energies and interest in a small dress shop which turned into a highly successful venture. An equilibrium of sorts became established in the relationship between her and her husband. They both focused on their respective businesses while keeping up the semblance of a marriage. Physically the patient remained well. Neither she nor her husband were motivated to seek help for their individual emotional problems and incompatibility.

Thus, some 10 years passed. Then, the husband, who began to experience an involutional type of depression, attempted to escape from this by a series of affairs with much younger women. At first this was unknown to the patient, but then, finally, her husband blatantly confronted her with the news that he was through with the marriage, that he had found a younger, prettier woman whom he wanted to marry and that he wanted a divorce. Shortly afterwards he moved out and went off on a long trip with his girlfriend. These events had a most stressful impact on H. P., but she clung tenaciously to the marriage and refused to consent to a divorce. She insisted that her husband and herself should see a marriage counsellor or seek psychiatric help. For a while he refused. Several months went by, during which the patient was under great strain, and for the first time in 10 years didn't feel "physically right." But she had no particular physical symptoms and did not consult with her physician.

She was not aware of it, but the hostile side of her ambivalence toward her husband was constantly intensifying. Finally, he returned and agreed to continue with the marriage and get help for his emotional difficulties. The patient experienced a temporary sense of relief, but became more aware of feeling emotionally hurt and not herself. At the same time she noted recurrent dull pain over the upper part of her back, a symptom which persisted and was unrelieved by aspirin and other analgesics. Finally, some three weeks after her husband's return and apparent stabilization of her marital situation, she consulted her internist and on his recommendation was hospitalized for a medical survey. X-rays of the thoracic spine revealed the presence of carcinomatous lesions in several vertebrae.

Patients like H.P. with a history of cancer, successfully treated, may be alert to somatic signs of recurrence but are unaware of the significance of psychologic stress as a factor in their physical health. This warning signal of the possible reactivation of the hitherto latent cancer is then overlooked, and only when some discrete physical symptom or sign enters awareness does the patient seek medical help. Such individuals need to be expecially aware of the influence of psychologic stress on their physical as well as mental health. When so exposed they should immediately be checked over both physically and psychologically, and at frequent intervals thereafter. Again, short-term psychotherapy aimed at modifying the emotional stress and its potentially upsetting effect on this patient's psychophysical equilibrium would have been useful. Consequently, the reactivation of cancer might have been prevented or at least detected at the earliest possible time, and appropriate counter-measures could then have been instituted immediately. A perceptive comment about recurrence of cancer has been made recently by a nonpsychiatrist (Mitchell, 1960). He notes that tumor cells dormant for years after successful surgical and/or radiation treatment start to grow again, with clinical evidence of recurrence becoming manifest within a year, sometimes within a few months after bereavement. Another non-psychiatrist (Stevenson, 1964) states that the time measurement between a critical stress and the appearance of cancer has been found sufficiently constant to be statistically significant. "Failure to recognize this temporal factor has delayed confirmation of this important causal relationship. In visceral malignancy the period averages 12 months and in connective tissue malignancy usually 6 months or less. . . . A point of interest is that the recognition of this relationship is often helpful in the diagnosis of occult cancer where the physical signs may be equivocal."

L. X., a 28-year-old, single man, whose character neurosis had both obsessional and depressive features, had completed dental school and after a year's internship undertook to cover his older brother's dental practice during the latter's absence for a month abroad. The patient had always been jealous of and competitive with this sibling, his only close living relative. The month went badly for the patient, and he experienced great tension, but was unaware of the intensity of his resentment at being put in such a difficult position. His physical health seemed good but he was troubled with insomnia and occasional nightmares. The brother on his return found things "fouled up." He convinced the patient that he should give up general dental practice and return to dental school as a graduate student in orthodontics. L. X. agreed to do this only with great reluctance and found himself resisting the school work and studies. His sleep continued to be disturbed and began to be characterized by dreams in which he was constantly messing things up, appearing as dirty and unwanted. The most frightening ones were those in which he was ill and no one, including his brother, would take care of him. As the school year progressed he began to have recurrent abdominal cramps and loose stools. He had had episodes of such physical difficulty when he was in college. At that time he was thoroughly examined, and he was told that he had a "nervous colon" related to his anxiety over his class standing. He recalled this now and considered his current condition to be similar and did not do anything further about it. Several months passed and the patient, facing midyear exams, felt physically "under par." He meanwhile had become friendly with an airline hostess, and they were discussing plans for their engagement. However, a mutual friend informed his brother who voiced strong disapproval, and the patient found himself unable to decide what to do about the relationship with his girlfriend. A week later he noted blood in his stools but explained it to himself as being due to hemorrhoids. When the bloody stools persisted, he finally saw an internist who hospitalized him. A diagnosis of ulcerative colitis was then made.

The early warning signals of possibly severe physical dysfunction had been principally psychologic. These were unknown to the patient. He was aware in only a general and vague way that he was under tension, but he did not seek medical advice then or even after the first physical symptoms had begun to appear. The opportunity to shift the impact of powerful psychologic stresses from impact on the soma through psychotherapeutic measures was not available to the patient who had waited until gross physical signs finally forced him to acknowledge the need for medical help. The defense of denial here had put the patient's health in grave jeopardy. Schaeffer (1968) reports that in ulcerative colitis patients given dispensary treatment after their symptoms had been controlled, the relapses could be correlated less with those major conflicts close to consciousness than with the small, everyday conflicts involving the individual's closest social relationships from which he derived his basic feelings of security.

K. S. is a 38-year-old manager of a food store. He has been obese since childhood, when his mother literally stuffed him with food. For many years he has presented himself as extremely active, giving and self-sacrificing. These are major reaction formations against underlying strong hostile-dependent needs. He is the youngest of five siblings and the only one not married. His father died of cirrhosis of the liver, after a lingering illness, about 10 years previously. Shortly thereafter his mother, mildly diabetic, developed lesions in her left leg which ultimately required midthigh amputation. The patient had been living with her, and for the next eight years the burden of her financial and medical expenses fell on him. A heavy indebtedness resulted. The patient had "become used" to this way of life. When his mother died, he had a markedly ambivalent reaction to her death, feeling free and yet at a loss about what to do with himself. He "resolved" his uncertainty by going to live with his oldest married sister who represented a mother-substitute. At the prodding of his relatives, he reluctantly began a limited social life and met a younger woman, a widow to whom he unwillingly became engaged. Actually he was afraid to assume the responsibilities of marriage, but he finally agreed to it. The psychologic stresses which these changes in his way of life had imposed on him were, however, constantly denied by the patient. He maintained an outwardly calm, pleasant demeanor, but he began to eat more than ever and gained 30 pounds in a two-month period. He also began to ruminate about the death of his parents and became concerned with his state of health, focusing on his obesity and the possibility that he might become invalided, though he had had no major illness for many years. He refused, however, to seek medical advice about his overweight condition or even to limit his food intake. For the first time he began to show flashes of anger, a change which was very noticeable to his relatives and fiancee, though the patient denied being irritable. One month before the wedding, the patient began to experience anorexia, although he was still gaining weight. Thereafter in rapid succession he developed a variable fever, epistaxis, bleeding gums, jaundice, and his urine became very dark. At this point he entered a hospital and a diagnosis of acute hepatitis was made.

Buffeted by one stressful event after another, this patient's psychologic equilibrium could not be maintained, and regressive shifts in it began to occur. Denial and affect block were impressively present. A major change in the patient's adaptation was being signaled and the psychologic cues pointed to major physical dysfunction. However, because these were not known to the patient, the earliest preventive measures to relieve the internalized impact of intense, unmodified, aggressive drives through psychotherapy could not be taken. When the gross physical signs of body malfunction became apparent, the disease process had already become well established. Rowland (1968) reports on the psychotherapy of hyperobese adults during total starvation. In five males, obesity had started early in life at a time when the father was actually or emotionally distant and the patient's relationship to a mother who was frustrated and food-conscious had become a close one. All the subjects had characterologic difficulties and difficulty in directly expressing their hostility. However, those who, during the starvation period were able to externalize these feelings, responded in a more favorable way.

Summary

It has been demonstrated in this work that there are groupings of specific psychologic manifestations which are of help in forecasting the imminence or development of somatic dysfunction before it reaches awareness through gross physical symptoms and signs.

These psychologic cues have not necessarily been elicited either quickly or easily: they have been derived from the intensive study of eight patients in psychoanalysis. More data from other psychoanalytic patients will be helpful in confirming, refining, or essentially modifying these findings. The predictive cues should also be tested in large subject populations. Here, obviously, a more superficial approach will have to be used. Wherever possible, a search for the specified psychologic indicators should be made, using a dynamic type of interview (such as the associative anamnesis) or at least a questionnaire (verbal or written) which attempts to elicit the relevant information. These data then can be compared with the individual's current and subsequent physical status. For general guidance and use in such clinical and research work, a summary of the pertinent psychologic factors, together with their variations and significance, is now presented.

PSYCHOLOGIC STRESS

Psychologic stress originates from interaction between human beings and from responses to the socioeconomic, political, and cultural institutions created by man. It may be sudden or cumulative, but, in most instances, its significance in terms of the individual's internal emotional conflicts is masked. Anniversaries and successes are particular groups of potential stress that are often not recognized as such. Everyday happenings, myriad in their manifestations, represent lesser, often transient and elusive forms of stress.

Sexual impulses, which for varying reasons become associated with anxiety or guilt, may become stressors, regardless of whether they occur in fantasy or are acted out.

Actual or threatened loss of a significant human relationship is a most frequent form of stress in the absence of adequate substitute objects. Losses of significance to the individual often do not appear directly in terms of human relationships. Instead, they may be symbolically represented by parts of the body and various physical functions (lost or altered because of illness, operation, injury, or mutilation), money, position, prestige, reputation, or other externals maintaining self-esteem, including alcohol, drugs, and obsessive hobbies. One type of loss frequently overlooked is that of the familiar sights and sounds of an habitual and "safe" environment. This may cause serious psychophysical regression especially in older people and in those with a phobic predisposition.

Personal loss may be followed by relief at having a burden removed by "fate"—or there may be, instead, a sense of abandonment. When loneliness is persistent and unrelieved, it becomes the supreme psychologic predator. It is experienced by countless millions causing much emotional and physical damage in their lives and, in turn, exerting an uncalculably destructive effect on socioeconomic development.

The more narcissistic an object relationship is, the more stressful is the loss, the greater the impact on the individual, and the more pressing the tendency to identify with the lost object which has been seen as essentially part of the self.

The basic difficulty in understanding the meaning of losses or any stresses is due to the fact that the psychologic conflicts they activate are often outside the awareness of the involved individual or the comprehension of the untrained observer. All emotional stress has unconscious (symbolic) as well as conscious meaning. What on the surface appears to be an ordinary or even trivial event may have great significance in the emotional life of the person who has experienced it. The intensity, frequency, accumulation, and duration of stress should be specified in order to assess its impact on the individual's current psychophysical equilibrium. Stress is frequently unspectacular, hidden from public view in the private life, thoughts, and feelings of the individual. Then, even those closest to him are surprised to learn that he has been under stress, when the "secret" is revealed.

While noxious psychologic stress does not lead inevitably to physical illness, it. The intensity, frequency, accumulation, and duration of stress should be illness. Detailed examination of the economics of a loss situation is necessary to determine whether there are compensatory substitute objects—current or future—which otherwise might be overlooked in a search for data focused only on the negative. The presence of such replacements is another reason why not all loss situations are necessarily traumatic. Furthermore, not all psychologic stress is unhealthy. A certain degree of stimulation and excitation—of the right kind and under the right conditions—is essential for normal functioning.

Stresses activating unmodified aggressiveness precede more serious physical dysfunction than those associated with insufficient sexual discharge. Loss of or disappointment in a sexual relationship has less impact on physical systems than when the lost object is a source of oral, narcissistic satisfactions necessary for maintenance of self-esteem and ego intactness. In the latter instance, the shadow of the object may fall either on the ego or on the vulnerable organ or organ system.

However, despite its invariable prior presence, stress is neither the only psychologic factor involved in physical illness nor the only one available in forecasting its development. It is an invaluable signal that changes in organismic functioning, of one kind or another, are in the offing.

LIFE STYLE OF ADAPTATION IN PSYCHOLOGIC STRESS

Despite the modifications and fluctuations that occur in an individual's mode of response to stress, there is a basic adaptive pattern of somatic and/or psychologic reactions, which has important roots in his genetic endowment and which is influenced by his earlier psychophysical development and prior stressful situations. It might be called the individual's life style of adaptation. Since this basic pattern of response is unique for each individual, it may be useful as a predictive cue. By itself, its value as an indicator of minor physical illness is limited. If the response to stress in the past has been through psychologic mechanisms, such will probably be the current reaction. However, severe and persistent stress points to the possibility of a major adaptational shift. Here, the determination that critical blocking of psychologic outlets of tension is developing will tend to confirm the likelihood of somatic disease. If an individual has responded to stress previously by developing major physical illness, this may provide a clue to the vulnerable organ or organ system that again may be involved, especially if the illness is of the "chronic" or "recurrent" type. However, another genetically predisposed body area, "silently" or less obviously sensitized by psychologic trauma in the past, may become the site of dysfunction. If psychologic shifts and episodes of physical sickness have occurred variably in response to stress in the past, an examination of the circumstances of these adaptational shifts is in order.

Many individuals respond to stress with frequent somatic symptoms that are, however, self-limited and transient. These may represent anxiety, depressive equivalents, or conversion phenomena. Though such persons often refer to physical discomfort, they do not have organic disease and may not for very long intervals. These somatic complaints are in effect by-products of primary psychologic modes of adaptation. However, the need for regular physical check-ups in these individuals must not be submerged by rationalizations that "it's psychosomatic or hypochondriacal," especially when there is a change in the character and frequency of the physical symptoms.

PSYCHOLOGIC EQUILIBRIUM — EGO ASPECTS

When external emotional stresses activate already existing internal conflicts and the habitual ego coping mechanisms are unable to maintain a relatively steady state in psychologic functioning, regressive shifts of varying kind and intensity will take place. Regression, a mental mechanism of primary importance, may result in an increase of psychologic dysfunction or the development of a major somatic response.

The dynamic fluctuations in psychologic equilibrium may occur within a brief period of time, such as an hour, as well as during longer intervals such as day-to-day, week-to-week, month-to-month, etc. There are shifts between dysfunction in which physical manifestations predominate and dysfunction in which psychologic symptoms are most prominent, as well as varying mixtures of both types. At times the equilibrium may be unstable, but this will not be directly obvious to the individual. Signs that it is shaky, e.g., persistent insomnia, greater than usual irritability, recurrent minor somatic complaints, etc., are often disregarded.

The capacity of the ego mechanisms of defense to cope through changes in their long-term or short-term alignments with stress-activated instinctual drives influence, but do not determine whether the outcome will be in a psychologic or physical direction. This coping capacity has important economic aspects which can, as yet, be estimated only grossly. However, the qualititative nature of these defenses is also of significance. How much do they interfere with perception of reality and to what extent do they block discharge of affect as such? Persistent affect block and tendencies toward denial of certain realities, if of sufficient degree, in the face of *increasing stress* and in the *absence of other worsening psychologic symptoms* are signals to be on the alert for possible major somatic dysfunction. This activity of the mechanism of denial *before* the development of somatic illness has to be differentiated from the way denial may operate after physical sickness has become established. Physically ill patients utilize this denial to enable them to cope with the anxiety and/or depression activated by the regressive pull often associated with their sickness.

The increased appearance of somatic references in the associations of an individual in whom they are ordinarily absent or minimal suggests instability of the psychologic equilibrium and may be a cue that physical dysfunction is developing, even though it is at a state where clinical manifestations in the form of symptoms and signs are not evident either to the patient or examining physician. However, in some persons, these references are equivalents of anxiety and depression, represent conversion symptoms, or else maybe a heightened awareness of body functioning which is not indicative of early somatic disease.

SUPEREGO FUNCTIONS

Superego disturbances precede and follow physical dysfunction and, thus, may be involved in its evolution primarily, secondarily, or both ways. Superego pathology is expressed psychologically through verbal references in content, disturbances in affect and behavior, or combinations of these responses. Even when guilt is so expressed, it often may appear as a generalized sense of discomfort or tension, or as a powerful need to ingratiate oneself with others, or a persistent expectation of the worst, or as a sacrificial attitude with unnecessary involvement in situations bringing only misery and suffering. The lessening of such manifestations following recurrent stress, when activated guilt might be expected, suggests that the impact of superego disturbance is being shunted onto physical systems. The psychopathology has not abated, but has become less obvious as it exerts its disturbing, possibly destructive influence more directly on the soma.

INSTINCTUAL DRIVES

Repressed, insufficiently discharged sexual drives have a relatively less disruptive impact on somatic functions, resulting in the more transient and reversible kinds of physical manifestations, e.g., the conversion symptoms, anxiety equivalents, minor somatic illnesses, etc., whereas unmodified aggressive drives under repression are associated with physical dysfunction of greater severity.

If attempts to cope with the loss of a narcissistic object are through its symbolic representation in already sensitized body parts, and if, concomitantly, the individual's habitual mode of discharging hostility through psychologic channels becomes insufficient, then the redirected energies of the blocked emotion will disrupt the functioning of that body area. If the unmodified aggression released is extensive, the physical disorder may be a serious one, because the patient, identifying with the object, bodily sustains the full impact of the sadism formerly directed against that object.

DREAMS

In persons in whom somatic dysfunction is in the larval phase of development, regressive psychologic changes, the significance of which are outside the individual's awareness, and an increase in physical sensations which may be largely subliminal become part of the residue of the day woven into their dreams. The internal stimuli from somatic malfunctioning continue during the night and also influence dream-formation. The latent content of such dreams may provide clues about the developing illness, even before the individual becomes aware of the discrete physical symptoms caused by the malfunctioning organ or organ systems. Dreams assume significance as predictors of physical sickness when they occur in the presence of other such psychologic indicators.

Parapraxia may also be early signals of somatic dysfunction before gross physical symptoms themselves are actually perceived.

SOMATIC IDENTIFICATION

Somatic identification appears as a manifestation of reactions in the physical systems to the impact of psychologic stress, especially losses, deprivations, and disappointments experienced by the individual. It represents an attempt to compensate for the loss, manifesting itself in the form of activated sensory perceptions from a sensitized body area, organ, or organ system similar to one actually involved in the key object or fantasied by the patient as being so involved. The notation of any physical characteristics or details of illness in these objects as they appear in the patient's associations will prove useful in cross-checking later against possible somatic responses following stress involving one or another of these figures. They may then provide clues about the site and type of physical dysfunction which subsequently develops. The elements identified with may be posture, gait, body build including deformities, and somatic symptoms, signs, or illness. There may or may not be *direct* verbal reference in current associations to these physical features. If there is none, the identification becomes more evident only when the individual's bodily manifestations show similarity to those of the involved object.

Conclusions

The psychologic manifestations which are very early signals of physical dysfunction have been generally overlooked or simplistically specified in the past. However, in this study with its prospective and in-depth observations, these cues have been described and discussed in great detail. It appears that they may have great value in the earliest detection of physical illness. The more of the following characteristics that appear together in a single individual, the greater the likelihood that they are forecasting the development of somatic disease: (1) exposure to critical psychologic stress inadequately compensated for by other environmental factors of a favorable nature; (2) some degree of physical dysfunction (ranging up to major illness) as part of a general style of adaptation to psychologic stress in the past, with previously sensitized body areas representing potential current target organs; (3) evidence of increasing instability and regressive shifts in psychologic equilibrium; (4) blocking of affects from *adequate* emotional expression or insufficient awareness of their significance if they are being so discharged; (5) presence of denial as a prominent psychologic defense; (6) existence of a high degree of ego-superego tensions *despite lessening psychologic manifestations* of their presence; (7) build-up of unmodified aggressiveness which is internalized; (8) a persisting increase in awareness of physical sensations and perceptions compared with previous levels; (9) recurrent dreams (and parapraxia) whose latent content contains prominent physical references especially to some form of dysfunction; (10) verbal references to somatic identification with an emotionally significant object, reinforced by actual occurrence of similar or related organ dysfunction in that person. The last three factors, especially, may provide clues to the site or type of the developing illness.

The findings of this study indicate that persons exposed to critical psychologic stress should seek medical consultation even though no gross somatic signs or symptoms are evident following such exposure. A psychologic profile including the cues listed above, as well as a careful physical examination and the necessary laboratory tests should be done. If there is no evidence of somatic illness, but a large number of suggestive psychologic manifestations are elicited, it would be advisable for the individual to be followed from the physical standpoint at monthly or more frequent intervals until such time as a less regressed emotional equilibrium has become established. Optimally, during this period, psychotherapy of the limited goal type could be instituted, aimed at relieving the tensions generated by the exposure to stress.

Although the described psychologic cues are still unquantified, they do represent relatively detailed clinical characteristics which can be observed and listed. Such data are necessary for a more comprehensive and meaningful approach to the detection of physical disease in its earliest phases of development. They are a basic supplement to those physical tests which have already been found to be useful for the purpose.

References

Alexander, F., French, T. M., and Pollock, G. H., eds. Psychosomatic Specificity. Chicago, The University of Chicago Press, 1968, Vol. 1.

Bahnson, C. B., and Bahnson, M. B. Cancer as an alternative to psychosis: A theoretical model of somatic and psychologic regression. *In* Kissen, D. M., and Le Shan, L. L., eds. Psychosomatic Aspects of Neoplastic Disease, London, Pitman Medical Publishing Co., Ltd., 1964, pp. 42-62.

—— Denial and repression of primitive impulses and of disturbing emotions in patients with malignant neoplasm. *In* Kissen, D.M., and Le Shan, L.L., eds. Psychosomatic Aspects of Neoplastic Disease, London, Pitman Medical Publishing Co., Ltd., 1964, pp. 184-202.

Bergmann, T. (in collaboration with Anna Freud). Children in the Hospital. New York, International Universities Press, 1965.

Bibring, E. Therapeutic results of psychoanalysis. Int. J. Psychoanal., 18:170, 1937.

Chassan, J. B. Statistical inference and the single case in clinical design. Psychiatry, 23:173, 1960.

Deutsch, F. The sense of reality in persons born blind. J. Psychol., 10:121, 1950.

—— Body, Mind and the Sensory Gateways. New York, Basic Books, Inc., Publishers, 1962.

—— and Murphy, W. F. The Clinical Interview. New York, International Universities Press, 1955, Vol. 1.

Dubos, R. Man Adapting. New Haven, Yale University Press, 1965.

—— So Human an Animal. New York, Charles Scribner's Sons, 1968.

Engel, G.L. Psychological Development in Health and Disease. Philadelphia, W.B. Saunders Company, 1962.

Fisher, C. A study of the preliminary stages of the construction of dreams and images. J. Amer. Psychoanal. Ass., 5:5, 1957.

Freud, S. 1895. Project for a scientific psychology. Standard Edition: The Complete Psychological Works of Sigmund Freud, 1:282 London, The Hogarth Press, Ltd., 1966.

—— 1915. Mourning and melancholia. Standard Edition: The Complete Psychological Works of Sigmund Freud, 14:239 London, The Hogarth Press, Ltd., 1957.

Gifford, S. Transient disturbances in perception. J. Amer. Psychoanal. Ass., 5:108, 1957.

Glover, E. The Birth of the Ego. New York, International Universities Press, 1968.

Greene, W. A., Jr. Role of a vicarious object in the adaptation to object loss. I. Use of a vicarious object as a means of adjustment to separation from a significant person. Psychosom. Med., 20:344, 1958.

—— Role of a vicarious object in the adaptation to object loss. II. Vicissitudes in the role of the vicarious object. Psychosom. Med., 21:438, 1959.

Grinker, R. R., and Robbins, F. P. Psychosomatic Case Book. New York, The Blakiston Company, Inc., 1954.

Hartmann, H. Essays on Ego Psychology. New York, International Universities Press, 1964., pp. 105-108.

Imboden, J. B., Canter, A., and Cluff, L. Separation experiences and health records in a group of normal adults. Psychosom. Med., 25:433, 1963.

Inman, O. B. Development of two different types of cancer in a patient undergoing psychoanalytic treatment. *In* Kissen, D.M., and Le Shan, L.L., eds. Psychosomatic Aspects of Neoplastic Disease. London, Pitman Medical Publishing Co., Ltd., 1964.

Kaufman, I. C., and Rosenblum, L. A. The reaction to separation in infant monkeys: Anaclitic depression and conservation-withdrawal. Psychosom. Med., 29:648, 1967.

Knapp, P. H. Sensory impressions in dreams. Psychoanal. Quart., 25:325, 1956.

—— Models and methods: A psychodynamic predictive approach to bronchial asthma. J. Nerv. Ment. Dis., 135:440, 1962.

Lewin, K. A. A Dynamic Theory of Personality-Selected Papers. New York, McGraw-Hill Book Company, 1935.

Linn, L. The role of perception in the mechanism of denial. J. Amer. Psychoanal. Ass., 1:690, 1953.

Mason, R. E. Internal Perception and Bodily Functioning. New York, International Universities Press, 1961.

Mitchell, J.S. Studies in Radiotherapeutics. Cambridge, Harvard University Press, 1960.

Pond, D. Epilepsy in adolescence. *In* Hambling, J., and Hopkins, P., eds. Psychosomatic Disorders in Adolescents and Young Adults. Oxford, Pergamon Press, Inc., 1965, p. 93.

Rowland, C. V., Jr. Psychotherapy of six hyperobese adults during total starvation. Arch. Gen. Psychiat. (Chicago), 18:541, 1968.

Schaeffer, G. Experiences as to relapses in the psychotherapeutic dispensary treatment of ulcerative colitis. Psychiat. Neurol. Med. Psychol. (Leipzig), 20:29, 1968.

Schmale, A. H., Jr. Relationship of separation and depression to disease. I. A report on a hospitalized medical population. Psychosom. Med., 20:259, 1958.

Silverman, S. Psychological Aspects of Physical Symptoms. New York, Appleton-Century-Crofts, 1968.

Solomon, P., et al. Sensory Deprivation. Cambridge, Harvard University Press, 1961.

Spitz, R.A. Hospitalism. *In* Fenichel, O., Freud, A., et al., eds. The Psychoanalytic Study of the Child, I. New York, International Universities Press, 1945, pp. 152-158.

Stevenson, D. L. Evolution and the neurobiogenesis of neoplasm. *In* Kissen, D. M., and Le Shan, L. L., eds. Psychosomatic Aspects of Neoplastic Disease, London, Pitman Medical Publishing Co., Ltd., 1964, pp. 152-158.

Titchener, J. L., and Levine, M. Surgery as a Human Experience. New York, Oxford University Press, 1960.

Waelder, R. Basic Theory of Psychoanalysis. New York, International Universities Press, 1960.

Weinstein, E.A., and Kahn, R.L. Denial of Illness. Springfield, Ill., Charles C Thomas, Publisher, 1955.

Author Index

393

Subject Index